This book makes a profound contribution. Bassam Tibi's analysis is both wide-ranging and incisive, covering the rise of contemporary political Islamism and its relationship with Islam, as well as explaining how its key concepts are to be understood in the appropriate historical, cultural and theological context. Based on over three decades of research, Tibi provides a critical, often fearless, assessment of political Islam which defies conventional wisdom and ignores political correctness without losing any of its intellectual rigour. Yet, Tibi not only evaluates and critiques, he puts forward an inspiringly positive vision of how Islam and democracy in Europe can prosper and enrich each other. In doing so, he addresses perhaps the most important political challenge in Europe today, making this book indispensable reading for anyone with an interest in how to overcome the threat from cultural division and religious conflict.

Dr Peter R. Neumann, Director, Centre for Defence Studies,
King's College London

A deeply honest and courageous account, written by a European Muslim scholar, of the challenges posed by political Islam to European values and institutions. Equally committed to democracy and pluralism as well as to his Islamic heritage, Tibi combines erudite scholarship with sharp political analysis, and calls for a transformational reform within Islam which would enable civilizational co-existence both globally as well as within Europe. A must for all who are worried by recent outbreaks of religious fundamentalism but nonetheless hope to avoid a clash of civilizations

Shlomo Avineri, Hebrew University of Jerusalem, Israel

This courageous book identifies Europe as the central location of the 21st century struggle for world cultural and political hegemony. Tibi deepens his well-known historical, cultural, political, and religious arguments for cross-cultural accommodation between Muslims and non-Muslims. For him, the solution is a European civil society that is both democratic and respectful of cultural and religious differences. He argues that this accommodation must be political, cultural, and religious because the conflicts are not caused by mere misunderstandings; they are about fundamental conflicts in worldview and political strategy and must be mediated authentically. Tibi's personal style is combined with a strong analytical framework that links him as a Muslim believer and a social scientist in precisely the way he argues one must link religion and politics to create "Euro-Islam". For Tibi, the alternative to Euro-Islam is to descend farther in to violent conflicts over attempts to "islamicize" Europe.

Davydd Greenwood, Goldwin Smith Professor of Anthropology,
Director, Institute for European Studies at Cornell University and
Corresponding Member, Spanish Royal Academy of Moral and
Political Sciences.

Bassam Tibi is a twenty-first century Martin Luther of Islam. His plea for a return to the open, tolerant, creative Islam that served as a beacon of progress for humankind a millennium ago offers the only real alternative to a jihadism that not only threatens world peace but also reinforces the root cause of jihadism–humiliation, as the Islamic world falls further behind the West, East Asia, and now India.

Lawrence E. Harrison, Director, Cultural Change Institute, The Fletcher
School Tufts University, USA. He is the author, most recently, of
The Central Liberal Truth: How Politics Can Change a Culture
and save It from Itself.

Political Islam, World Politics and Europe

Is political Islam compatible with democracy?

The rise of political Islam, as a new force in world politics, has prompted questions and theories concerning its nature and compatibility with democratic values and with the present world order. Not least have been discussions and conflicts within Islamic communities, particularly in Europe where choices of identity and allegiance are growing acute.

Bassam Tibi provides a broad-ranging assessment of political Islam in the world, in all its various manifestations. In particular he focuses on Europe which is also home to a significant Islamic minority. Whilst rejecting the "clash of civilizations" theory the author clearly demonstrates the growing conflict and incompatibility between Islamist movements and European democracy. A devout Muslim himself, Bassam Tibi makes clear the vital importance of developing a Euro-Islam that will peacefully accommodate religious beliefs within an inclusive democratic European culture of citizenship.

This is an innovative and challenging work that will give readers a clearer understanding of political Islam, particularly in Europe where the issues of religion, identity and democracy are pressing. *Political Islam, World Politics and Europe* will be of interest to students and scholars studying Middle Eastern and European politics, political Islam and international relations.

Bassam Tibi has been Professor of International Relations at the University of Goettingen since 1973 and is a non-resident A.D. White Professor-at-Large at Cornell University, USA. Professor Tibi has taught and lectured at thirty universities in five continents including tenures at Harvard, Princeton, UC Berkeley, IRIC/Yaoundé, Cameroon, Khartoum/Sudan, St. Gallen/Switzerland, The Islamic University of Jakarta/Indonesia and at the Diplomatic Academy in Vienna. His work has been translated into 16 languages. Among his six books in English are in new editions: *The challenge of Fundamentalism* (2002) and *Islam between Culture and Politics* (2005). The president of Germany Roman Hetzog decorated him in 1995 with the highest Medal/State Decoration for his "bridging between Islam and the West."

Political Islam, World Politics and Europe

Democratic Peace and Euro-Islam versus Global Jihad

Bassam Tibi

Routledge
Taylor & Francis Group

LONDON AND NEW YORK

First published 2008
by Routledge
2 Park Square Milton Park Abingdon Oxon OX14 4RN

Simultaneously published in the USA and Canada
by Routledge
270 Madison Avenue, New York, NY 10016

Routledge is an imprint of the Taylor & Francis Group, an informa business

Typeset in Times New Roman by
Taylor & Francis Books
Printed and bound in Great Britain by
Antony Rowe Ltd, Chippenham, Wiltshive

British Library Cataloguing in Publication Data
A catalogue record for this book is available from the British Library

Library of Congress Cataloging in Publication Data
Tibi, Bassam.
   Political Islam, world politics, and Europe / Bassam Tibi.
      p. cm.
Includes bibliographical references and index.
1. Islam and politics. 2. Islamic fundamentalism. 3. Harakat al-Jihad al-
Islami fi Filastin. 4. Islam–Europe. 5. Muslims–Europe–Politics and
government. I. Title.
   BP173.7.T563 2007
   320.5'57094–dc22
                                          2007012391

ISBN 10: 0-415-43780-6 (hbk)
ISBN 10: 0-415-43781-4 (pbk)
ISBN 10: 0-203-93484-9 (ebk)

ISBN 13: 978-0-415-43780-6 (hbk)
ISBN 13: 978-0-415-43781-3 (pbk)
ISBN 13: 978-0-203-93484-5 (ebk)

Contents

Acknowledgements

This is a Cornell University book, even though I began writing it in Jakarta, Indonesia. However, the invitation extended to me by Professor Peter Katzenstein to lecture at Cornell on Islam in Europe and also to join the project he chaired on "Religion in an Expanding Europe" created a momentum for the emerging book. The Cornell impetus was a major one. In fact, the completion of this book would not have been possible without the unfailing support of many persons and institutions throughout the world received in the years 2003–6.

First, as an old scholar of a different age of writing, I acknowledge that I am fully computer illiterate. I put my thinking as research on paper while undergoing the ordeals of old-fashioned handwriting. Therefore, it is a fact that the most important person in technically helping me to complete this book was my staff assistant, Elisabeth Luft. In the years 2003–6 she most patiently word-processed numerous drafts and revisions with great professionalism. This book was written in four continents and completed in all its drafts in handwriting. From all over the world these drafts were faxed to Elisabeth Luft in the course of my work and research. She always faxed the texts back a few days later after word-processing them, to allow further revisions in handwriting. The birthplace of this book stretches from Jakarta, Indonesia, to other continents, whether Brisbane or Melbourne in Australia, Singapore in Southeast Asia, or Harvard and finally Cornell University in the USA. Of course, this encompasses Europe as well, primarily my home German university of Goettingen.

The next person to thank is my editor at Routledge, Joe Whiting, without whose commitment this book would not have seen the light given twists that would not be relevant to describe here.

Next, I acknowledge the great contribution of my research assistants in Goettingen, Vera Weidemann and Nicole Klitzsch.

In 2003 I started writing this book in Jakarta during my tenure as DAAD-Visiting Professor at the Hidayatullah Islamic State University, teaching Indonesian graduate students a daily course on Islam and world politics while introducing my ideas on a reform Islam. I owe these students and my colleagues there, as well as the president of that Islamic university, great gratitude for helping me to understand the civil Islam of their country, which has the largest Muslim population in the world (230 million). I have always admired this Indonesian civil Islam and found it more appealing than the Salafi Islam of the Middle East, my own background. I left Jakarta in late summer 2003 to move to a completely different part of the world: California. In Montclair I assumed the visiting position of Erma Taylor O'Brian Distinguished Professor at the European Union Center of California at Scripps College. There I continued writing this book and presented its material in numerous public lectures also attended by colleagues and students from other related colleges.

In the following year, 2004, I returned after the special leaves in Indonesia and California to my home university of Goettingen, where this book was word-processed in every stage of its completion by Elisabeth Luft. Despite all my criticisms of Germany and its retarding university system, I am constantly grateful to the University of Goettingen for the modest Center for International Affairs it has given me, along with its foremost staff. I repeatedly mention Elisabeth Luft and two great research assistants, Vera Weidemann and Nicole Klitzsch, who provided unfailing assistance and great help in the completion of this book.

In the academic year from September 2004 through spring 2005 I enjoyed a sabbatical from Goettingen which allowed me to go back to Harvard, where between 1982 and 2000 – with a few interruptions – I had a variety of affiliations at the WCFIA (the latest 1998–2000, Bosch Fellow of Harvard). Those years were the richest and most inspiring part of my entire scholarly life. In fall 2004 I worked on this book at Harvard, this time as a Visiting Scholar at CMES. I continued the research in 2005 as a Senior Research Fellow at Asia Research Institute (ARI) at the National University of Singapore (NUS) until the end of my sabbatical. In the second half of 2005 I returned to Cornell, this time with the great honor of an appointment as A.D. White Professor-at-Large, becoming a faculty member there. At Cornell I held a dozen public lectures on the themes of this book and was based at the Center for European Studies (CES), which supported this book. In adding names of colleagues related to the institutions listed, the next colleague for whom I am most grateful is the Director of the Cornell Center for European Studies, Professor Davydd Greenwood. He nominated me for the A.D. White Professorship, supported by Professor Peter Katzenstein, who first brought me to Cornell in 2003, and then included me as an author in his book *Religion in an Expanding Europe* (Cambridge University Press, 2006).

The list of persons I am indebted to is too long and therefore I have to restrict it to the following, after my associates in Goettingen, my Routledge editor Joe Whiting and my Cornell colleagues just mentioned. In Jakarta I am grateful to the president of the Islamic University, Azyumardi Azra, and his deputy, Professor Masykuri Abdillah; at Scripps College, CA, to Dr Martina Ebert, who made my research and lectures there possible and most memorable; at Harvard, to my friend Professor Cemal Kafadar, by then Director of the Center for Middle Eastern Studies (CEMES) – Cemal not only facilitated my return to Harvard, but also like me lives "between two worlds" (the title of his seminal book). Next to Harvard I need to mention the Fletcher School, Tufts University, where Professor Lawrence Harrison included me in his "Culture Matters Research Project/CMRP", at which I acted as a co-author of the resulting two volumes, also published by Routledge. Furthermore, I need to thank Professors Y. Raj Isar and Helmut Anheier for an inclusion of my research in the "Cultures and Globalization" project of UCLA/American University of Paris (our book: *Culture, Globalization and Conflict*, was published 2007 by SAGE in London). In Singapore Prof. Anthony Reid was my host and best source of inspiration. My gratitude goes also to Professor Kostas Ifantis of Athens, Greece, and his Hellenic Center for European Studies for which I completed a research paper on Islam and Europe published as EKEM-Paper 2007. The study of Islam and conflict in this book owes insights won in cooperation with two Muslim colleagues in Melbourne, Professor Shahram Akbarzadeh of Monash University, and Professor Fethi Mansouri of Deakin University, and with my Jewish colleague Efraim Inbar of Bar Ilan University. My work on Islam and democracy was integrated in a project at the Centre for European Policy Studies, Brussels, led by Michael Emerson and in an other project chaired by Professor Allan Olsen of Boston University. I co-authored books at both institutions on this subject and related insights are included in the present book. I also need to add the Madrid enterprise on "Terrorism, Safe Democracy and Security," repeatedly mentioned in the book. In this context, I thank Professors Peter Neumann and Leonard Weinberg for including me as a co-author in their book on Islam and democracy in the Middle East.

At the top of the list of people who promoted my work, I must again mention my editor Joe Whiting and his assistant Natalja Mortensen. Next to Elisabeth Luft, they were the foremost supporters not only of this book but also of the freedom of academic research practiced on the following pages. I also want to express my gratitude to my production editor Paola Celli, who superbly supervised the printing process and also Liz Jones for straightening my English in their careful copy-editing.

The book was partly completed in Ithaca, New York, October 2006, at Cornell University, and finalized in Goettingen, Germany

Bassam Tibi
February 2007

Preface

On my way to Ithaca, New York to resume my A.D. White Professorship-at-Large at Cornell University and to complete the final draft of this book, I stopped off in Cambridge, Massachusetts to lecture at Harvard's J.F. Kennedy School of Government on political Islam. This was at the invitation of a British baroness, who shares with me the faith of Islam, though unlike me, a humble scholar, she is a member of the parliamentarian House of Lords. Baroness Kishwer Falkner – her forename discloses her Pakistani origin – also shares with me being a Muslim in Europe who is concerned with bridging Islam and Western culture. Both of us believe the ultimate bridge is sharing the political culture of democracy, which is much more than a voting procedure. During her Harvard tenure on leave from the British Parliament, Kishwer Falkner organized a lecture series on "Political Islam and Democracy." In fact, this is the major theme of this book. At Harvard I was expected to answer the question whether political Islam – that is Islamism, or the Islamist variety of religious fundamentalism – is compatible with democracy. This book deals with this question, while pointing not only to global conflict but also to inner conflicts within Islamic civilization between those Muslims who embrace democracy as a political culture and others who adhere to Islamism as a totalitarian ideology.

To be sure, Islam could accommodate democracy on grounds of religious reforms which need to be more than a reinterpretation of the scripture. Islamism, in contrast, could not achieve this task. This is a most sensitive issue and needs to be addressed most carefully in view of the bad image of Islam in Western media. Therefore, the distinction between political Islam and the Islamic faith has to be kept in mind throughout the analysis, for strategic as well as for analytical concerns. On these grounds, I strictly distinguish between the religion of Islam (faith and ethic) – which I share – and Islamism as a political totalitarian ideology represented by a movement based in transnational religion. I refer to this distinction so frequently that once an anchorman in German television shouted at me in a live debate: "Professor Tibi, stop repeating yourself! We've got it!" This seems, however, not always to be the case, as some of my readers in the process of peer-group reviewing of this book raised the accusation of "Islam-bashing," overlooking not only the fact that this author is a devout Muslim committed to an understanding of reform Islam compatible both with democracy and individual human rights, but also that this book reflects this commitment in the research for an exit strategy in a peaceful conflict resolution. Therefore, let it be quite clear that the subject-matter of this book is political Islam, not Islam as a faith. This is reflected in the title.

Despite the pivotal distinction outlined, I do not fall into the trap of the politically correct allegation that Islamism has nothing to do with Islam. In fact, the movement of an Islamist internationalism placed at the center of this book is a political reality in all societies of Muslim civilization. Moreover, it is also a popular choice based ideologically on the resentment of the West and socially on a real material and normative crisis. I acknowledge that not all Islamists are jihadists and therefore put forward another distinction, that between peaceful institutional Islamism (e.g. the AKP of Turkey) and the jihadist branch of political Islam represented by a variety of movements committed to violence. These are no "crazed gangs" as Edward Said once contended, but a movement based on transnational religion with global networks.

Under these conditions and in this setup all people of Islamic civilization are exposed to dealing with two pending challenges. One is within their own civilization as they face a militant minority – albeit a well-organized one – that pretends to lead them as an imagined *umma* in a remaking of the world, be it through global jihad or institutional Islamism. The other challenge Muslims are confronted with is the need to come to terms with democracy and its pluralism in an international environment in their relations to others. As stated, secular democracy can be embraced by Muslims and accommodated to Islamic civilization. In the context of the return of the sacred, Islam is revived not only as a religion but also as a system of life in a political shape, and this is the obstacle.

While grappling with the question I was exposed to at Harvard – that is, political Islam and democracy – I operate in this book on the firm view that democracy is neither simply the rule of the majority nor a mere procedure of voting; it is a political culture of pluralism. Despite my conviction of compatibility I contend that an Islam based on a worldview of a universal *umma* united vis-à-vis non-Muslims (in a variety of categories) has a problem with democratic pluralism. This problem is addressed in terms of a predicament, and it can be solved peacefully. To be sure, cultural pluralism as based on popular sovereignty and democracy is secular and is not rooted in religious precepts. Is it then compatible with Islam? My answer in this book is: for the world at large, yes, but conditional to the will of Muslim believers to allow what my fellow Muslim Mohammed Arkoun addressed as a "rethinking of Islam." It is thus dependent on their will to engage in reforming Islamic thought on a path towards a civil Islam put in line with democracy. I state candidly that, for Muslims in Europe, even more is required. In the world of Islam one may reform the shari'a, but to rethink and reform Islam in Europe requires an abandoning of the shari'a altogether – as well as jihad and *da'wa*/proselitization – in favor of a concept of Euro-Islam. I claim this concept and state, against those who present it in a distorted version, that Euro-Islam is based on a Europeanization and on embracing pluralism. On the grounds of shari'a there can be no place for Islam in a democratic Europe. The Islamization of Europe that Islamists envision – and some do not like to acknowledge – is a threat to European identity and to the civil open society. In this context I present to my fellow Muslim immigrants the alternative of a European Islam based on the values of civil society, to be shared by all who want to live in Europe as citizens of an open society.

This book deals with Islam in the context of both world politics and the European Union, home to an ever increasing community of Muslims – more than 20 million in 2006. At Cornell we addressed this issue in terms of "religion in an expanding Europe." I look at these issues through the lens of a Muslim migrant committed to democratic pluralism seeking a place for Islam within the European culture of open society. Against the vision of a European Islam (Euro-Islam), Europe is becoming a battlefield for determining the future of Islam – with regard to its compatibility with democracy – and of the West itself. Having been an active member of the "Culture Matters Research Project" at the Fletcher School, I see in Islam a "developing culture" compatible with democracy through reform: that is, through cultural change.

One major focus of this book is Islam in Europe. I argue for the acceptance of democracy by Muslim immigrants as a minimal requirement. Years ago, I participated in a research project "Islam and the Changing Identity of Europe" at the University of California Berkeley and co-authored the resulting volume, edited by Nezar AlSayyad and Manuel Castells and published under the title *Muslim Europe or Euro-Islam?* In my view, this question is posed for Muslims, for Europeans and for the world in the twenty-first century. In the Cornell project already mentioned on the role of transnational religion in an expanding Europe, I coined the slogan "Europeanizing Islam vs Islamization of Europe?" This is based on a political concept for the integration of Islam in Europe. For the other domain of world politics I draw on the revived debate on the Kantian idea of democratic peace for bridging between the Islamic civilization and the rest of the world within the framework of cultural pluralism.

Given the focus on Europe, the story begins with 11 March 2004, not with 9/11. One year on, the Club de Madrid summoned more than a thousand people, including hundreds of statesmen and experts, to commemorate the victims of that jihadist action. Also at issue was an effort to think about the roots of terrorism with religious legitimation, which is an indication of global jihad, of course, in the understanding of jihadism. As one of the invited experts to the Madrid meeting, I was saddened to see a Saudi shouting at a Western expert and demanding that she abandon the use of the term "global jihad," alleging that there was "no such thing." I grew even more concerned when the attending Egyptian philosopher Hasan Hanafi, the author of the term "*al-usuliyya al-Islamiyya*/Islamic fundamentalism," which he uses as a title to one of his major books, suggested that Europe is in crisis and unequivocally stated that the solution would be to apply the model of "*al-Andalus*/Islamic Spain" to present-day Europe. The implication of this recommended "solution" would be, in plain language, the Islamization of Europe. And indeed, Europe is becoming the battlefield on which the struggle for the direction of the world in the twenty-first century will be fought. Therefore this book first outlines the overall conflict between the competing options of democracy and global jihad in Part I. In Part II the book offers a detailed description of the vision of an Islamization of the world guiding the pursuit of Islamist internationalism. Part III is devoted to a discussion of the European situation with regard to Islam. In this final part, as well as throughout the book, it is made clear that the ill-guided term "clash of civilizations" is not useful for explaining the relations of Islam and Europe. It can be conceded that in the post-bipolar world politics of the twenty-first century there is a conflict between all varieties of political and jihadist Islam and the system of international affairs (that continues to be structured along the Westphalian interstate system), but this is by no way a clash of civilizations. Underlying this argument is the view that Muslims themselves are involved in the choice between democracy and Islamist shari'a rule. The challenge of jihadism as a new variety of an irregular war in world affairs is also a challenge to Muslims themselves in many ways, and they are the foremost victims of it.

The work on this book started in an Islamic place back in 2003 when I was teaching at the Hidayatullah Islamic State University of Jakarta, Indonesia, and this process of four years is described at length in the acknowledgements. In this context I also worked in 2005 at the Asian Research Institute of the National University of Singapore (NUS), where I came across a report published in Singapore's *Straits Times* under the headline: "Muslims Must Speak Up about Jihad" (*Straits Times*, 28 January 2005, p. 14). The story covered a meeting of fifty Islamic scholars invited by the Organization of the Islamic Conference (OIC) and sponsored by the Malaysian Prime Minister Abdullah Ahmad Badawi. The Prime Minister opened the meeting by stating: "Speak out against militant extremism or share the blame for the world's misunderstanding of Islam." Two months later, in Madrid, I very much missed this true sentiment among many of that meeting's Muslim participants, who presented themselves as victims of the West instead of joining the call for "safe democracy" against Islamist jihadism. Instead of debating the issue seriously, some participating Muslims deplorably engaged in blame-games amounting to anti-Westernism. And in abandoning the rhetoric of a clash of civilizations, we need also to abandon the confrontational polarization of Islam vs the West. The conflict is, rather, between democracy and totalitarianism.

The cited call of Badawi is enlightening and courageous, but it stops short of acknowledging the fact that we are dealing with a movement *within* Islam. The chairman of the OIC asked that Muslims seek to correct "misperceptions about the concept of jihad, which has often been distorted to justify violence" (ibid., p. 14). He insisted that the exclusive meaning of jihad was "self-discipline." Unfortunately, even on a scriptural level this statement is wrong. In the Qur'an, the concept of *qital*/physical fighting is a part of jihad, as shown in Chapter 1 in this book. In Islamic history, the wars of Islamic expansion, called *futuhat*, were legitimized by reference to fighting a jihad against the infidels. What we are witnessing now is a new jihadism, not classical jihad. This jihadism is not only restricted to Islamic militancy, but also – as Sayyid Qutb put it in his *Signposts along the Road* – an effort aimed at remaking the world by establishing a new world order based on Islam. It was most disturbing in the above-mentioned Madrid meeting to listen to an Egyptian envoy telling the audience: "Qutb stated this half a century ago. Today he has no impact." Again, this is a distortion. The new Islamist interpretation of jihad as an "Islamic world revolution" (Qutb) is a popular public choice. The founder of the first fundamentalist movement in Islam, Hasan al-Banna, detaches the idea of jihad as *qital*, i.e. as "violent struggle," from the rules limiting the jihad-actions as prescribed in the Qur'an by the traditional concept. This is not a mere "misunderstanding," but an indication of a new phenomenon, one which Islamists themselves call "global jihad" and which is unfortunately much more than a new form of religious extremism. In Europe it is a popular idea among young European-born Muslims who feel discriminated against and socially excluded. The French intelligence service, Direction Générale de la Sécurité Extérieure (DGSE), completed a report ahead of the London jihadist assaults in July 2005, in which the strike was predicted. The report stated that al-Qaeda "will take the advantage of the pro-jihad sympathies within the large Pakistani community in the United Kingdom" (quoted by *International Herald Tribune*, 9 August 2005, front page). This report was submitted to the British authorities, but ignored. The best strategy for Europe for countering this challenge is to make it possible for young Muslims to join the democratic open civil society. If integration fails, the result is a ghettoizing of oneself in Islamic enclaves awaiting the Islamization of Europe through fighting jihad. For dealing with the conflict a policy of "better-informed Muslims correcting other Muslims" is needed. This is the phrasing of the OIC chairman in the Malaysian meeting mentioned above. In this mindset, this book is written by a Muslim with a clearly normative approach. Being trained in the West in philosophy, social sciences and the historical study of Islam, with a professional focus on International Relations (IR), I see two needs, one political, one methodological. Politically, I would advise abandoning the Huntingtonian rhetoric of a "clash of civilizations," even though I do not overlook the conflict over values and ideas between the Islamic and the Western civilizations. I believe that confrontation can be averted in world affairs in the twenty-first century if we succeed in a cross-cultural bridging based on commonalities, at the top of which is secular democracy as a political culture.

On both sides one needs to be honest and acknowledge that the issue is not a "misunderstanding of Islam," but rather a conflict. The present book is a scholarly contribution, although imbued with personal references for addressing this conflict. Some Westerners may not like this. I have had the repeated experience of scholars and many Western "peer-group" readers – acting as judges on intellectual merit and summoned with the power to decide on a work's appropriateness for publication – deeming this personal style inappropriate. Therefore, I ask for cultural tolerance and for a cross-cultural understanding. In order to ease such possible differences of literary expectations between me and my readers, a justification for my personal way of addressing objective issues is needed. To do so, I allow myself to refer to two authorities beyond dispute: to Thomas Kuhn and his *Structure of Scientific Revolutions* and to René Descartes and his *Discours de la méthode* to underline and support my concern pursued in this book.

Thomas Kuhn was a scientist and he dealt with the place of established paradigms within the sciences. In his view, the lack of an overall accepted paradigm in the humanities is related to the very character of the related disciplines themselves. In Kuhn's understanding, social sciences – even if quantified to the bone – could never become a science like physics or chemistry. In the social-scientific disciplines, where no paradigm could ever be shared by the entire community, one encounters divergent schools of thought that must at least be tolerant to one another within a scholarly pluralism, as is the case concerning differences existing in culture and politics. The same principle of pluralism applies to writing styles characterized by diversity. Without a culture of pluralism applied to scholarship, in a culturally diverse world academia would become totalitarian. Far from being naïve, I see the power structure inside academia (of which "peer" assessment is a part) and argue that if a paradigm is subsequently imposed on others, then the overall endeavor becomes a power-based game, not a scholarly one based on the freedom of speech. In the social sciences, scholarly views can be compared with beliefs, as described in the Qur'an: "*lakum dinakum wa liya din*/you have your religion and I have mine." One expects in this situation to be exposed to a practice of scholarly tolerance – along the lines of general religious tolerance – a practice which accepts disagreement, and within which there is restraint from using clichés, such as "Orientalism," "Islamophobia" or "right-wing," in order to avoid defaming those scholars of a different mind. Unfortunately I have reason – based on experience – to refer to these issues in a context in which political positions were confused by readers as being presented as expressions of scholarly schools of thought, and used for rejecting submissions. In short, just as there is not one religion for all of humanity, there is no single true paradigm, school of thought or writing style for all social scientists and students of Islam. We need a real pluralism to be practiced both among religions and among divergent scholarly schools of thought.

When it comes to my second authority, René Descartes, the reference is more succinct. I have encountered readers who question the scholarly character of my work simply because I write in a personal manner (e.g. "I think" and not "one thinks") and refer to personal experience. Subsequently, some ask me to depersonalize my arguments. However, René Descartes' *Discours de la méthode* is based on "*cogito*/I think" and not on "one thinks." I act along the term "thinking is research" coined by Hedley Bull, a scholar who in the IR discipline enjoys my greatest respect. Only individual humans think. For Max Weber, rationality is a reason-based *Entzauberung*, which means disenchantment. Rationality is an achievement of individual reasoning based on the capability of individual recognition. Jürgen Habermas addresses this rationality as *Subjektivitaetsprinzip*/principle of subjectivity which is not to be confused with objectivity, as some do. Subjective thinking is a rational thinking and also – in Bull's understanding – research. Scholars are thinking subjects studying the objective world. Their objectivity is no more than a claim. Immanuel Kant described the objective world as a *Ding an sich*/objectivity – something we could only venture into when recognizing it for good and all on an individual level. Nevertheless, I do not believe in postmodern narratives. There is objective knowledge that can be reached by individuals on subjective levels.

Within such an understanding and positioning, I offer the present study as a scholarly contribution for understanding contemporary political Islam, written by a Muslim living in Europe and experiencing the inter-civilizational conflict on the ground and under issue on a personal level. Therefore, I refuse to comply with the depersonalization of knowledge, and ask readers to honor the need to include personal background in this inquiry. The problems I face in this context are not restricted to some Westerners who want – in a paternalistic Euro-centric manner – to "teach me" not only objectivity and scholarship but also my own Islamic culture. I also have problems within my own Islamic community with some of my fellow Muslims, who prefer to preach instead of arguing, and in the case of disagreement often threaten and even excommunicate those who disagree from Islam, using the obnoxious Islamic tradition of "*tafkir*/declaring a Muslim an 'unbeliever'." There is an Islamist narrative of "Islam under siege" and this book is a scholarly contribution to its understanding.

The methodology employed in this book for studying Islam is based on looking at religion as a *fait social*/social fact. One needs to study religious jihadist terrorism as such a fact. This is the way in which I was trained as a social scientist – that is, underpinned by the mindset of cultural modernity that evolved in Europe. Facts are to be distinguished from beliefs, even though beliefs themselves are social facts to be studied accurately. For example, the belief in jihadism by young Muslims, presented as their way of religious faith, is a social fact in the Durkheimian sense of a *fait social*. The view of Islamic jihad as "a permanent Islamic world revolution" has undeniably become a reality, shaping one direction of Islam in the twenty-first century. The effects of this doctrine are now spilling over beyond the world of Islam, touching on world politics in general and, through migration, on Europe, as home to 20 million Muslim migrants, in particular. True, the jihadists are a minority, as they are among migrants in Europe; however, their thought is on all levels a powerful doctrine. It gains its strength not only by way of its tremendous appeal to a generation of hopeless Muslim youth, but also through its considerable mobilization of support systems, stretching from mosques and various religious associations to welfare societies, foundations and efficient financial infrastructures. Europeans unwittingly contribute to this strengthening through the exclusion and marginalization of Muslim immigrants.

At this stage, the argument of pluralism could be turned against me. I state openly that the Weberian and Frankfurt School perspective of social sciences, in which I was socialized as part of my own education, is my frame of reference for studying global jihad as well as Islam in Europe. My ideas could therefore be contested by some Muslims as an imposition of Western social sciences on Islam. In fact, Islamists not only want to remake the world through jihad and thus Islamize it, they also engage in an Islamization of knowledge. It follows that epistemology is also involved in this war of ideas. In an article published in *Theory, Culture & Society* (1995) I respond to the challenge to my European–Western social-scientific study of Islam. Having stated this, I refrain from defending Western scholarship. I regrettably fail to find guiding help from any of the schools of thought currently dominating the discipline of International Relations while addressing the issues covered within this book. As Stanley Hoffman rightly put it, this discipline of International Relations is an "American science," i.e. dominated by a US perspective. IR scholars educated in the US tradition are not trained to deal with the changed world after the demise of bipolarity, nor are they equipped with scientific tools for dealing with other cultures. When it comes to Islam and the need to reform it, as I write on this in English and German I have been intrigued by people asking the question: "Why are you not writing this in Arabic?" thus overlooking the pertinence of these reforms to Europe. In this critical mind toward both Euro-centric arrogance and the Islamo-centrism of my co-religionists, I have been in search of new outlooks while not claiming to have found the solution, but I assert that the pains undertaken in seeking new outlooks have been individual efforts, as described by *ijtihad* in Islam or, to put it in the Cartesian tradition, "*cogito ergo sum.*" Despite my Islamic socialization, my worldview is rooted in cultural modernity. I also openly profess that I do not share the post-modernist cultural relativist belief in "multiple modernities," nor the dichotomic Islamic view of the world splitting the globe into *dar al-Islam/* house of Islam, as opposed to *dar al-harb/*house of war, or house of the unbelievers. One finds this worldview even among European-born Muslims who disparage Europe as the abode of *kufr*/unbelief (see the report: "Jiha-dist Self-portrait" in *International Herald Tribune*, 9 August 2005, p. 2). This book seeks other options based on reason.

Cultural modernity, as outlined in a major book by Jürgen Habermas and intellectually rooted in the thinking of René Descartes, Immanuel Kant and Max Weber, is a European idea. In addition to it, I have learned in my European education that Europe itself is "a beautiful idea," a term coined by Rob Riemen, the director of the Dutch Nexus Institute. This institution ran a research project on this topic, supported by the Dutch government during its presidency of the European Union in the second half of 2004. The dialogue had both a European (The Hague, Berlin, Warsaw, Rotter-dam) and a transatlantic (Washington, DC) orientation. I was in charge of the discussion on Islam, for which the guiding question was: How could Muslims living in Europe embrace the idea of Europe? To be sure, this goal cannot be reached without changing the dichotomic Islamic worldview just described.

The project mentioned had an impact on this book, as reflected in Part III. The argument raised was that Europe is challenged by Islam, equally through migration and through Turkey's bid for accession to the EU as a full member. It is asked whether the idea of cultural modernity that estab-lishes the self-awareness of man as a thinking subject and the possibility of contributing to the *Entzauberung* (Max Weber) as disenchantment of the world can be appealing to Muslims, in particular to those living in Europe. My argument is: As Islam was Hellenized in medieval times, so this "ratio-nalization" as an accomplishment of cultural modernity in terms of the *Subjektivitaetsprinzip*/principle of subjectivity (Habermas) can also be incorporated into contemporary Islam. Sadly, I feel compelled to note that there are "peer-group" readers, devoid of philosophical education, who misread this notion of "subjectivity" to mean "subjectivism" in contrast with objectivity. With such an awareness of *cogito* – as the subjectivity of man – I write my book and therefore do not remove my individuality (as a subjectivity) while studying the objective world in which I act as a thinking Muslim engaged in rethinking Islam. Unlike the constructivists, I continue to follow Kant in believing that there is an objective world – as "*Ding an sich*" – not constructed by us, even though Kant concedes that we are not fully in a position to capture this objectivity.

On a personal level, my study of Islam results from a process of returning to a belief in enlightened Islam after a decade-long venture into Marxism. When I came from Damascus to Europe in 1962 at the age of eighteen, I became (under the impact of Adorno's and Horkheimer's Frankfurt School) a follower of *Kritische Theorie*/critical theory, a light variety of Marxism. After those years (1965–75), which included education in European philo-sophy and a journey through the *tiers mondisme*/third-worldism of Frantz Fanon, in around 1975 I started – after a severe identity crisis – to study Islam, this time no longer as scripture, as had been the case in Damascus.

Among my early inspirations for engaging in this pursuit was an encounter with the distinguished Jewish-German philosopher Ernst Bloch, who was not on good terms with my academic teachers in Frankfurt, but in contrast to them – though himself a Marxist – was highly knowledgeable about Islam. I first met Bloch in 1965, when he gave me his book *Avicenna und die Aristotelische Linke* (1963), in which he praises the Islamic rationalism of Avicenna against "the mufti world" of Islamic orthodoxy. Six years later – influenced both by Marxism and by Bloch's line of reasoning – I published my own first book, *Die Arabische Linke* (1969). That book was the grounds for Edward Said to invite me to the USA to speak on the Arab left, and to contribute to his book *The Arabs of Today. Perspectives for Tomorrow* (1973). The Arab left was critical of Salafist Islam and of Islamism. The point of departure was the shattering and humiliating Arab defeat in the Six-Day War in 1967, which opened the eyes of my generation and provided impetus for a new thinking that would go beyond the illusions and irrational romanticism of pan-Arab nationalism. In this new context, the reference to the "Aristotelian Left" (Bloch) was an inspiration for a new Enlightenment by the post-1967 Arab left, correctly described by Said as "perspectives for tomorrow." Islamic rationalism is regularly associated with Averroës and therefore the term "Averroëism" is established for covering this tradition. This Averroëism failed in medieval Islam. The failure of the Arab left resulted in a success for political Islam.

In an essay published in November 2005 in the German weekly *Die Zeit*, I drew a parallel between the failure of Averroëist medieval rationalism and that of the post-1967 Arab left – both indications of Islamic Enlightenment. To understand these failures, we need to grasp the meaning inherent in religion. In his outstanding biography of Thomas Muentzer as a theologian of the medieval peasant revolution, Bloch warned that religion would be ill perceived if reduced to economic and social conditions, for religion is an entity in itself. Though it is embedded in social realities, it is not simply a reflection of them and can affect both social and economic conditions of life. In addition to Emile Durkheim, this Blochian view has had a great impact on my understanding of religion. It is true, as I learned from Adorno and Horkheimer and their *Kritische Theorie*, that every example of economic reductionism, i.e. explaining everything within a reference to economic constraints, is an expression of vulgar Marxism. But the Frankfurt School approach itself was not helpful for a proper understanding of religion. Therefore, I was compelled in my study of Islam to put aside Marxian theory – and later abandon it from my thoughts altogether. The Frankfurt School taught me to think rationally and critically and not to refrain from subjecting everything – even my Islamic beliefs – to reflection in the course of critical reasoning. I continue to be loyal to this approach, but beyond this the Frankfurt School gave no further guidance. So what is to be done in the search for a bridging between cultural modernity and Islam, both in the world at large and in Europe? What solution can be found for overcoming the pending predicament? The present book claims to be a modest contribution to this end, with a focus on Islam and world affairs on the one hand and Islam in Europe on the other.

Those who accuse me of "Islam-bashing" fail to understand my work as a continuation of efforts by enlightened Muslims at "rethinking Islam" (M. Arkoun). My earlier books – *The Crisis of Modern Islam* (1980, US edition 1988), ten years later *Islam and the Cultural Accommodation of Social Change* (1990) and after another eleven years *Islam between Culture and Politics* (2001) – deal with the politicization of Islam as a misleading perspective for Muslims and their future. In this context I reiterate my contention: The problem is not Islam as a religion, but its politicization as a belief system. However, a religious belief is also at work, as dealt with as politicized religion. The politicization of religion is not simply an instrumental use of religion. At issue is a reference to the meaning of religion for political ends. In my view, a civil Islam can be put in harmony with secular democracy as the better choice for our Islamic civilization. In Europe, the variety of such a civil Islam compatible with democracy is characterized by the concept of Euro-Islam, which I claim to have unfolded since a presentation made in Paris back in 1992. This book is committed to rethinking Islam and ends with a concluding chapter on Islam and democracy as the *al-hall*/the solution for Muslims in their current *mihna*/crisis. This is my commitment.

Bassam Tibi
Ithaca, New York
Institute for European Studies at Cornell University

Introduction

The impact of the politicization of Islam on world politics as a context for Europe and Islam in the 21st century

In a pre-modern sense, i.e. in an understanding of world politics prior to the creation of the Westphalian system[1] of sovereign states, the Mediterranean[2] was the center of world history. At present, the combination of an expanding European Union in the North and continuing surge of political Islam in the South has been contributing to making this region pivotal for contemporary international politics. Historians are familiar with the civilizational centrality of the Mediterranean that predates the rise of Islam in the past and of Islamism at present: The Roman Empire viewed the Mediterranean as *mare nostrum*/our sea. This understanding was challenged when the foundation of Islam took place not only as a religion, but also as a competing civilization. The new monotheist message of the Prophet Mohammed[3] (610–32) changed the Mediterranean. The ensuing rise of an Islamic empire based on Islamic *futuhat*-expansion[4] aimed at mapping the globe into *dar al-Islam* and transferred the Mediterranean into an Islamic sphere. This Islamic model of globalization was the first of this kind in world history.[5] Following the conquests in the Mediterranean, Arab-Muslims invaded Europe from the south-west (Spain) in a first wave and, centuries later, in a second wave from the south-east (the Balkans). The Turk-Muslims were able to accomplish what Arabs failed to do: to conquer Constantinople in 1453 and to bring Byzantium to an end. Is this a model for the present? Some believe they see Islamic civilization threatening to engulf Europe by Islamizing it. The announced end of history has proven to be a fallacy, given the lie by a return of history. This book asks whether massive Islamic migration to Europe is creating a third wave related to the history just outlined, or whether Europe will be able to absorb Muslim immigrants by integrating them as citizens. Could Islam become European, as a Euro-Islam? In the spirit outlined in the preface, I have been writing this book as a scholar who combines a Muslim background of immigration with the will to embrace the idea of Europe, and who thus rebukes the rhetoric of a clash of civilizations. To be sure, European realities of other-ing Muslims and marginalizing them are not in line with the idea of Europe. Both Europeans and Muslims need to change, to avert an unfolding of the announced clash of civilizations in a self-fulfilled prophecy. The present book is a contribution to this needed change on both sides.

The issue: not the end, but the return of history

Despite all the romance of medieval Islamic Spain, the heritage of that historical experience is not a model for European–Muslim relations, either in Europe itself or in the Mediterranean neighborhood of the European Union. The moderate Egyptian Islamist Hasan Hanafi – as quoted in the preface – proposed, in all seriousness, in the Madrid meeting of March 2005 that Europeans consider the model of Andalusia, i.e. of an Islamized Iberia, as a solution for the whole of "crisis-ridden" Europe in the twenty-first century.[6] Underlying this proposition is the coincidence of the end of bipolarity, with both an intensifying Islamic migration to Europe and a civilizational identity crisis in Europe. Does the claim expressed by Hanafi hold? Does it reflect the return of history as a return of Islam to Europe?

Muslims – like myself – no longer come to Europe as part of a classical jihad, but instead peacefully, within the framework of *hijra*/migration. Students of Islam will know that the Islamic *futuhat*-wars of the classical jihad were traditionally accompanied by the *hijra* of entire tribes from Arabia to the conquered and Islamized areas.[7] The history of combining jihad with *hijra* is related to a practice of the Islamic faith which urges Muslims to migrate in order to spread Islam (*da'wa*). This very history seems at present to return to Europe, putting the prediction of the end of history into question. As quoted in an editorial in the *International Herald Tribune*, Francis Fukuyama acknowledged in view of Islamic migration that Europe is under pressure to defend the validity of its values within Europe itself. According to this report, Fukuyama asked Europeans in Berlin not to let themselves be intimidated by Muslim migrants demanding the recognition of Islamic values as a space for Islam at the expense of European ideals. Is this "the end of history" that Fukuyama proclaimed after the end of the Cold War, or rather the return of it?

To reiterate, in Islam migration is a religious duty with much greater meaning than simply technical migration, i.e. moving from one geographical place to another; rather, it is linked to *da'wa*/proselytization and also to creating *amsar* as *hijra* settlements. In relation to this Islamic process, migrants are claiming Islamic values for Europe, and some of their leaders draw instrumentally on the ideology of multi-culturalism to put communitarian views at the service of creating a space for the Islamic *da'wa*. The earlier failed Islamization of Europe by jihad from the south-west and from the south-east between the eighth and seventeenth centuries can therefore now be seen as resurfacing peacefully in the twenty-first century. The context is the increasing Islamic migration to Europe and the related creation of Islamic parallel societies as "enclaves" (Kelsay) emerging throughout Europe. In short, at issue is not "the end of history,"[8] but rather the return of the history of civilizations,[9] both to Europe and to world politics. The core question once again is how Islam is challenging Europe. This is a major theme of the present book, alongside proposing an accommodation for averting any polarization on the grounds of maintaining the identity of Europe.

It is regrettable that this debate – as resumed in this book – is highly burdened by the work of Samuel P. Huntington, which is itself unfortunately biased and in many ways flawed through many misinterpretations of the history both of civilizations and of Islam. The work of the founder of the science of civilization/*ilm al-umram*, namely Ibn Khaldun, is completely ignored in Huntington's *Clash of Civilizations*.[10] In contrast, Arnold Toynbee's inquiry about civilizations acknowledges the centrality of Ibn Khaldun.[11] This distinguished Muslim philosopher of the fourteenth century was the first to conceptualize the history of humankind as *ilm al-umran*/science of civilization. The twentieth-century seminal historian Arnold Toynbee,[12] who considered himself a disciple of Ibn Khaldun, perceived his own study of history as a study of civilizations in the path of this Muslim philosopher. Two other major scholars pertinent to this inquiry are also missing in Huntington's thinking. The first is the Belgian historian Henri Pirenne, who related the rise of Europe under Charlemagne to the challenge of Islam. The Islamic incursion into the Mediterranean contributed to the decline of the Roman Empire – which was basically Mediterranean rather than European. In a sense, Western Christendom shaped Carolingian Europe in the process of this formation of Europe, which would have been inconceivable without the impact of Islam. As Henri Pirenne put it forcefully: "*Sans Mahomet, pas de Charlemagne.*"[13] Nevertheless, at issue are not the rival religions of Christianity and Islam, as is often contended, but rather the civilizations related with each. The historical product has been their competition with one another. The other scholar missing in Huntington's work is Raymond Aron, who in his *Paix et guerre entre les nations*[14] rightly notes that the real division of humanity lies not in the "blocs" of the Cold War but rather in the heterogeneity of civilizations. In that book, published in 1962 (i.e. at the height of the Cold War) Aron predicted that bipolarity – a veiling of the heterogeneity of civilizations – could not be a lasting divide, and that with its disappearance the true civilizational divide would emerge. This is, in fact, what is happening at present and is determining world politics in the twenty-first century, as described in this book in terms of the return of history as a history of civilizations.

In my view, the surge of political Islam, viewed by its exponents as a civilizational *sahwa*/awakening,[15] is ill perceived if it is viewed merely as, negatively, a case of religious extremism or fanaticism, or, positively, a religious renaissance. Both interpretations are flawed. At issue is a revival of a civilizational worldview, based on the vision of a new idea of an Islamic world order[16] in which a reinventing of the historical tradition of jihad takes place. In Chapter 1 this revival is addressed as a rise of "a deadly idea" that does harm equally to Muslims and to others. The goal of the Islamists is to replace the existing order based on the secular foundations of the 1648 Peace of Westphalia with *Hakimiyyat Allah*/God's rule. Thus the targets are the nation-state and subsequently the existing world order.

At present, world politics is being shaped by US-American hegemony. The concept of "the West" consists, however, of both Europe and North America, and therefore while Islamic anti-Western attitudes may reflect an anti-Americanism on the surface, Europe is much more affected by the civilizational claims of political Islam targeting the "crusaders," who were in fact Europeans. In contrast to the propaganda of the new conservative right in the US, there is no trace of Islamization in North America. In Europe, on the other hand, this issue is a genuine concern, reviving collective memories – on both sides – be they of the efforts for an Islamic mapping of Europe, or the crusaders conquering the world of Islam. A "war of memories" is at issue. As quoted above, Hasan Hanafi's words in Madrid voiced what many Muslim migrants in Europe have in their minds. In this book, however, I pointedly refuse to contribute to such divides and strive to study the conflict on its own terms, avoiding a mindset of conquest. Instead, when exploring the "Islamization of Europe," I adopt a mindset of accommodation and consider the "Europeanization of Islam"[17] as the alternative.

In Islam, the mindset of conquest is that of jihad. In every case, jihad is an effort to spread Islam for mapping the world into *dar al-Islam*. This may be done peacefully through Islamic *da'wa*/proselytization, or – as at the present time – by resorting to "terror in the mind of God"[18] – a term coined by Mark Juergensmeyer. As will be shown in Chapter 1, according to the Qur'an jihad becomes an expression of violence when it is combined with *qital*/physical fighting, but it is definitely not "terror." However, today's jihad, called *jihadiyya*/jihadism or global jihad/*al-jihad al-alami*, is something new based on a reinvention of tradition[19] and it heralds the return of history in the addressed sense. The packaging and language are traditional but the substance is new, and this is precisely what makes this return of tradition not merely a revival, but a reinvention. In this new language of global jihad is expressed the return of Islam – not as a religious faith – and of the historical claims of its civilization to world politics. The target of this jihadism is not only the US (9/11), but also, and most significantly, Europe (Madrid on 11 March 2004; Amsterdam on 2 November 2004 and London in July 2005). The Club de Madrid has responded to this challenge with a call for "safe democracy and security" (see note 6). Does democracy prevent jihadism? In Chapter 2's discussion of democracy and Islam, I ask how Muslims could embrace the idea of democracy and of democratic peace as the alternative to political Islam. Civil Islam is compatible with democracy, but Islamism is not.[20] The message of political Islam to Europe is conveyed in an Islamist expression of the new "revolt against the West"[21] bringing history back to the fore!

The deadly idea of global jihad – used here interchangeably with jihadism – can be traced back to Hasan al-Banna;[22] a new concept is at issue, no longer the same as classical jihad. The grandson of al-Banna, Tariq Ramadan, presents his grandfather not only as an "anti-colonialist" but also as one of the major sources of *Renouveaux musulman*. This is utterly wrong. Sayyid Qutb[23] is the other authority for jihadist political Islam. The major point is twofold: First, global jihad is not only and simply jihadist terror, but also implies a concept of new order; second, it is directed not only against Western hegemony, but also primarily against the idea of the West as perceived to be opposed to the idea of Islam. This polarization is the content of the war of ideas at issue related to a process of remaking the world[24] in the context of the return of history.

In a nutshell, the contemporary post-bipolar "revolt against the West" supports the already stated assumption that it is directed not only against Western hegemony, but foremost against secular Western values and the rational worldview underlying them. Conceptualized in traditional International Relations (IR) terms, the Islamist revolt is a global jihad against the present world order and the secular structure of authority on which it is based. It is true that non-Western civilizations were exposed to modernity within the framework of European expansion. In a colonial context they also encountered cultural modernity, but the difference was that decolonization movements actually *embraced* European ideas – such as the right to self-determination and to national sovereignty – to legitimize their fight against colonialism. This is not the case with the new revolt of religious fundamentalisms, as it is directed against Western values altogether. In contrast to early decolonization, this revolt refuses to honor the distinction between Western hegemony and cultural modernity. One can reject Western rule and at the same time embrace cultural modernity. Religious fundamentalist movements are based on cultural purisms and reject any hybridity. In bringing "culture" into the debate, I would argue that neither cultural relativism nor so-called post-colonial studies can help in understanding the conflict-triggering dichotomy between purist jihad in pursuit of "Islamic world peace" (*Pax Islamica*) and an Islamic embracing of the Kantian principle of democratic perpetual peace/*ewiger Friede*. Global jihad reflects a variety of neo-absolutism, opposed to "democratic peace" underpinned by cultural pluralism. In addition, cultural modernity can neither be equated with "colonial Orientalism," as some Westerners and Islamists jointly do, nor should it be undermined by the flawed concept of "multiple modernities." It is argued in this book that this conflict matters to Europe becoming the battlefield described. The project of integrating Muslim migrants as European citizens has not been successful, as the Muslim uprising in the *banlieues de l'Islam* of Paris, France (October/November 2005) demonstrates.

The outlined context makes clear that the call for a global jihad, viewed by Sayyid Qutb as an Islamic world revolution for the introduction of a new world order, is a concept that predates the end of the Cold War. This jihadism is no longer classical jihad and it can be traced back to Hasan al-Banna and his *Risalat al-jihad*/essay on jihad. This neo-jihad is essential to the foundations of the movement of the Muslim Brotherhood[25] as the very first movement of political Islam. This legacy, as well as the ideas of Sayyid Qutb, currently enjoys great appeal under conditions of post-bipolarity, and this mobilizatory ideology brings back history. Though only a fringe phenomenon when the Muslim Brothers were founded in Egypt in 1928, the movement eventually moved towards the center to become the mainstream of political opposition in the post-1967[26] context. However, it was not until the assaults of September 11 in New York and Washington, and the chain of 11 March in Madrid to 7 July in London that people in the West developed an awareness of global jihad lying at the hub of world politics. It is sad to see that Islam in general and political Islam in particular have since that time been wrongly associated with an understanding of jihad as terrorism. Let us not forget: the religion of Islam does not endorse terrorism, but forbids it. In addition, political Islam is not identical with jihadist terrorism. All Islamists are Muslims, but not all Muslims are Islamists involved in a "revolt against the West" for the restoration of the history of Islamic dominance. To be sure, not all Islamists are jihadists who resort to violence. Despite all of these differentiations, it is clear that the world at large, Europe and the people of the Islamic civilization need other options than political Islam,[27] in its both jihadist and its peaceful institutional varieties. In an effort to counteract flawed understandings, this book suggests options for Islamic civilization in its contemporary crisis.[28] A distinction is made between two levels: world politics and Europe. On the first level a global move for democratic peace is needed. For Europe a Euro-Islam for the integration of Muslim immigrants is recommended.

In addressing these issues one finds that the Middle East continues in a Mediterranean tradition to be the civilizational core of Islam. All events and developments there have a spillover effect, not only on the rest of this civilization but also on the neighborhood, i.e. on Europe. The competing options presented by the neo-jihad of an "Islamic world revolution" are the creation of the divine order Qutb termed *Hakimiyyat Allah*/God's rule. This is viewed as an alternative to the democratization of the Arab world as a neighborhood of Europe. The option touches greatly on the future of the European Union.[29] It is known to me that some contemporary Islamists believe that political Islam could peacefully achieve its concepts of the "Islamic state" viewed as a nucleus for an Islamic world order. The idea of an Islamic world revolution, as taught today in madrasas/Islamic schools has, however, never been abandoned. I do not buy into this trading. Islamists in the world of Islam and in Europe continue to be dedicated to the concept of the classical Islamicate[30] being revived in an "invention of tradition." This revival replaces not only the needed rethinking of Islam in the new international environment, but also the needed democratization in the neighborhood of Europe.

The Islamist vision of the state and of a new world order compels us to look at the systemic structure of international relations in a historical perspective. The bipolar age was shaped by the existence of two competing quasi-empires, the United States and the Soviet Union, both embedded in a global structure concealing the existence of another structure, namely the "heterogeneity of civilizations." In pre-modern times, there were no such global structures. Instead, there existed a diversity of regionally competing civilizational empires, which were not connected with one another nor able to become completely global. The one exception in world history was the period of *futuhat* or "opening" of Islamic civilization, which occurred between the seventh and the seventeenth centuries and ended the dominance and rivalry of the Byzantines and the Sassanides. During that period, Arab and Turkish Islamic empires successively dominated major parts of the world, with the goal of enhancing the territoriality of *dar al-Islam* through classical jihad and ultimately of mapping the entire globe in accordance with this model. But while the then established Islamicate (see note 30) was successful in its own terms as an effort at globalization, it was not so to the extent of becoming fully global. Therefore its order was never a world order in our modern understanding. By contrast, the later military revolution in Europe,[31] based on modern science and technology, paved the way for an emerging West to become the civilization that would succeed at establishing the global world structure.[32] The Islamic civilization had failed to accomplish this goal through processes of what is often called globalization. In view of the inflationary use of the term "globalization" it is important to state firmly that the understanding of globalization is limited here to an "ability" of a structure and the related idea to map the entire globe. In this understanding, Islamic expansion was the first globalization in history, even though it never reached the completion it envisioned.

The history of the international system shows that only the Westphalian order of sovereign states – as both a structure and an idea, and as determined by Western standards – gained global dominance. In the twenty-first century, political Islam is challenging these realities and is at pains to reverse them. This is the meaning of de-Westernization for a remaking of the world along a return of history. It can be viewed as a backlash against Western dominance and as an indication of a return of the history of civilizations in the shape of reinvented traditions. De-Westernization is not to be equated with political Islam, for it is also a sentiment shared by other non-Western civilizations, which were subjected to the Western-dominated globalization.

It is true that the issues discussed are not only pertinent to the world of Islam. The Islamic civilization is, however, the only one that – next to the West – claims universality. Therefore the effort of political Islam to mobilize Islamic civilization as an expression of a return of history matters most to post-bipolar developments in world politics and to Europe under conditions of Islamic migration. Since the time of bipolarity and the decline of Europe as the perceived core of the West, the world has radically changed. Today, people who blame the USA for globalization and its effects seem to forget that the origins of these globalizing processes lie in events and factors triggered by European expansion (see note 32) and conquests worldwide. Therefore, globalization is not a *Pax Americana*. In the meaning suggested earlier, globalization is a process for mapping the globe around one model and one structure, and in this understanding we are not only dealing with a contemporary phenomenon. The Islamic *futuhat* expansion as well as the European expansion were the earlier competing models of globalization. The Islamic expansion of an expansive jihad was halted and replaced by a Western model of globalization, which subsequently extended into the world of Islam itself. Here we find the roots of today's Islamic outrage directed against US hegemony. The origin of this process was, however, a revolt against Europe as a resistance to the colonial rule of the nineteenth century. The first revivalist Muslim leader al-Afghani[33] called for jihad against the West – but only to deter European expansion. Unlike the expansive jihad from the seventh to the seventeenth centuries, this pattern of the nineteenth-century jihad was basically an anti-colonial and culturally defensive mobilization, definitely not for expansive ends. The jihadism of today is a new pattern in a situation that has changed yet again. This global jihad or jihadism is neither classical nor anti-colonial jihad. It is an instrument in a strategy to replace the existing world order with an Islamic one. Therefore the anti-colonial jihad of al-Afghani in the nineteenth century has to be dissociated from the global jihad of Hasan al-Banna and his Muslim Brotherhood. There is a significant distinction between the two that belies the claimed continuity, contended for instance by the grandson of al-Banna, the Swiss-born Tariq Ramadan,[34] a person often accused, rightly or wrongly, of Islamism.

In concluding this preliminary debate – focused on Francis Fukuyama's premature conclusion that, after the breakdown of communism, a triumph of Western values and thus "the end of history" is taking place – an update is needed. It is suggested that the visions and values related to global jihad rather indicate a return of history of civilizational conflict determining the present. An insight into this change led Fukuyama to reconsider his assumption and to express his concern over the claims of some leaders of the growing Islamic diaspora in Europe. In considering this background he joined me in proposing a European *Leitkultur* (culture of guiding values) for Muslim migrants to share with Europeans as an alternative to jihad. At a summit meeting of European and US opinion leaders addressing the question of "Europe – A Beautiful Idea?" under the EU presidency of the Netherlands, I presented my ideas[35] and received the support of Fukuyama when he recommended in his presentation that Europeans "embrace the views of Bassam Tibi." His words were of great comfort to me, both on a personal level and for the sake of Europe's future as a continent shared by Muslims and Europeans. I conclude by stating that, instead of an Islamization, a secular-democratic, cultural and religious pluralism needs to be the basis for the guiding values. This is not multi-culturalism but a civic culture also shared by Muslim migrants, and it is the meaning of the slogan coined in a Cornell project (see note 17): "Europeanizing Islam" as an alternative to the "Islamization of Europe." At issue is a competition as a war of ideas in the context of a return of history.

The major theme of this book and its structure

The major theme of this book is the competition of global jihad and the secular culture of democracy in Europe, both in world politics and in view of a diaspora of Islam. Despite allegations by some Muslim apologists, who deny any relation between jihadism and Islam or tensions with democracy and pluralism, this book deals in honesty with a current political and cultural reality in Islamic civilization reaching out to Europe. At issue is a message originally given by Sayyid Qutb and continued at present. The preoccupation with al-Qaeda and its terror is misleading: the challenge under issue is not restricted to an organization, since a "deadly idea" elevated to a popular public choice is also involved. In March 1997, the religious zealot Osama bin Laden told Peter Arnett, then a CNN reporter, that "the most important experience we made in the war in Afghanistan [against the Soviet Union] is that we have been able to defeat a superpower." The implication of his message was clear: Having brought the Soviet Union to its knees, the Islamist global jihad was ready to turn against the USA. On the invitation of the Club de Madrid, the Islamist Hasan Hanafi repeated this idea (see also note 16), now upgraded to a mobilizatory ideology. To be sure, the real issue is neither a push for anti-globalization nor a call for more justice in the world, but rather an effort at remaking of the world within the framework of a *Pax Islamica*. Even if bin Laden were to be captured or killed and even if al-Qaeda subsides, the vision and the claim for Islamic supremacy as a "deadly idea" remain. It is acknowledged that this vision cannot be accomplished in the foreseeable future. Nevertheless, it creates disorder in world politics and undermines the integration of Muslims in Europe.

Two steps are taken in this book: the first is to establish the place of Islam in world politics and the second is to determine its space in Europe. In this succession, I refer to security problems related to global migration. Problems of the world of Islam are transferred to Europe. In Afghanistan under Soviet occupation, the Soviet Empire received a tremendous blow. That jihad was providing the backdrop for an ultimate Soviet breakdown was made clear by experts such as Anthony Arnolds, who on the one hand acknowledges the great "social and political problems in the waning years" of Soviet history, yet on the other points to the war in Afghanistan as the "pebble" that brought down the Soviet Union.[36] Could such a destructive process be repeated against the US Empire in its post-9/11 exposure to the challenge of global jihad?

In an earlier book I addressed this question and reached the conclusion that for a number of reasons such a crashing defeat of the USA could not materialize. In that 1998 book, *The Challenge of Fundamentalism*, I maintained, however, that political Islam was in a position to destabilize existing political structures equally at home and internationally, and that it could contribute to shaking US dominance. Since then, the actions of the jihadist Islamist movement have contributed to a trend earlier described as a "new world disorder." The developments following 11 September 2001 in the USA and 11 March 2004 and 7 July 2005 in Europe are supportive of this prediction. In this line of events, the war in Iraq did not lead to the envisioned reordering of the Middle East, but rather to a strengthening of the power of global jihad and to more destabilization as well as to disorder. It is really the case that the irregular war labeled an "insurgency" is leading to still greater disorder, not only in Iraq but throughout the world of Islam through spill-over effects. Another concern is the link to Europe. It is a fact that French- and British-born Muslims are participating in the jihad in Iraq and that the recruitment of so-called "insurgents" includes immigrants in countries like Germany. This is not the "safer world" President George W. Bush promised when he launched his "war on terror." The world has become less safe than it was before.

Given the IR character of this book, it is asked what theories are helpful for the present enquiry. Most IR theories are based on abstract models not derived from the study of realities and therefore they often prove to be of little relevance. To be sure, this great flaw is not remedied by models of statistical correlations established indiscriminately on quantified data. There are prominent US scholars who quantitatively study the so-called "Islamic insurgency" who never have been to Iraq or ever dealt with Islam. These scholars prove to be a joke even though the scholarly community continues listening to them. The models on which they operate do not explain the cultural factors involved. In contrast to IR discipline, traditional Islamic studies are largely uninterested in theory. Moreover, many scholars refrain from dealing with jihadism for reasons of political correctness. They compensate for their Orientalism by becoming Orientalists in reverse. This unpromising state of the field explains existing gaps of knowledge, difficulties, and also the confusion of political Islam with terrorism and at times with Islam itself.

Political Islam consists of two directions, jihadism and institutional Islamism, both constituting different pathways for accomplishing the goals of Islamism, i.e. an Islamic order. Unlike jihadists, institutional Islamists are peaceful and represent a movement willing to participate within a democratic format. Both, however, share the same worldview, i.e. the way of viewing oneself and looking at the other. Traditionally the dichotomy of believers/Muslims versus unbelievers has never ceased to determine the

Islamic worldview. Therefore it is also shared by jihadist and peaceful Islamists, although in different political shapes. Among the commonalities one finds the concept of order in pursuit of a new world order shaped by Islam. In the main, they diverge on the employed means: jihadism as a form of terrorism or participation in existing institutions. As much as I warn against identifying Islam with political Islam, it is equally important to beware of confusing jihadism and Islamism. Both directions, jihadism and institutional Islamism, exist equally in the world of Islam and in its diaspora of Europe, distinct from one another. In world politics, an adherence to democratic peace is required from Muslims for living in peace with peoples of other civilizations. In Europe much more is needed, namely a Europeanization of Islam. This is not only the best choice, but also the bottom line. These contentions reflect the major ideas on which the assumptions of this book rest. In terms of methodology and discipline, I propose that this study, which as far as possible combines IR theory with both Islamic and European studies, integrates the cultural factor in a new post-bipolar approach to IR in acknowledging that culture matters.[37]

This book is organized into three parts. In Part I I introduce the basic notions underlying the civilizational competition in world politics: the envisioned *Nizam Islami*/Islamic order and the vision of democratic peace for a post-bipolar world order. I first inquire into the classical Islamic concept of jihad and how Muslims have debated it, both in the past and in the present, as an instrument of an Islamic world revolution (Chapter 1). This chapter is fundamental to the rest of the book, given the often false contentions made on this issue both by Salafist Muslim and biased Western commentators. Living with Islam requires abandoning not only any education in global jihad, but it also demands to abandon Western Orientalism. This sounds tough, but violence cannot be admitted in a global civil society. Casting accusations of Islamophobia on those who criticize global jihad is no contribution to the dialogue but is part of the war of ideas. In making such contrasts, I attempt to reinterpret Islam alongside the concept of democracy (Chapter 2) in supporting the idea of a civil Islam compatible with democracy. In acknowledging the cultural factor and the cultural turn, I also recognize cultural diversity. However, I put democracy above it. I admit that people of different cultures have different ways of thinking and thus adhere to different ways of looking at democracy. But culture is always in flux and one should beware of essentializing cultural diversity. There are limits to it. For this kind of study one needs to establish epistemological grounds for an inter- and cross-cultural understanding that seeks commonalities. This goal cannot be reached through quantitative methods. In short, in studying Islam and democracy, one needs also to address the question of cultural diversity without abandoning the need for commonalities. As much as a reason-based universal understanding of knowledge is required, one needs to be sensitive to cultural differences, but never to put these above political democracy. In my work I beware of the traps of both cultural relativism and essentialization. It is most disturbing to see cultural relativism being put at the service of neo-absolutism. Islamism is an indication not of difference but rather of a totalitarian neo-absolutism.[38] Therefore I preclude any real democratic pluralism on the grounds of Islamism. In contrast, Islam can be put in harmony with pluralism on the grounds of religious reforms for overcoming the view of others as subjected minorities within the framework of *dhimmitude*.[39]

In Part II, I move on to deal with Islamist internationalism as an expression of the politicization of a transnational religion bringing the sacred to the core of world politics. At present Islamism is replacing communist internationalism in world politics. Throughout history, the world of Islam has been subdivided along sectarian lines (Sunni and Shi'ite) while simultaneously being characterized by ethnic-local cultural diversity. These real inner differentiations within the ideal of an universalist *umma* are also reflected in the ideology and realities of Islamist internationalism. Chapter 3 deals with the Sunni variety of jihadist internationalism. Originally it was an Arab phenomenon articulated and represented (1928) by the Muslim Brotherhood of Egypt as a non-state actor. Similar global aspirations are to be found in the more recent Shi'ite internationalism, represented by a nation-state, the Islamic Republic of Iran, analyzed in Chapter 4. This state has aimed at exporting its model of governance, and in this pursuit has also promoted jihad in the understanding of terrorism. Many people took at face value the call of the then president of Iran, Mohammed Chatami, for a dialogue of civilizations. They were shocked, however, when the new president "elected" in 2005 revived Khomeinism as an ideology of jihadist terrorism. The "critical dialogue" between Europe and Iran has so far been based on the ignorance and naïveté of EU politicians, who confuse business with intercultural communication.

Part III of the book focuses on Europe; it addresses the relationship between Islam and Europe in two steps. In Chapter 5 it is shown how much Europe and the Mediterranean core of Islamic civilization are historically intertwined, both in terms of mutual threat of conquest – be it jihad or crusade – and in positive terms of inter- and cross-cultural fertilization. Chapter 6 moves to the present, characterized by a massive Islamic migration to Europe creating a sizable presence of Islam as a diasporic enclave within Western civilization. In view of this expanding demographic and religious-cultural presence, it is asked whether Muslim migrants would continue to be aliens living in parallel societies (ghettos) enhancing *dar al-Islam* in Europe as an enclave, or whether they could embrace the idea of Europe and become European citizens at heart instead of quasi settlers aiming at Islamizing Europe. This task is not only a Muslim one; it is also incumbent upon the Europeans themselves to determine whether this project of integration ever succeeds.

In all three parts of the book I operate on the assumption that Islamic civilization and the West as a whole (Western Europe and USA) stand at the center of post-bipolar world politics. In contrast to the USA, Europe is the battlefield both for possible rapprochement and of political conflict with cultural undercurrents. Islam's relations with Europe are burdened historically with an ambiguity. Islam faced Europe with a predicament with cultural modernity and simultaneously the political-military challenge of Western hegemony. The incursion into the world of Islam by expanding colonial Europe preceded the American–Islamic rivalry. Muslims equally emulate Europe and repel it. At present, the US politics of the "war on terror" distorts the conflict and gives it the shape of a US–Islamic rivalry that distracts from basic realities. The Europe of the EU is now a continent for massive migration from Islamic civilization – a home to some 20 million Muslims – creating a complex array of issues more pertinent to Europe than to the USA. Europe needs its own distinct approach; it cannot and should not treat every Muslim as a suspect. As a friend of the USA, I am deeply disturbed every time I enter the USA and am treated as a suspect on the grounds of religion and ethnicity, only because I am a Muslim who was born in Damascus. This is counter-productive, for there is a desperate need to incorporate Muslims into a pluralistic world both on the level of international community and within Europe itself. The West needs to beware of a derailed "war on terror" that alienates Muslims and makes them feel that they are the target of this war.

Europe today with 20 million Muslim migrants needs to engage in a Europeanization of Islam and to differentiate between ordinary Muslims and Islamists. Since Madrid 11 March 2004, the slaying of Theo van Gogh as an unbeliever by an Islamist in November the same year and London 7 July 2005, European governments and civil societies have started to perceive the challenge. To be sure, the Islamists are a tiny minority (3 to 5 per cent) within the European diaspora of Islam. But it is acknowledged that we are in reality dealing with a very powerful minority, at times controlling major institutions of the diaspora including mosques, faith schools and so-called religious welfare associations engaged in "alms for jihad."[40]

To sum up the presentation of this book, it is in its structure and content a study of International Relations, including European and Islamic studies in a radically changing world. The book ends in its Chapter Seven with a proposition: democracy as a political culture is the solution to be shared by the conflicting parties. I believe the established discipline of IR has not yet met the current challenge, perhaps because the discipline has been predominantly a narrow-minded American social science preoccupied with the study of state and power from a Western point of view, a study that overlooks the place of religion in world politics.[41]

Ironically, theories share certain aspects of religions – in religion you pay dearly for suspicion of disbelief, just as you may in scholarship if you happen to stand outside the "mainstream" and do not share the views of the dominant schools of thought believed to provide "robust theories and models" – in other words, the true belief. To state it bluntly: Peer-group-reading is a power game, not a scholarly assessment and evaluation. I take this risk, just as I do within my own religion as a reform Muslim. The birth of this book supports this assessment.

The study of religion is a recent addition to world politics, and it is the subject-matter of this book. Today in the USA and in Europe, no prudent scholar of International Relations would deny the relevance and significance of the study of religions, such as Islam as a transnational religion, to international studies. However, scholarly and professional contributions from an IR perspective to the field of religious studies are rare, a shortage reflected clearly in scholarly journals. Religion is a "cultural system." The growing prominence of the insight that "culture matters" (see note 37) is a head-start and continued efforts are needed. There must be a change in cultural attitudes, not just by Muslims but also by the Western academic establishment itself. IR scholars strive to preserve their "theoretical" heritage, while scholars of the Middle East and Islam waste their energies on accusing each other of the sin of "Orientalism." It is most regrettable that even the propaganda of political Islam now finds its way to the scholarly language of US Islamic studies. Despite all its flaws, the "war on terror" is not "the new crusade" that the title of a book published by a prominent US university press suggests. With few exceptions, there is little grasp of the politicization of religion in post-bipolar international relations heralding the "return of the sacred." In the world of Islam, the "sacred" is returning in the form of political Islam rather than as a religious renaissance.

The concluding chapter of this book focuses on the difficulties of democratization in the present age of Islamism. The major slogan of the Islamists is "*al-Islam huwa al-hall*/Islam is the solution." In Chapter 7 I argue that democratization is the solution. Various deliberations are needed to establish a cultural-Islamic underpinning of democracy in the world of Islam.

The present contribution claims to belong equally to the diverse fields of Islamic, European and international studies and I do not wish to see it classified as an Islamic-area study only. In my own experience, gaining acceptance for this kind of inquiry and approach is becoming very difficult. However, I continue to speak out and write with a belief in academic freedom and the civil right of free speech, even though – regrettably – realities in Europe and the USA run counter to this belief for a Muslim, like this author. I am acting in a Western environment seeking to bridge the two worlds without, however, overlooking existing conflicts, which I approach candidly.

Transnational religion and world politics: the scope of the study and its approach

Sadly, in the aftermath of 9/11 and 11 March 2004, as well as 7 and 21 July 2005, only a few IR scholars have recognized the role of Islam in the new development of world politics in a professional manner of the discipline. Among them is Daniel Philpott, who argues, "radical Islamic revivalism . . .

challenges the authority structure of the international system. This is the tradition behind al-Qaeda's attacks."[42] In a broader sense, the rise of Islamism as an indication of the politicization of religion is related to a global phenomenon of religious revival articulated as the "return of the sacred" – a challenge to the secular worldview established in Western societies, but not yet in non-Western civilizations. The study of religion and politics has also become an area of concern for the discipline of IR in view of the impact of transnational religion. The ascendance of Islamist movements as non-state actors makes clear that the overall issue is the "return of the sacred" taking place as a politicization of religion. This process also affects International Relations based on secular foundations. When it comes to Islam, the study of jihadism as terror (professionally phrased: the violence of irregular warfare) is important; however, more pertinent are the differences in worldviews and values. At stake is not simple terror, but rather the quest for a new world order. In this context, the distinction between the international system and the international society is of fundamental importance for understanding the "return of the sacred" and the related discord with regard to world order. As Bull argues:

> a *society of states* (or international society) exists when a group of states, conscious of certain common interests and common values form a society ... bound by a common set of rules in their relations with one another ...

> An international society in this sense presupposes an international system, but an international system may exist that is not an international society.[43]

In relating this distinction to the "revolt against the West" (see note 21) articulating a contestation of European values, it becomes clear that this revolt is "best exemplified" (ibid.) in the case of Islamic fundamentalism, as Bull contends. In this understanding there can be no stable international system or perpetual world peace if the related values are not shared. The same applies to inner peace in Europe in the age of migration. The call for global jihad in the pursuit of an Islamic order – in contrast to the need to incorporate the world of Islam into a system of democratic peace or, more specifically, Muslim migrants into European citizenry – is the source of tension. This issue of the "return of the sacred" with a concept of order is of crucial importance to the West. This matter is related to the question of shared values. To put it in Bull's language, the world of Islam is a part of the present international system, but not yet of an international society sharing common values. To reiterate the concern: While such an understanding is useful in exploring the nature of war and peace in world politics, it is equally valid for the case of Muslim migrants living in "enclaves *in* the West, but not *of* it."[44] As a continent of rising Islamic migration, Europe is beginning to feel the heat of the conflict between secularity and politicized religion. Islamists call upon civil rights, in particular freedom of faith, to ensure their safe havens. The accusation of Islamophobia has become a most useful instrument to beat any critique in the respective war of ideas.

Europe is a recipient or an importing place of political Islam. The movement of the Muslim Brotherhood, established in 1928 in Cairo, was the beginning. Egypt was the birthplace of this development and continues to be the core place of political Islam. In addition, the Muslim Brotherhood of today has its mosques and infrastructure in Germany and throughout Europe. This movement is an example of a transnational religion. Despite all differences between Salafi-Wahhabi and political Islam, the notion of transnational religion applies to both. Islam in Europe is being promoted today through Saudi funding of mosques and madrasas. Islamists throughout the world do not mind receiving Wahhabi petrodollars. What do Islamists want, and why Europe?

One of the diaspora Islamist movements, Hizb al-Tahrir, established in Jordan in the early 1950s but now acting in the UK and Germany (despite its ban), rejects the existing secular nation-states established in the Muslim world following the dissolution of the Ottoman Empire. This movement, an offspring of the Muslim Brotherhood, claims from London to be re-establishing the Islamic order of the caliphate. It is, however, utterly wrong to conclude that the "restoration of the caliphate" is the foremost goal of political Islam. Unlike Hizb al-Tahrir the majority of the Islamists adhere to the notion of *Nizam Islami*/Islamic system.

When the caliphate was dissolved in 1924, the context was one of colonization and de-colonization. Today, Islamists want to reverse this process by de-Westernizing the world at large within the framework of an Islamic system. When it comes to the diaspora in Europe, they seek to undermine the integration of Muslim immigrants into European society, because they want to use the diaspora as an enclave and logistics base for their two-step strategy. The first step is to topple the nation-state at home, while the second is to topple the present international order, which is to be replaced by an alternative Islamic one. The aim is justified in the belief that Islamic principles of order are universal. Therefore this section began with "the return of the sacred" viewed as a challenge to the "authority structure of the international system." In relating this phenomenon to political Islam and Islamic migration to Europe I determine the scope of the present study. Again, a new Islamic order and not the restoration of the caliphate is at issue.

The addressed "return of the sacred" runs counter to any "disenchantment of the world/*Entzauberung der Welt*" (Max Weber). The outcome of this process of "disenchantment" is cultural modernity as a secular discourse. Secularization has been an essential part of cultural modernity (the term "multiple modernities" is misleading) and de-secularization is the "revolt" against it. Any inclusion of Islam in European democracies within the framework of the proposed Europeanization of Islam requires coming to terms with Islam's predicament with cultural modernity. Can Muslims share secular values with non-Muslims?

Unlike Christianity, which underwent a process of secularization and then privatization of faith, Islam never ceased to have an impact on politics. In modern times, however, Islam has been exposed not only to Western hegemony but also to secular cultural modernity. Jürgen Habermas, the pre-eminent European theorist of cultural modernity, identifies modernity with secularization by borrowing the Weberian formula of "the disenchantment of the world/*die Entzauberung der Welt*." Weber – and in his footsteps Habermas – sees the separation of the worldly and the divine as one of the foundations of cultural modernity. In this sense, there exists only one reason-based modernity and the claim of "multiple modernities" is left meaningless. As Habermas puts it: "Weber described ... as rational the process of disenchantment which led in Europe to a disintegration of religious worldviews that issued in a secular culture."[45] In acknowledging cultural diversity, it is to be asked whether this Western notion is based on a universally valid knowledge. Does this knowledge underpin a worldview that can be shared on cross-cultural grounds by all of humanity? Is cultural modernity – as Islamists contend – an "epistemological imperialism"[46] of the West? The epistemological aspects of this issue are discussed elsewhere and therefore put aside here. In drawing on it, only one aspect has to be addressed, namely the political ramifications of the rejection of modern Western knowledge by the Islamists.

In fact, the Islamist accusation of "epistemological imperialism" serves as a denunciation of cultural modernity and subsequently of the secular concept of order. There are also those Western cultural relativists who give in and speak of "multiple modernities" in applying their relativism to their own culture. These Westerners are blamed by Ernest Gellner for continuing to overlook the neo-absolutism of the others.[47] It becomes clear that an analysis of political Islam and world politics encroaches on issues of dealing with knowledge (see note 46). This issue leads us to cultural analysis, and dealing with it requires breaking taboos. This subject is pertinent to broadening the scope of international studies for including the role of transnational religion in world politics – especially in view of the "return of the sacred" and related conflicts between religious and secular values with regard to political order. Back in the 1960s, when the American-inspired modernization theory[48] dominated social sciences, Westerners believed that all societies, regardless of their civilizational origins, were heading towards secularism, which would be the natural outcome of the development of society toward more complexity and functional differentiation. Since that time the world has radically changed. Today we most assuredly know that this is not happening. Secular legitimacy is questioned and transnational religion is back as "a return of the sacred" in political guise. In Europe this development is one of the great obstacles in the way toward integrating

Muslims as European citizens of a secular polity. Leaders of the Islamic diaspora demand a redefinition of the relationship between religion and the state, as well as a "place for Islam in Europe," in a power game. In this context even Habermas suggested considering a "post-secular society" in Europe itself. The Islamic uprising of October/November 2005 in France illustrates the pertinence of the issue.

During the Cold War era IR scholars were even more blind to religion and culture. They thought that the only obstacle to the equating of universalization and Westernization was to be found in world communism and the related structure of bipolarity in international politics. With this mindset, the breakdown of the Soviet Union prompted triumphal sentiment as expressed by Francis Fukuyama's *End of History* – earlier quoted – and also by Huntington's "third wave of democratization,"[49] suggesting an overall victory of the secular democratic nation-state. The latter process was believed to be of global magnitude. It took only a few years to see one of these authors revising his concept radically in a claim of a "clash of civilizations." Among the results of this revision has been Huntington's coming to believe in the uniqueness of Western accomplishments such as democracy and human rights. Fukuyama is both more balanced and more subtle than Huntington, restricting himself to the effort of protecting Western democratic values against the claims of Islam in the European diaspora. In this debate Fukuyama thus indirectly concedes that "the end of history" was a premature contention and he acknowledges that Europe is becoming a battlefield for the fight over the validity of Western values, now challenged by the Islamic diaspora in the continent itself. This introduction therefore began with addressing the return of history in the twenty-first century and continues in addressing the "return of the sacred." In fact, the return of history is a return of civilizations to the fore; each civilization has its own distinct values and worldviews. However, fault-lines should be avoided, even though politicized religion contributes to this very end in challenging the existing secular order.

Given the fact that we live in one world structured by a comprehensive order of nation-states, there is a need for common values that not only underpin the international system but also make a global civil society possible. These values need to be cross-cultural and therefore secular. Even though some – even Western-educated – Muslims argue that "civil society does not translate into Islam,"[50] Muslims cannot be part of an international society which is intrinsically secular and based on an authority structure reflected in the "Westphalian synthesis" if the values on which it rests are rejected. The continued rise of political Islam and its extension to Europe challenges these foundations of the existing international order. In this situation one must ask: What is at stake and what is to be concluded for the future? Is Huntington's "uniqueness" argument correct, or despite diverging cultures is there – conversely – a hope for a universality of values on cross-cultural grounds? Does transnational religion undermine this pursuit?

It is within the scope of the present study to deal with questions regarding "the return of the sacred" and the related de-secularization. This issue compels us to inquire into the conflict and the commonalities between Islam and the West in order to avert the divides presented by Huntington as fault-lines. One way of doing so, as a contribution to bridging, is to revive the early heritage of Islamic rationalism. Unlike contemporary Islamists, medieval Islamic rationalists affirmed universal knowledge. In drawing lessons from Islamic history for the present, the precedents of Western–Islamic cultural borrowing can be offered as proof against the assumption of "cultural fault-lines" that has been made both by Islamist and by some Western authors. I have chosen the battlefield "Europe" in the context of Islamic migration to propose Euro-Islam as an alternative, both to the "clash of civilizations" and to the envisioned Islamization of Europe. Regrettably, a chapter on Islamic heritage had to be taken out of this book in order to comply with page limits. It suffices to summarize its substance: Islam had in its medieval glory a tradition of Enlightenment, of being open to learning from others. In contrast, today's political Islam closes the minds of contemporary Muslims. It presents neither a case of "multiple modernities" nor a post-secular society, but rather a new form of totalitarianism.[51] An essential part of the heritage of Islam that cannot be discussed at length in this book is its Hellenization. Muslim rationalists adopted the Greek legacy. Given the very roots of democracy in the Greek polis which the great political philosopher of Islam, al-Farabi, embraced as a model in his magnificent work *al-madina al-fadila* [The Perfect State], Muslims of today could embrace democracy and the idea of democratic peace on similar grounds. Could the return of history be shaped by earlier cross-cultural fertilization instead of being shaped by jihad and crusades? These are the two competing sides of the coin presented here as the history of civilizations.

In repeating the notion that culture matters and subsequently in including transnational religion as a cultural factor, I distinguish between a globalization of structures and a universalization of norms and values. The claim that globalization is sweeping and encompasses all aspects of life fails to recognize this distinction. The message is: cultural modernity can be universalized (norms and values), but structures are to be globalized. This is not the same process. To claim that both are the same is belied by the reality in which global economic structures are converging while cultures are diverging. In my work, I address existing tensions in terms of a simultaneity of *cultural fragmentation* (divergence over norms and values) and globalization (convergence of structures). The argument follows that structures are globalized, but with no cultural acceptance underpinning this globalization. The term "cultural globalization" is thus based on a wrong concept and is a contradiction in terms because culture by definition (a system of meaning) is always local. In view of the lack of a cultural underpinning, i.e. indigenization, for these globalized structures, there is the perception of an imposition from outside – a case in point is the introduction of secular democracy in post-Saddam Iraq, related to an unfavorable perception. Applying this to the secular nation-state and to democracy in the non-Western world in general, and in the world of Islam in particular, one is in a position to understand the repeatedly addressed "revolt against the West" (see note 21). In much of the Muslim world there is a crisis – both normative and structural – in which the appeal of political Islam and the alternatives it presents to the nation-state is growing and anti-Western sentiments are running high. It is too simple to view this revolt as an indication of an anti-globalization, because, rather, a legitimacy crisis of the international order is at issue. The crisis reflects the existence of an international system (interaction between states) that lacks necessary commonalities needed to establish an overall international society (shared rules, norms and values). This is the distinction made by Bull, introduced at the outset of this section. The described situation leads to world disorder and to the conclusion that a new approach is needed. Islamists state "*al-Islam huwa al-hall*/Islam is the solution." Enlightened Muslims must reject this claim in a plea for democracy, as done in the concluding chapter to this book.

These deliberations on the return of religion challenging the mostly secular international environment focus on the world of Islam and on the new pattern of transnational religion, because this is the most pertinent case for world politics. The Middle East is, next to Europe, the prominent region in point.[52] In this context the nominal nation-states in the world of Islam stand in conflict with the inherited dichotomous religion-based division of the world into the house/abode of Islam/*dar al-Islam* and the house of unbelievers/*dar al-kuffar* or house of war/*dar al-harb*.[53] This dichotomy is based on a *Weltanschauung*/worldview not supported by political structures. But now these states are also exposed to the demand of Islamists to be replaced by a divine order of an "Islamic state" consonant with the Islamic worldview. Until the rise of political Islam as articulated by Sayyid Qutb, the world of Islam seemed to have succumbed to the realities of a world of nation-states. The current rise of political Islam – both institutional and jihadist – reflects the crisis of the nation-state in the world of Islam. Some Western scholars, such as Mark Juergensmeyer, grasp this conflict between religious and secular concepts of order well, while others – such as James Piscatori – contend that no problem exists between Islam and the nation-state and thus fail to understand that the call for global jihad is not simply terrorism.[54] It is a call against the nation-state in current world affairs. In Qutb's book *Islam and World Peace* we read that the goal of political Islam is "to defeat any power on earth that prevents the mapping of the world under the 'call to Islam/*da'wa*'."[55] This is the contemporary definition of Islamic global proselytization. Jihadism attaches this *da'wa* to military action heralding the context of religion and world politics in a bid for a remaking of the world.

The succinct phrase by Qutb for determining the Islamic uprising reads: "Islam needs a comprehensive revolution ... being a jihad prescribed on

Muslims to lead this revolution to success for establishing the '*Hakimiyyat Allah*/rule of God'."[56] In short,

> jihad envisions a world revolution/*thawra alamiyya* ... for the realiza-
> tion of (Islamic) peace ... for the entire humanity ... These are the
> outlines for world peace in Islam ... This does not mean to avoid war/
> *qital* at any price ... Islam is a permanent jihad which will not cease
> until Allah's mission rules the world.
>
> (ibid., pp. 172–3)

In fact, this declaration of an Islamic world revolution is tantamount to a declaration of war on the present world order and is therefore, regardless of what it claims, most definitely not a message of peace, neither for global Islamic–Western relations nor for Europe's relations with its Islamic diaspora. This is what is meant when one talks about transnational religion in world politics and in Europe.

Transnational religion in a political shape is a challenge creating fault-lines. Is *Preventing the Clash of Civilizations*[57] feasible? Yes, if my fellow Muslims join in and bid farewell to jihad. I have presented this option in many parts of the world of Islam, for instance in Indonesia, where "civil Islam" is partly a reality, and also in Turkey. Despite all odds, there seem to be no alternatives to democracy as the most promising option for the world of Islam (Chapter 7). In addition, I maintain that "Europe is a beautiful idea" (Chapter 6), also, for Muslim immigrants. In educating Muslims for democracy, for embracing Europe as "citizens of the heart" (Charles Maier, Harvard, September 2001), secular, neither Islamic nor Christian values are the common grounds for living together peacefully. Transnational religion is a reality, but it is not imperative to accept the attached political claims. Democracy could be established on ethical Islamic grounds in the world of Islam, but one should beware of the confusion with an Islamist state that runs counter to democratization.

From bipolarity to uncertainty: political Islam, global jihadism and the "new Cold War"

Instead of dealing with the changed world after the end of bipolarity one encounters ridiculous allegations put forth since the end of the East–West conflict. Some argue that with the breakdown of communism, the West lost the enemy it needed to maintain its unity. This conspiratorial approach suggests that the West was on the lookout for a substitute enemy, and has supposedly found one in political Islam. No doubt, "the revolt against the West" as defined by Bull (see note 21) and exemplified by the rejection of the secular nation-state by Islamic fundamentalism is a reality and nobody's invention. The existing conflict can be seen as the triggering of a "new Cold War" (see note 54). World peace, much desired for the twenty-first century, needs to be combined with European inner peace in the age of cultural diversity. Through migration, transnational religions touch also on Europe in the context of politicization and the world-wide drive towards de-secularization, thus threatening peace. Political Islam is a phenomenon documented by facts, and not an invention in a search by the CIA or Mossad for a substitute enemy. An analysis of political Islam and its jihadism in the age of "the new Cold War" clearly has to be free of any such conspiratorial approaches to open our eyes to occurring uncertainties creating the real challenge.

As consistently argued, the rise of political Islam and the uncertainties it engenders are related to the overall phenomenon of the "return of the sacred." Not merely an indication of a renaissance of religion, this move-ment serves as an articulation of the "revolt" against Western values pre-sented in religious garb. In this process of politicization of religion in Islamic civilization, Islamists unfold a new anti-Western ideology engen-dering a "new Cold War" with the rest of the world at large. In the Islamic ghettos in Europe one encounters hatred-Imams undermining the integra-tion of Muslim immigrants into society. An international security dimen-sion is involved. Having said this, I do not wish to indiscriminately defend "secularism" against religion nor do I dismiss the "return of the sacred" in simple terms. The concern is to accommodate the "return of the sacred" for a better future without a "clash of civilizations."

Clearly, the areligious European secularism of the nineteenth and twen-tieth century is no longer a useful venue for the twenty-first century's crisis of meaning, particularly not in the hub of Islamic civilization, the Middle East. There was once, however, an opening for secular thought during the age of "Arab liberal thought." At that time, secularism appealed to Western-educated Muslim elites, but today it has lost its spell. The emerging counter-elites have a religious worldview. Again, a rejection of the militancy and the proselytizing spirit of political Islam does not lead to accepting whatever dogmatic secularism. At issue is the need for an establishing of a religio-cultural underpinning that smoothes an embracing of cultural mod-ernity and democracy in a culturally and religiously diverse world. The great diversity of religious communities precludes that one religion-based order of a single community can be accepted by all others, let alone imposed on them. In view of this fact, it is not an indication of a dogmatic secularism to argue that religious pluralism needs to be based on a separa-tion of religion and politics and thus be acceptable to all religious commu-nities. Such a policy reflects strategies for conflict prevention and no pursuit of secular beliefs. Clearly, today's non-Muslims are not willing to live as *dhimmi* – as explained above – under Islamic rule. In the context of "the return of the sacred," the choice therefore falls between the secular inter-national order of democratic peace and the jihadism of political Islam for a *Pax Islamica*. There are no solutions in between, such as the vague concept of "post-secular society" proposed by Habermas.[58] The end of bipolarity combined with "the return of the sacred" to politics has led to an age of uncertainty in world order. There is nevertheless no alternative to an Islamic embracing of cultural modernity of which pluralism is part and parcel. This kind of thinking has been pursued by, for example, the reform Muslim Abdullahi An-Na'im[59] in his efforts to create cultural grounds for an Islamic acceptance of human rights. If such innovations are not accepted in Islamic civilization, then "the new Cold War" related to *Weltanschauungen*, i.e. a war of ideas, cannot be prevented. If religious-cultural concepts and world-views that naturally create divides among people were to prevail, the outcome would be more uncertainty.

For overcoming existing divides, commonalities can be constructed such as a separation of religion and politics that could serve as a bridge between people of different religions. In contrast, politicized religions of all kinds present their own concepts of order unacceptable to others and thus contribute to "the new Cold War" based on the pattern of conflict addressed in Mark Juergensmeyer's work (see note 54). This conflict is not restricted to Islam and the West in that it can be observed internationally in regional and local conflicts. We can see this in India, Russia, China and Indonesia, the Philippines and Malaysia, where tensions involve other religious communities and their civilizations. In Europe, however, the related conflict is domestic and focused on Muslim immigrants placed in the triangle of Europe, the world of Islam and its diaspora. The overall context is the networking of transnational religion.

The addressed "new Cold War" is a general issue related to the return of the sacred. In the world of Islam this war is ignited by the Islamist concept of a neo-Islamic order (*Hakimiyyat Allah*/Allah's rule) that adds fuel to the fire in the war of ideas. The concept originates in the writings of Qutb, who prescribes fighting jihad to establish a new world order based on an "Islamic world peace."[60] At issue is a global enhancing of *dar al-Islam* to map the entire world. Non-Muslims aside, there are also millions of Muslim women and men who not only reject this vision of Sayyid Qutb, but also refuse to live under the conditions of a totalitarian Islamic shari'a state. In post-Saddam Iraq, Muslim women's groups have been most vocal in opposing the shari'a. It is unfortunate that at present the vision of an Islamic state does attract a few million active Islamists, though they remain a minority, albeit a politically most powerful one. In positive terms Europe holds the potential to become an example of an Islamic embracing of cultural modernity on cross-cultural grounds. If Euro-Islam were to become a reality, incorporating Muslims into a citizenship-based polity and secular democratic peace, it could set a precedent for the world of Islam at large. To be sure, the opposite negative scenario, i.e. Europe as a battlefield between jihadism and democracy, could also set a precedent if Euro-Islamic perspectives fail. Sad to say, a negative scenario is currently at work. The Islamic uprising of Paris in 2005 is not only a case in point, but also a warning valid for all of Europe.

In facing the challenge there is a need to rethink secularism, although without giving up the separation of religion and politics. I need to add my discomfort with all forms of *isms*; therefore in this case and for this reason I prefer to speak of "secularity" or to use the French term *laïcité*. A rejection of the effort of de-secularization[61] by political Islam should not amount to a dismissing of religion. I emphasize that the present analysis is not at all anti-religious. Thus, I restrict my commitment to secular modernity as a decoupling of religion from politics. At the same time, I accept religion as a source of ethics for a cultural underpinning of international morality. This is no contradiction. In this spirit, I draw on the Hellenized tradition of Islamic rationalism, addressed earlier as a positive heritage of Islam, to support the argument that religion – as ethics, *not* as a concept of order – in a cross-religious and cross-cultural morality could contribute to a bridging between Islam and other religions and civilizations. However, this task is not fulfilled by the contemporary revival of religions arising in a political shape. On the contrary, "political religions," since they are clearly based on a concept of order, actually hamper peaceful pursuits. The politicization of religion contributes to establishing civilizational fault-lines. I would call, in the name of Islamic Enlightenment, for an "open civil Islam" analogous to Karl Popper's call for the defense of "open society" against its enemies. This position is compatible with the Islamic tradition of Averroëism that once placed Islam in harmony with the rational worldview of Hellenism. One could establish an analogy between Hellenism in the past and cultural modernity at present in order to provide legitimacy for the much needed spirit of cultural innovation and religious reform. This is not an imposition of secularity and modernity on Muslims, but a double-track effort, first to revive the heritage of Islamic rationalism in order to present it as a variety of an "open Islam," and second to view it as an Islamic model in contrast to political Islam. Is this promising perspective real for averting the "new Cold War" and the related "clash of civilizations"?

The age of uncertainty that gives rise to political religion is not coming to an end, as some experts prematurely announced; the assumed failure of political Islam[62] did not lead to its decline and will not do so as long as the related uncertainties continue to prevail. The truth is that political Islam will continue to be with us for decades to come, waging its "new Cold War" as a "revolt against the West" in the outlined meaning. Political Islam is not only alienating Muslims from non-Muslims, i.e. from the rest of humanity, but also creating rifts within the Islamic *umma* itself. It is an illusion to believe that jihadism can be extinguished by a military US-led war on terror, because at issue is a war of ideas and the related worldviews, in addition to this being an irregular war difficult to win. The task of change must fall to Muslims themselves. A model for such an effort is the work done at the Hidayatullah Islamic State University of Jakarta where a dialogue between Islam and the West – not only as dialogue between civilizations but also as a security dialogue – has been taking place.[63] There it was also possible to conduct an experiment with graduate students and other liberal Muslims favorable to democratic peace and critical of global jihad. These students welcomed democracy, rejected jihadism and showed themselves to be willing to accept the separation between religion and politics as well as to learn from others in the tradition of the medieval Islamic rationalists who embraced the Greek legacy. These individuals represent a variety of Islam existing in Indonesia, earlier addressed in a general manner as "civil Islam." Unfortunately, Wahhabi Islam[64] and other varieties lacking such a civil-society-based understanding of religion are spreading from Saudi Arabia throughout the world of Islam and – as already stated – are even reaching out to the Islamic European diaspora. In Europe, Wahhabi Islam can be countered by the concept of Euro-Islam.[65] To be sure, Wahhabi Islam is a reality in Europe's mosques; Euro-Islam, however, is only a vision and a policy proposal waiting to be implemented.

In dealing with political Islam one finds it sometimes erroneously associated solely with jihadist views, but there are of course Islamists who are not jihadists. Earlier, I made the distinction between jihadists and institutional Islamists, who pursue a peaceful variety of political Islam. Some Western experts refer positively to the new Islamists as they exist in Turkey's ruling Justice and Development Party (AKP) and in Egypt[66] and take their approval of democracy at face value, but I admit to a strong degree of skepticism. Though it is true that in Turkey there is a political Islam in power under conditions of parliamentarian democracy, I nevertheless contend that all Islamists share the same worldview centered on Islamic order, even though they differ on the instruments employed. When it comes to the Cold War of ideas, both jihadists and institutional Islamists share the goal of de-Westernization. The worldview of Turkey's AKP is definitely not European.

Under conditions of post-bipolar uncertainties related to what has been earlier addressed as cultural fragmentation,[67] there is a need today for pluralism of cultures and religions. This requires a combination of diversity and consensus over core values. Muslims need to abandon jihad and *da'wa/* proselytization altogether. They also need to engage in an Islamic reform based on a new reasoning in this direction to avert the shari'atization and jihadization of Islam in favor of an Islamic embracing of cultural and religious pluralism in world politics and in Europe.

Neo-Jihad, world politics and Europe's jihadist dilemma; the place of civilizations

The meaning of the return of history is that in the twenty-first century Europe is again encountering Islam, even though under very different conditions and circumstances. Historical references to positive encounters are useful but insufficient, even misleading, if they bypass the real issues of conflict.[68] Along with Islamic migration to Europe the old world faces a "jihadist dilemma."[69] For Ibn Khaldun every civilization is based on *asabiyya*, i.e. awareness of itself. Europe's *asabiyya* is challenged. This concept, first established by the last great philosopher in Islam, Ibn Khaldun, becomes equally pertinent and topical when asking the question: Does the concept of *asabiyya* matter to Europe in the new encounter with Islam? I seek to establish my concept of Euro-Islam as a Euro-Islamic *asabiyya* on these grounds to respond to the Islamic and Islamist challenge now creating fault-lines in the heart of Europe. This is admittedly my wishful thinking in establishing an accord with reality; I leave it to one side in order to address the real issues and ask: Where does the Europe of today stand? After two world wars Europe ceased to be not only a center of world politics, but also a center of international scholarship. The academic study of Islam was first centered in Europe, but the international studies' related interest in Islam as well as the political attention given to the world of Islam is now based in US academia. Two events – stretching over a time span of almost a quarter of a century – brought Islam to the center of world politics with a slight but continuing impact on Europe. Both events were distorted through sensational media coverage that failed to transmit the deeper meanings behind them. Below the surface of the media barrage, one finds in each case the reality of a tragic situation emanating from the inability of a civilization to cope with a predicament with modernity, resulting in a crisis (see note 28). The two events triggered off a variety of responses, none of which were related to Islam as a religion, but rather to it as a civilization.

The first event was the "Islamic revolution" in Iran in 1979. Academically speaking, this event gave a boost to the study of Islam in world affairs.[70] Among the reasons underlying the pertinence of that revolution to world politics was its claim to universality, accompanied by the pronouncement of its leaders' intention to export it to the rest of the world of Islam, first and foremost the neighboring Arab states. The Mullahs compared their uprising with the French Revolution and claimed a universal place in history at large.[71] In emulating the universality, but not the values of the French Revolution, the Iranian leaders of the Islamic revolution envisioned a remaking of the world. However, despite its universalist rhetoric, the revolution had an overtly Shi'ite character. This is the theme of Chapter 4 of this book.

Conversely, the second major event, the jihadist assault of al-Qaeda in the USA on 11 September 2001, was a Sunni challenge in its character. In their respective cases, the Shi'ite Ayatollah Khomeini and the Sunni-Wahhabi bin Laden each claimed for these events the character of an Islamic internationalism. In view of these claims, Part II of this book has a chapter on each of the two events, documenting these two different varieties of Islamic internationalism in world politics. Given their character as watershed events, they continue in the twenty-first century to be a challenge for Europe, although with little awareness of the issue by the Europeans themselves. The nuclear proliferation of Iran is a threat to world politics and foremost to

Europe itself. The so-called Iran–EU dialogue did not bear fruit, but instead helped the Mullahcracy of Iran to win time for their "Islamic revolution" and to establish the legitimacy internationally claimed. In the years 2004–5 the appeasement approach of the EU proved incapable of preventing Iran from continuing its nuclear proliferation.

Europe faces political Islam as a state – i.e. Iran – and as a transnational movement of the radical political Islamism – committed to global jihad as the expression of a new internationalism. Islamists come to Europe as asylum-seekers. Europe has not been successful[72] in dealing with them. It is intriguing to see jihadism ignored by the Europeans, who provide a safe haven for the Islamists in the name of human rights. In the Madrid meeting mentioned earlier, Hasan Hanafi took the liberty of stating – as already quoted – that Europe should become a new *al-Andalus*, i.e. in other words a territory under the banner of Islam. He also interpreted the "physical missiles" of suicide bombers as a resort of the weak to their bodies to face the strong with their sophisticated technology. Islamists seem to be more favorable to Europe than to the USA. The reason is not only their belief that Islam is more likely to take hold of Europe than of the USA, but also the safe haven Islamists enjoy in Europe. Will Europe become Islamized?

In the study of the twenty-first century, world politics needs to deal with the challenge of an Islam with a mindset of religious conquest facing a Europe that is relinquishing its civilizational identity in the name of multi-culturalism, indifferent tolerance and dialogue. As hinted at the beginning of this section, Europe is uncertain about its *asabiyya* in the age of Islamic migration. No wonder that Hanafi's message failed to elicit contradiction or criticism from the Europeans present, even as he proposed Islam as a solution for Europe's crisis of identity, clearly meaning an Islamization of Europe. Is this polemics or a real issue?

Post-bipolar world politics is characterized by civilizations competing for a new world order. The dichotomy of secular democratic peace and of an order envisioned as a *Pax Islamica* for the world is the expression of this competition, heralding "the new Cold War" now reaching the heart of Europe. The historical background is that Islam and Christianity are transnational religions that share a centuries-old history of mutual conquests, cultural borrowing and, on the basis of these, a mixture of reciprocal admiration and antagonism.[73] Today this special relationship between both civilizations becomes – through contemporary Islamic migration to Europe and the drive of Muslim Turkey to join the European Union – an even more compelling issue for Europe. The head-scarf is viewed as a fault-line.[74] As John Kelsay suggests, we are in a situation in which we can no longer speak of "Islam *and* the West, but of Islam *in* the West."[75] Clearly, this message matters more to Europe than to the USA. Political Islam seeks to establish itself on all levels in the European Islamic diaspora and has proven successful in doing so. To be sure, Europeans have no policy for dealing with this challenge, nor a civilizational awareness of its meaning.

In the age of terrorism, Myron Weiner's effort to introduce the study of migration to the themes of international security also gains great topicality.[76] The existence of al-Qaeda cells and the related logistical elements of Islamist movements in the safe haven of Western Europe contribute to an obstructing of average Muslim migrants' integration into European citizenry. So while it is the USA that has created a department of homeland security, the real problem is a European one, for it is in the core of Europe that global jihad is taking hold. The perpetrators of 9/11 came from Europe, not from the world of Islam.

Long before Huntington announced his famous formula, Islamists have been reversing his formula "the West and the rest" into "Islam and the rest." In the words of one of the Indonesian jihadists involved in the Bali assault of 2002, speaking in front of the Indonesian court: "Islam is at war with the rest of the world." For me and for most of my fellow liberal Muslims, this jihadist declaration of war is unacceptable, as we refuse the alleged fault-lines between Islam and the West – whether they come from Huntington or the Islamists themselves. The rejection of the "clash" approach should not, however, amount to ignoring the place of civilizations in world politics, nor to overlooking the war of ideas taking place. The stated or alleged deplorable fault-lines, though constructed, can no longer be ignored by the state-centric discipline of International Relations. Jihad in Europe matters for world politics, but is not a state-centered matter. It indicates, and also compels us to acknowledge, that "culture matters" to the study of International Relations (see note 37). Religion is a cultural system and its return demands reasoning about Islam's predicament with modernity becoming a political concern in the twenty-first century that touches heavily on Europe. The context is a war of ideas in which fault-lines between the civilizations are established. For a countering strategy, bridges for democratic peace are needed.

Within Islamic civilization and its diaspora in Europe there is a need for a revival of the reason-based view of the world established by the Islamic rationalism that thrived between the ninth and fourteenth centuries. This would be most helpful to legitimate cultural borrowing. Medieval Muslim rationalists, from al-Farabi to Ibn Sina (Avicenna) and Ibn Rushd (Averroës), up to Ibn Khaldun, were able to base their thinking on Hellenized Islamic foundations.[77] In referring to these historical records of cross-cultural fertilization I draw on Leslie Lipson's work on civilizations[78] to underpin two major arguments:

1 The introduction of Hellenism to Europe took place via the rationalist line of thought in Islamic civilization.
2 With the assistance of Hellenism, adopted from Islamic rationalism, the first civilization of Europe based on Christendom was developed into a new civilization named "the West," which has ever since been a secular one.

These references to the history of ideas in an ongoing war of ideas have been made in a book on International Relations not simply to show that relations among civilizations also include cross-cultural fertilization through cultural borrowing. It is too simple just to talk of a "clash." In this regard I refer to the authority of Hedley Bull, who in his book *The Anarchical Society* made it crystal clear that the history of ideas is most essential for establishing consistent foundations of thinking for IR scholars. References to the Hellenization of Islam support the conclusion that Muslims of today could embrace cultural modernity (Habermas) much as their Muslim ancestors were receptive to Hellenism. To reiterate: cultural modernity is secular and not a reflection of Christianity. Hellenism belongs to the heritage of Islamic rationalism,[79] as much as it does to Europe's own Renaissance. In so arguing, I refer to the Muslim adoptions from Hellenism in a positive manner as a civilizational encounter that creates a precedent which – if revived – could provide a cultural underpinning for embracing modernity and its vision of democratic peace as an alternative to global jihad. These references contribute to clarifying the meaning of the concept of Euro-Islamic *asabiyya* earlier introduced.

In the outlined tradition of medieval Islamic defenders of reason, the contemporary Islamic rationalist Mohammed Abed al-Jabri has argued that a "promising future can only be Averroëist."[80] In so doing, al-Jabri means that a reason-based or a rational worldview has to be established in contemporary Islamic civilization. Without a doubt, rationality is the meaning of modernity. I reiterate my serious concerns about the notion of "multiple modernities," seeing it as a baseless postmodern construction. What is at stake are Muslims and modernity, in the understanding of primacy of reason, not some postmodern Western fashion. Cultural modernity can serve as the best bridge between the rival civilizations. Muslim civilization had known rationalism, but never underwent cultural modernity in its entity, so how could it adopt the construction of postmodernity?

In summing up the argument, I contend that the development of jihad to jihadism is an invented tradition. Muslims should counter it with a revival of the tradition of Islamic rationalism, which flourished in medieval Islam. The underlying argument is that establishing a rational worldview would ease the acceptance of democratic peace. The Islamic civilization of today needs to emulate medieval Islam. Rationalism was by then largely in conflict with the *fiqh* orthodoxy, which succeeded in preventing the institutionalization of a scientific view of the world established by Islamic philosophy, without which no cultural innovation could endure.[81] It was able to prevent this institutionalization via orthodoxy-controlled institutions of learning, which undermined the introduction of the reasoning of Islamic philosophy into the curriculum.[82] This tradition of *fiqh* orthodoxy is comparable with the work of the Wahhabi orthodoxy, which today fulfills the same task. Wahhabi education of the madrasas promotes the mindset of global jihad, not of democratic civil and open Islam. I contend the pertinence of this issue to world politics and to Europe. It is sad to see Europe tolerating political and Wahhabi Islam, not promoting Euro-Islam.

For bridging between civilizations in world politics, be it in Europe or worldwide, education for democracy – instead of global jihad – is a paramount concern. Europeans need to understand that education is and must be one of the foremost weapons against political Islam and therefore this book concludes with a discussion of this topic. In Europe Imams trained in the spirit of Islamic rationalism and Euro-Islamic *asabiyya* can teach Muslims born in Europe how to become European "citizens of the heart," instead of importing Salafist and Islamist hatred-Imams who preach jihadist anti-Semitism and anti-Westernism. This hatred is more than an anti-Americanism: it is also directed against Europe. The European Union needs a policy for dealing with the civilizational challenge of Islam in world politics and also for coming to terms with "Europe's jihadist dilemma" (see note 69), ignored for reasons of political correctness.

Islamic civilization between cultural modernity and the vision of an Islamic world order

The debate pursued in this introduction makes clear the contention of this book, namely that world politics in the twenty-first century is about the politics of civilizations, i.e. the return of history. Europe is the battlefield of the new development. It makes sense to refer to the philosophy of Ibn Khaldun and forget about the work of Samuel Huntington. Ibn Khaldun is my source of inspiration. Huntington not only misses the point when he establishes the argument of "fault-lines" between Islam and the West, but also shows his lack of historical knowledge about Islam and Hellenism forming a synthesis of civilizations in the past useful as a model for the future. Fault-lines between the civilizations – even constructed ones – are detrimental to living in peace with one another. Not only the ideas of Huntington but also those of global jihad are a point in favor of fault-lines; the alternative is cross-cultural bridging. The concern behind this discussion is not merely an intellectual undertaking, as is the nonsense theological idea of a "world ethics." In reality, each civilization has its own ethics. It is feasible, however, to establish a consensus over a political order for the world. Hedley Bull's understanding of world politics as evolving around the concept of "order" is central to this book. Viewed in this manner, at issue is a competition between two concepts of order for the twenty-first century. This is the substance of the contended war of ideas. In his inspiring book *Islam and War*, John Kelsay asks the pc-free question: "Who will determine the future of world order?" This question is certainly not a rhetorical one and justifies quoting the statement underlying it at length:

> Much of the contemporary return to Islam is driven by the perception of Muslims as a community ... having a mission to fulfill. That this

perception sometimes leads to conflict is not surprising. In encounters between the West and Islam, the struggle is over who will provide the primary definition of world order. Will it be the West, with its notions of territorial boundaries, market economies, private religiosity, and the priority of individual rights? Or will it be Islam, with its emphasis on the universal mission of a trans-tribal community called to build a social order founded on the pure monotheism natural to humanity? The question for those who envision world order, then, is, "Who determines the shape of order, in the new international context?" The very question suggests a competition between cultural traditions with distinctive notions of peace, order, and justice. It thus implies pessimism concerning the call for a new world order based on notions of common humanity.[83]

If this perspective is considered, then the conclusion would be that the relationship between world politics and Islam in the twenty-first century revolves around the competition between two conflicting understandings of order for the future of humanity: Sayyid Qutb's popular Islamist vision of global Islamic expansion, by means of jihad or peaceful proselytization, to map the entire globe along an Islamic order of *Hakimiyyat Allah*/God's rule, and the Kantian vision of "democratic peace" as a secular order for the world. This is the real issue and nothing else. Avoidance of acknowledging this reality for reasons of political correctness only conceals the real conflict. A choice must be made by Muslims themselves between Qutb and Kant, or, in the case of Europe, between a Muslim Europe or Euro-Islam – that is, the Islamization of Europe or the Europeanization of Islam (see note 17). If Islamic civilization embraced pluralistic democracy as an essential part of cultural modernity in the context of a reform Islam, then the war of ideas over the question "Who determines the shape of order in the new international context?" would end.

In this book it is argued that an Islamic embracing and acceptance of democracy need to be attached to a proper understanding of cultural modernity. To be modern is more than the ability to use modern instruments like computer technology. Similarly, democracy cannot be reduced to just a process of voting. Modernity is based on a worldview related to secular values and democracy is a political culture. In the twenty-first century we need to abandon the twentieth century's extreme universal choice between Islamization and Westernization. Kemalism and similar varieties of secularisms – equating progress/*tarakki* with Westernization – have failed,[84] because they overlooked Islam, but that does not mean that the political Islam of the AKP is the right alternative. The approach of Islamist de-Westernization as a response to Westernization, such as the Egyptian Islamist al-Sharqawi's rejection of Kemalism as a strategy for Westernizing the world of Islam, is not a promising option. Moreover, it contains the intriguing, some might say ironic, call for Islamists to both resent the West and at the same time adopt Western weaponry for fighting jihad against it:

> Our goal cannot be to Westernize (as Kemalism envisions), but to learn from the West how to deal with modern weapon systems, and even more: to produce these systems by ourselves to be in a position to beat the West as our enemy.[85]

The quote clearly shows that the Islamist al-Sharqawi accepts modernity as techno-scientific instrumentality[86] but rejects it as a value-system. In reviving the nostalgia of Islamic growth, his nostalgic mindset is not simply an expression of cultural self-assertion, as some Western experts believe, but rather a dream of restoring and reinventing the medieval *Pax Islamica* in a modern vision of an Islamic world order. This is – as argued earlier – not the restoration of the caliphate. Among the very few Western scholars who grasp this reality is again John Kelsay, who repeatedly deserves being quoted at length:

> it would be wrong ... to understand the contemporary call for revival among Muslims as simple nostalgia ... Some authors long for the glory of the past ... [and] have argued that the ascension of European and North American civilization in world affairs has been based on a failure of leadership in the Islamic world and on the Western willingness to shamelessly exploit, in the name of profit, the human and material resources of the developing countries. The mood of such writers is not nostalgia but outrage over the state of the world, in particular the state of the Muslim community.[87]

The outrage mentioned does not stop at voicing nostalgia and is not limited to an Islamic romanticism. It results in a call for global jihad aimed at toppling the existing order within a strategy of remaking the world. That strategy would see the pursuit of an Islamic world order for mapping the entire globe in *dar al-Islam* as a primary goal. To counter this endeavor, the West, in particular Europe, needs a dual strategy: a new security approach combined with an effort at an inter-civilizational dialogue with liberal and open-minded Muslims as a means of conflict resolution. This double-track strategy is the most promising pursuit in this costly and mutually detrimental conflict. However, the needed inter-civilizational dialogue[88] does not mean talking in the sense of *l'art pour l'art*, but rather addressing the real issues in a kind of peaceful conflict resolution aimed at establishing and accepting core shared values, led by those for religious and civilizational pluralism. We also need to assume a security dialogue to cope with the threat jihadists pose.

In this context, a revival of the heritage of Islamic medieval rational philosophers,[89] as called for by Mohammed Abed al-Jabiri, is a more helpful route for contemporary Muslims to consider than nostalgia for a former era of Islamic superiority. Self-assertive and defensive-cultural responses do not contribute to a "coming to terms" with others. Among the positive contributions one can locate in the heritage of Islam is al-Farabi's *al-Madina al-fadila* [The Perfect State], referred to earlier.[90] In contrast to the concept of *Hakimiyyat Allah*/God's rule, al-Farabi's secular understanding of the state is also acceptable to non-Muslim parts of humanity, because it revolves around a rational order. The *madina al-fadila* as a perfect state is ruled by a philosopher (in the Hellenistic sense), not by an Imam in the understanding of shari'a. On the contrary, any imposition of a *Hakimiyyat Allah* on non-Muslims – which is, by the way, mentioned neither in the Qur'an nor in the *hadith* – is tantamount to a declaration of war, be it rhetorical (war of ideas) or a practice in jihadism as irregular war of terror. Obviously, non-Muslims would never accept their own subordination as *dhimmi* to an alien Islamic order in which the Muslims are considered to be superior to them, even if done in the name of "Islamic world peace" (Qutb). The alternative to such totalitarian rule must be democratic pluralism on the grounds of equality and mutual acceptance of all religions in a setup with shared rules.

Sudan is a case in point[91] for illustrating the situation of the non-Muslims under Islamic rule. In the past and present this country has continued to provide a strong case of the problem at issue. The shari'a was imposed on non-Muslim Sudanese peoples in September 1983, and since that time Muslims in the north have been fighting a jihad against the non-Muslims in the south.[92] The 2004 crisis in Darfur, continued 2005, has resulted from the unabated attempts to subdue the non-Muslims living there to an Islamic order under the shari'a rules. In Europe, on the other hand, Muslims find themselves in the opposite position: they are the minority, but they are offered the equality of citizens. The acceptance of reason-based knowledge by Muslims would for them smooth the way to secular democracy, human rights, peace among democratic nations and above all cultural-religious pluralism. If Muslim migrants embrace these values and the related rules, it matters little whether Muslims constitute a minority or a majority. Some leaders of the Islamic diaspora are not favorable to this embracing and make the accusation of Islamophobia every time the shari'a is rejected. This accusation becomes an instrument for deterring any call for change and for incriminating any rational criticism. A call for an embracing of cultural modernity as a platform of peace between civilizations becomes in this perception an expression of Islamophobia.

Preliminary conclusions

Ahead of the analysis to follow in the seven chapters of this book on Islam in world politics and in Europe, the tensions between democracy and jihadism have been outlined in this introduction. In candor and sadness I acknowledge that the views presented in the following chapters are shared by only a minority of enlightened Muslim liberal thinkers (e.g. al-Jabri, Arkoun, al-Azm, An-Na'im, Shahrur, etc.), and are not among the popular public choices unfortunately shared by the majority of Muslims, including the diaspora of Islam in Europe. To pretend the opposite would be to over-look existing realities. I also disclose the fact that my life has been repeatedly threatened, because of my commitment to the ideas of civil society, secular democracy and human rights against political Islam. Ideologues like Yusuf al-Qaradawi,[93] who incites on al-Jazeera TV as a global mufti and argues in favor of shari'a and jihad, are more popular and far more influential than al-Jabri. These ideologues are the source of contemporary public choices in the world of Islam and its diaspora in Europe. In contrast to civil and open Islam, the Islamist internationalism of global jihad and global shari'a pre-sently enjoys great popularity – though of course to varying degrees – among young Muslims. Education in the Islamist and Wahhabi interpretations of Islam does not favor a remaking of Muslim politics along the lines of a "civil Islam."[94] Therefore, policies of further Islamization continue to prevail while an embracing of cultural modernity combined with a rethinking of Islam remains an unrealized hope. Without cultural innovations leading to cultural change, no successful coping with a structurally changing world will be on the horizon. Successful transformation requires that the Arab-Islamic mind-set as it dominates Islam honors the insight that culture matters (see note 37), that Islam is changeable, and that cultural change is as important as eco-nomic, political and social change.

The UNDP reports on the Arab Middle East[95] make it shatteringly clear that existing grievances are basically homegrown. A culture that lacks democracy and human rights and promotes authoritarian regimes is itself responsible for existing deficits. The Moroccan philosopher al-Jabri coined the phrase: "*takwin al-aql al-Arabi*/the creation of the Arab mind"[96] to depict cultural attitudes existing in the Arab world. Another enlightened Muslim, the Syrian Mohammed Shahrur, demands a radical cultural change. He criticizes Arabs for being committed to what they have inherited unquestioned from their forefathers, and therefore of being unwilling to welcome innovation and change. In supporting his argument, he cites the sura *al-baqara* of the Qur'an (2:170) which reads: "When asked to follow what Allah revealed, they answer, no, we only follow what our forefathers have passed to us."[97]

In this verse, the Qur'an is speaking of *al-kafirun*/unbelievers, but Shahrur extends this argument to most contemporary Muslim Arabs, concluding that: "there is no one single nation on earth like we Arabs which is infected by this disease on a permanent basis, i.e. unquestioned submitting to what is inherited from the ancestors" (ibid.).

At the end of 2004, Shahrur was among a group of Muslim intellectuals meeting in Cairo to discuss the Qur'an. At that gathering he rightly argued for the primacy of reason in the tradition of Islamic rationalism. According to an *International Herald Tribune* report of December 2004, he received in response shouts and name-calling, including accusations of being "a liar" and even a *kafir*/unbeliever. Such is the culture that has spread in the Middle East and is now spilling over via the Islam diaspora to Europe. I acknowledge being exposed in Europe to what Shahrur experienced in Cairo. To state this is not an "Orientalism." As an Arab Muslim living in Europe, and as someone who has been exposed physically to threatening experiences similar to Shahrur's – or even worse – within Europe, I strongly object to the admittance of such a culture to Europe in the name of "tolerance," or multi-culturalism. This "Arab Islam" is being exported not only to Europe, but also to Asia and Africa with Wahhabi support. I would wish for the reverse, i.e. for an exporting of Southeast Asia's "civil Islam" to the Middle East. The exportation of the "Arab Islam" comprising the belief in the authority of the text is pursued by the Wahhabi education in Europe, which also focuses on teaching Arabic among the European diaspora. The New Yorker inventor of tradition, the late Edward Said, and his followers would discriminate against any critique of such teachings as an expression of Orientalism – and in fact they have done so repeatedly. My response remains firm: Without criticizing this way of thinking and arguing in favor of reason-based modernity, one cannot establish the kind of cultural innovation that could smooth the way for accomplishing the needed democratic freedom for the people of Islam. I reiterate, it is possible to establish democracy in Islam, but political Islam – as Islamism or the Islamic variety of religious fundamentalism – does not contribute to this end. Islamists make use of democracy as a voting procedure, as in Palestine, Iraq and Lebanon, but reject its political culture of dissent and pluralism.

In concluding this introduction to the conflict over the choice between jihadist Islamism and democratic peace in general, and between Wahhabi-inspired ghetto-Islam and Euro-Islam in particular, I make an addition to the argument that culture and modernity matter by noting that security matters, too. In the French Declaration of Human Rights paralleling the French Revolution, one finds in the same clause that the "right to security" is among "the rights of man." Therefore there can be no democratic peace under the insecure conditions of global jihad. If we consider the fact that among the victims of global jihad are more Muslims than Westerners (e.g. in Iraq and Algeria), the conclusion is clear that the necessary security must matter to Muslims as much as it does to Westerners. As already argued, a security approach should be added to the discourse of dialogue outlined in this introduction. Let it be reiterated: This combining of dialogue with security constitutes the needed double-track strategy for coping with jihadist Islamism[98] applicable in world politics to both Islam and the West in general, and to Europe in particular.

In Europe, where major countries are challenged by increasing Muslim migration, the situation is more complex. It is certainly an exaggeration when Bernard Lewis states in an interview that "by the end of the century" Europe will become "an Islamic space." It is, however, certain that Muslims are on their way to becoming in the next few decades a very powerful and major segment of the European population. The Islamic uprising in France in winter 2005 and the ensuing Danish cartoon crisis of 2006 were just a warning. For this reason, it matters whether a political jihadist Islam or a civil Euro-Islam will prevail among Muslims living in Europe and will affect their worldview.

It is not only Muslim homework, but also a task for the Europeans themselves to think what can be done to help insure that Muslim migrants embrace the idea of Europe and become European citizens of the heart. This is the most crucial question facing Europe in the twenty-first century, as addressed in Part III of this book. Given Europe's centrality in the West, it is of vital importance to world politics in general to help accommodate the predicament of Islam with freedom and modernity, which is in view of Islamic migration also a European problem on the soil of Europe. I refrain from joining those who predict a Europe as "Eurabia," but do not close my eyes when I see the culture of Islamization (see note 17) pursued in a variety of mosques throughout Europe. The issue is a burning one and blame-games are just the wrong approach. However, in pointing at the inappropriate way Europeans deal with Muslims a way which is itself a source of the malady – next to the ills of political and jihadist Islam – I do not engage in these blame-games. My life in Europe is a case in point. After spending most of my life in Germany, the balance that I can best draw is most unpromising. I acknowledge with all clarity that I have failed to become a European in Germany. Despite all assurances to the contrary, European societies continue to be ethnically exclusive entities unable to integrate non-European immigrants to citizens heart.[99] This is not in line with the idea of Europe as an "open society" (Popper) and "island of freedom in an ocean of violent rule," and therefore I do not give up referring to the idea of Europe from the perspective of being equally against ethnic as well as Euro-centric Europeans and against totalitarian Islamists. The present book is written in this spirit. Not only Muslims need to become European citizens of the heart, also Europeans themselves are challenged to deliver what the "idea of Europe" promises.

Part I

The conflict within Islamic civilization between jihadism and democracy

Its pertinence to world politics and to the Islam diaspora in Europe: obstacles and solutions

Introductory remarks

The bottom line for living in peace and with mutual respect in the twenty-first century is the acceptance of people of all cultures and civilizations of the values as well as the institutional safeguards of religious and cultural pluralism. This pluralism that combines diversity with a consensus over core values should be the house order for the entire world, but this goal cannot be achieved without the participation of the people of Islamic civilization who count as one quarter of humanity.

To set the record straight: Cultural and religious pluralism – as an essential part of democratic peace – is an adoption from the political theory of multiparty parliamentarian democracy. Political pluralism acknowledges diversity, but requires the acceptance of shared rules and common values. This idea is applied to religion, but this undertaking is hampered by the obstacles related to religious absolutism shared by all religions. The foremost Islamic revivalist of the nineteenth century, al-Afghani, called for anti-colonial jihad not only to reject a foreign rule, but also in contesting the fact that world political realities are not in line with Islam's self-image of being superior to others in its claim for ruling the world. In al-Afghani's view the "*ghalab*/superiority" is among Islam's central features. As a young boy born in Damascus to the centuries-old Damascene "*ashraf*/notables family" – according to the history of Damascus by Taqiul-Din al-Husaini – of Banu al-Tibi, I learned at school along with the respective Qur'anic verse that we Muslims are the *khair umma*/best community God created on earth (sura *al-Imran* 3:110). This is the inherited image that Muslims have of themselves. It follows that not only are *Pax Americana* and hegemonic US unilateralism obstacles in the way of global pluralism, but there are also Islamic barriers. Muslims lack power, but nevertheless adhere to a powerful Islamic worldview which teaches "*al-Islam ya'lu wa la yu'la alayhi*/Islam is superior and no one can stand above it." Muslim preachers teach this formula, which runs counter to the need for cultural and religious pluralism.

When I was taught this Muslim self-image as a young schoolboy in Damascus, I contradicted our teacher, who was preaching Islamic superiority to us. To support my objection I referred to the facts perceived by the media. Our teacher responded, however, in a self-righteous manner and had no other argument to present than the scriptural one he gave to us in quoting the Qur'an. The tension between reality and the Muslim self-image was explained by the reference to a *mihna*/crisis that we are undergoing. In Arabic, *mihna* also means a test: in this case a kind of civilizational exam. The message is: Muslims are expected to prove that they are really better than the realities, and of course better than the others, i.e. the non-Muslims classified either as *dhimmi* (Christians and Jews living as protected minorities under the banner of Islam) or as *kafirun*/infidels. Again, this inherited worldview stands in contradiction to any religious or cultural pluralism. The reported Damascene story is the personal background for my dealing with Islam. Therefore, my first book on Islam in 1980 bore the title *The Crisis of Modern Islam*. To be sure, any objective scholarly findings always have a personal background. I have addressed this issue at length in the preface and refrain from repeating it. It is self-deception to think that scholars can keep their "selves" out of their work in terms of objectivity.

The question I asked my Damascene teacher never left my mind. In 1962, I moved from Damascus to Frankfurt to study philosophy, history and social sciences with, among others, Theodor W. Adorno, Max Horkheimer, Iring Fetscher and Jürgen Habermas. For a young Muslim that meant a window of opportunity, the opening of an avenue. The conservative education I received as a Muslim in Damascus was not much help in finding convincing answers to questions that stemmed from thinking about Islam. The education of the Islamic tradition internalized in Damascus, combined with the cultural modernity of the Frankfurt School which I perceived in Europe, built up my background when I switched from philosophy to international studies. In following the philosophical approach of "thinking is research" introduced by Hedley Bull, I came to the conclusion that contemporary Muslims in their exposure to cultural modernity and the related globalization are torn between the tradition of jihad – including its present reinvention as jihadism – and the need to incorporate their civilization into international society based on shared values and a culture of democratic peace. This is the theme of Part I of this book.

The study of Islam as a civilization in a scholarly but not in an Islamic apologetic or an Orientalist manner (and, to be sure, also not in the Saidian way of Orientalism in reverse) helped me to understand the history of Islamic civilization and its current dilemmas. Islam succeeded in ruling most parts of the world in its imperial history after the Islamic conquests. The latter were conducted as jihad in the form of *qital*/physical fighting and contributed to an Islamization of vast parts of Asia, Africa and parts of Europe. Between the seventh and the seventeenth centuries Muslims formed the leading civilization.

As a student of history in Europe and the USA, I learned in my academic studies that the decline of the Islamic civilization was related to both an emerging inner weakness and the rise of the technologically superior West within the framework of "the military revolution," as Geoffrey Parker puts it. In contrast to what I had learned in Damascus, I was exposed to the telling story of the consequences of new industrial power translating its capabilities into warfare, characterized by the "industrialization of war," as Anthony Giddens argues. This new power underpinned the European expansion. Through its technological advantage, the West was in a position first to contain the jihad expansion, then to overtake the place of the earlier superior Islamic civilization, and later even to conquer the abode of Islam itself while subjecting it to European colonial rule. This development caused deep wounds, to the extent that Muslims in their collective memory relate colonization and crusades to one process of humiliation of Islam by the Christians of Europe. When colonial rule ended, decolonization never meant more than an inclusion into the system of sovereign states. Europeans had successfully managed "to impose [this system; B.T.] on the entire world," to put the story in the phrasing of Charles Tilly.

The twenty-first century is characterized by a Muslim revolt. A distinction between early decolonization based on European ideas and the contemporary civilizational "revolt against the West" (H. Bull) continuing in the twenty-first century is needed in order to understand the issues involved. There is a contestation of the European pattern of the nation-state that prevails throughout the world, i.e. also in the world of Islam. Given the fact that the imposed European nation-state in a civilizationally alien environment lacks the needed substance and basically exists therein as a nominal nation-state, a crisis is the outcome. Unlike early anti-colonial nationalists who were seeking inclusion, the jihadist Islamism is a challenge to the secular nation-state as such. Most of the nation-states in the world of Islam are undergoing both a structural – i.e. development-related – and a legitimacy crisis. In this crisis of modernization Islamists speak of a *sahwa Islamiyya*/Islamic awakening, which is nothing other than an effort to reverse the development that has been taking place in the past few centuries since the universalization of the principles of Westphalian peace. As Daniel Philpott rightly argues, this return of a vision of an Islamic political order is targeting the structure of the "Westphalian synthesis" (*World Politics*, 2002). The envisioned shift from Europeanization to de-Westernization is not only directed against Western dominance, but is also a neo-jihad against the present world order and its expanded Westphalian system mapping the entire globe. This jihadism is no longer the classical jihad, as shown in

Chapter 1. In Chapter 2, I ask: Could Muslims instead embrace democracy and democratic peace?

At issue is an "invention of tradition" and not the tradition itself. The neo-jihad – or jihadism – is an irregular war, which means a war with no rules, and can therefore be addressed as a variety of modern terrorism. However, it would be wrong to use the terms Islamism and terrorism interchangeably, as is done in the media for describing acting jihadists. The concern is the *mihna*/crisis of Islamic civilization, not terror itself. Jihadism is a bid for the remaking of the world.

The chapters of Part I refer to Islamic civilization at a crossroads seeking its future. I normatively envision these future prospects: a choice between global jihad as an invented tradition, and joining democratic peace to become a part of the entire human community on an equal footing within the framework of pluralism outlined in the outset of these introductory remarks. It is argued that these choices pertain equally to world politics and to Europe affected through massive Islamic migration. The existing Islamic enclaves in Europe, called "parallel societies," indicate that Muslim immigrants are not integrated and are not yet a part of Europe. Some of them read the works of the intellectual father of political Islam, Sayyid Qutb, who teaches all Muslims that their civilization is in crisis and needs "*ma'alim fi al-tariq*/signposts along the road." Are the solutions he offers, including an "Islamic world revolution" to map the entire globe into this divine order, envisioned to replace the Westphalian one also valid for Europe?

As a European Muslim I contest, but acknowledge, the tensions between the envisioned Islamization of Europe by the Islamists and the Europeanization of Islam as an alternative to it proposed by the concept of Euro-Islam to be introduced in Part III. At the level of Part I, the focus is on contrasting jihadism and democratic peace as competing options. In subscribing to the view of Hedley Bull that "thinking is research," I look first at the development of jihad to jihadism and then question the Islamization of democracy. In my view, there can be no Islamic epistemology, because knowledge is human and universal. Along these lines, I argue that there is no specific Islamic democracy. In contrast, there can be with nuances a democracy in the world of Islam, as in any other civilization.

1 From classical jihad to global jihadism in an invention of tradition for mapping the world into Dar al-Islam

As much as Khomeini made the Islamic term *fetwa* popular, so did bin Laden with jihad. Today, one barely finds a Westerner who has not heard these Islamic terms. However, *fetwa* is not a death sentence, just as jihad is not terrorism. These are the wrong meanings spread in the West along with many misconceptions of Islam itself. The present chapter will elucidate, explain and claim to change the described situation. The development of the classical jihad to jihadism lies at the center of the analysis. It is asked: Is the jihadist path a promising option for the future of the Islamic civilization? In Chapter 2, I present democracy as a competing option.

The different meanings of jihad and jihadism

It is true that at present Islamists think of violence and fighting when they speak of whatever practice of jihad. However, in the Qur'an jihad does *not* mean terrorism, but it is also not simply a peaceful "self-exertion," as some suggest. In most Western contemporary popular writings on jihadist actions – particularly since 9/11 – the readers are exposed to an equation of Islamic jihad with terrorism. In this distorted context, jihad[1] and jihadism are consistently confused. In contrast, this book subscribes to the clear distinction between classical jihad and modern jihadism. Jihad combines *qital*/fighting with proselytization in wars for Islamic *futuhat*/expansion. This fight is subject to binding rules that also limit the targets. In contrast, contemporary jihadism is a pattern of the new irregular war waged as global jihad by those Islamists who subscribe to violence for fighting against the West and its believed Islamic allies. It is a war without rules. The distinction between jihad and jihadism pertains to the other basic distinction between Islam and Islamism. This is most crucial. To be sure, not all Islamists are jihadists. There are peaceful Islamists who believe in pursuing their goal within institutions. These are the institutional Islamists who reject jihadist terrorism. After these distinctions I hasten to add that it is not enlightening when – as is sometimes done, with misleading intent – some translate *jihad* as pure peaceful "self-exertion." In fact, *jihad*[2] is also related to *qital*, which means physical fighting that includes the use of weapons.

However, long before Clausewitz, the Qur'an made it obligatory on those Muslims fighting jihad-wars to honor prescribed rules during the *qital*, as will be shown in this chapter. It follows that classical jihad, unlike jihadism, is a regular war subjected to clear rules and limited targets; it does not allow ambush fighting and prohibits the killing of civilians in general and fellow-Muslims in particular. In short, a war without rules is strictly forbidden in the Qur'an. In the history of Islam, jihad stood always in the service of *da'wa*/proselytization and therefore it was and continues to be in conflict with pluralism and democratic peace. On these grounds the plea is presented to Islamic civilization to move forward from global jihad to democratic peace as a positive perspective for the twenty-first century.[3] Professedly, this is the normative commitment of this book, which nevertheless is at pains not to confuse analysis with wishful thinking. I acknowledge the spread of the present understanding of jihad as jihadism and qualify this as a deadly virus which is also detrimental to the people of Islam.

In turning to the analysis of the Islamic concept of jihad, it is clear that it is equally based on both normative and real grounds, by which the scripture as well as historically practiced Islam are to be considered. On normative grounds, the concept of jihad is scriptural as it is derived from Islamic revelation. To orthodox scripturally minded Muslims, the Qur'anic revelation is the divine source of knowledge which includes the obligation to jihad. This is viewed as the ultimate source of any knowledge of the world. It is for this reason that the study of jihad as contrasted with pluralistic democracy also touches on the problem of knowledge. Religious knowledge – determined in Islam by the discipline of the *fiqh*/sacral-juridicial knowledge, i.e. knowledge *par excellence* – is mostly an interpretation of the scriptural revelation. Logically it follows that *fiqh* as an interpretation is human knowledge, too, but nonetheless often presented as Allah's knowledge by the Salafists, who dismiss any objection as a heresy. This is one of the major obstacles to an Islamic reformation and it also matters to rethinking the Islamic concept of jihad. This reasoning in the context of clarifying the terms creates the starting point of the ensuing analysis.

In moving away from the normative to the historical meaning of jihad, one no longer faces any peaceful effort at proselytizing for Islam (*da'wa*), but rather war. In historical Islam, Islamic proselytization was carried out within the framework of jihad-wars.[4] It included the use of force in the service of Islamic expansion legitimated by spreading Islam. At issue, in the pursuit of globalizing *dar al-Islam*, is the mapping of the entire world.[5] This is the Islamic idea of world peace that can only be achieved when the globe becomes identical with *dar al-Islam*. This Islamic utopia is part of classical Islam, but it has been given a new shape by Sayyid Qutb (see note 23). He argues that world peace presupposes jihad, including *qital*. This is a reinvention of the classical Islamic concept of peace, attached to a new doctrine of jihadism and becoming a mobilizatory ideology in the service of jihadist

Islamism. Having clarified the terms under issue, we now have to go back to history in order to understand the present.

The context and the sources of jihad, past and present

In classical Islam the concept of jihad is based on ethical foundations. The Islamic tradition of jihad legitimates waging war, although clearly for ethical reasons, and it determines the rules for its conduct as an Islamic ethics of war (see note 3). Jihad is among the basic beliefs underlying the Islamic worldview as a *Weltanschauung* that seems to be resistant to change[6] because it is believed to be immutable as it was revealed by Allah. However, the real world is in flux and keeps changing, to the extent that the believed and text-based dichotomy that divides the world in a rival Islamic and a non-Islamic territoriality is no longer a reality of our world in the twenty-first century. In ignoring the realities, jihadists revive the jihad in a new meaning, abandoning the perceived dichotomy through establishing an Islamic peace uniting the world under the banner of Islam.[7] In this perception imagination and realities are confused with one another. What origins do these concepts have in the basic scriptures of Islam, the Qur'an and the *hadith*? And what is their pertinence to the present?

Islamic thinking on war and peace mostly refers to the Qur'an and to the authoritative interpretations of Islamic tradition. Of course, there are basic differences between Sunni Islam, as the expression of the major stream in Islam, and Shi'ite Islam, represented by a sectarian minority in Islam. These differences are crucial in our present examination of the transformation of classical jihad into a jihadist internationalism. This contemporary manifestation of transnational religion is extremely important and is the subject of Part II.

In keeping up with the sources of jihad, both past and present, the Arabic Qur'an is acknowledged as the major source. In recognizing Sunni Islam as the mainstream and looking for institutions of Islamic thought and meaning, one finds the al-Azhar University of Cairo to be the most authoritative. The focus on authoritative Arab sources in this chapter definitely does not reflect any Arab-centric view, but rather a consideration of the prevailing and major tradition in Islam, as well as the related dominating worldviews and historical realities.

In this chapter the interpretation of the Qur'an by Maxime Rodinson[8] is adopted. It views this scripture as chronicles of the establishment of Islam in Arabia between the years 610 and 632 AD. In early Meccan Islam, before the founding of the first Islamic polity at Medina, in a Bedouin culture hostile to state structures, one fails to find Qur'anic precepts related to war and peace. Most Meccan verses focus on spiritual issues. It is for this reason that Islamic reformers like Abdullahi An-Na'im[9] prefer to draw on Meccan Islam for establishing new ethical foundations for an Islamic embracing of individual human rights.

In an Islamic understanding, history begins with the Islamic *hijra*, which is the migration of the Prophet and his supporters to Medina in 622. There he established the first Islamic political community (*umma*), which was not a state, as contemporary Islamists wrongly read Islamic history. The term "*dawla*/state" never occurs in the Qur'an nor is it used in the *hadith* (the sayings and deeds of the Prophet). Those Qur'anic verses revealed between 622 and the death of the Prophet in 632 all speak of the polity of Medina addressed as *umma*, not as state. The fact that the Prophet never employed the term "state/*dawla*" and that it is not included in the language of the Qur'an uncovers the term "Islamic state" as a recent invention.

In the formative years of Islam, jihad as physical fighting/*qital* was waged against hostile tribes surrounding the polity of Medina. Jihad was aimed at subduing these tribes to the new supra-tribal community of the *umma*. In this historical Medina context we find a variety of Qur'anic verses pertaining to jihad. It is by no means an essentialization or an Orientalism when one refers to the persistence of Muslim thinking towards change, since it is related to an Islamic belief in the absolutely eternal validity of the Qur'an and the *hadith*. But in reality, the understanding of these texts is subject to time and space. Therefore, there is no essential Islam in that this religion and its civilization are always placed in a time–space context. However, common Muslims are generally reluctant to take a historical view of their religion and its culture. It is not only some Western Orientalists but also many Muslims themselves who are inclined to essentialize what is truly historical. During the Madrid summit (March 2005) on safe democracy and terrorism, it was a pleasure to listen to an Israeli, supported by a prominent Indonesian Muslim, correcting the claim made by an Egyptian participant that "There is only one immutable Islam" and stating diversity within Islam.

While acknowledging the primacy of the text for Muslims, it is argued that the first step in a thinking oriented towards a reform Islam is to subscribe to historizing Islamic sources. This is also to be applied to the scriptural concept of jihad. The point of departure for presenting the religious sources of jihad needs, however, to be based on scriptural Qur'anic traditions themselves, while placing them in a historical context. In pursuit of this, it can be shown that these verses are related to particular events and therefore are not general provisions. When Qur'anic verses at times seemingly contradict one another, then different historical circumstances are at issue. It follows that it is not easy to reconstruct a single Islamic overall concept of jihad from these verses. Instead, there are a number of different traditions, each of which draws selectively on the Qur'an to establish legitimacy for a human view of war and peace, even though it is claimed that this is divine in the meaning of a revelation by God. In the following – despite these differentiations – I shall try to synthesize these elements in an effort at outlining an overall Qur'anic concept of jihad.[10]

In Islam the concept of jihad is based on the already mentioned division of the world into an abode of Islam, viewed as the house of peace/*dar al-salam* (Qur'an, sura *Jonah* 10:26),[11]and the non-Muslim world, the house of war/*dar al-harb*. The politics of jihad was related to this distinction, and it determined world history for one millennium until the rise of the West[12] and the expansion of its European society[13] at the expense of Islamic jihad-expansion. At this stage, I wish to make it clear that the rejection of the outlined Islamic dichotomy consequently leads to abandoning the concept of jihad. The anticipation of this conclusion, to be made at the end of the analysis, is not premature but logically consistent.

The evolution of the modern international system is related to basic developments introducing a change in the structure of the world.[14] In this historical context, the dichotomic division of the world, created in medieval Islam, lost all its foundations. The scriptural reference to it today by political Islam and by Salafism is belied by the historical realities. This way of thinking – perceiving historical realities through religious doctrines fixed in the scripture, and not the reverse, i.e. juxtaposing doctrines to the realities themselves – existed long before the incursion of Europe into the Muslim world. An example of this thinking is the belief in Islamic unity contradicted by the facts of the Middle Ages, showing that *dar al-Islam* was already at that time dismembered into a "multiplicity of separate, often warring sovereignties," as Bernard Lewis rightly notes. It is utterly wrong to view this dismemberment as "territorial pluralism," as for instance James Piscatori does, thereby overlooking the meaning of "pluralism" in political science in which this term is based. The issue is, as Lewis maintains, that "in international ... matters, a widening gap appeared between legal doctrine and political fact, which politicians ignored and jurists did their best to conceal."[15] However, in terms of Islamic perception and the prevailing worldview, the unity of the *umma* has been a hallmark of Islamic thought, and no "territorial pluralism" whatsoever has ever been acknowledged. To this day, Muslims commonly believe that this unity was first shattered by the Christian crusaders and the colonizing West, who destroyed the Islamic order of a united *umma*. In contemporary writings of political Islam, a historical continuity between the crusades and colonial rule is established. It is argued that the appropriate response to this still perceived challenge is best achieved by combating it through jihad. The revival of jihad occurs in the guise of "the revolt against the West" (Bull), discussed at length in the introduction. Religious sources are read in the light of the present leading to a new understanding of jihad currently interpreted as jihadism/*jihadiyya* on the grounds of an invention of tradition. Therefore, the reading of the sources needs to be contextualized and historicized.

In going back to the classical history of Islam as an Islamic expansion between the seventh and seventeenth centuries, the jihad of Muslims against the other, conceived as *kuffar*/infidels and thus the enemies of Islam, was the centerpiece. Islamic jurists never dealt with relations with non-Muslims under conditions other than those of "the house of war," except for the temporary cessation of hostilities under a limited truce, when *dar al-ahd*/

house of contract was allowed.[16] The superiority of Islam existing in medieval history ceased in reality when the "military revolution" of the West (see note 12) took place between the years 1500 and 1800. It signaled the start of modern times, and ultimately contributed to the rise of the new, militarily most powerful civilization of the West. This rise touches mostly on Islamic civilization. In this context, the concomitant decline of the world of Islam is the substance of the question: "What went wrong?" asked by Bernard Lewis.[17] The West took over the place of Islam, and this is the problem of what went wrong. Muslims have tried ever since to establish armies along the European model[18] to offset the increasing weakness of the abode of Islam. In this historical context, the globalization model of the Islamicate was replaced by the one of European expansion. The changed historical balance exposed Muslims to a major challenge, but it never changed their worldview based on their image of themselves as superior. As noted in the introductory remarks to this Part I, I grew up in Damascus as part of a generation educated in this thinking. This education has never changed, but I changed through my European education and therefore read the sources in the light of the historical facts, not vice versa.

In international relations since the "Westphalian synthesis," the believed dichotomy between *dar al-Islam* and *dar al-harb* has become incongruent with the existing realities. Following the Peace of Westphalia, the modern world was composed of sovereign states that further developed into nation-states in the aftermath of the French Revolution. Muslims were challenged to rethink their dichotomic worldview and consider new approaches in the light of changed realities. But despite its incompatibility with the modern world order, there has not yet been any authoritative revision of this worldview, as the Muslim scholar Najib al-Armanazi rightly argues (see note 16). In the nineteenth and twentieth centuries, ideologies of Islamic liberalism and the ensuing military praetorianism failed to cope with the challenge. They did not contribute to the needed cultural accommodation and to the cultural modernization of the world of Islam. This failure triggered a crisis addressed in the introduction to this book. The crisis contributed to the revival of the jihad-doctrine, though in a revised version, which is jihadism. Those who reduce jihadism to a response to the US unilateralism during the war against Iraq, or trace it back to al-Qaeda, lack knowledge about the historical background and about sources much older than this phenomenon and pre-dating bin Laden, Saddam Hussein and all of the related topicalities.

Having contextualized the scriptural source of the Islamic religious doctrine of jihad in both the past and the present, it becomes clear that the belief that Islam is a religious mission to all of humanity is a driving force. Muslims are religiously obliged to disseminate the Islamic faith through jihad throughout the world. As the Qur'an pronounces: "We have sent you forth to all mankind" (sura *saba* 34:28). If non-Muslims submit to Islam through conversion or subjugation, this call/*da'wa* can be pursued peacefully.

If they do not, Muslims are then obliged to wage jihad-war to subdue them. It is only in this meaning that jihad is understood as a defensive action of violence. In Islam, peace requires that non-Muslims submit to the call of Islam, either by conversion or by accepting the status of a religious minority of *dhimmi* obliged to pay an imposed tax/*jizya*. This "privilege" of "dhimmitude" applies, however, exclusively to Christians and Jews, i.e. to monotheists. Peoples of other non-monotheist religions are considered to be *kafirun*/infidels. World peace is perceived as the result of successfully carrying out the *da'wa*, being the Islamic proselytization, leading to the submission of all humankind to Islam, thus mapping the entire globe. In this context, it is important to note that the expression "*dar al-harb*/house of war" is not Qur'anic; it was coined in the age of Islamic military expansion and thus relates to historical Islam, when Islamic jihad-wars were waged to spread Islamic faith through the enhancement of *dar al-Islam*.

Contemporary Islamists use the term "*dar al-kuffar*/house of infidels" for Europe and the USA, even though Christians and Jews – in the scriptural understanding of Islam – are *dhimmi*, not *kafirun*. Moreover, in Europe Muslim immigrants themselves are a minority, a fact that creates a challenge to inherited Islamic thinking of viewing only non-Muslims as minorities.

In summing up the context of the development from the classical jihad-doctrine, when historically jihad was the instrument of war for Islamic expansion, to the present of jihadism, it can be stated that a fulfillment of the Qur'anic command to spread Islam is understood as a message of peace. Consequently, the relations between *dar al-Islam*, as the abode of peace, and *dar al-harb*, as the world of unbelievers, were defined in terms of war, according to the authoritative commentaries of Islamic jurists. An exception is allowed to be applied when Muslim power becomes weak; then a temporary truce/*hudna* is permitted. In passing it can be noted that Islamic jurists differ on the definition and length of "temporary." This notion of temporary peace as a truce defined in the terms *dar al-sulh*/reconciliation or, at times, *dar al-ahd*, dominates Islamic thought even today.[19] It is true that the religious doctrine of jihad determines the attitude of common Muslims and that there is, except in Sufi Islam, no Islamic tradition of non-violence. However, the violent jihad as a war has never been glorified in Islam. At issue is the obligation of *da'wa* to disseminate Islam for which jihad is considered an instrument. The aggressive language of jihadism and its glorification of violence are recent and have no roots in classical Islam. It is therefore wrong to describe Islam in general as a "religion of the sword." The late Edward Said would have described this formula as "Orientalism." However, contemporary jihadists speak the language of the sword, and Hasan al-Banna can be considered the Georges Sorel of Islam with regard to the glorification of violence, a language alien to classical Islam. Qadhafi of Libya is not an Islamist, but he gave his son the name of *saif al-Islam*/the sword of Islam. Is Qadhafi infected by Orientalism? At issue is a Muslim, not a Western, mindset.

Jihad and the doctrine of just war

In view of the fact that Muslims do not see their jihad as a war of aggression, but rather as a defensive measure, it has been suggested that jihad can be interpreted as a just war. Students of Islam know, however, that the Western distinction between just and unjust wars, as discussed by Michael Walzer,[20] is unknown in Islam. This can be safely stated although these very terms are at present employed by some Western-educated Muslims, as by Islamists as well. However, this is often done within a different frame of reference. In Islam, war against unbelievers, whatever its immediate ground, is in general morally justified and in this sense perceived to be a just war, even if the term itself is not used. In the past, when Muslims waged wars for the spread of Islam, labeled as *"futuhat/*openings," they did not believe themselves engaged in a war of aggression, despite the fact of the conquest and killing of those who resisted them. In the Muslim view, when non-Muslims fight against Muslims, then an unjust war/*idwan* (or aggression) is perceived to be at issue. In the West, jihad is interpreted by some as an Islamic concept of "just war." One of the sources for the use of the terms "just/unjust" with regard to Islam is an old pioneer study by Majid Khadduri – albeit now outdated. In this study, one encounters the benign interpretation of jihad as *bellum iustum*. Khadduri's contention is:

> The universality of Islam provided a unifying element for all believers, within the world of Islam, and its defensive–offensive character produced a state of warfare permanently declared against the outside world, the world of war. Thus jihad may be regarded as Islam's instrument for carrying out its ultimate objective by turning all people into believers.[21]

From this point of view, the Western concept of *bellum iustum* in the sense of a just war may apply to Islam. Khadduri's writing back in 1955 was dealing with history. By then, there existed no mobilizing ideology of global jihad: even though the intellectual seeds already existed in the writings of Qutb and al-Banna, they were not known to Khadduri, who prematurely stated that "at the present it is not possible to revive the traditional religious approach to foreign affairs ... The jihad has become an obsolete weapon."[22] This assessment and the related prediction proved to be utterly wrong: Jihad is back as jihadism, and it has proved to be a successful threat of irregular war against the West, destabilizing world politics in the twenty-first century.

A closer look at the classical religious doctrine of Islam reveals two ways of dealing with war. The first refers to war in the concrete situation of fighting a battle/*qital* as a resort to jihad in following the Qur'anic precept to proselytize for the spread of Islam, usually when non-Muslims hinder the effort of Islamization. The other understanding is more general, namely war as a permanent condition between Muslims and non-believers which can only be brought to an end by an accomplishing of the global dominance of Islam after a victory over the infidels. We find this understanding of "global" and "permanent jihad" revived in Qutb's booklet *World Peace and Islam*,[23] which Khadduri should have known by 1955 but did not. This booklet is among the most popular writings in the contemporary world of Islam. Together with the *risalat al-jihad* of 1930 by Hasan al-Banna (see note 40), it never ceased to enjoy broad dissemination.

In ethical terms the Qur'an makes a clear distinction between "fighting/ *qital*" and "aggression/*idwan*" and asks Muslims not to be aggressors: "Fight for the sake of Allah against those who fight against you, but do not be violent, because Allah does not love aggressors" (sura *al-baqara* 2:190). However, the very same Qur'anic passage continues with this phrasing: "Kill them wherever you find them. Drive them out of places from which they drove you ... Fight against them until idolatry is no more and Allah's religion reigns supreme" (sura *al-baqara* 2:190–2). Is this a contradiction? The Qur'anic term for fighting is here *qital*, not jihad. The Qur'an prescribes fighting for the spread of Islam: "Fighting is obligatory on you, much as you dislike it" (sura *al-baqara* 2:216). The *qital* of Muslims against unbelievers is also a religious obligation: "Fight for the cause of Allah ... how could you not fight for the cause of Allah? ... True believers fight for the cause of Allah, but the infidels fight for idols" (sura *al-nisa* 4:74–6). It follows that *qital* is the more concrete implementation of jihad. In the logic of the Qur'an, there is no contradiction between condemning the *idwan*/aggression of unbelievers and prescribing jihad in the form of *qital* as a religious duty/*farida* on Muslims. In this context, it seems to be justified to interpret *idwan* as unjust war, whereas *qital* for Islam could be seen as *bellum iustum*. This is, however, clearly a modern, not an authentic, reading!

In addition to engaging in multiple interpretations, it is also possible to refer to the Qur'an selectively for supporting one's own standpoint. These practices combined have caused a loss of specificity of the meaning of jihad used by Muslims themselves. Some Muslims allege that jihad is merely a self-exertion, while contemporary jihadist groups legitimize their action against the West, carried out as terrorist attacks, as jihad. Literal references to the Qur'an are made in each case. The Islamic fundamentalist groups invoke the idea of jihad to underpin their view of the fight "against crusaders and Jews" as a just war.

In the nineteenth century, al-Afghani called for jihad against colonial powers.[24] This violent "Islamic response to imperialism"[25] is, however, quite different from the Sorel-like "*action dirécte*"[26] of the contemporary jihadists; they mostly lack intimate knowledge of Islamic sources and politicize Islam to justify their atrocities of terror as jihad. Nevertheless, this reference cannot be played down as merely instrumental, for the simple reason that Islamists view themselves as true believers, and this is honest. This new understanding of jihad and the related practice first occurred in Egypt, then Lebanon, and also in the civil war in Sudan, not to forget Afghanistan, Palestine and Iraq.[27] Through respective interpretations, the concept of jihad has been identified with the related Islamic concept of "armed fighting/*qital*" and, moreover, a *qital* without rules and with unlimited targets, i.e. an irregular war of terror, which is the dominant case in our present. Those who continue to view jihad exclusively as self-exertion help the jihadists to legitimate their action as divine terror, as "terror in the mind of God."[28] This is a formula coined by Mark Juergensmeyer for conceptualizing religion-based terrorism, of which jihadism is a major variety, but the phenomenon as such is not restricted to the world of Islam.

In focusing on the scriptural references to jihad while placing them in a historical context, one encounters again and again Islam's self-image as a mission of peace for all of humanity. In this universal understanding, the *da'wa*/proselytization is justified as a declaration of war on unbelievers. Therefore, the *da'wa* includes a call to jihad. Literally, jihad means "to exert oneself." In this pursuit, one can involve either military or non-military efforts and means. However, jihad can definitely become a war/*qital* against those who physically reject or oppose the spread of Islam. Fighting against these people is considered in Islam to be defensive, not aggressive, in the sense of removing the obstacles in the way of the spread of Islamic faith. This is the doctrine in history. In the present, jihad has predominantly become a jihadism. It is not only terrorism, but also an expression of a religious imperialism of the "Wahhabi International," as shown in the work of Stephen Schwarz.

Again going back to history, the reader is reminded that the Meccan years of Islamic revelation (610–22) can be indicated as referring to the fact that the Meccan parts of the Qur'an are basically spiritual and contain no reference to violence as a use of force. For instance, in the Meccan sura *al-kafirun*/the unbelievers of the Qur'an, the supporters of the new religion are asked to respond to their contestants by advocating their faith in this manner: "You have your religion, and I have mine" (sura *al-kafirun* 109:6). In another Meccan verse, the Qur'an simply demands from the believers that they will not obey unbelievers, and that they will refrain from attacking them. Qur'anic verses from this Meccan period use the term jihad to describe efforts to convert unbelievers peacefully, i.e. not in connection with any *qital*/fighting. To be sure, there is no mention of *qital* in the Meccan Qur'an. By then, Muslims were, in fact, a tiny powerless minority not yet able to wage wars. The verse "Do not yield to the unbelievers and use the Qur'an for your jihad/effort to carry through against them" (sura *al-furqan* 25:52) clearly illustrates this mindset of a persuasive rather than a military jihad: In the Meccan formative years of Islam, the foremost undertaking the Qur'an requires from the believers is to engage in presenting the argument of faith. Again, this is history. After the death of the Prophet, Muslim rulers engaged in violent global conquests (see notes 4 and 5), not in a discourse of persuasion and argumentation. The *futuhat*-wars in Asia, North Africa and Europe were, like any war, an act of violence, albeit within prescribed rules. In contrast, contemporary global jihad is a war without rules: it is an irregular war and therefore a variety of terrorism.

With the gradual move from Meccan to Medinan times in early Islam comes the emergence of new precepts in which jihad assumes the shape of global *qital*/fighting. The *futuhat*-wars, as an Islamic expansion, should not distract from the existing ethical justification of war. The Qur'an provisions: "You shall not kill – for that is forbidden – except for a just cause" (sura *al-an'am* 6:151). This verse might tempt the scholar to read this Qur'anic expression in a modern way and to see in it – as earlier discussed – a concept of just war. Even though this procedure, as already noted, is not quite accurate – since the distinction between just and unjust war is a Western view alien to Islam – it is legitimate to engage in a modern interpretation. There is also a need to outline the other distinction: The "just cause" (Qur'an) of killing is only permissible along rules prescribed by the Qur'an. Therefore, it is incumbent upon us to distinguish between allowed "killing" during war waged on ethical grounds and the unethical slaughtering of "infidels" by the jihadists in acts of terrorism. In Iraq – and earlier in Algeria – jihadists were primarily killing fellow Muslims, accusing them of collaboration with the "infidels." These are crimes committed in the name of jihad. The perpetrators in Algeria, Chechenya and Iraq believe they are waging an Islamic jihad and view themselves as jihadists. For a sociologist of religion, faith is not a text but rather a *fait social* (Emile Durkheim). The confusion of justice and terrorism is a "social fact" today. If one views jihadists as criminals one denies one self an understanding of the image these Islamists have of the self.

The conduct of jihad as *qital* is a war with rules, in contrast to the jihadism of irregular war

In covering Islam, Western journalists share with jihadists the obsession with jihad. In putting aside this disturbing observation, it is a historical fact that Muslims never waged jihad as an end in itself; they employed it as an instrument in the pursuit of *da'wa*/proselytization for mapping the world into *dar al-Islam*. In addition to this end, traditional jihad prescribes rules for the conduct of this kind of war and puts moral constraints on military warfare in the fight against non-Muslims. As in other traditions of waging war, in Islam two categories of restrictions can be distinguished: restrictions on weapons as well as on methods of war, and restrictions on permissible targets. Having done justice to the doctrine of jihad, the historical truth obliges us to add that, despite the rules, in extreme situations it is allowed by Islamic law/shari'a to practice the precept that "necessity overrides the forbidden/*al-darura tubih al-mahzurat*." In short, this precept allows moral constraints to be overridden and to be put aside in emergencies. It is true that the Islamic criteria for determining whether an emergency exists are vague; however, this is not to the extent of putting the jihad-doctrine aside altogether and making out of jihad a jihadist terrorism in the understanding of a war without rules, as in the case of political Islam of our time.

In apologetic Islamic writings we often read that jihad-wars were not violent. This is presumptuous, because Islamic jihad-wars were violent. In history, non-violent warfare does not exist. Despite the high ethical standards imposed by the classical doctrine, Islamic jihad-wars were also related to blood-letting. The distinction between the normative and the historical level in the study of jihad reveals many self-deceptions most Muslims continue to believe in, and are still at work in, the view that jihadism is a resurgence against US globalism.

It is true that the Islamic doctrine regarding the conduct of war was developed in an age in which the destructive weapons of industrial warfare were not yet available, and therefore the Qur'anic doctrine on the conduct of war does not take this into account. It is also shaped by pre-Islamic tribal notions of honor. The Qur'an asks believers to honor their promises and agreements: "Keep faith with Allah, when you make a covenant ... Do not break your oaths" (sura *al-nahl* 16:19). And: "Those who keep faith with Allah do not break their pledge" (sura *al-ra'd* 13:19). It also prescribes that the enemy is to be notified before an attack. Surprise attacks or acts that one addresses today as terrorism are therefore prohibited by the Qur'an. These are binding rules for the conduct of jihad-war. In this understanding, the contemporary global jihad waged by the jihadists as an irregular war is not in line with the code of honor prescribed by classical jihad, as ruled in the Qur'an. A war without rules and ambush fighting are not permissible according to the classic jihad-doctrine. *Ghadr* – that is, deceptive fighting – is unlawful in the teaching of the Qur'an.

In classical jihad there also exists another category of restrictions, i.e. permissible targets of war. Here, the Qur'anic doctrine is in line with the pre-Islamic norm of "man's boldness/*shahma*" in strictly prohibiting the targeting of civilians, in particular children, women and the elderly. This prohibition is consistent with the pre-Islamic tribal belief that it is not a sign of honor for a man to demonstrate his power to someone who is weaker. Therefore, the precept follows that prisoners have to be fairly treated (sura *al-insan* 76:8–9). And because the goal of war waged against unbelievers is not to kill them but to compel them to submit to Islam, one finds among the rules of war the precept to honor life and the banning of plundering as well as destruction. All of the jihadist actions of al-Qaeda worldwide, as well as the so-called jihad of the Zarqawi group in Iraq, are pure violations of the classical jihad-doctrine.

Having outlined how the Qur'an determines jihad as governed by strict rules of conduct and by limiting targets, the question arises: Why, then, have 11 September and all the ensuing assaults been legitimized as an act of jihad violating the outlined rules and the indicated restrictions? The answer is simple: At issue is a new understanding of jihad, a kind of neo-jihad or, better, jihadism/*jihadiyya*. As argued earlier, the origin of the new concept goes back to the movement of the Muslim Brothers and to its foundation by Hasan al-Banna in 1928. There existed another earlier reference to jihad in Islamic history. It was made when al-Afghani in the nineteenth century called for an anti-colonial jihad. That jihad was, however, a real defensive war against colonial rule, not terrorism. Afghani and al-Banna do not belong to the same school of thought; there are extreme differences. An equation would only contribute to legitimating the terror of 9/11. Even though the irregular war of jihadism is not in line with the Islamic conduct of jihad, it would be wrong to deny that the jihadists are Muslims acting in this belief. Truly, jiihadists are not scriptural scholars, but men acting in the belief of "terror in the mind of God."

The outlined historical development of the Islamic doctrine of jihad, legitimating Islamic expansion and the related conquests for one millennium between the seventh and the seventeenth centuries as well as contemporary jihadism, has to be placed in the Islamic decline which began in Vienna back in 1683. It was the beginning of the story of one defeat after another in a series of wars. Islamic armies were not in a position to hold their own against their technologically superior enemies in a time described by Anthony Giddens as an age of "industrialization of warfare."[29] In this asymmetrical situation, jihadism, a war without rules, becomes the weapon of the weak against technologically superior foes.

The other option: Islamic conformism as an attempt to pacify jihad in order to adjust to Islamic weakness

Prior to the development of jihad to jihadism, Muslim *ulema*/scribes engaged in conformist thinking in the nineteenth century to adjust to the new situation. The Islamic Moroccan scholar Ahmed bin Khalid al-Nasiri (1835–97) was a pioneer of this, and his thought was followed in the late twentieth century by several sheykhs of al-Azhar. This kind of conformism seeks, in an altered world, to perpetuate the traditional religious doctrine of jihad, i.e. to reinterpret it under the changed conditions but definitely not to rethink it or to speak of abandoning it altogether, as this book suggests. The new effort focused on absolving the Islamic rulers from the obligation of conducting jihad as a war of expansion for the spread of Islam.

In the following, I shall illustrate this conformism through the example of the nineteenth-century Moroccan Islamic thought of al-Nasiri. To understand this thought, it is useful to have some information about the historical situation. Unlike most Islamic countries, Morocco has a continued centuries-old tradition of statehood. It also enjoyed independence for more than three centuries prior to its colonization and it was not subjected to Ottoman rule. Moroccan dynastic history is state history, and in this capacity Morocco was the only Arab country the Turks had failed to subdue to their empire. Political rule in Morocco was legitimized by Sunni Islam in the sultanate, just as Ottoman rule was legitimized by Sunni Islam in the caliphate. Most of the nineteenth-century Muslim thinkers were in a general situation of uncertainty caused by the ongoing decline of the jihad-project in the context of a changing global balance of power to the benefit of the technologically superior West. In considering the change, the Moroccan *ulema* were more realistic in their reasoning and were the first to unfold a conformism which would put them in a position where they were able to come to terms with the new reality. In this situation, Ahmed bin Khalid al-Nasiri was the first Muslim *alim*/scribe of his age to honestly acknowledge the lack of unity in the Islamic community/*umma*, as well as Islam's weakness in the face of its rival powers. The conclusion of the Islamic Moroccan conformists was to admit the *umma*'s inability to pursue jihad for the expansion of the Islamicate. However, their conformism never went as far as abandoning the concept of Islamic superiority. The Islamic scribe al-Nasiri restricted his thinking to legitimizing the politics of his Moroccan sultan, Hassan I, who was no longer in a position to fulfill the obligation to jihad as expansion. The issue therefore was not to abandon the concept, but merely to dispense with the duty of waging war against unbelievers in a historical situation of weakness. This is the nature of Islamic conformism, exemplified in the thinking of al-Nasiri, that remains to date the typical pattern among Muslim statesmen and their advisers, many of whom do not even know of al-Nasiri. This pattern is characterized by pragmatic submission to international standards of law and order among states, and by the acceptance of peaceful relations with non-Islamic countries; it is not a commitment of heart in the sense of accepting the substance within a context of rule of (un-Islamic) law, but is rather an adjustment. The compliance with modern international law, which includes law of war, takes place without submitting to the "*esprit de loi*" in Montesquieu's sense. In short, the principle of Islamic *ghalab*/superiority has never been abandoned. This is a real Islamic problem that hampers an embracing of a real pluralism. Islamic conformism to diversity is not an acceptance of a real pluralism. Yet, this pattern of conformism determines Islamic thinking.

The belief in the moral superiority of Islam and the validity of its law over non-Muslims is to be placed in the dichotomy related to separating the world into Islamic and non-Islamic realms. It is maintained by al-Nasiri, who constantly refers to the "abode of Islam/*dar al-Islam*," even though he has only his own country, Morocco, in mind.[30] At present, this Islamic territoriality is formally united in the Organization of the Islamic Conference (OIC), the only one in our time based on religion. The Organization has refused to condemn contemporary jihad – such as the jihad of Hamas – as terrorism, even though this practice does not comply with the outlined Islamic conduct of jihad-war. The call of Malayan Prime Minister Badawi, cited in the preface, remains an exception in our age in which the world of Islam is moving from Islamic conformism back to jihad. The Islamist movements, being at present the major political opposition, do not provide any solution to this predicament. Islamic conformism as represented by the Islamic establishment of scribes/*ulema* still exists. The *ulema* continue to argue on twofold grounds, one scriptural, the other expediential. Along these lines, the already cited al-Nasiri selectively and repeatedly refers to the Qur'anic verse, "if they incline to peace then make peace with them" (sura *al-anfal* 8:61). In so doing, he recommends on a normative basis to his sultan that he should establish peace between his state, Morocco, and Europe. The expediential argument of al-Nasiri pertains to the conditions of the Islamic community/*umma*:

> No one today can overlook the power and the superiority of Christians. Muslims ... are in a condition of weakness and disintegration ... Given these circumstances, how can we maintain the opinion and the politics that the weak should confront the strong? How could the unarmed fight against the heavily armed power?[31]

A close reading of this statement shows that the obligation to jihad is suspended through *darura*/necessity, but not abandoned. In his reasoning al-Nasiri maintains that Islam is equally a "shari'a of war" and a "shari'a of peace." He argues that the Qur'anic verse, "if they incline to peace then make peace with them," rests on the notion of Islamic interest/*al-maslaha*. Under contemporary conditions, in al-Nasiri's view, the interest of Islam forbids Muslims to wage war against unbelievers, because they are not in a position to win it. As al-Nasiri states:

> The matter depends in the main on the Imam who is in a position to foresee the interest of Islam and its people with regard to war and peace. There is no obligation that Muslims must fight forever or accept peace forever ... The authority that cannot be contested by anyone is the ruling of the Sultan Hassan I ... whom we trust, because Allah has assigned him to run our affairs and to fix our destiny; Allah authorized him to decide for us.[32]

The ruler obliged to jihad has the right to determine the Islamic interest/ *maslaha*. The conformist shari'a-related interpretation of *maslaha* is strongly reminiscent of the Western IR-realist school's idea of the "national interest" of the nation-state, even though phrased in divine language. It reflects the view of a then leading *alim*/scribe on matters of war and peace, voicing Islamic conformism as a response to the challenge of a changed world.

Even in Islamic conformism the ethics of peace is implicitly determined by the view that non-Muslims are enemies with whom Muslims can, at best, negotiate a truce/*hudna*. The belief that lasting peace with non-Muslims is not possible persists to date. Islamic conformism does not make a reasonable effort at placing Islam in a pluralistic, secular international society, it simply adjusts Islamic views to a changing environment, although without rethinking Islam or ever revising the Islamic concept of jihad or of dhimmitude. Thus, the idea of democratic peace remains alien to the Islamic *ulema*, because they insist on Islamic dominance/*taghallub*. Seen from the intellectual frame of reference of this book, this is a core issue of Islam's predicament with modernity. In narrowing the scope from the world at large to Europe as a continent for Islamic migration, we face similar problems. The fact that the Muslims, not the others, are the minority does not alter the worldview. It is not explicit: at issue is a transition. In the future, Muslims believe be the majority, and in this spirit no rethinking takes place.

The development from colonial rule to the creation of sovereign states in the world of Islam[33] brought conditions leading to a need for a new variety of Sunni Islamic conformism. It was provided by the Islamic establishment, as reflected in the scholarship at the al-Azhar University. The new variety continues the tradition of Islamic conformism in reinterpreting the Islamic notion of jihad, this time, however, to discourage the use of force: At issue is an effort at pacification of jihad. This development as a pacification of jihad has never led to questioning the concept of jihad itself, nor to abandoning the believed dichotomy existing between the *dar al-Islam* and the *dar al-harb*. This new thinking can be found in the authoritative textbooks of al-Azhar which are characterized both by the selective use of religious scripture and by an arbitrary interpretation of it. These are the confines of Islamic conformism even when it aims at pacifying jihad.

In the most authoritative textbook of this school of thought, the then head of al-Azhar, sheykh Mahmud Shaltut, reasserts the universal claim that Islam is a religion for all humankind, but nevertheless contends – contradicting himself – that Islam is open to pluralism.[34] Shaltut quotes the Qur'anic verse, "we have created you as peoples and tribes to make you know one another" (sura *al-hujrat* 49:13), that acknowledged diversity in supporting the claim for a pluralistic approach to interpreting the scripture. Yet, the diversity in existing realities cannot be equated with pluralism as a discourse. It is fine that Shaltut rejected any imposition of Islamic belief again by quoting the Qur'an: "Had Allah wanted, all people of the earth would have believed in Him, would you then dare force faith upon them?" (sura *Jonah* 10:99). The conclusion that war is not a proper instrument for pursuing the call to Islam/*da'wa* is new. Shaltut states that "war is an immoral situation,"[35] and Muslims must adjust the *da'wa* to the need of living in peace with non-Muslims. Shaltut takes pride in the fact that centuries ago Islam laid the foundations for a peaceful order of relations among peoples, whereas

> the states of the present [that is, Western; B.T.] civilization deceive the people with the so-called public international law ... Look at the

human massacres which these people commit all over the world while they talk about peace and human rights![36]

Shaltut pleads for peaceful coexistence and goes to the furthest extent possible in stretching the opening for an Islamic conformism, but he does not go beyond it. The intention of putting aside violence is, however, not accompanied by a mechanism for revising the concept of jihad. Today, the return to jihad is determined by a variety of reasons: one of them is certainly the failure of the Islamic *ulema*-establishment to provide the theological grounds for historicizing jihad and consequently abandoning it as a legitimation of violence from Islamic thought.

Among the valuable pronouncements of the religious Sunni establishment is the work of a later sheykh of al-Azhar, Jadul-haq Ali Jadulhaq, composed in a two-volume textbook, which is a most powerful work.[37] It includes a more significant conformist reinterpretation of the concept of jihad. Also, there is no mention of states: At issue is the Islamic community/*umma* as a whole on the one hand and the rest of the world on the other, thus the division of the world into Islamic and non-Islamic continues to prevail. The Islamist paradigm of world affairs is charged with contradictions: on the one hand the Islamists do not acknowledge the international system as a system of states, while on the other they call for an Islamic state. In a chapter on jihad in the first volume of the quoted al-Azhar text, Jadulhaq emphasizes that jihad in itself does not mean war. If we want to talk about jihad as a war, he argues, we would have to add "armed" and speak of "*al-jihad al-musallah*," to distinguish between this kind of armed jihad and the everyday "Jihad against ignorance, jihad against poverty, jihad against illness and disease … The search for knowledge is the highest level of jihad" (vol. 1, p. 277).

Having made this distinction, the al-Azhar textbook downgrades the importance of "armed jihad" in arguing that the *da'wa* can be pursued without *qital*/physical fighting:

> In earlier ages the sword was necessary for securing the path of the *da'wa*. In our age, however, the sword has lost its importance, although the resort to it is still important for the case of defense against those who wish to do evil to Islam and its people. However, for the dissemination of the *da'wa* there are now a variety of ways … Those who focus on arms in our times are preoccupied with weak instruments.
>
> (vol. 1, pp. 278–9)

The al-Azhar sheykh Jadulhaq dissociates the *da'wa* from violent proselytization as an imposition of Islam on others: "The *da'wa* is an offer to join in, not an imposition … Belief is not for imposition with force" (vol. 1, p. 281). To support this, earlier Meccan spiritual verses are repeatedly quoted in an effort to downgrade the notion of *qital* as armed jihad: "Islam was not disseminated with the power of the sword. The *qital* (fighting) was an exception only for securing and also for the defense of the *da'wa* (call) to Islam" (vol. 2, p. 268). Despite this most significant reinterpretation the al-Azhar textbook insists on the uncompromising traditional claim of Islam to universality, i.e. as a mission for all of humanity (vol. 1, p. 280), in quoting the Qur'an: "We have sent you forth as a blessing to mankind" (sura *al-anbiya* 21:107). Instead of jihad carried out as *qital* for the spread of Islam, this sheykh of al-Azhar calls on Muslims in the modern age of communication to use the networks of this medium to avoid armed conflict for the pursuit of the *da'wa* without giving up the worldview that humanity should adopt Islam.

The outlined effort at an appeasement of jihad is combined with an encouraging abandonment of violent proselytization; however, it fails to lay grounds for perpetual democratic peace between Muslims and non-Muslims. According to al-Qurtubi's classical commentary of the Qur'an, quoted by Jadulhaq (vol. 2, p. 371), treaties creating an armistice/*hudna* between Muslims and non-Muslims can be valid for a period of no more than ten years, but never forever. If the Muslims are powerful, they may not hold an armistice for more than one year; if they are militarily weak, a truce can be extended up to ten years. There is silence on what occurs after a time of limited peace. It is viewed as heretical to revise the classical doctrine of permanent jihad. Even in this al-Azhar handbook we see no desire to thoroughly rethink the jihad-doctrine in the light of changed international circumstances. The result is conformity to or acquiescence in the new international system, but no effort is made at altering the classical categories standing in contrast to international legal and ethical standards. Scriptural Islam again proves an obstacle in the way of Muslims coming to terms with modernity and abandoning global jihad for embracing democratic peace. Given the conformism on the surface, the pacification of jihad by al-Azhar did not last long. The contemporary jihadist movements (see note 27) had their head-start in Cairo, the seat of al-Azhar. Today, they also exist in Europe. The challenge is tremendous, and not least for Muslims: in the deceptive rhetoric, jihad is only peaceful self-exertion, and if it turns violent, then this is only for defense.

The road to jihadism: al-Banna and Qutb were no Islamic revivalists, but Islamist precursors of the "Islamic world revolution"

In contrast to Islamic conformism as a way of accommodation, the reinvention of jihad as irregular war indicates a return to the Islamic claim of supremacy. The failure of the al-Azhar-*ulema*, and of the Islamic establishment in general, to subject the scripture to reasoning in the light of changed conditions restricted their conformism to an adjustment that was merely superficial. This Islamic tradition is challenged by the representatives of contemporary political Islam in an inclination to reverse the procedure: A true Muslim has to measure reality by the text itself. Unlike the Islamic establishment, these Islamists read the scripture selectively in a new mindset. The roots of political Islam can be traced back to the year 1928, when the movement of the Muslim Brotherhood/*al-Ikhwan al-Muslimun* was created in Egypt.[38] The leading authorities of the political thought of this Islamism are the founder Hasan al-Banna and later on Sayyid Qutb; these ideologues continue to date to provide the prominent intellectual guidelines of political Islam.[39] In addition, the works of both are the political pillars of jihadism.

In his *Risalat al-jihad* al-Banna laid the grounds for the reinterpretation of jihad as irregular war, not for an Islamic revival as his grandson Ramadan suggests. The quoted essay by al-Banna is the major source for the orientation of contemporary jihadism.[40] In the mentioned treatise of al-Banna on jihad, he makes literal use of the Qur'an and the *hadith* to support conclusions opposed to those made by authorities of Islamic conformism. In contrast to pacifying jihad, al-Banna argues first that jihad is an "obligation [*farida*] on every Muslim" (p. 275), adding that jihad and *qital* can indiscriminately and interchangeably be referred to in the meaning of "use of force." The targets are existing regimes in the world of Islam as well as unbelievers. In the Islamic non-state-centered tradition, contemporary jihadists view "war" to mean fighting, basically between non-state-related parties of believers and unbelievers, no matter how they are organized politically. This new approach reflects an Islamist thinking adopted by al-Qaeda. The distinctions between regular war, i.e. jihad subjected to rules, and other patterns of violence are fully blurred in jihadism as a doctrine of irregular war. The idea that the basic conflict is between "*iman*/the faith of Islam" and "*al-kufr al-alami*/international unbelief" was put forward by Osama bin Laden in a speech ahead of the 2001 Afghanistan war in retaliation for the al-Qaeda 9/11 assault. As argued earlier, this thinking is new, and it transforms classical jihad into the contemporary idea and practice of jihadism.

The precursor of the new interpretation of jihad, al-Banna, begins the treatise referred to above by quoting from the Qur'an, from the sura *al-baqara*: "Fighting is obligatory on you, much as you dislike it" (2:216). He continues with two other quotations from the Qur'an: "If you should die or be slain in the cause for Allah, his mercy will surely be better than all the riches you amass" (sura *al-Imran* 3:158). And: "We shall richly reward them whether they die or conquer" (sura *al-nisa* 4:74). These and similar quotations are selectively chosen by al-Banna for a glorification of fighting and death in *fi sabil Allah*/the path of Allah. The close resemblance to Georges Sorel's fascist glorification of violence (see note 26) in his *Réflexions sur la violence* is most obvious. In their context, the cited verses do not glorify violence.

In rejecting al-Banna in Islamic terms one can cite the tolerant Qur'anic verse from the sura *al-kafirun*: "You have your religion and I have mine" (109:6). Instead of honoring this Qur'anic provision, al-Banna extended the obligation to a *qital* against unbelievers to a fight against the "people of the book/*ahl al-kitab*" – i.e. Christians and Jews – in quoting the Qur'anic verse: "Fight against these who neither believe in Allah nor in the Last Day ... until they pay tribute out of hand and are utterly subdued" (sura *al-tauba* 9:29). As al-Banna concludes, Allah "has obliged Muslims to fight ... to secure the pursuit of *al-da'wa* and thus of peace, while disseminating the great mission which God entrusted to them" (p. 287). The reader of the jihad-essay by al-Banna misses all of the Qur'anic verses included in the work of al-Nasiri quoted above. Nor does one find in al-Banna's essay any reference to the Islamic call for tolerance and peace, for he is preoccupied with the armed jihad/*jihad al-musallah*, to refer to the cited al-Azhar formula. In contrast to al-Azhar, al-Banna does not downgrade the status of fighting/*qital* for the benefit of upgrading the non-military jihad against such evils as ignorance, poverty and disease. In fact, he does exactly the opposite in drawing a distinction between "low jihad/*al-jihad al-asghar*" and "high jihad/*al-jihad al-akbar*," ridiculing those Muslims who consider the physical fighting of *qital* to be a "low jihad." Any downgrading of *qital* to a "low jihad" is a misunderstanding of the duty of *qital*, al-Banna believes, and for him the true essence of the jihad is this: "The great reward for Muslims is to fight, to kill or to be killed for the sake of Allah" (p. 289). This is the spirit of jihadist Islam, which provides the religious foundations for terrorism "in the mind of God" put forward in al-Banna's treatise. Those who are at pains to rehabilitate al-Banna by presenting him as an anti-colonial Muslim thinker – as does his grandson Tariq Ramadan – overlook this dimension of his thinking, documented in the cited quotes from his major essay on jihad.

Instead of drawing a wrong line – as I believe – from al-Afghani to al-Banna, I would rather establish commonalities with Georges Sorel (see note 26), based on those thoughts from al-Banna permeated with a rhetoric glorifying violence and death. The clandestine work of the Muslim Brothers between the 1930s and 1960s included killing and assassinations. At the beginning of the twenty-first century, more than half a century after the slaying of al-Banna (1949), jihadism in the understanding of irregular war spilled over the world of Islam and has become a central issue in international affairs. It looks as if the dreams of the perpetrator are coming true.

When jihadist Islamists today preach to Westerners, boasting: "You love life and we love death," in justification of the "heroic deeds" of suicide bombers, one is reminded of al-Banna's statement in his quoted jihad-essay reflecting this mindset: "Allah rewards the *umma* which masters the art of death and which acknowledges the necessity of death in dignity ... Be sure, death is inevitable ... If you do this for the path of Allah, you will be rewarded" (p. 291).

Being a Muslim myself and a student of Islam, I fail to find this glorification of death and terror in the Qur'an or in the *hadith* of the Prophet. Islam honors life, and it is no contradiction to be a Muslim and to prefer life to death. The quoted death poetry of al-Banna reflects neither the mindset of Sufi Muslims nor that of those bright Muslims who established Islamic rationalism.

Despite their rhetoric of death and glorification of violence, jihadist Islamists argue that their jihad is a message of peace. This creed can be traced back to al-Banna, who waged jihad for Islamic peace. However, Islamic peace is viewed on the basis that peace is only possible under the banner of Islam. Monotheistic non-Muslims should be permitted to live only as members of protected minorities/*dhimmi* under Islamic rule.[41] In all other cases, war against unbelievers is a religious duty for Muslims. This is not new. What is new, however, is the definition of jihad-war which ends in justifying terrorism. This is also the spirit of Sayyid Qutb, who has politically revived the dichotomous Islamic division of the world into the abode of peace/*dar al-Islam* and the world of unbelievers/*dar al-harb*. Qutb employs this dichotomy to establish the view that war against "unbelievers" is a religious duty for Muslims. Giving the old dichotomy a new twist, he coins the expressions "the world of believers" and "the world of *neo-jahiliyya*" (*jahiliyya* is the Islamic term for the pre-Islamic age of ignorance). For Qutb, modernity is nothing more than this new form of *jahiliyya*,[42] a setback for the world and also for Muslims attracted to its spell and sympathetic to it.

Qutb claims that "the battle lying ahead is one between the believers and their enemies ... Its substance is the question *kufr aw iman*? (unbelief or belief?), *jahiliyya aw Islam*? (ignorance or Islam?)."[43] The confrontation, then, is "between Islam and the international society of ignorance"[44] – a civilizational confrontation in which victory is reserved for Islam, as Qutb believes. Qutb invented this "clash of civilizations" ahead of Huntington. One finds these phrases copied almost word for word in many of the jihad speeches of Osama bin Laden. The idea of the "clash of civilizations" is an essential part of the Islamist repertoire.

The thoughts of jihadist political Islam are documented in a great number of pamphlets industriously produced during the decades since 1970. In substance, this literature rarely goes beyond quoting passages from al-Banna and Qutb. When an Egyptian representative to the Madrid summit on safe democracy and terrorism told the audience that "Qutb's writings have no impact today," he was clearly lying to them, relying on European ignorance of the issue. Contemporary Muslim fundamentalists often cite passages from his writings, like the following:

> The dynamic spread of Islam assumes the form of jihad by the sword ... not as a defensive movement, as those Muslim defeatists imagine, who subjugate themselves to the offensive pressure of Western Orientalists ... Islam is meant for the entire globe.[45]

It is most intriguing to see this polemic against Western Orientalists adopted in the West itself as a discourse wrongly qualified as a critique of Orientalism: this is, however, nothing other than reversing the arguments of

Orientalism. This mindset does disservice to Islamic and Middle Eastern studies in the West, and it helps to distract Muslims from doing their homework by blaming the West for their home-made ills. The three UNDP reports of 2002, 2003 and 2004 suggest that the truth is otherwise. At issue here is jihad, neither "Orientalism" nor the development ills in the failed Arab-Islamic states. The pertinence of the Orientalism debate to the pending issue in a war of ideas is its belittling of the intellectual impact of jihadism, which is spreading like a virus through Islamist and jihadist teaching as a means of indoctrinating frustrated young Muslims in related schools. The writings by Qutb, and not those produced by the conformists willing to accommodate, are taught in the Islamist madrasas. This is becoming the basic religious training of the jihadists, once assembled in the al-Qaeda camps in Afghanistan. The influence of Qutb is sweeping and can be illustrated with reference to a vast literature on this topic. An example is Muhammed Na'im Yasin's 1990 book on jihad. The book establishes an understanding of a global war between believers and unbelievers as a gradual process in which, at the last stage, "regardless of an attack of the Muslim lands by unbelievers, ... fighting of Muslims against them ought to take place."[46] Yasin then quotes the Qur'anic verse: "Fight against the unbelievers in their entirety as they fight against you in your entirety" (sura *al-tauba* 9:36), commenting on the verse as follows: "The duty of jihad in Islam results in the necessity of *qital* against everyone who neither agrees to convert to Islam nor to submit himself to Islamic rule."[47] This jihadist Yasin then concludes that the ultimate "return to Allah cannot be pursued through wishful thinking but only through the means of jihad" (ibid.).

According to another jihadist thinker, Colonel Ahmad al-Mu'mini, an officer in the Jordanian army, this offensive view of jihad must determine the military policies of all Islamic states.[48] The book by al-Mu'mini, first published in the Mashreq/Arab East, enjoys a wide circulation and was also reprinted in the Arab West in the Algerian city of Constantine and used by the jihadists. I obtained it in 1992 while doing fieldwork in Algeria. This jihadism cannot be fought by armies, but rather by an alternative Islamic education favorable to democracy and pluralism. In a valuable recent study by the Pakistani diplomat Husain Haqqani, published by the Carnegie Endowment for International Peace in 2005, the role of the madrasas spreading shari'a[49] and jihad is rightly presented as a great concern, both to the people of Islamic civilization and to the international community.

Conclusions: Whither the world of Islam? What future for jihad?

World politics is the overall context of the return of jihad in the new guise of jihadism reflected both in the world of Islam and in Europe. The phenomenon is incorporated into political Islam (Islamism), being an Islamic variety of the religionization of politics, the politicization of religion and the culturalization of conflict in the post-bipolar international environment.

This development creates a challenge to Muslims themselves. They engage in pragmatic adjustments but stop short of rethinking the doctrine of jihad itself. It is true that the states of the world of Islam comply with the rules of international law by virtue of their membership in the United Nations and their accepting of its charter. But while they are committed to international law that prohibits war, their educational system teaches Islamic law/shari'a that prescribes jihad-war against unbelievers. Does their recognition of international law really indicate a revision of Islamic ethics of war and peace? Or does this recognition indicate no more than outward and temporal conformity as *hudna* complied with by the Islamic civilization in its present weakness within the international system?

To be sure, shari'a can be viewed as morality, not as a legal system or international law. There is a need for a decoupling of Islamic thinking from jihad, and from shari'a as well. In fact, the Muslim reformer Ashmawi asks us to consider that the term "shari'a" occurs only once in the Qur'an.[50] Looking at shari'a as morality would be an achievement in overcoming jihadism, with Muslims themselves doing their homework to change prevailing cultural attitudes in a changed international environment. This need also includes Muslims living in the diaspora of Europe, who are exposed to the challenge of jihadism.

What are the roots of jihad and jihadism? Many Western authors who write on concepts of war and peace in Islam overlook the fact that there is no consistent theory of the territorial state in Islam.[51] In general, Islamic thinkers view war as a struggle not between states but between Muslims as a community (*umma*) and the rest of the world, inhabited by unbelievers (*dar al-harb*). In contrast to this tradition, the French-educated Muslim legal scholar Najib al-Armanazi acknowledges that the international order established on the grounds of the treaty of Westphalia is based on relations among states and their mutual recognition of each other's sovereignty. This order is in contradiction to "the spirit that inflamed the great Arab conquerors, namely to impose their power all over the world."[52] But despite this tension, al-Armanazi argues, Muslims do in practice recognize the sovereignty of non-Muslim states with which they conduct relations on the basis of "the *aman*, customary law or the rule of honoring agreements (*ahd*, *'uhud*)" (ibid., p. 226). Nevertheless, "for Muslims war is the basic rule and peace with infidels is understood only as a temporary armistice. Only if Muslims are weak vis-à-vis their adversaries are they entitled to reconciliation with their enemies" (ibid., p. 157). As al-Armanazi continues, "for Muslim jurists peace only matters when it is in line with the *maslaha* [interest] of Muslims" (ibid., p. 163).

Given the provision of the Islamic shari'a doctrine that in the relations between Muslims and non-Muslims peace is only a temporary armistice and that jihad-war remains the rule until Islam succeeds in mapping the entire globe, it becomes clear that the problem is not restricted to contemporary jihadism. In short, not only for the jihadists but also for traditional Islamic scribes/*ulema*, permanent world peace is only possible under the rule of Islam, and only then could jihad subside. What can be done to make Muslims abandon this thought and to embrace democratic pluralism?

In view of the fact that the culturally diverse Islamic *umma* makes up only 1.6 billions out of a humanity comprising more than 6.5 billions one is inclined to ask: How could world peace be established if the universality of Islamic law is claimed? An Islamic shari'a order is certainly not acceptable for non-Muslims, nor for those Muslims who embrace democracy and pluralism. Therefore, the contemporary drive of political Islam to re-introduce the shari'a within a commitment to jihad alienates Islamic civilization from the international law community and its existing international order. The combined call for the shari'a and for jihad is also a threat posed by Islamism to world peace.

In considering the failure of Islamic conformism, Muslims need a "cultural accommodation"[53] that includes a rethinking of Islamic tradition in a process of cultural change. They are challenged to accept a more universal law for regulating war and peace on secular grounds to replace the inherited Islamic doctrine. In Islam, the will to such a "cultural accommodation" of the religious doctrine to the changed social and historical realities presupposes the will to engage in religious reforms. Therefore, the substance and the role of the religious doctrine itself as the cultural underpinning of the Islamic ethics of war and peace are at issue. If this statement is correct, then Elisabeth Mayer's conclusion that "Islamic and international legal traditions, long separated by different perspectives, are now starting to converge in areas of common concern"[54] is far too optimistic and – as wishful thinking – does not convey existing realities. This is a nice way of saying in plain language that Elisabeth Mayer is wrong in her views on Islamic law. The alleged convergence is pragmatic and only limited to practical matters. In short, it does not reflect more than a conformism and is definitely not the accommodation to the new international environment necessary to a basic rethinking of inherited conceptions of war and peace. The inherited Islamic perception of non-Muslims either as *dhimmi* (Christians and Jews as protected minorities) or as *kafirun*/unbelievers should be abandoned altogether and replaced by an Islamic acceptance of democracy and pluralism for overcoming the Muslim dichotomic worldview. In this book it is argued that the rise of political Islam and its jihadism as related to the crisis of the nation-state in the world of Islam are not a contribution to the needed change.

It is acknowledged that the issue is not merely cultural. There is a Middle East conflict leading a delegitimation of the nation-state throughout the world of Islam in an overall context.[55] In fact, there is no generally accepted concept of the state in Islam; the community of believers/*umma*, not the state, has always been the focus of Islamic doctrine. The idea of "the Islamic state" promoted by political Islam is a recent addition. With a few exceptions, Islamic jurists do not deal with the notion of the state/*dawla*. As the Moroccan scholar Abdullatif Husni writes in his study of Islam and international relations, recent defenders of the classical Islamic division of the world

> confine themselves to quoting classical Islamic jurists. In their writings we do not even find the term "state." This deliberate disregard indicates their intention to ignore the character of the modern system of international relations. They refuse to acknowledge the multiplicity of states which are sovereign and equal in maintaining the notions of *dar al-Islam* and *dar al-harb*.[56]

In the context of the exposure of the world of Islam to the West, many adjustments to the modern international system have been made, but none of these conformist efforts were accompanied by a will to a cultural accommodation. Apart from a few individuals (al-Jabri, al-Azm, Shahrur), one cannot find any rigorously critical rethinking of Islamic tradition. Throughout this book I suggest a view of Islam's predicament with cultural modernity. The related crisis of development has contributed to the evolution of jihad to jihadism. In the past, the ground for jihad-war was always the envisioned dissemination of Islam throughout the world. Truly, in their conduct of war, early Muslims were at pains to avoid destruction and to deal in fairness with the weak. This is no longer the case for the combatants of neo-jihad, who are waging an irregular war of terror.

Islamic civilization, despite its universal religious mission of Islam, is today institutionally embedded into an international system but without accepting its values. If this attitude is extended to the diaspora of Islam in Europe, then great conflicts are ahead. There is only one international system in the history of humankind which became global as it grew from the expansion of the European model. As Charles Tilly puts it:

> All of Europe was to be divided into distinct and sovereign states whose boundaries were defined by international agreement. Over the next three hundred years the Europeans and their descendants managed to impose that state system on the entire world. The recent wave of decolonization has almost completed the mapping of the globe into that system.[57]

In their "remaking politics," contemporary jihadist Islamists envision undoing the mapping of the world into a European system that also includes the world of Islam itself and reviving the doctrine of war and peace. Their thought continues to be scriptural and pre-modern[58] and fails to take into account the reality of changed conditions based on relations among sovereign states, and not on the religion of the people living therein. However, their bid for a return of history in a jihadist world revolution becomes a source of conflict. The real world is not based on a division into *dar al-Islam* and *dar al-harb*, as the Islamic shari'a law suggests and Islamists reinvent in their dichotomic worldview.

The alternative to the outlined conflict is democratic peace both for the world of Islam and for Europe's Islam diaspora. The present international crisis is also a crisis of Islam itself,[59] and democratic pluralism is suggested as a solution for Islam's relations to non-Islamic civilizations. In the next chapter an embracing of democracy and its related concepts of pluralism and peace are presented to the Islamic *umma*-civilization as an alternative to the empty promises of jihadism.

2   Polity and rule

The Islamic quest for civil society and for democracy against Hakimiyyat Allah as the Islamist system of totalitarian government

The French-Muslim contribution to end the riots in the *banlieues de l'Islam* in France made the point clear that a coming to terms of civil society in Europe with Islam is an essential joint task. Globally, it is argued, there can be no democratic peace in the twenty-first century without Muslim participation, given the fact that Muslims constitute one quarter of humanity. In setting the focus on Europe, one can establish the existence of an increasing Muslim population of 20 million in Europe in 2007, doubling and even tripling in the foreseeable future. A positive Muslim contribution to democracy globally and in Europe requires a rethinking of the concept of expansionist jihad provisioned by the shari'a and its contemporary development to a terrorist jihadism. In order to counter mere rhetorical pro-democracy pronouncements, a rethinking of Islam aimed at supporting religious-cultural reforms has to be placed on the agenda. To put Islam and democracy in harmony, an Islamic cultural acceptance of the political culture of democracy, as underpinned by a civil society, is the basic requirement.[1]

Is this feasible? Can Islamic civilization deliver? Are Muslims who live in Europe willing to cooperate towards this end? My response is positive, conditional on a Muslim honest will to engage in this endeavor.

It is a fact that competition exists between the idea of a civil society combined with the culture of democracy and the concept of *hakimiyyat Allah*/God's rule of the Islamic state as constructed by Islamists. A debate on this competition should not be silenced in the name of political correctness. Muslims living in Europe are challenged when a co-religionist like Şerif Mardin blatantly states that "civil society does not translate into Islamic terms."[2] In facing this challenge I argue in Islamic terms for an acceptance of the culture of democracy and of democratic peace. I do not engage in philological eyewash through single-mindedly pointing at jihad as self-exertion and thus do not share the belief in the fallacy of an "Islamic jihad for democracy" limited to *shura*/consultation. I avoid distraction from the pending issues and clearly state the bottom line: democracy is a political culture of civil society that requires the establishment of a religious-cultural pluralism. In contrast, the culture of political Islam is based on a proselytization for Islam on the grounds of an envisioned Islamic order. Ambiguities are to be avoided.

Throughout this book, I look at religious beliefs in the Durkheimian sense as a *fait social*, not as a text. Seen through these lenses, one can be disillusioned and in the situation of discerning that in today's Arabic "*jihadi*" means terrorist, not a self-exerting pious Muslim. The terms "*jihadi*" and "*mutatarif/extremist*" – or even "*irhabi/terrorist*" – are often used interchangeably in the Arab press. The core argument of Part I states that a competition between the project of democratic peace and global jihad is the closest to reality. This competition requires not only mediation, but also the search by Muslims, both in the world of Islam and equally in Europe, for a cultural acceptance of democracy based on an Islamic-cultural underpinning for facilitating a heartfelt commitment. To be sure, this underpinning does not mean an Islamization of democracy, as some suggest. This would be an additional fallacy.[3] At issue is a rethinking of Islam[4] and a venture into religious-cultural reforms aimed at putting Islamic thought in harmony with democracy. This cultural change is to be viewed as a democratization of Islam, which is something different from an Islamization of democracy. The bottom line is that democracy as a notion of cultural modernity has never existed in any religious tradition. Islam is no exception. Therefore, I strongly dismiss the notion of the Christian roots of democracy,[5] because this disturbing argument is also used by Islamists, albeit for other reasons. For in rejecting democracy they argue that democratization is a hidden agenda for Christianization.[6] Instead of this conspiracy-driven thinking, I engage throughout this chapter in deliberations on the three levels of analysis covered in this book: world politics, the world of Islam and finally Europe. A differentiation between these levels of analysis is to be kept in mind even though they are linked to one another. The strategies needed for each discrete level are different. In world politics, one needs a joint Islamic–Western response to the challenge of global jihad. In the world of Islam, democratization is not only a pending issue, as shown in this chapter: it is also the solution for the people of the Islamic civilization, as will be argued in Chapter 7. In Europe, the Europeanization of Islam is the solution, an idea which creates the focus of Part III.

The quest for an Islamic-civilizational underpinning for democracy and democratic peace

Muslims favorable to the cultural acceptance of democracy, and to democratic peace to be shared by all humanity on cross-cultural grounds, are confronted with the competing revival of the vision of an Islamic peace, once unfolded by Sayyid Qutb. In an invention of tradition, the vision of an Islamist peace aims to remake the world through global jihad. As Qutb phrases the issue, jihad is the "Islamic world revolution" for re-establishing the rule of Islam, viewed as a prerequisite for world peace. In the introduction to this book I dealt with this vision and have shown clearly how much it stands in contrast to the Kantian concept of democratic peace. Having stated this tension, I hasten to add that, being a Muslim myself, I am at pains to mediate and therefore continue to dismiss the confrontational style, be it of the rhetoric of an alleged "clash of civilizations" or the misleading polarization "Islam vs democracy." Both Huntington and the Islamists have been arguing in favor of this clash. Instead, I argue for an analysis-based pursuit of cross-cultural bridging.[7] This preference by the author is not only a personal one, but a rational choice. At issue is the insight that Muslim societies need democracy for themselves and democratic peace to live peacefully with others. World peace could never be accomplished without the participation of the people of the Islamic civilization, as put forward at the outset. After all, the international system includes 57 Islamic states, organized in their own terms in the Organization of the Islamic Conference (OIC) – as already stated, the only world organization based on religious grounds.

In concrete terms, to achieve the pursuit of democracy as a perspective for the Islamic civilization in the twenty-first century requires an effort at making this order of life culturally and politically acceptable to Muslims themselves. As argued, this can only be accomplished through working out an Islamic-civilizational underpinning for the introduction of democracy into the world of Islam that supplants existing patriarchal rule,[8] and also the mindset related to it. One cannot reiterate enough that an imposition of democracy from outside would always be doomed to failure. This insight is supported most notably by the experience of the failed democratization of Iraq after the toppling of Saddam Hussein.

It is no contradiction to simultaneously turn down the rhetoric of a clash of civilizations and state the existence of conflict between democracy and the idea of a *global* jihad[9] (jihadism) for establishing an Islamic world order. The challenge of religious fundamentalism is real as a threat, and political Islam is not an invention of Western media "covering Islam" (Said). The existing world political challenge[10] of Islamism is not about religion, but is an invention of tradition transforming religious faith into a political ideology. At issue is also Salafist-Wahhabi Islam mobilized to confront the secular authority structure of the "Westphalian synthesis."[11] It follows that the conflict is not between Islam in general and the West as such,[12] but rather between competing value systems related to the identity politics of civilizations. Based on this contention, this chapter aims to continue the earlier efforts to establish harmony between Islam and democracy.[13] The pursuit of this project requires honesty, straightforwardness and scholarly integrity, so that one can state with candor what this endeavor requires and recognize the real obstacles standing in the way of making it feasible. Consequently, I do not overlook or play down civilizational values-related differences, nor do I essentialize any tensions, but rather I cope with the conflicts they engender. This is done in an effort at an accommodation, wary of the risk of essentialization which jeopardizes the entire endeavor and is therefore always kept in mind.

Having stated the issue at hand, I now move on to addressing the realities. At present, the most advanced understanding of a "civil Islam"[14] is not to be found in the Middle East, but rather in the Islamic civilizational periphery of Indonesia. It is an Islam which subscribes to creating a democratic and pluralistic polity, i.e. a real civil society. This project also needs to include efforts at reforming the state by civilizing its structures. In this regard, I share the view of Robert Hefner that the creation of

> a public culture of democratic civility will be impossible unless it can build on the solid ground of civil Islam ... civil Islam rejects the mirage of the "Islamic" state, recognizing that this formula for fusing religion and state authority ignores the lessons of Muslim history itself ... Civil society and civic culture are required to make democracy work ... a healthy civil society requires a civilized state.[15]

The ensuing arguments are based on these deliberations. In this regard, it is important that we take a look at the ways Indonesian intellectuals view democracy in an attempt at a cultural accommodation of this Western concept. At first, one needs to ask whether these intellectuals recognize the fact that an Islamic system of government based on the shari'a is in conflict with civil society and democracy. The study of the Indonesian scholar Masykuri Abdillah[16] on this issue is highly interesting, but it is not informed by the major assumption that the concept of democratic peace is the requirement for world peace in the twenty-first century. In arguing that democracies do not wage wars against one another, one needs to dismiss the concept of jihad as incorporated into the idea of an Islamic state not organized along democratic principles. By definition, a democracy is based on popular sovereignty[17] and thus in conflict with Qutb's view that sovereignty is due only to Allah, i.e. not to the people. It follows that any effort at establishing a variety of a civil Islam automatically stands in conflict with a spreading of political Islam. The prominent Indonesian Masykuri Abdillah evades all these issues. This is a general problem in Islamic thought.

In his interesting book *Responses of Indonesian Muslim Intellectuals to the Concept of Democracy*, Abdillah tells us that Indonesian intellectuals overtly "accept the term democracy," which is fine. Now Abdillah adds that "their concept ... is not fully in line with the liberals' 'concept'." He points out the "differences ... concerning the idea of popular sovereignty ... (because) real sovereignty, according to them, is vested in God."[18] This does not reflect an intellectual contradiction, but rather a real predicament, a cultural one with modernity. What to do? Muslims need to deal with this predicament properly. Abdillah suggests the need to "differentiate between the absolute sovereignty of God and the political sovereignty of a certain state," but also maintains that one must keep up with the shari'a "as the basic standard." Does this mean that the issue is to Islamize democracy or to democratize Islam? Can there be something in between? Straightforwardness, not ambiguity, is needed for clear answers.

In the search for solutions to these major questions, there is no easy route in coming to grips with the pending issues. An inquiry on the grounds of free reasoning is an essential part of this endeavor. To outline and examine the concepts employed ensures a clear understanding of the problem with no inclination to bypass hot issues.

First, we need to ask questions related to the substance of democratic peace. Only after outlining this concept can we move forward and discuss whether or not, and how, Muslims could embrace this modern notion, seemingly so alien to their civilization but pivotal for the modern world. As Bruce Russett states in a seminal work on this subject, the idea of democratic peace rests on the vision of Immanuel Kant. The assumption is that:

> democratically organized political systems in general operate under restraints that make them more peaceful in their relations with other democracies ... in the modern international system, democracies are less likely to use lethal violence toward other democracies ... the relationship of relative peace among democracies is importantly a result of some features of democracy ... Exactly what those features are is a matter of theoretical debate.[19]

Russett engages himself in such a debate and also addresses "democratic norms and culture" (pp. 30–8), but he ends up subscribing to democracy as a procedurally fair election, not as a political culture. In so arguing, Russett is aware of the fact that

> A Muslim fundamentalist movement might achieve power in the name of democracy ... But, conceivably, such a regime could have been both stable and somewhat democratic; i.e. while promoting Islamic values of a majority it might have respected minority rights and tolerated the expression of secular opposition under domestic and international pressures. Such a government probably would not be seen as a major security threat to nonfundamentalist neighboring regimes.[20]

This statement displays the problem of established IR scholars, already addressed in the introduction. This IR community discovers Islam as an issue area while regrettably knowing very little about this subject. The assessment reveals not only the lack of familiarity with the general Islamic concept of war and peace, but also a lack of general knowledge about the concept of the Islamic state as based on a totalizing understanding of Islamic shari'a law. In Islamic tradition, minorities were viewed as *dhimmi*[21] and this will continue in an Islamic state. It follows that the concept of perpetual peace diametrically contradicts the worldview of the *dar al-Islam/* abode of Islam and of its values.

This is not the place to lament the gap between IR and Islamic studies earlier addressed in the introduction. In focusing on the issues, suffice it to state that Russett reveals almost no knowledge about religious fundamentalism. In overlooking all of the findings of the Fundamentalism Project of the American Academy of Arts and Sciences, he bypasses established research. In volume 3 of that project, the political visions of fundamentalists concerning order are dealt with under the titles "Remaking Politics" and "Remaking the World through Militancy."[22] The problem is that, on the one hand, general theorists in the IR discipline rarely read the works of area studies while, on the other hand, students of Islam rarely care about IR theory, and may even resent it. It is a welcome exception when, in contrast to this tradition, a knowledgeable scholar like Mark Juergensmeyer closely watches the emergence of a "divine order" directed against the secular state leading to a "new Cold War."[23] Had Russett and other IR scholars read Sayyid Qutb's booklet *World Peace and Islam* (see note 9), these people would have learned that in political Islam there is a different understanding of peace and order. As shown in the introduction and in Chapter 1, this "Islamic peace" would be accomplished through a global jihad for establishing the divine order of *hakimiyyat Allah*. Therefore, the assumption regarding the possible incorporation of Islamic fundamentalism into a democratic peace is flawed to the extent that it can be assessed as an utterly wrong view, based on ignorance.

In the search for a cultural underpinning for democracy in Islamic civilization, one finds that the Salafist or Islamist concept of world peace clearly contradicts cultural and religious pluralism. Those who advocate an inclusion of political Islam in the name of relativism and diversity not only miss the point that one is dealing with an absolutism – as Gellner argues[24] – but also fail to see the distinction between political and civil Islam. It is imperative to address this differentiation when talking about a global democratic peace encompassing within it the world of Islam. If we fail to go beyond "black and white" – that is, to differentiate them – then ill-informed and thus false conclusions will be the outcome. In this regard, general and thus indiscriminate talk about Islam is misleading. In focusing on the potential for a civil Islam and on its likelihood to culturally accommodate the concepts of civil society and democracy, we encounter the first sticking point. It relates to the fact that the concepts of democracy, civil society and the vision of democratic peace rest on European origins. How can Muslims embrace European ideas rooted in a civilization alien to them? And, moreover, how would they respond if some (see note 5) emphasized the Christian roots of these concepts?

To complicate the matter, there is the "cultural turn" of our time, in which we encounter the attitude of cultural self-assertion spreading and thus creating obstacles to inter-fertilization generated by inter-cultural mutual recognition. In this situation, it becomes difficult to be receptive to learning from others – something that may even be discredited. Therefore, when it comes to a universalization of democratic concepts the decisive "final enemy of civil society" is a cultural one, as John Hall puts it (see note 2). In the volume edited by Hall we read with regard to Islam that it "possesses a civilizational vision of its own, radically opposed to that of the West." In the same volume a leading Muslim scholar, Şerif Mardin, who spends his life between the USA and secular acclaimed Turkey, elaborates on this notion in arguing in his contribution that "civil society is a Western dream ... part of the social history of Western Europe ... civil society does not translate into Islamic terms" (see note 2). If these allegations were true, then the idea of democratic peace would be devoid of cultural foundations in non-Western cultures and thus not feasible, perhaps even irrelevant for the world of Islam. In short, in this case it would make no sense to write this book. The fact of writing this book is an indication that I do not share this view. Democracy and civil society are not an illusion for Muslims, and therefore I continue with passion to write this book, where I opt for a global civil society[25] in which people of Islamic civilization are supposed to participate.

To be sure, democracy needs to be based on a civil society. As John Hall argues, democracy is "not equivalent ... to more familiar and valued notions; democracy can be decidedly uncivil." Therefore I follow Hefner, who establishes a synthesis between Islam, civil society and democracy based on an Islamic legitimacy for the civilianization of the state which prevents "uncivil" action done in the name of democracy.

A closer look at the political order of the Salafist orthodoxy or, even worse, at the Islamic state that Islamism envisions, leads to the finding of an "uncivil state." Therefore, the choice when talking about "order" is: a democratic one or none. The exclusiveness of Islam is best and most forcefully expressed against democracy and civil society, as in the works by Abu al-A'la al-Mawdudi. He argues for the incompatibility of Islam with democracy, unequivocally stating,

> I tell you, my fellow Muslims, frankly: Democracy is in contradiction with your belief ... Islam, in which you believe ... is utterly different from this dreadful system ... There can be no reconciliation between Islam and democracy, not even in minor issues, because they contradict one another in all terms. Where this system [of democracy] exists we consider Islam to be absent. When Islam comes to power there is no place for this system.[26]

In contrast, there are other Muslims who envision a synthesis between Islam and democracy, but their impact is professedly weak. At issue is therefore – as Jean François Revel phrases it – not only "the inability of Islam to adopt itself to democratic civilization, but also ... the inability of democratic civilization to find an appropriate response to totalitarian attacks upon itself."[27]

While defending Islam, as both a religion and a civilization, against the Islamophobia spreading in the West, I cannot deny and overlook "fundamentalist Islam's offensive against the freedom of the rest of humanity," as Revel phrases the issue while arguing against those Western democrats who believe they could accommodate anti-Western Islamist totalitarianism: "The morbid wish of the enemies of the open society finds support among politicians ... who think they can come to terms with fanatics ... If you give all, they cannot be grateful, because morally you no longer exist."[28]

In a similar manner, I have argued in an earlier work (1998) that the civilizational identity of Europe is at peril, and I continue this argument, although without other-ing Islam, in the chapters of Part III of this book. Revel joins those who acknowledge the distinction between formal democracy and substantial civil society: "calling a state secular does not make it democratic, when only the ... state and not civil society benefits from this secularism."[29]

Without engaging in a digression, there is a need to underline the fact that a Muslim acceptance of democracy and civil society is not a matter exclusive for the world of Islam. As will be shown in Part III, there exists in Europe an increasing community of Muslim migrants not integrated in the existing polity, but rather living as an "enclave" in parallel societies.[30] In addition, there is a Muslim country, namely Turkey, seeking accession to the European Union. Based on these facts it is argued that Islam and democracy are not a matter exclusively pertinent to Muslims themselves. The acceptance of democracy and civil society or its rejection by Muslims becomes a European concern. Therefore, establishing Islamic foundations favorable to democracy and civil society in competition between global jihad and democratic peace is not only a subject for international but also for European studies.

Islamic civilization in its medieval glory days proved to be in a position where it was able to embrace Hellenism, i.e. the source of the idea of civil society, as addressed by the historian of ideas, John Ehrenburg. In his study of civil society Ehrenburg traces the idea back to Plato's "vision of a political leader who would unite knowledge with power,"[31] and adds his conviction that this is "the classical effort to rescue humankind from barbarism and secure for it the possibility of a politically organized civilization. The transition from polis to republic ... described a man-made civil society where reason and civilization would be safe" (ibid.). Yet, this interpretation of Plato by Ehrenburg is not alien to medieval Islam. To engage in this debate is not simply to conduct an exercise in the history of ideas, because the quoted Platonian requirement is at present highly topical in culturally underpinning the idea and reality of a civil society as the Islamic civilization of today lacks both. Readers knowledgeable about Islamic history are reminded that Plato's cited vision was shared in medieval Islam by the

Islamic rationalists, and foremost in al-Farabi's *al-madina al-fadila*.[32] If this was the case, then why cannot contemporary Muslims refer to this Islamic heritage for legitimating a modernity-oriented embracing of civil society? Knowledge for al-Farabi, as it was for Plato, was human- and also reason-based, and thus was not restricted to a revelation of a religion or to the exclusive worldview of one civilization. It follows that the concepts referred to in this book to promote democratic peace, presented as the alternative to global jihad, are universal: they are not purely Western. With this line of reasoning this book gives more credit to this intellectual background which is both Hellenistic and Islamic.

If the reference to the European origins of democracy and civil society is used in a discourse aimed at a de-Westernization of knowledge, this becomes a dangerous undertaking. Islamists who engage in it want to establish fault-lines between their civilization and the rest of humanity. In this situation, present-day Muslims are challenged to emulate al-Farabi and other great Muslim philosophers in discrediting the options presented by Sayyid Qutb, Hasan al-Banna and Abu al-A'la al-Mawdudi, in order to pursue an Islamic quest for a better future. At this point, the debate on knowledge as the source of worldview[33] and values is most pertinent to the present inquiry into Islam and democracy. If rational knowledge about the secular organization of the polity is dismissed as alien, then one could proceed in a similar manner and repudiate the political culture underlying civil society as alien to Muslims. Then, the claim of democracy to universality would be questioned as well.

Islamic liberal authors[34] admit that historical Islam did not give space to individual freedom, but insist that the idea of freedom lies at the hub of the Islamic scripture. In responding to the critique that such ideas were never implemented, these authors concede the lack of institutions needed for bolstering the Qur'anic idea of freedom – and indicate this as a reason for such deficits.[35] Elsewhere, in an overall intellectual history of Islam, I have supported the contention with evidence that in Islamic history the just order was never an issue for itself, in that the concern was associated with a "just Imam/*Imam adil*" in contrast to an "unjust Imam/*Imam ja'ir*." The person, not the institution, was the concern. Throughout their history Muslims have been directed by their yearning for an *Imam adil* in the footsteps of the Prophet,[36] not for the proper institution as a safeguard for protecting freedom. However, this ideal has never materialized. To date, the first four caliphs in Islam continue to be considered as "*rashidun*/righteous rulers," though three of them were assassinated by Muslims who accused them of deviating from the right path of being a just Imam.

Unlike Bruce Russett, I do not simply view democracy as a voting procedure that leads to the rule of the majority (see Chapter 7). As much as there is an *esprit de loi* (Montesquieu), there is a culture of democracy (democracy is not simply a voting procedure) without which no democracy could ever thrive. The rule of the majority could be very uncivil without a culture putting civic restraints on it. This culture is the very one of civil society and its rules. The case of Iraq 2002–6 makes clear that the toppling of a dictator and the installation of voting makes for little democracy, just as "nice words do not make ice-cream." This is one of the lessons of the war in Iraq. Neither the Bush administration nor its foe, the French government of President Chirac which opposed the war, was in a position to grasp that democracy cannot be introduced from outside, whether by order from Washington or through the UN, as Paris requested. Elections are not the substance; they create only one aspect of establishing the rule of democracy. An election is no more than a formal procedure and it cannot be equated with democracy itself. Elections make little sense if they are not underpinned by a political civic culture giving democracy legitimacy, supporting it by civil society and a civilized state that institutionally provides safeguards for individual freedom. All of these requirements were and still are missing in Iraq and in most countries of Islamic civilization. It required generations to accomplish this task in the West. Taking Iraq as a case in point, one needs to ask how people of Islamic civilization can cope with secular democracy as the substance of modernity and lay grounds for a civil society. Only if free thinking/*tafkir* is allowed and not dismissed through the accusation of unbelief/*takfir*, may one find a way out of this impasse in Islamic civilization. It is not a digression to end this section with a parallel of suppressing free expression in Western Islamic and Middle Eastern studies. Instead of the accusation of *tafkir*/unbelief, one faces the accusation of Orientalism if one speaks of Middle Eastern despotism and Islamist totalitarianism. This is damaging to democratic scholarly culture in the West, much as Islamism undermines "free civil Islam."

Rethinking Islam and democracy in Islamic and global contexts

A major argument of this book is that a predicament with modernity is at work when focusing on incorporating democracy into Islamic thought. Without rethinking Islam, and without a wholehearted willingness to engage in this endeavor free of restriction and without fear of being accused of *tafkir*, there can be no progress. Among the questions to be asked in this manner is one concerning the compatibility of Islam and democracy as a political culture of pluralism and civil society. One could state that democracy has Greek origins and point to Plato's concept of the state and the Hellenistic culture of the polity (*polis*). To hark back to these roots may seem like stating a reminiscence of traditional wisdom. However, in our time this reference has deep meaning. Those Muslims like Mawdudi, who argue that Islam and democracy are at odds in referring to the non-Islamic sources of democratic thought and who state that democracy is alien to Islam, overlook the fact that the Hellenization of Islamic civilization has contributed to its growth in the past. The same can be said concerning the work of the contemporary Islamist Yusuf al-Qaradawi, who rejects democracy as an imported solution/*hall mustawrad*.

There are also Westerners who – with a reference to its classical Greek origins – think that democracy does not apply to the world of Islam. This allegation is based on ignorance of the history of Islam and it certainly amazes well-informed students of Islamic heritage. The reason is simple: These students are familiar with the extremely positive attitudes of the medieval Muslim philosophers in the classical age of Islam vis-à-vis the Greek legacy.[37] Aristotle was named by these philosophers the *"al-mu'allim al-awwal/*the first master,"* whereas the most significant Muslim philosopher, al-Farabi (already quoted) was ranked as *al-mu'allim al-thani*, only second to Aristotle.[38] In awarding the top ranking in intellectual history to a non-Muslim thinker, Islamic rationalists proved how open-minded and flexible Islam can be. As the Hellenization of Islam was feasible in the past, so the opening for a democratization of Islam in our time should be possible, too. From this perspective, the exposure to the choice between global jihad and democratic peace could result in a more favorable decision for the Kantian model.

Unlike religious traditions in classical Islam that encouraged learning from other cultures, one finds the opposite in very influential writings of political Islam. Earlier, the book *Islam and Modern Civilization*[39] by the late Abu al-A'la al-Mawdudi was quoted, in which an outlawing of democracy is expressed as a firm conviction in the strong phrases that there is no democracy where Islam rules and that "Islam is absent" where democratic rule is in place (see note 26). No US-American or European, liable to be accused of "Orientalism," is making these statements. If the alleged incompatibility of Islam and democracy were correct, then Muslims would stay out of the so-called third wave of democratization,[40] believed to be global. Islamic and global contexts would contradict one another. In contrast to this polarization, a view of an intellectual open-mindedness of Islam vis-à-vis other civilizations, as the one in medieval Islamic history,[41] must start with renouncing Islamism and continue with rethinking Islam. For this and other reasons it is most disturbing to see Esposito and Voll confusing Islam and Islamism when they deal with democracy while engaging in blurring generalities.[42]

In the Islamic rhetoric employed when playing to the gallery (especially with Westerners), one hears the message that there is only one true Islam. True, in terms of pillars of *iman*/belief there exists only one Islam. In Islamic history, however, there have been many different approaches to understanding Islam, and thus various schools of thought. This applies also to the present day, so that we can see diverse positions in contemporary Islam. One of them is reflected in the quoted statement by Mawdudi, adverse to democracy, which is clearly an expression of political Islam,[43] being the Islamic variety of religious fundamentalism based on the politicization of Islam. In contrast, one finds Muslims expressing liberal and civil Islam, like

Mohammed al-Jabri and Mohammed Shahrur. There can be a democratic Islam, but there definitely can be no "democratic Islamism," as suggested by Voll and Esposito.

To be sure, there is also another source of diversity in Islam based on local cultures which this civilization encompasses. These cultures rally in terms of civilizational outlooks to an Islamic worldview as the expression of a cultural system, not of a system of government. Now, the contention that Islam is a specific system of government opposed to democratic rule is a quite recent phenomenon. As repeatedly stated, the term *"nizam Islami/* Islamic system" occurs neither in the Qur'an nor in the legacy of the Prophet, the *hadith*. It is rather a misconception of Islam when it is identified with political Islam. It is most important to draw a clear distinction between these two totally different understandings of Islam. On these grounds, the argument that political Islam of global jihad stands in the way of democracy and democratic peace is conceivable. The question over the compatibility or incompatibility of Islam and democracy as related to the exposure of Islam to a global context can be answered in many ways. Positively, the first step of rethinking would be an identifying of the obstacles. A proper solution to them could result in a favorable synthesis of Islam and democracy. The other perspective is that of political Islam either accepting democracy as a tool (voting procedure) for seizing power (e.g. Hamas) but rejecting its political culture, or dismissing it by global jihad (e.g. Taliban).

The issue in rethinking Islam is not the diversity based on a great variety of local cultures. More pertinent than this diversity is the claimed unity of ethical standards related to similar norms and values shared by all Muslims, much like the corresponding worldview. The Islamic unity in terms of *Weltanschauung* addressed as the Islamic civilization is a universalism claimed for the world of Islam. The Islamic and the Western civilizations both claim universality for their worldviews and the related concept of order.[44] This is the source of the constructed conflict between democracy and *hakimiyyat Allah*. A rethinking of Islam could replace this clash through cross-cultural bridging.

The international context of the twenty-first century compels people who belong to divergent civilizations, but who at the same time share the essence of belonging to one humanity, to establish a consensus over a common core of ethical values that can unite this very humanity. To do this, one needs to go beyond local contexts to make democratic peace possible, yet not overlook differences. It follows that global democracy and universal human rights based on a global civil society constitute the core issues in this international morality for bridging on cross-cultural grounds. Certainly, the shari'a cannot be the framework for this endeavor,[45] because it alienates Muslim minorities from others in concrete societies (e.g. India and Western Europe) and the Muslim population as a whole from humanity in general. Instead of the call for shari'a, Muslims need the call to rethinking Islam. In this global context, Muslims are challenged to question the claims of the shari'a to universalism and to honor cross-cultural pluralism instead.

Change within Islam matters to the West in general and to Europe in particular. In the West, opening up to other cultures assumes the shape of cultural relativism. Islamophobia moves to Islamophilia without the limits of pluralism. In the encounter of Islamist neo-absolutism and European relativism[46] cultural relativists are the losers. In the search for world peace European relativism and fundamentalist neo-absolutisms seem to be the extremes opposed to one another, but they do not clash because the relativists give in, in the name of tolerance.[47] It is regrettable that post-modernists, who subscribe to cultural relativism, fail to see how consequential their position is, i.e. how it undermines the needed cross-cultural bridging between competing world civilizations. The notion of a united humanity goes beyond relativism in furthering the conviction that a shared international morality essentially requires a cross-cultural underpinning of an ethical core of binding values, such as individual human rights and secular democracy. This value-based commitment is valid for all humanity on cross-cultural – neither universalist nor relativist – grounds. In this understanding, an effort at establishing a political culture of democracy in Islamic civilization is a contribution to promoting democratic peace while denouncing Islamism as "the new totalitarianism."[48] This effort pre-supposes an effort at rethinking Islam, a process that matters to all humanity across the globe, and in particular within the European context of a growing Islamic diaspora. The Islamic context is pertinent to others.

Cultural requirements for overcoming Islam's predicament in the process of learning from other civilizations

The earlier Islamic responses to the exposure to modernity were basically defensive-cultural. The rejection of the West by the contemporary Islamists is based in nothing less than a drive toward a wholesale de-Westernization. Islam has a rich history of opening itself to others and of basing its own achievements on learning from other cultures and civilizations. The addressed attitudes, stretching from defensive culture to rejection, are therefore not typical of Islamic civilization. In contrast to their predecessors' open-mindedness during the early encounters with Europe in the nineteenth century, Muslims of today do not have this spirit vis-à-vis cultural modernity. Can democracy as a political culture of modernity be introduced to the world of Islam in spite of the prevalence of this mindset?

Given the fact that the final version of this chapter was completed at the Asia Research Institute in the National University of Singapore, in answering this question I shall focus on Asia as another place where these questions are asked and answers are being looked for. Even in Southeast Asia, though – yet less than in the Middle East – a hostile attitude towards the West affects the overall atmosphere. Three cases in Asia are pertinent as models. One is India, a secular state with the largest Islamic minority (ca. 130 million) in the world; it provides a model for the peaceful coexistence of people belonging to diverse religions, all living under secular democracy as the common umbrella. But India's model is flawed and has potential to become a model for "the coming anarchy,"[49] if this secular multi-religious setup were to break down. In contrast, we see the other model of Pakistan, which claims to be "Islamic" but is not in a position to accommodate non-Sunni Muslim ethnic and sectarian minorities – indeed, Pakistan is not even able to integrate the minority of Sunni Mauhajirs, i.e. Indian Muslims who immigrated to an "Islamic diaspora" after the partition of 1947. The third model is Indonesia,[50] another Asian country where a relatively enlightened and tolerant (i.e. civil) Islam is embracing democracy and providing a secular state as an institutional guarantee for inter-ethnic and religious peace, and above all for religious pluralism (*pancasila*). An early version of this chapter was completed in 2003 in Indonesia itself, while the final revisions were done in 2005 in Singapore, giving a distance of time and space with regard to Islamic Southeast Asia.

To begin with Indonesia: one may ask whether the Indonesian example provides significantly favorable conditions for democratization in the world of Islam as a model for civil Islam despite its flaws. This model could generate demonstrative effects throughout the Islamic civilization, including West Asia, i.e. the Middle East, as the center of the Islamic civilization. But this is not the case. Why? A renowned expert on Indonesia, Fred von der Mehden, subjected the interaction between Southeast Asia and the Arab Middle East, i.e. West Asia, to closer scrutiny. As a result he states the telling facts:

> Middle Eastern religious ideas still dominate the exchange between the two regions. There is relatively little influence by Southeast Asian Muslim intellectuals on the rest of the Muslim world ... Religious education in the Middle East, and in Cairo in particular, remains a major source of Muslim thought in Southeast Asia, especially in Indonesia.[51]

Despite the Asian focus of this chapter, the quoted observation compels us to give West Asia – or, as it is called in the West, the "Middle East" – more weight, since it is the cultural core of the Islamic civilization even though its record is poor. It is not democracy but rather global jihad, as the ideology born in the Middle East, that enjoys great appeal; it has been exported to Indonesia from the Arab world. During my work in Indonesia in intervals between 1995 and 2003, I encountered Saudi Wahhabi education (madrasas) and learned that Indonesian students go to Egypt and Saudi Arabia to study Islam. In the Middle East, I never came across Muslims studying Indonesian civil Islam. In Indonesia one encounters the fact that thousands and thousands of *pesantrens* (Islamic boarding schools) teach *aqida*-Islam.

The Bali bombing in 2002 was related to the worldview taught at these schools. The founder of this madrasa-pattern, Abu Bakr Bashir, is an Indonesian Islamist with Wahhabi views and al-Qaeda links.

The search for *asalah*/authenticity is much more pertinent to the Middle East than to Indonesia. Therefore, issues related to the cultural underpinning for the adoption of democracy as the alternative to global jihad are highly relevant. With reference to *asalah*, some Arab Muslims argue that there is no need for a Western model of democracy, because Muslims have their *shura*/consultation, as provisioned in the Qur'an. In reverse, others are of the view that the reference to the *shura* could serve as a cultural underpinning for the adoption of democracy, thus establishing an accepted frame of reference compatible with Islamic views. In this debate, there is the need to honestly reiterate the fact stated by the late Hamid Enayat, that democracy is a cultural addition to the traditional political concepts of Islam.[52] The Islamic awareness of this cultural novelty is unfortunately still weak, despite all the lip-service paid to it. At this point there is no difference between the Middle East (West Asia) and Southeast Asia.

With regard to the context of globalization, Western hegemony and the exposure of Islamic civilization to "cultural modernity," there is no doubt about the place of the Middle East as the core of Islam's predicament with modernity. It is not an expression of Arab-centrism to state that neither Indonesia nor Pakistan or India (an entity only split after partition in 1947) is the center of Islamic–Western encounter.[53] At the outset, Arab Muslims were receptive to an embracing of democracy and to reconciling it with Islam. The first Muslim Imam and student who went to Europe was the Egyptian Rifa'a Rafi al-Tahtawi; he expressed his deep admiration for the French democracy. He was to witness the July revolution in Paris in 1830, and was both amazed and impressed to see that the representatives of the toppled regime were not killed but instead were treated lawfully and with dignity, being granted basic human rights. For Tahtawi this was evidence – as he says – "for how civilized the French are and how their state is bound to justice."[54] This modernist Tahtawi was followed by other Muslim modernists and reformists who were critical of Europe for its colonial incursion into the abode of Islam; but despite their criticisms, they were receptive to learning from the West. Following these Muslim liberals who pursued the reconciliation of Islam with cultural modernity came another Egyptian, Mohammed Abduh. In the Islamic liberalism[55] of the early twentieth century, democracy was at the top of the agenda of Muslim thinkers like Abbas Mahmud al-Aqqad[56] and others. However, this liberalism of Arab Muslims failed to trigger the needed cultural innovations, and so it waned as a mindset in the wake of the emergence of the radical-secular praetorianism (Nasserism) of the military, by then viewed as the embodiment of modernizing elites. In fact these elites did not fulfill what has been attributed to them. At issue was a superficially secular variety of Islamic authoritarianism that can also be labeled a neo-patriarchy (see note 8), continuing old patterns in a new garb. These cultural changes spilled over from the Arab Middle Eastern core to the Asian fringe. However, there are differences between both regions of the Islamic civilization, related to the fact that Southeast Asians are characterized by openness to learning from other civilizations.

In the discussion of the embracing of modernity, it was asked why Japan succeeded and countries of Islam failed. In their medieval Islamic history, Muslims were open to other cultures, as is Japan today. Islamic rationalism of that historical period was in fact a synthesis of the Greek legacy and the Islamic civilization.[57] Western historians of civilization – such as Leslie Lipson (see note 58) – remind us of the fact that this Islamic rationalism was one of the major sources of inspiration for the European Renaissance. In European philosophical discourse, it is acknowledged that the legacy of the Renaissance has been one of the basic pillars of cultural modernity. It can further be argued that this very modernity is the major source of democracy. We should remind ourselves of the historical fact that the Renaissance is a part of the very same legacy that grew from the interaction between Islam and Europe. I refer to this legacy in order to legitimate the plea for an adoption of democracy. I turn again to Leslie Lipson's analysis of the European awareness of Hellenism via Islam:

> Aristotle crept back into Europe by the side door. His return was due to the Arabs, who had become acquainted with Greek thinkers ... The main source of Europe's inspiration shifted from Christianity back to Greece, from Jerusalem to Athens.[58]

This very Athens was also the source of inspiration within the earlier civilizational interaction, which led in the course of inter-cultural fertilization to the Hellenization of medieval Islam. Hellenism is a shared legacy between Islam and the West. This reference has two meanings: First, the spirit of Western civilization is Hellenistic (Athens), not primarily Christian (Jerusalem). Second, this very legacy belonged to Islamic civilization while it was at its height. Islam succeeded through inter-fertilization and it has decayed through civilizational fault-lines that Islamists continue to construct at present.

Islamic medieval philosophers shifted in their outlooks and worldviews "from Mecca to Athens."[59] Enlightened contemporary Muslims view a revival of this rationalist legacy as a requirement for promoting a cultural underpinning for embracing modernity.[60] It is unfortunate to see that this is not happening. Instead, this Greek legacy, once transmitted to Europe by Muslim philosophers, continues to vanish along with the Islamic heritage of rationalism. The rival Islamic orthodoxy gathered forces around the *fiqh*/Islamic sacred jurisprudence. In medieval Islam this Salafism contributed to the banning of rationalism from the institutions of learning,[61] just as Wahhabi Salafism does today in the madrasas. In the past, the Islamic *fiqh*-orthodoxy took over after suppressing Islamic rationalism of the *falsafa*.[62] One asks: Did Islamic rationalism fail to have a lasting impact? The answer is: Without an institutionalization (e.g. in the educational system) no cultural innovations can be enduring in society.[63]

Again, in the core of contemporary Islamic civilization there have been some efforts to revive this tradition of Islamic Enlightenment and rationalism, but they have not been very successful and have waned.[64] The defenders of reason had an outreach in Indonesia, and their reference to this tradition of Islamic rationalism was not an exercise in intellectual history. Those early Muslim liberals[65] who were at pains to revive this legacy for coming to terms with democracy, and for facilitating the adoption of its norms and values in an Islamic environment, failed. To be sure, the failure was not only due to poor performance: it was caused not so much "by conceptual incoherence as by absence of specific social and economic formations,"[66] as the late Oxford scholar Enayat puts it. He argues that on domestic grounds the constraints were "educational backwardness, widespread illiteracy, and the prevalence of servile habits of thinking and blind submission to authority" (ibid.) and adds to these major obstacles the fact that the West, despite all its lip-service, has not been favorable to the process of democratization in the world of Islam. Enayat was a reasoning Muslim and refrained from putting the blame on Western policies. He also acknowledges the cultural shortcomings of Muslims themselves. In this sense we need not only to establish a balance between the cultural factor and the structural constraints, but also to relate each to one another.

In discussing the cultural requirements for overcoming Islam's predicament with modernity, a reference was made to three non-Middle Eastern Asian models with a record of procedural democratization in the early postcolonial period. Then, after acknowledging the cultural prevalence of the core of Islamic civilization, I turned to the Middle East – or West Asia or whatever you choose to name it. Unlike South and Southeast Asia, the Middle East is an underachiever in democratization. The rule of praetorian one-party authoritarian regimes, legitimated by the populist ideology of pan-Arab nationalism,[67] marked the end of futile democratization. Ever since, the levers of power have been residing in the hands of lifetime presidents and other tyrants of all shapes. The de-legitimation of these authoritarian regimes, in particular since the shattering defeat in the Six-Day War,[68] contributed to the rise of political Islam being presented as the alternative (*al-hall al-Islami*). The few cases of electoral democratization, i.e. democracy as a procedure without the political culture of democracy (e.g. in Algeria, Jordan, Morocco and most recently Iraq), produced only poor results.

The reasons for the lack of democracy are multifaceted, a point that is not ignored while we focus on the cultural underpinning as a requirement for democratization in countries of Islamic civilization. The alleged Islamization of democracy via political Islam by so-called "new Islamists without

fear" is not the needed new avenue for democratization in terms of introducing a political culture for democracy.[69] The actions and pronouncements of the exponents of political Islam stand in contrast.[70] I share the
view that the Islamists are "committed to using the fragile reemergence of
democratic processes to destroy any decisive move in this direction of
liberal democracy itself."[71] My own observations in Algiers during the
democratization process in 1991–2 in Algeria and similarly in Egypt, Morocco and also in Indonesia support these conclusions. In two reference
articles, first 1995 in the *Encyclopedia of Democracy* (The Congressional
Quarterly 1995) and, a decade later, in the *Encyclopedia of Government*
(2004), I express the view that all varieties of religious fundamentalism are
at odds with democratic rule.[72] To be sure and to reiterate, Islam and Islamism are two different issues. In rethinking Islam one can reach positive
conclusions about the compatibility of democracy and Islam, but this
option cannot be achieved by Islamism. The Turkish experience of the
AKP related to the rise of this party while democratically playing the
power game after the election of November 2002 continued 2007 is a great
challenge to this view. To be sure, the AKP presents itself as secular and
"conservative-Islamic," and no longer as an "Islamist" party. For an evaluation of this experiment the norm would be to "wait and see." It is too
early for a mature statement. More details will be provided in Part III of
this book.

In assessing the relationship of political Islam and democracy I refer to
the major authorities of contemporary Islamism – from Qutb in the past
through al-Qaradawi in our own time. They argue against democracy, stating that it is alien to Islam. I have already cited the late Pakistani Abu al-
A'la al-Mawdudi (see note 26), who is the major ideological source of political Islam next to the Egyptian Sayyid Qutb. By the same token, Qutb
(executed in 1966) believed that Islam would replace the West in the leadership of the world. This belief continues to be with us in the new direction
of global jihad. On the Islamic front, Qutb was also the precursor of the
idea of a clash of civilizations. Like Huntington, Qutb supports the alleged
incompatibility of Western and Islamic views and contended decades earlier
that a conflict on a global scale is looming: "After the end of democracy to
the extent of bankruptcy the West has nothing to give to humanity ... The
leadership of the Western man has vanished ... It is the time for Islam to
take over and lead."[73]

The quoted statement makes clear that, for taking over, global jihad is
required. In this tradition combined with Mawdudi's legacy Yusuf al-Qaradawi, the most influential Islamic writer of our time, has coined the phrase
"*al-hall al-Islami*/the Islamic solution" as opposed to "*al-hulul al-mustawradah*/the imported solutions." In al-Qaradawi's view, democracy is among
these imports to be rejected. In this mindset there is no opening for learning
from other civilizations and subsequently no sign of overcoming Islam's
predicament with modernity.

A brief discussion of al-Qaradawi's views supports the stated assessment. In his major book al-Qaradawi states: "Democracy is a Greek term which means the government of the people" and then continues that "democratic liberalism came into the life of Muslims through the impact of colonialism. It has been the foremost dangerous result in the colonial legacy."[74] As the reader will notice, al-Qaradawi's dismissal of the Greek legacy deliberately overlooks the positive record of Hellenism in classical Islam. In contrast to al-Qaradawi, it is argued here that any synthesis of Islam and democracy needs to be based on this very record of Islamic rationalism and Hellenism as a cultural underpinning. If this is dismissed, the cultural bridging aimed at will, as a consequence, be dismissed too. It is wrong to classify the Islamist al-Qaradawi as a representative of "liberal Islam" or of an "Islam without fears,"[75] as some Westerners do, who claim to be "experts on Islam."

The cultural synthesis of democratization of Islamic thought

In Islamic political ethics the Qur'anic idea of *shura* could determine the ethical level in the search for commonalities in the attempt to establish a synthesis between Islam and secular democracy. This political-ethical approach is both authentic and flexible and need not to be of a scriptural nature. In this pursuit of an international cross-cultural morality, I read Islamic sources and hereby share the position of Hamid Enayat that it is "neither ... inordinately difficult nor illegitimate to derive a list of democratic rights and liberties"[76] from Islamic provisions. Thus the contention that Islam and democracy are at odds does not hold, since it is based on an arbitrary reading. In addition, we have to consider the fact that the fundamentalist notion of *hakimiyyat Allah* is definitely not an authentic Islamic concept, for it does not exist in the authoritative sources. As repeatedly stated, one finds it neither in the Qur'an nor in the *hadith*, i.e. the tradition of the Prophet. On the grounds of both these authoritative sources of Islamic faith, one can dismiss most concepts included in the ideology of political Islam. However, on this scriptural level no problem can be solved. In order to overcome Islam's predicament with modernity, to which the embracing of democracy belongs, Muslims definitely need to go beyond the scripture and the arguments based on it. Coping with the tensions between open civil and political Islam is also part of the broader range of problems involved.

The first obstacle in the way of a synthesis between Islam and democracy resulting in a democratization of Islam is the complementary call for the *tatbiq al-shari'a*/implementation of Islamic law for establishing an Islamic state. Shari'a law has traditionally been civil law, but it is advanced in the current Islamist ideology to a state law or alleged constitutional law. In the Islamist view, shari'a is a decisive criterion for determining the character of a *dawla Islamiyya*/Islamic state or its constitution. Students of Islam who are familiar with the concepts of Islamic shari'a law[77] will have some major corrections to the fundamentalists' claims. These scholars know that legal norms of the shari'a have never been codified as a legal system. The simple reason for this is that codification runs counter to the nature of the shari'a as an interpretative divine law. There are four Sunni Islamic legal schools, each of which has its own tradition of law-making. Thus Islamic law has been a law of the divergent Hanafi, Shafi'i, Hanbali or Maliki religious Sunni communities. In Islamic history, shari'a was separated from *siyasa* as politics of the state, as we learn from the authoritative book by Joseph Schacht.[78] In addition, Enayat tells us that the shari'a "was never implemented as an integral system, and the bulk of its provisions remained as legal fictions."[79] In other words, the *tatbiq al-shari'a* aspired to by Islamists is virtually based on a fiction expanded to the view of how the state should be conducted and how its affairs are to be dealt with. This fiction of an Islamic shari'a state is an agglomeration of inconsistent constructions and consequently leads to rejecting all realities of the existing international order of states based on secular foundations. This rejection happens to the extent of putting Islamic civilization in conflict with the rest of humanity, i.e. not only with the West. Asia is a case in point: It is neither part of the West nor fully Islamic. It would not succumb to Islamic claims.

To avert a polarization, Muslims need to establish harmony between Islam and democracy. At issue is a process of conflict resolution which encompasses dealing with the existing differences and real tensions. Having stated this, it is not only for the sake of honesty and integrity, but also for the sake of a synthesis between Islam and democracy, that these tensions are addressed as real and fundamental. One has to address them in plain language, beyond ambiguities. Again, I am in agreement with the late enlightened Muslim Hamid Enayat when he states: "If Islam comes into conflict with certain postulates of democracy it is because of its general character as a religion ... An intrinsic concomitant of democracy ... involves a challenge to many a sacred axiom."[80]

It is tough, but imperative, to develop a full awareness of this challenge. The mistake of early Muslim reformers committed to the search for the aspired synthesis was to evade any addressing of – not to say coping with – hot button issues. Obviously, these reformers were concerned that such an unpopular endeavor could jeopardize their plea for democracy. However, an adaptation of religious doctrine to changed historical realities requires a reform which is more than the conformism discussed in Chapter 1. There is a challenge which compelled the contemporary Algerian Muslim thinker Mohammed Arkoun to call for a "rethinking of Islam."[81] This needed reasoning involves, as I argue in an earlier book,[82] not simply indulging oneself in some kind of conformism in a pragmatic manner, but rather a substantial cultural accommodation to changed social conditions.

For joining democratic peace it is not enough to suspend the jihad, for reasons of convenience, through conformism. Muslims need to venture into a rethinking of jihad. The late Oxford Muslim scholar Hamid Enayat describes the state of affairs as follows:

> What is blatantly missing ... is an adaptation of either the ethical and legal precepts of Islam, or the attitudes and institutions of traditional society, to democracy. This is obviously a much more complex and challenging task than the mere reformulation of democratic principles in Islamic idioms. It is because of this neglect that the hopes of evolving a coherent theory of democracy appropriate to an Islamic context have remained largely unfulfilled.[83]

Instead of continuing this unfinished business, Islamists abuse these obvious shortcomings of Islamic liberals and modernists for promoting their own vision. They denounce an alleged deviation from the true religious doctrine, and some of them argue for an Islamic democracy. To introduce democracy into Islamic civilization in unequivocal terms requires a full awareness of the fact that

> efforts to synthesize Islam and democracy are bound to founder on the bedrock of that body of eternal and unchangeable doctrines which form the quintessence of every religion. Those Muslim thinkers who face this issue boldly, and free of any compulsion to keep their faith abreast of ephemeral political fashions, normally come up with the open admission that Islam and democracy are irreconcilable.[84]

The only way out is to reconsider and rethink the claim of the doctrine to eternity and to immutability, placing it into a historical context that renders it positive and makes it changeable; merely to engage in a reinterpretation in the spirit of conformism is not sufficient. In honestly facing these problems, the pending question relates to an opening for an alternative to the existing options of superficially phrasing democratic principles in Islamic idioms (e.g. *shura*) or to surrender to the Islamist challenge in stating the irreconcilability. This question best reflects the addressed predicament of Islam with democracy. It refers to the limits of a morality and political ethics based on religion.

In other words: Any exclusive religious underpinning of democracy expressed in doctrinal Islamic terms would fail. Existing approaches are either selective and limited in their scope or mostly apologetic in their nature. The way out would be a secularization of politics as a requirement for overcoming the conflict between Islam and democracy in the states of Islamic civilization. I see no "Islamic democracy" emerging, because democracy is based on popular sovereignty, not on religious precepts, even though democracy can be underpinned by religious ethics (e.g. *shura* in Islam). Popular sovereignty is a universal principle. The democratization of Islam is a better formula than the Islamization of democracy.

With an awareness of the unpopularity of the secular approach in Islamic civilization, it is important that we clear up the understanding of secularity. Radical-dogmatic or state secularism can be areligious, a position that I dismiss in admitting religious ethics while maintaining secularity.[85] In short, the secular argumentation is not areligious in that – as argued – it admits religion as a source of ethics for a cultural underpinning of democracy. In my understanding, *laïcité* is no more than a separation of religion and politics, but never a wholesale abandonment of religion from public life. However, religion is specific. The Qur'an states: "You have your religion and I have mine," but democratic institutions and the culture of democracy are universal and this is exactly the argument underlying the secular approach for an Islamic–democratic synthesis. I refer to the Islamic *shura* as an ethics of democracy, because it is in line with the culture of democracy.

Rethinking Islam in the pursuit of an Islamic–democratic synthesis is a reasoning, and not a scriptural undertaking that can be accused of deviation from Islamic precepts. In my plea for real democratic freedom, I find myself in conflict not only with orthodox-scriptural Muslims, but also with Western cultural relativists who contend that democracy, as a Western political model, is of only limited interest for non-Western cultures. As argued earlier in this chapter, cultural arguments can be the foremost enemy of civil society.

In moving from the general to the empirical level and acknowledging the Indonesian background of some parts of this book (see the introduction), I shall, in the remainder of this section on an Islamic–democratic synthesis, focus on Asia. Some of my major ideas, including this chapter, were exposed to my graduate students at the Islamic State University of Jakarta, and also to the community of the Asia Research Institute at the National University of Singapore. Sharing the experience of Robert Hefner in Indonesia, I agree that there are some seeds of a "civil Islam" as contrasted to the Islam of a "totalizing shari'a." On the normative level the possibility is suggested of establishing harmony between an enlightened Islam and democratic ideas. Of course, more important are the institutions that safeguard living up to these ideas of a democratic culture in Islam. I agree with Hefner in his statement that "democracy ultimately requires a public culture ... to promote universal habits of participation and tolerance. This civic culture ... the culture of civility remains vulnerable and incomplete, if not accompanied by a transformation of state."[86]

These arguments are much more pertinent than the cultural-relativism this reservations presented by the Turkish-American Şerif Mardin (see note 2) vis-à-vis the universal validity of democracy in the world of Islam. In addition, these arguments make it clear that for democratization in the world of Islam to take place, the envisioned Islamic–democratic cultural synthesis is not enough: It is true that culture matters, but one needs to add that institutions as a safeguard matter, too (see Chapter 7).

In arguing for a culture of democracy and for the institutions of a civilianized state, I establish a combination of a cross-cultural underpinning of democracy and institutional democratization, both being requirements on the level of the state for the pursuit of democratic peace. With this understanding in mind, the current state of affairs in the world of Islam is to be addressed. The questions that I shall ask are based on a commitment to democracy. This is an ethical basis for a global institutional democratization as a precondition for a global civil society. It is argued against cultural relativists that democracy is not a fond Western dream – as Mardin contends – but rather a necessity for world peace that can only be pursued seriously on realistic grounds. To reach this end, not only ethical but also structural requirements are to be fulfilled in order to strengthen democracies along with nation-building.

In honoring the fact that the Muslim Arab Middle East is the core of Islamic civilization, I return to this region to discuss the findings of a project published in Beirut[87] two decades ago. The story of the project is pertinent. It goes back to November 1983, when a group of 70 Arab scholars, journalists and former politicians, myself included, addressed issues dealt with in this chapter under the formula: "*azmat al-demoqratiyya*/crisis of democracy" in the Arab world. This gathering took place in Limassol, Cyprus, after we were denied permission to meet in Cairo or in any other Arab city under Saudi petrodollar pressure. In Limassol I presented a paper on the structural requirements of democracy.[88] The published volume enjoyed wide dissemination in the Arab world, through both legal and underground means and editions. In the ensuing two decades, the concern for democracy and democratization has become more urgent, and equally the means of repression employed against it have become more brutal. After the demise of bipolarity the Arab world continues to be the center of despotic rule. The reference to the unjust behavior of Israel as an explanation for this state of affairs is no more than a distraction from the real issue. The basic missing requirements, such as institution-building, the economic underpinning of democracy and a supportive social system, as well as education in a culture of democracy, are related to home-made shortcomings, as the UNDP reports of 2002, 2003 and 2004 clearly reveal.[89]

In arguing for democratization in the Arab world, a cultural core of the world of Islam is to go for a change in two major fields:

First, changing Arab political culture (worldview, values, behavior) requires the development of favorable pluralistic attitudes towards democracy as a political culture of its own. This "civil Islam" runs counter to Arab political, quasi-tribal collectivism and to neo-patriarchy. Citizenship as the bedrock of a democratic polity is something other than loyalty to a clan or a sectarian group.[90] A democratic polity cannot be based on a tribe, such as the Saudis in Saudi Arabia, nor on a sectarian or ethnic community, be it Sunna, as was the case in Iraq under Saddam, or Shi'a as in the course of de-Saddamization. At present and since the elections in December 2005, the Shi'a majority rules the country while discriminating upon the Sunni minority.

Second, political development in the sense of institution-building has to take place in Arab societies now characterized by varying degrees of low institutionalization and a high degree of personalization of power.[91] The legacy of these obstacles has deep roots in Islamic history: the Prophet and his Sunna were to be emulated; no institution was the model. After the death of the Prophet the search was accordingly for the *Imam salih*/just Imam, not for a proper institution. In the UNDP report, we are informed that political development is a requirement for promoting democratization which is still virtually absent in the entire Arab world. It was very sad to read in an article by Edward Said, prior to his death in 2003, that he and his followers accused this UNDP report of "Orientalism."[92] To state it frankly: such goings-on made the entire Orientalism debate, a serious matter, into utter nonsense.

Following the cited democracy debate of the 1980s and in the aftermath of the Gulf War of 1991, the West was blamed for not having resorted to pressures to compel Middle Eastern states to introduce democratization.[93] Again, a decade later the democratization of the Middle East served as a legitimization for the Iraq war, which instead of being a contribution to democratization gave jihadism a boost. The lesson is that democracy cannot be imposed, and it cannot thrive if the local underpinning is lacking. Of course, there is a need to promote democratization, and Western policies vis-à-vis the world of Islam should support this. But this is not tantamount to imposing democracy, even though in some cases some pressure needs to be exerted on US allies, for instance in the Middle East, although not by the use of military force. All in all, it is a sign of the ignorance of Western missionaries of democracy that they address this issue without taking into consideration the debates[94] people of the region have been conducting for decades.

The problems of introducing democracy to the world of Islam in general and to the Middle East in particular can be illustrated in the case of Iraq. The state there is basically a nominal nation-state without a democratically designed political community. After the liberation of Iraq from Saddam's despotism, all political groups seeking to replace the Ba'th Party by their own power have been divided along ethnic and sectarian lines related to the artificial emergence of the Iraqi state in 1921. Iraq is mainly composed of three rival ethnic and religious communities and their corresponding territories: the former Ottoman province of Mossoul, inhabited by Kurds; the Sunni province of Baghdad; and the Shi'ite southern province of Basra. The Ba'th Party of Iraq[95] was secular only on the surface. In contrast to its pan-Arab ideology, it was basically a representation of the Sunni minority with the Takriti clientele at its core. In Iraq not only the ruling elites under Saddam, but also the counter-elites, were based on political communities formed on the basis of religion and ethnicity. In this regard Iraq is just one case in point. Therefore, at issue is not only Islam's predicament with democracy and the lack of institutions, but also the religio-sectarian ethnic determination of communities as rival collective identities. These are among the major obstacles to nation-building and democratization, both in Iraq and elsewhere in the Middle East. In going beyond the Middle East, we see this problem with variations throughout Islamic civilization. Ethnic and sectarian subdivisions, at times – illogically – combined with Islamic universalism, are preventing nation-building and democratization in the non-Arab cases of Indonesia, Pakistan, Malaysia and India, presented earlier. And it is not only the nation-state, but also the proclaimed unity of global jihad, that is being undermined by this ethnic-sectarian fragmentation. The existing and prevailing political ethnic–tribal culture creates great obstacles in the way of the introduction of a culture of democracy and its institutions. In view of these facts, efforts at democratization need to be combined with ethno-politics[96] in the understanding of a political culture of power-sharing as a component of democracy in multi-religious, sectarian and multi-ethnic societies. In the Middle East, this power-sharing is essential to any ethno-politics of democratization. In the first place, Sunni Arabs need to learn how to view others as equals, as human beings entitled to rights, and also as being members of the community as a polity. When Shi'a come to power, as in Iraq, they should not turn the tables on the Sunni; this is no democratization.

In all Islamic societies in Asia, and particularly in the Arab world, collective entities are virtually a functional equivalent to the old Arab tribes or ethnic community. Being a Sunni Arab myself, I state this and underline the need to respect ethnic and religious minorities living in Arab societies and to share political power with them. At present there are many cases that strongly demonstrate the violation of rights of minorities. In Iraq and the Sudan these consistent violations are most obvious. The minority rights of the Kopts in Egypt as well as of the Berbers in Algeria are other examples. The Ibn Khaldun Center, established in Cairo by Saad Eddin Ibrahim, did substantial research on violated rights of minorities in the Arab world.[97] This was not welcomed, and a pretext was found to close the Center, to outlaw its founder and to jail him until – under international pressure – he was eventually released and acquitted. Today, going for democracy in the world of Islam is a personal risk. As a Muslim living in Europe, I have misgivings that Islamists of the diaspora are making the issue most perilous in Europe itself, threatening pro-democracy Muslims who disagree with their agenda.

Conclusions

Global democracy and democratic peace have become a universal vision for the twenty-first century in post-bipolar world politics. Under the conditions of an Islamic awakening and the related call to global jihad/jihadism as an

Islamist solution in contrast to democracy, the people of Islam and its civilization are facing tough choices. The issues also touch on the existing secular authority of the international system determined by the secular rules of the Westphalian Peace.

The twenty-first century commenced with 11 September 2001, followed by the wars in Afghanistan 2001 and Iraq 2003. Then global jihad was extended to Europe after 11 March 2004 and the London assaults in the following year. For countering Islamist jihadism in a war of ideas, democracy and democratization are presented as the proper solution next to security. In this context, the Marxist slogan "the liberation of the proletariat can only be the work of the proletariat itself" is pertinent to the people of Islamic civilization. Therefore, I conclude by stating that democracy and democratization can only be accomplished by Muslims themselves. They have the choice to engage in cultural change to overcome the culture of neo-patriarchy. Muslims would be alienating themselves from humanity if the global jihad of the Islamists were to prevail. For the people of the Islamic civilization in the world of Islam and in Europe, it is more promising to become part of democratic peace. Instead of quoting Marx here, I refer to the Qur'an and its provision: "And Allah does not change people until they change themselves" (sura 13, verse 11).

Without playing down the effects of globalization I argue that culture matters and that cultural change is needed in Islamic civilization. What happens in the world of Islam matters to the future of Europe. Due to Islamic migration there is a long-term possibility – clearly envisioned by some leaders of the European Islam diaspora – of an Islamization of Europe. In anticipating the debate in Part III, I state the opposite strategy: Europeanizing Islam matters for Muslims in Europe, who could provide a model for the acceptance of democracy. In Europe, Europeans have the right to actively participate in determining the future of Islam on their continent. The rest of the book is written in this spirit. Islam and democracy are also a European concern. To avoid wishful thinking I first return to world-political realities and address Islamist internationalism in both its Sunni and Shi'ite directions. The political agenda of this Islamist internationalism presents options that stand in competition to the culture of democracy and to a new world order based on democratic peace.

Part II

Political Islam enters world politics

Global jihadism as an Islamist internationalism in its Sunni and Shi'ite varieties as a challenge to safe democracy and international security

Introductory remarks

This Part II moves from the analyzed inner predicament of Islamic civilization – torn between the revived spirit of jihad and the one of a quest for democracy – to deal here with the contemporary post-bipolar entry of Islam into world politics. At issue are competitive civilizational options, one of which is the Islamist alternative for the future consisting of a divine order for the world. However, global jihadism of political Islam predates the post-bipolar developments. It existed earlier, but the end of the East–West conflict has given it a boost. In this context, 9/11 has been a watershed event, often wrongly related to an exclusive uprising against US hegemony and thus viewed in this context as a revolt against the *Pax Americana*. This view is considered partly wrong, because Europe is the historical source of the conflict, and equally at present it forms one of the major pillars. The fact that the world of Islam constitutes the neighborhood of Europe is honored in the foreign policy concepts of the European Union. In addition, Islamic presence as a diaspora in the West is more visible in Europe (ca. 20 million Muslims within the EU) than it has ever been in the United States. As will be shown in Part III, Europe is becoming the battlefield for the conflict, in parallel to the continual growth of this diasporic presence.

Given this reference to Europe, this section begins with the first anniversary of the assault on 11 March 2004 in Madrid, viewed as the European version of 9/11. The Club of Madrid organized a huge event to commemorate the tragedy and to mourn its victims in an effort to understand what was going on the ground and to learn lessons from it. European and Muslim statesmen, scholars and opinion leaders were among the participants, coming not only to mark the commemoration, but also to engage in a debate on a new phenomenon related to the role of terror legitimated by religion in world politics. Unlike the "war on terror" declared by US President George W. Bush as a response to 9/11, the European approach to 11 March was designed as a combination of two concerns: "safe democracy" and "security." A dialogue between the opinion leaders and politicians of the Islamic civilization and those of Europe is seen as a tool to avert the "war on terror" sliding into an alleged "war on Islam." The equation of these two wars is a prevailing Islamic perception incorporated into the prevailing Islamic narrative of Islam under siege and also used by political Islam in a war of ideas not to be simply dismissed as propaganda. This perception constitutes a distraction from the pending concerns, in that it rather strengthens and exacerbates the sense of victimhood cultivated by Muslims. In contrast, to engage in a Euro-Islamic cooperative venture against jihadist terrorism one needs a security dialogue, not a counterproductive perception of the self within the framework of self-victimization.

In dissociating the thoughts presented in this book from the rhetoric of the "clash of civilizations," a clear distinction is made between the Islamic faith and the ideology of political Islam as Islamism. The challenge dealt with here emanates thus from political Islam and its jihadism. In the preface to this book, the Malaysian Prime Minister, Abdullah Ahmad Badawi, is quoted as stating that Muslims need to do their homework in the existing world-political situation. Instead, Saudis and Egyptians attending the European anti-terrorism meeting in Madrid in March 2005 not only flatly denied the existence of global jihad altogether, but moreover moved to an offensive approach in an effort at turning the tables on the West. Those who relate global jihad to terrorism were defamed and accused of Islamophobia. As a result, it looked as if the Madrid commemoration would shift from being a forum for reasoning about "safe democracy" in the pursuit of countering terrorism and establishing security and would become a forum for Europe-bashing. The accusations and the condemnation of Europe were combined with Islamic efforts at proselytization. This was a version of the ongoing war of ideas, not a proper inter-civilizational dialogue. Within the context of these blame-games a prominent Islamist attending the summit suggested that Europe is suffering an identity crisis and proposed, as a "remedy," the adoption of Islam as a "the solution" for the Europeans. Unfortunately, none of the attending Europeans repudiated this proposal. That was a great disservice, not only to any "Islamic–Western understanding," but also to a serious countering of terrorism. The silence reflected the state of Europe.

In the following two chapters of this Part II on Islamist internationalism, the issue is frankly addressed without any silence in the name of political correctness. As a scholar of the Muslim faith, I value Europe for providing me with the right of free speech and of practicing the idea of "thinking as research" (Hedley Bull). On these grounds, I continue to reject the silencing

I face – as in the publication of this book – whenever I tackle the issues addressed. This happens to me throughout my research activities.

To begin with, I address the challenge of an Islamist internationalism represented by a movement based in the global networks of transnational religion. The target is the existing Westphalian order based on the "authority of a secular synthesis" (Philpott), to be replaced by an Islamic one. This is the subject-matter of the present Part II written in a draft completed prior to the Madrid debate on "safe democracy, terrorism and security." The text had to be rewritten later, not only in the light of the Madrid debate but also to include further events in Europe (from 11 March 2004 through the slaying of Theo van Gogh on 2 November 2004 to the London assaults of 7 and 22 July 2005 and the uprising in the *banlieues de l'Islam* in Paris in October/November 2005, continued globally during the conflict over the Danish Mohammed cartoons in early 2006 and again in the outrage over Pope Benedict) in the never-ending story of the challenge addressed.

In the ensuing introductory remarks, pains are taken to place the addressed issue in an overall context. I am aware of the risky nature of this undertaking in an environment of a European shift from one extreme sentiment to the other, i.e. from "Orientalism" (Edward Said) to an "Orientalism in reverse" (Sadiq al-Azm). In this poisoned atmosphere old-style racism, Islamophobia and prejudice about other world cultures are certainly not overcome, but rather reversed. This is the truth, like it or not. The new opposite attitude forbids any critique of other world cultures by establishing rules of censorship called political correctness. Despite the positive intention of this sentiment it is clearly not helpful at all, and it has created great damage to scholarship on Islam. It also has hampered an uncensored inter-civilizational dialogue. Any serious dealing with the significance of jihadism and its call for an "Islamic world revolution" (Sayyid Qutb) in the pursuit of an Islamic world order is often ill presented as panicking and is combined with the weak argument that "it is un-Islamic" to state that jihadist terrorism "has anything to do with Islam." This attitude was discernible in March 2005 in Madrid and elsewhere throughout Europe. It is for this reason that I feel the need to protect the analysis provided in this part from any of the currently prevailing accusations in the public debates. Existing ideological bias in scholarship hampers any analysis of issues under scrutiny. This is often combined with a lack of awareness of existing threats. In order to understand this I refer to the concept of *asabiyya* of the great Muslim medieval philosopher Ibn Khaldun, who died in 1406. His model, meaning *esprit de corps* of a civilizational entity, continues to be relevant for the twenty-first century. In fact, the European *asabiyya* of today is a weak one as proven by the silence vis-à-vis the cited accusations made in Madrid. To be sure, tolerance and understanding of other cultures are precious. However, we need to distinguish between true tolerance on the one hand and sentiments of indifference and self-denial on the other. Europe needs a combination of self-awareness (*asabiyya*) and tolerance to come to terms with the Islamic civilization in a changed environment, to be described in this Part II.

With its jihadist internationalism legitimated by a reference to religion, political Islam tries to mobilize the Islamic civilization to make it enter the theater of world politics. The context is transnational religion parallel to a culturalization of conflict and a religionization of politics. Given the fact of Islam as a universal religion, the articulated claims are equally universal. If this universalism is politicized and if its transnational links are mobilized to a networking, then the grounds for a new internationalism will be at work across borders. The new process taking place and resulting in this novelty is related to the original Islamic universalism, although in an invention of tradition. In this new shape, politicized religion contributes to the "culture of violence" pursued in a "cosmic war" (Mark Juergensmeyer) against an imaginary enemy. Therefore, the issue is not only the new place of religion as a cultural system in world politics, but also the fact that those people adhering to this new interpretation view themselves as "true believers" while denying most co-religionists and other believers an equal standing.

The analysis of global jihadism as an Islamist internationalism acknowledges the fact that jihadists are non-state actors. However, it also takes account of involved states like Iran and Saudi Arabia. The Islamist state of Iran presents its Islamic revolution as a model for export. The other state, Saudi Arabia, also exports its ideology of Wahhabism. In both cases the state-related networking of a transnational religion is at work in world politics. Unlike the new Iranian president Mahmoud Ahmadinejad, who revived revolutionary Shi'ite Khomeinism in 2005, the Saudis for their Sunni part promote Wahhabism abroad mainly for the sake of convenience and not fully from conviction. The fact of a Wahhabi internationalism is not related to a Wahhabi call for a world revolution. There is no such thing as a vision of a Wahhabi world order comparable to the one once envisioned by Ayatollah Khomeini or by the Sunni Islamists in the mind of Sayyid Qutb, both outlined in the ensuing chapters. Nevertheless, Saudi Arabia continues to be more dangerous than Iran has ever been, the threat of nuclear proliferation notwithstanding. Why? Saudi Arabia provides financial support for the networks of a worldwide Islamism even though the Islamist–jihadist ideology of internationalism is not shared, at least not in public.

Contemporary jihadist internationalism is rooted in political Islam and its culturized politics matters to world politics in general as well as specifically to Europe. It is well known that Islamists use the Islamic diaspora in Europe as their logistic base in the pursuit of jihadist internationalism in the context of globalization. The following analysis is aware of the flaws of reductionism and of culturalism. Therefore it is argued that for a proper understanding of jihadist violence any reductionist thinking would be misleading. Religion needs first to be viewed in its own terms as meaning employed in discourse, and only then can it be contextualized. Two issues need to be accounted for: Religion is embedded in society, economics and politics, but equally based on a tradition and on a related meaning that stands for itself. Traditions are reborn by a reinvention which also applies to religion as a cultural system. The Islamic revival is shaped by such a reinvention of traditions. This process takes place in a context of structural embedding and it brings the old and new into one package. In considering both the meaning of religion and its embedment into a structural context, the flaws of cultural essentialism and sociological reductionism are avoided.

In this section and throughout this book the reference to "religion" is persistently made in the Durkheimian sense of a *fait social*, not to religion as a faith. This is a social-scientific study and not a theological analysis of the scripture documenting religious provisions. However, I engage in this inquiry without overlooking the meaning of religion. Therefore, the jihad of religious activism is viewed as a social fact, even though not in line with an authentic understanding of the scripture, but without ignoring the self-image of the jihadists as "true believers." No doubt, religious texts are important for the scholar, but the scripture in itself does not provide any guidance for a social-scientific analysis. At issue is a useful explanation of the realities of religious movements and their culture of violence. For this reason most Western Islamic studies are lacking, be they inspired by an Orientalism or an "Orientalism in reverse." This is the point of departure of the present Part II, being an effort at a proper understanding of contemporary religious activism in Islam legitimated in sacral terms for justifying a "cosmic war" (Juergensmeyer) on non-Muslims convicted of *kufr/* unbelief. Religious activists fight against the infidels not for personal benefit, but in the service of their religious beliefs. Whether these are a right or a wrong interpretation of religion is not the concern of this study, which is focused on existing realities. The worldview, not a material interest, of the actors is at stake, even though the worldview itself is subject to change underpinned by material constraints. Therefore, the reference to religion – and to all culture-related ideas, ideals and attitudes – is always incorporated or embedded in ever-changing societal realities, economic, social and political. Nevertheless, religion as a faith and a cultural system is never a mere reflection of those realities. Since humans are not automata, they do not mechanically reflect the socio-economic environment in their worldviews and related thoughts. When it comes to religion, there is a need to grasp it as an intrinsic body of beliefs on which a cultural view of the world is grounded. If the meaning of religion is ignored no proper grasp of this issue will be possible. To state this is definitely not an essentialization of religion or of culture. In short, religion is an entity in its own terms even though embedded in realities. To draw attention to this fact is simply an effort to beware of reductionism, in order not to fall into the trap of reducing religious views and beliefs to acknowledged socio-economic situations and circumstances.

The complexity lies in the duality that religion is both a body in itself and simultaneously embedded in society. There is an interplay between both. In this understanding, jihadist internationalism is not a mere protest against an unjust globalization. It is true that Islamists hate the West, because of its present hegemonic power which also extends to the world of Islam. However, in its substance political Islam is much more than simply a rejection of the West because it has its own intrinsic views, as well as concepts of order and aims for a remaking of the world. Islamists do not simply lament existing conditions; it is therefore wrong to reduce the Islamic "revolt against the West" (Bull) to an anti-globalism. Stated in a nutshell: A new world order shaped by *"hakimiyyat Allah/*God's rule" and not just an expression of anti-globalism is at issue. In Europe, the matter is more complex. The marginalization of Muslim immigrants is a social reality. Yet, for Islamists the issue is not equality, but rather promoting the shari'a in secular Europe, first as a cultural right, and later as a totalizing order.

It is not a contradiction to acknowledge the great appeal of the religion-based culture of violence reflected in the jihadist movements and to state simultaneously that the jihadists constitute a minority among Muslims. However, if one condemns jihadists and then excommunicates them as "un-Islamic" – on the basis of making scriptural references – one ends up sharing their way of dealing with the other. It is more productive to follow Juergensmeyer's proposition, presented at the international conference in Madrid (8–11 March 2005): namely, to deal with the question: "Why is religion involved with terrorism?" In an effort at providing an answer one can point to three issues pertinent for understanding the culture of violence promoted by Islamist internationalism:

First: Jihadism as "terror in the mind of God" is based on "ideals and ideas" which are "authentically and thoroughly" religious. In relating this general statement to a serious reading of Sayyid Qutb's declaration of an "Islamic world revolution" in his *al-salam al-alami wa al-Islam*, or of Hasan al-Banna's *Risalat al-jihad*, the conclusion can be drawn that the religious-Islamic character is inherent in such pronouncements. The commitment to violence and terror in the name of religion results from a specific – of course questionable – understanding of religion. Islamists deny their Islamic critics membership of the Islamic *umma*. Similarly, one would play the same game if the jihadists were – in reverse – called "un-Islamic" and excluded from the Islamic community in whose name they believe they fight their jihad!

Second: The idea of jihadism as religiously motivated terrorism enjoys growing popularity. In employing the concept of "public choice," I argue that within the generation of young Muslims, who are mostly "no-future kids," there is an increasing admiration for bin Laden and moreover a consent to his ideas symbolizing the Islamic "revolt against the West." The phenomenon of bin-Ladenism becomes a virus. Clearly, in this context the related religion-based worldview is definitely endorsed by those prone or susceptible to this appeal. It follows that the "minority argument" is relative and ought to be placed within a context. In other words, the reference to the minority argument should not serve as a belittlement of jihadism.

Third: It is the idea of bin-Ladenism that a cosmic sacred battle between *al-iman*/belief and *al-kufr al-alami*/international unbelief is the legitimacy of an Islamic world revolution. This claim is the pending core issue and it pertains to the non-negotiable claim to establish a *siyadat al-Islam*/supremacy of Islam which will replace the hegemony of the West after it has been de-centered (de-Westernization). In this understanding *al-iman* is non-negotiable and it would never accommodate itself to what is considered to be *al-kufr*/unbelief, as seen from the point of view of "true believers." The sacred battle in a cosmic war is waged by people who have no concept of time and who believe they are not dependent on specific or limited practical resources; therefore this war can continue until the envisioned goal is reached. Sacrifice/*al-tadhiya* is viewed by these believers as a permanent act. For Europeans this is often difficult to understand; they seem to have lost their beliefs to the extent that they cannot imagine a human sacrificing his life for religious ends. Certainly, the Islamist ideology reflects extremist views, but in a specific environment – as is the one of post-bipolarity – it functions as an *idéologie mobilisatrice*/mobilizatory ideology, a term coined by Maxime Rodinson. This process is taking place in our time, providing fertile environment for the neo-jihad as a kind of "holy terror." The overall atmosphere is overloaded with the mind and spirit of millenarianism.

The listed issues need to be grasped beyond culturalism and reductionism in recognizing an interplay between religion, politics, society and economy. In this context "religion has become politicized" and "politics have become religionized" in the process of a culturalization of the conflict. This intrinsic combination of religion and politics via a culture of violence/terror determines the belief in neo-jihad, or jihadism as a new concept of irregular war in the pursuit of an Islamic world order. The fight for the latter is regarded as a sacred battle on cosmic grounds. The worldview underlying the enduring absolutism under issue ignores an awareness of time. The belief prevails that the fight will end in a millennialistic sense with the ultimate victory of *al-iman* of the true believers over *al-kufr al-alami* of the infidels. Again, for the jihadists the pronounced claims are not negotiable. Therefore it is utterly impossible to dialogue with them in an effort at accommodating them. In contrast to the jihadists there are institutional Islamists (e.g. AKP of Turkey), who are willing to share the game of power and to refrain from a resort to jihad-violence. Of course, negotiations with them are at least conceivable, however without falling into the trap of believing that their lip-service to democracy can be taken at face value. They accept democracy as a procedure of voting, but are unfavorable to its culture of democracy. This debate will be resumed in the concluding Chapter 7.

This book subscribes to the notion of cultural change and applies concepts of development to culture. There are "developing cultures" (L. Harrison).

Therefore, an awareness of the trap of essentialism is always on my mind. Being among those Muslims committed to change and equally committed to "preventing the clash of civilizations" I plead for a two-track strategy that combines a security approach against jihadist Islamism with a real dialogue between civilizations over pending issues. I refer to dialogue in the understanding of an effort at a peaceful conflict resolution. In Western–Islamic general dialogues pursued in Jakarta (2002, 2003), I asked my fellow Muslims to participate in a security dialogue in the pursuit of countering terrorism, which can never be successful without an Islamic contribution. Such participation in a security dialogue also frees the people of Islam of the bad image imputed to them, and it could accomplish even more than that. In Jakarta, the Islamic response to this call for a security dialogue was most favorable. Western policies that fail to be inclusive and that give the impression of demonizing Islam play into the hands of the jihadists, who want to promote exactly this perception to ignite polarization for the sake of jihad on cosmic grounds. The ensuing two chapters on Islamist internationalism are guided by these insights, and therefore it would be a misconception to view this analysis as a panicking contribution. The intention is to inform and to enlighten about facts on the ground, as related to Islam and world politics in the post-bipolar age of the cultural turn. This is done with a view to Europe.

The following two chapters also consider the existing divide within the Islamic civilization. The rift between Sunna and Shi'a is currently revived. The distinction between state-sponsored terrorism in contrast to the irregular war of non-state actors is embedded in this political context. At first, jihadism was a Sunni phenomenon established by the Muslim Brotherhood. However, the Sunni suicide bombing as one of the practices in irregular war has grown from the Shi'ite impact of martyrdom on Sunni Islamism and is shaped by it. Sunni internationalism is carried out by the irregulars of underground groups (non-state actors), whereas the Shi'ite variety is a state-sponsored phenomenon and is incorporated into the Islamist foreign policy of Iran. Of course, it makes use of these irregulars.

Some moderation which occurred in the rhetoric during the two presidential terms of Mohammed Khatami contributed to the false impression that Iran had abandoned its self-perception as the "center of the universe" and as "the model" designed for others. In practice and with regard to its worldview, however, it never did so. Even though the term "Islamic world revolution" (Qutb) is not used by Iranian cleric-politicians, they never shied away from exporting their system into the neighboring Islamic countries (e.g. Iraq, Lebanon, Gulf states, Palestine). The Iranian politics of Shi'ite internationalism is a reality contrasted with the competing Sunni internationalism, which, however, predates Khomeinism. The virus of bin-Ladenism, spreading in Europe among socially marginalized young Muslims in a context of a war of ideas and of collective memories, is nothing more than giving the Muslim Brotherhood's ideas of Hasan al-Banna and Sayyid Qutb a practical shape.

3 The world-political Sunni fallacy

Jihadist internationalism as a cosmic war of irregulars for remaking the world

The contemporary Islamist call for global jihad in world politics follows the view of the foremost thinker of political Islam, Sayyid Qutb, that an "Islamic world revolution" is at issue. This call has given birth to a real political movement based on transnational religion. Jihadism can no longer be discarded as mere rhetoric of political Islam. During the lifetime of Qutb the diaspora of Islam in Europe was fairly negligible in quantity. Therefore, at its beginning the movement aimed to topple regimes at home which were charged with being "un-Islamic." Over the course of time this has changed. From the first assault on the World Trade Center in New York back in 1993, followed by 9/11 and combined with the assaults in Europe between 2004 and 2006, jihadism took a global shape. In this time span there were 31 global jihadist strikes extending from the USA to Asia and Africa. From 11 March 2004 and 2 November of the same year in Amsterdam (the murder of van Gogh) this process started mapping Europe. It also inspired the Islamic uprising of October/November 2005 in the *banlieues de l'Islam* of French cities, and furthermore affected the global conflict over the Danish Mohammed cartoons. One may infer that if Europeans continue to fail to include Muslim immigrants as true citizens in their societies, Europe could become a battlefield of jihadism. The foiled plan to blow up ten US-bound planes in London in August 2006 was one of the alerts that should be taken seriously.

In this book a distinction is made in the study of Islamism between the institutional, i.e. peaceful variety of political Islam, and jihadism in Qutb's understanding as a violent world revolution. This neo-jihad emerges from a new interpretation that gives a new design to classical jihad within the framework of an "invention of tradition" (see note 14). The overall context is the contemporary politicization of religion in the countries of Islamic civilization as they are undergoing a severe crisis situation, both structural and moral. In reiterating the critique of the reductionist approach, it is emphasized that the phenomenon under issue is related to, but definitely not reducible to, a structural crisis. Precaution against any reductionism needs to be at the top of the agenda in any analysis of religion in the context of globalization and terrorism. In addition, it has been noted that the phenomenon of religiously legitimated violence is not restricted to Islam: it can be observed in other world religions as well. Some scholars are reluctant to conceptualize the cross-religious politicization of the sacred in terms of religious fundamentalisms. It is, however, a fact that terror legitimated by a reference to a religious belief grows from this very context, and it therefore does not take place outside of Islam or of any other religion. Those involved in practicing "terror in the mind of God" view their action as "sacred terror." It is based on a religious interpretation to be related to the emergence of the global phenomenon of religious fundamentalisms (see note 9) resulting from the politicization of religion and the religionization of politics within the framework of the contemporary "return of the sacred."

The issue: an introduction to the study of Jihadist Islamism in International Relations

In its formative years jihadist Islamism was an exclusively Sunni phenomenon first aimed – as stated – at toppling local regimes and at establishing a shari'a state in the world of Islam. However, the idea of an Islamist world order was articulated in the writings of Qutb. Contemporary jihadists subscribe to a kind of "direct action" reminiscent of Georges Sorel's glorification of violence. Some leaders of political Islam learned to make use of democracy in Europe and in the world at large, and thus paid lip-service to abandoning jihad as a violent action. Nevertheless both the so-called democratic new Islamists and the jihadists envision a shari'a-based order that stands in all terms against the idea of an "open society" based on the culture of democracy and its pluralism. Therefore, I do not see any democratization coming from Islamism, as some believe. A peaceful pursuit of political Islam does not make a democracy. It only makes use of the voting procedure. Islamist movements that came peacefully to power, like the Sunni Hamas, or that just participate in democratic rule, like the Shi'ite Hezbullah of Lebanon and the Mahdi Army of Iraq, continue to have their militias as terrorist irregulars and thus engage in irregular war while others of their movements participate as members of the elected parliaments. This is by no means an endorsement of democracy.

The focus of this chapter is on jihadism, not an institutional peaceful Islamism. Therefore the analysis centers on the Sunni idea of global jihad and its manifestation as a major theme of world politics in the twenty-first century. This phenomenon predates the spectacular actions of the jihadists of al-Qaeda. The related terror was well known to Muslims themselves much earlier. The Muslim victims of jihadism, be it in Algeria, Egypt, Pakistan or other Islamic countries, were ordinary Muslims accused of deviation. Since the 1980s Muslims have been victims of the violence exerted by a variety of jihadist groups. The "sacred terror" is expressed in two ways. *First*, there is the call to topple the locally existing order of the nation-state in the world of Islam. Fellow Muslims who disagree with the jihadists' views are also targetted, being excommunicated from "Islam" to provide justification for killing them as infidels. In a *second* step, jihadists work towards a remaking of the international system. In this context a war of ideas and worldviews is also involved, and this equally touches on international security. The goal to be achieved by an "Islamic world revolution" (Sayyid Qutb) is the *Pax Islamica* of a new world order that replaces the present one based on a Westphalian synthesis. The implication is that violence is accompanied by a war of ideas. In short, the Sunni jihadist ideology of political Islam, which precedes the emergence of al-Qaeda by a few decades, can be viewed as an Islamist internationalism supplemented by the global networks of transnational religion. Its vision of an Islamic world revolution is a pertinent challenge to the idea and structure of post-bipolar International Relations.[1]

Post-bipolar developments have contributed to bringing the jihadist cross-border threat to the fore, and it is now becoming a major concern of international security. In a way, jihadism heralds a shift from Clausewitzian inter-state war to a new type of war waged by irregular warriors. This neo-jihad is a new pattern which I suggest should be viewed as an irregular war. At issue is a de-regularization of war pursued by internationalist jihadism in world politics which creates a challenge to the wisdoms of traditional security. In order to safeguard democracy under these changed circumstances, new strategies for dealing with the challenge of "terror in the mind of God" are needed. In order to understand the new violence of suicide bombers, I conceptualize the use of religion in an irregular war waged by non-state actors, while acknowledging the earlier contributions to this new warfare by Martin van Creveld and Kalevi Holsti.[2]

To be sure, jihadism is not simply terrorism. Given its political agenda, it is in a broader sense much more than a pure practice of violence. What is targeted by jihadist action is the international order of secular states known as the Westphalian order. Islamists envision replacing it by a global Islamicate, in which *dar al-Islam*/the house of Islam based on *hakimiyyat Allah*/God's rule is enhanced to map the entire globe. This is the real issue, and therefore the addressed war of ideas revolves around this competition over the future order of the world. Indeed, the Islamist vision looks like an expression of madness, but is nevertheless a policy that enjoys support as a popular public choice. In addition, the mindset of jihadism spreads among those susceptible to its ideology, including marginalized youngsters in the Islamic diaspora in Europe, who are ready for recruitment. Therefore, it has to be kept in mind that the logistics and networking of jihadism are based in the diasporic cells of political Islam in Europe, where Islamists use civil rights as an instrumental cover for the protection of their activities. The assaults in Madrid (March 2004) and London (July 2005) and the foiled plot of August 2006 are only illustrations of more to come, if countering strategies – also in the war of ideas – fail.

Islamist Sunni internationalism is analyzed in the following three steps to explain the background of jihadism and then relate it to international and European security. In looking at the networking of jihadism, Myron Weiner's approach, incorporating global migration into security studies, seems to be most pertinent and helpful.[3] As already stated, the al-Qaeda global networking is mainly based in the European diaspora of Islam. There, al-Qaeda and its offspring make full use of the openings which grow from global migration. This makes the jihad pronounced by contemporary Islamist groups a migratory theme embedded in International Relations. Political correctness creates obstacles to an inquiry into this field and to incorporating Islamic migration into a security approach. To be sure, at issue is not Islam as a religion, but Islamism as a totalitarian political ideology embedded in the networks of transnational politicized religion.

Not only in contemporary world politics, but also specifically throughout Europe, the call to global jihad is heard in some major mosques. On the surface it looks as though Islamism is becoming the heir of international communism, representing the challenge of a new internationalism. It is, however, a different phenomenon, though comparable. In addition, it is carried out by a minority among the Muslim world community, but has to be taken most seriously for a variety of reasons. Prior to the October Revolution of 1917 Lenin and his comrades were seemingly an insignificant Russian diaspora circle acting in Switzerland, but they managed to topple a mighty – though declining – Czarist empire in order to establish a new one. The Islamist jihadist vision displays great resemblance to Leninist thought: Just as the Leninist cadres acted in the name of an inactive proletariat, so jihadists believe themselves to be the spearhead of the revolution – comparatively speaking – representing the real *umma* itself, purifying it from the ills of Westernization. Their objective is to put it into action in the pursuit of a new order. The traditional study of terrorism[4] fails to provide the proper approach for grasping this new phenomenon.

There are two levels for dealing with the pertinence of political Islam to International Relations. First, there is the state level, related to the existence of states with Muslim peoples. Their assemblage in the Organization of the Islamic Conference (OIC) makes them present in the international system, with its fifty-seven members designed along the rules of international law as sovereign nation-states. They act in this capacity in international politics, even though their very state grouping on religious grounds heralds the return of religion to world affairs. This return of the sacred in a political shape creates a major challenge in ongoing post-bipolar developments. Second, the emerging non-state actors in international affairs are becoming a major concern demanding a new security approach (see note 2). To avoid any misunderstanding it is imperative to reiterate that jihadism is in line neither with the faith of Islam nor with the spirit of Islamic civilization, but nevertheless it is a social fact in both, pointing to a branch that clearly exists in it in the shape of one direction within contemporary political Islam. Therefore the distracting argument that it is "un-Islamic" does not hold, in politics or in scholarship. Jihadism is moving to center-stage in the International Relations of the post-bipolar age.

This part of the book looks at these issues with a European perspective focused in the context of the "global migration crisis" on security concerns combined with the need to integrate Muslim immigrants to keep them away from the spell of Islamism. The issue was addressed by Peter Neumann in the IISS's journal *Survival* as "Europe's Jihadist Dilemma" (2006). The study of jihadism and its Islamist internationalism should become a part of the study of Islam in contemporary Europe, as well as of the study of order in world politics[5] in the context of the rise of politicized religion, indicating the return of the sacred with the claim of a role in international affairs as a challenge to secular politics. Therefore, interest is focused here on the phenomenon in general and not on the concrete cases of terror legitimated as "jihad in the path of God." Among the major concerns is also the political discourse related to the use of religion for legitimating an Islamist world revolution. The use of religion is definitely not instrumental, since it reflects an inherited, civilizationally determined worldview based on a religious belief, albeit in a new shape. The goal of jihadist terrorism is, however, to establish a new divine political order outlined in the new discourse. In short, the reference to religion in politics underpinning the legitimization of an irregular war is placed in the pursuit of an alternative Islamic world order. This is the seminal issue area in post-bipolar security studies. Therefore, it is imperative to underline the insight that jihadist terrorism is not just a concern of military studies, not to mention the criminal policing some ignorant "pundits" suggest.

Political Islam is pertinent to European studies[6] and to International Relations, the latter, as Stanley Hoffmann once noted, being designed as an "American discipline." I hasten to add that it was a discipline of the Cold War era. All major schools of the discipline concurred with the Hobbesian view of the state as the basic actor in world politics and its power being the issue to consider. Yet, there were a few exceptions. Long before Samuel Huntington coined the disputed term "clash of civilizations," Raymond Aron, who was once in Paris the mentor of Stanley Hoffmann, drew attention to the fact that bipolarity has been the "veil" concealing the real source of conflict in international politics, namely "the heterogeneity of civilizations."[7] In Aron's view, people belong by nature and through cultural socialization to civilizations, and only formally to states. This belonging may have changed in modern citizenship as an identity pattern, but such a modern development is utterly restricted to the Western civilization. In the West, citizenship has replaced pre-modern parochial identities. In contrast, in the world of Islam, nation-states are a kind of "quasi state," i.e. only nominal states.[8] In view of this fact, citizenship in the world of Islam – compared to the deeply seated *umma* identity – lacks substance and thus is meaningless. Above all it fails to provide real identity. Accordingly, the identity of the people living in the Middle East is not bound by nation-states. Under these conditions, Islamism revives the concept of the *umma* in Islam as an identity pattern for opposing the existing nation-states, and this gives Islam as an imagined community a political shape. The decline of secular pan-Arab nationalism has been related to the crisis of the nation-state in the Arab world. The end of pan-Arabism then smoothed the way for the emergence of new identity patterns, of which the one provided by Islamist internationalism is the most prevailing. There are also ethnic and religious-sectarian identities, all of which are embedded in transnational religion.

At present the nominal nation-state is still there, but for non-state actors identity politics go beyond this nominal institution. In the study of international conflict one needs to acknowledge that "culture matters" for dealing with cultural worldviews, however without derailing the analysis to a "culturalism." Prior to 9/11 it was risky to maintain that cultural differences create fault-lines that could lead to violent conflict. Only a few scholars have dared to point to the potential for bloodshed in conflicts related to cultural-ethnic differences being politicized. For averting such an outcome, a combination of conflict studies with a policy-oriented effort at reviving the Kantian vision of perpetual peace seems to be promising. In acknowledging the existing impediments, the mobilizatory ideology of jihadist internationalism is presented as an ideology of violent conflict embraced by a political movement. The findings of the "Fundamentalism Project" of the American Academy of Arts and Sciences, the "Culture Matters Project" (CMP) of the Fletcher School, Tufts University, and the "Transnational Religion Projects" run at Cornell University have provided contributions that shaped my insights employed in this chapter.[9]

Understanding Islamist internationalism

In a first step of the analysis three interrelated issue areas, the new identity politics, the cultural turn and the return of the sacred in a political shape,[10] all imbued with ethnicity, are to be identified as the centerpieces of the study of conflict in an international environment. At issue is a competition over remaking the world[11] in the twenty-first century. In the pivotal case of Islamism the major goal is an establishing of *hakimiyyat Allah*/God's rule,[12] believed to be the ultimate divine political order. In this ideology one finds a combination of a new internationalism of a global *Pax Islamica* and particularisms related to an inter-Islamic sectarian and ethnic split as demonstrated in Iraq. Sunni Islamism claims universality for its worldview, which alienates Muslims from non-Muslims worldwide but at the same time creates rifts within Islam.

The described phenomenon reaches Europe via global migration. In this case the Islamist rejection of a pluralism of religions and cultures threatens internal peace. Without rethinking Islam and its doctrines for abandoning existing religious absolutism, Islam's predicament with pluralism will continue to trouble Muslims including their diaspora in Europe.[13] Islamist internationalism is the jihadist cosmic fight for *siyadat al-Islam*/supremacy of Islam; therefore it is not consonant with the need for pluralism and as such provides no plausible alternative to secular concepts.

In placing the present subject-matter among the basic issue areas of post-bipolar international security studies, the following analysis is pursued – as stated – in three steps. It intends *first*, to approach the theme in question in the pursuit of understanding Islamist internationalism; *second*, to shed light on the politicization of religion as the source from which the Islamist worldview emerges; and *third*, to outline jihadist action as a new pattern of an "irregular war" rooted in political Islam. The overall concern is the new divine order envisioned for this century by the Islamists, as the solution to the crisis of the present international order. At the very outset one is reminded of two facts: first, the roots of this movement in Islam are to be found in the Sunna, not in the Shi'a as commonly and wrongly believed; second, it is not an enlightenment but rather a deceit when some leaders of the Islamic diaspora excuse actions of jihadist terrorism as outrage over wrong Western policies and related occupation in Palestine, Iraq, Afghanistan and Lebanon. It is a fact that jihadism was born in 1928 when none of these issues existed.

In undertaking the first step in understanding Islamist internationalism, the inquiry compels us among other things to engage in breaking with established taboos. This is like entering a minefield. It is true, after 11 September 2001 in the USA and 11 March 2004 as well as 7 July 2005 in Europe, that it has become easier in a way to speak of jihadist Islamism as a security threat without running the risk of being accused of Islamophobia. However, the flawed policies of the Bush administration, in particular the questionable Iraq war, have contributed to a setback and to a revival of the obstacles in the way of dealing candidly with the roots of jihadist terror in political Islam, making the venture a thorny path. As a Muslim migrant living in Europe, I am aware of an existing Islamophobia and agree that there is a need to combat it, but I cannot overlook the fact that the Islamists – in the ongoing war of ideas – are exploiting current suspicions of Islamophobia attached to constructed images of Islam for camouflaging their own activities. Thus, the accusation of a demonization of Islam is used as propaganda against scholars engaged in uncovering political Islam. During the conflict over the Danish Mohammed cartoons, not only did it become obvious that there is a lack of understanding of other cultures, but it was also clear that the Islamists in action were pursuing their agenda to reduce freedom of expression. The protest movement was orchestrated, not spontaneous.

To begin with, jihadist Islamism as a new internationalism in world politics is not the religious faith of Islam nor does it reflect the classical doctrine of jihad. Islamism and its jihadism are an "invention of tradition."[14] Despite this distinction, it makes no sense to overlook the self-reference of these jihadists, i.e. their religion-based image of themselves. Again, one is reminded that Islamists view themselves as "the true believers"[15] and that they convict others of being "un-Islamic." It follows that jihadist Islamism is neither cynicism nor an instrumental cover for concealing political action in abusing religion. At issue is a sincere attitude of belief, even though, as an action of terror, it is clearly not in line with inherited religious doctrines. To reiterate: for a social scientist religion is a reality and not a scriptural belief. In this understanding it matters that the jihadists do not perceive their action to be "*irhab*/terrorism," but rather "*jihadiyya*/jihadism," i.e. a new interpretation of the Qur'anic jihad. Their claim to act as "true believers" in an effort at "remaking the world" compels us to study what they think and what they do. It is therefore abundantly clear that the scripture is not the subject-matter of the analysis, nor is it the source of Islamist inspiration. So what is Islamist internationalism all about?

To answer this question some methodological grounds should be clarified. First, the study of transnational religion needs to be introduced to the discipline of International Relations, and second, the study of war needs to go beyond legalistic constraints attached to an inter-state war (e.g. declaration of war by a sovereign state) as well as beyond the traditional wisdoms of the Clausewitzian thinking on war. These wisdoms are no longer helpful for grasping the recent current of irregular war, of which jihadism is a major case in point. In general, we are challenged to rethink the discipline of International Relations and established theories of war in the course of introducing needed innovations. The scholastic and the dividing debates in International Relations not only separate schools of thought from one another, but also distract from the issue itself. Quantitative methods are not useful for the study of political Islam because the subject-matter is not quantifiable. Understanding Islam and Islamism are matters of cultural analysis applied to social science.

Political Islam is based on reinventing religious concepts as jihad, shari'a, *da'wa*, etc., in a context of politicization under conditions of globalization. Of course, this phenomenon is embedded in a power structure, but explaining "revolt against the West" simply as an anti-globalism is pointless. Islamist internationalism is not an anti-globalism, for it is itself an ideology of a new globalization based on a political-jihadist interpretation of Islam as a global remaking of the world. The fact that jihadist Islamism is an idea – albeit embedded in a political movement – makes clear that in order to counter it as a source of modern terrorism, one needs also to engage in a war of ideas.[16] In Europe the issue is related to "open society and its enemies." It is a challenge to "safe democracy."

Jihadist internationalism is not "religious extremism," but a revolt against the West based on the politicization of Islam

Next to understanding jihadist Islamism, the focus in the second step is on the rise of new challenges related to the return of religion to world politics for the articulation of political goals. Max Weber's prediction of a disenchantment of the world/*Entzauberung der Welt*, as a process of rationalization of worldviews being an outcome of secularization, did not materialize globally as a universal outlook. The return of the sacred is related to reversing secularization into a de-secularization. This is the meaning of the politicization of Islam. A civilizational self-assertive "revolt against the West"[17] is quite different from the earlier phenomenon of decolonization. The targets of the new revolt are the secular values of the Westphalian order itself, and as such are no longer restricted to combatting the political hegemony of the West. This contestation of European values is a de-secularization; it has been militarized through the jihadization of the revolt.

In the present study the addressed revolt is placed in the study of civilization despite the contamination of the issue through Huntington's "clash." My reference to the study of civilization in the history of ideas is the fourteenth-century Muslim philosopher Ibn Khaldun. In the year 2006 we commemorated him 600 years after his death in 1406, in an event in Granada sponsored by the Spanish government within the framework of its project "Alliance of Civilizations." Without further specifications, Huntington speaks of a "clash between civilizations" in an essentializing manner. Instead I deal with conflict and cite the work of Hedley Bull – not quoted by Huntington who, moreover, does not know Ibn Khaldun's work. Bull unravels the fallacy of the so-called global village in stating that

> it is also clear that the shrinking of the globe, while it has brought societies to a degree of mutual awareness and interaction they have not had before, does not in itself create a unity of outlook and has not in fact done so ... Humanity is becoming simultaneously more unified and more fragmented.[18]

In considering Bull's insight and while stating a cultural fragmentation rooted in the reality of the "heterogeneity" of civilizations pointed at by Raymond Aron, I place the politicization of Islam in the context of the contemporary civilizational revolt against the West, for which jihadism is a prominent case in point. Western civilization is secular, and its structural globalization does not match with a universalization of its secular values; rather, a cultural fragmentation is the outcome. While the European expansion has contributed to the structural mapping of the entire world along the lines of standards designed and unfolded by the civilization of the West,[19] there was no successful overall universalization of Western values that matches with the degree of globalization reached. It was a fallacy of the early development studies to equate value-related Westernization with modernization and secularization. Western scholars continue not to distinguish between the *globalization* of structures and the *universalization* of values together with related worldviews. Such a distinction is the precondition for a proper understanding of the mindset of Islamist jihadism as a variety of the new "revolt against the West," also aimed at a de-secularization. This is the meaning of the return of the sacred contributing to a lack of consensus

over universally valid and accepted norms and values determining international behavior, and is the point of the politicization of religion. There is a
reversal from modernization to re-traditionalization, from secularization to
de-secularization and from Westernization to de-Westernization. The rejection of Western knowledge[20] is essential for this reversal. In this regard,
education is the battlefield of Islamism, using madrasas for disseminating
the jihadist mindset not only in the world of Islam but also in its diaspora
throughout Europe itself. In this regard, the new interpretation of Islam as
Islamism attached to civilizational claims is accepted by some in the name
of multi-culturalism and religious freedom, boosting the mushrooming of
Islamic enclaves of the diaspora that provide shelter to the Islamists. The
processes of de-secularization in the world of Islam are extended to Europe
through education, using the networks of transnational religion. The return
of the sacred in the guise of a politicization of Islam thus becomes a European phenomenon and also the subject-matter for studies both on Europe
and on education.[21]

The frame of reference of the politicization of Islam is a civilizational
understanding of all Muslims imagined as an *umma*-community[22] in international politics. This understanding of Muslims as a distinct international
community is not restricted to the irregulars of political Islam, but also
comprises the states that constitute their own grouping in the international
system as the Organization in the Islamic Conference (OIC). This is the
only one in the world based on religion. Since the rise of political Islam in
that part of the world, any dealings with Islamist movements have also
become a policy issue on international grounds and are no longer merely an
academic concern for the traditional students of Islam or for Islamic states
themselves. Neither those Orientalist philologians nor the others of cultural
anthropology are in a position to relate the return of the sacred as a politicization of religion to International Relations. To be sure, jihadist Islamism is
an internationalism pertinent to security studies that cannot be explained
with empty phrases such as "Islamic politics."

In historical terms it can be stated that the contemporary Islamist internationalism as a civilizational revolt against the West began with the establishing of the very first Islamist movement in Egypt. In the year 1928 Hasan
al-Banna founded the movement/society of the Muslim Brothers.[23] It was
al-Banna himself who, in a most authoritative essay, reinterpreted the doctrine of jihad, thus laying grounds for jihadism in the understanding of
terrorism against infidels.[24] However, at issue is not terror, but rather a fight
in a competition between an envisioned *Pax Islamica* and a hegemonic *Pax
Americana*. Yet, Europe is involved, too, because even though distinct it is a
part of the civilization of the West. The Westphalian order in world politics
challenged by the Islamist "revolt against the West" is a European order
that mapped the entire globe.

This section started with a reference to the Weberian formula of secularization as *Entzauberung*/disenchantment of the world, in order to point

out that a re-religionization of politics, i.e. the opposite, is taking place. This process takes shape in world politics as a conflict between the secular and the religious concepts of order leading to a "new Cold War."[25] In short, the civilizational conflict in world politics is not between Islam and the West as essentialized entities, but is rather an effect of the de-secularization.

One is inclined to wonder why Islamists who disparage the Europeans as crusaders/*salibiyyun* despite this contemp seek asylum in Europe. The explanation is quite simple and pragmatic: Islamists cannot act freely in their undemocratic home countries. In contrast, Western democracies provide safe havens for their activities. In most of the Islamic states there exists no opportunity to practice political opposition, be it by Islamists or others. Thus, the rise of political Islam is denied expression through institutional channels (Turkey and Indonesia are exceptions, even though with limits). Islamist movements are, however, the basic political opposition in the world of Islam; there, they operate underground as clandestine actors. In the search for outlets for free action, Islamist leaders resort to Europe as asylum-seekers, obtaining both refuge and benefits of the welfare state. They have been successful so far in establishing a hinterland for their activities in Europe. Why do European states tolerate Islamism? In a Chatham study published after 7 July 2005, one reads:

> The police were aware that London was increasingly used as a base for terrorism in the Middle East and elsewhere ... However, these individuals were not viewed as a threat to the UK national security and so they were left to continue their activities.
>
> (*International Herald Tribune*, 19 July 2005)

In his "Lipset Lecture," published in *Journal of Democracy* (2006), Francis Fukuyama identifies Europe as a battlefield of Islamism. This will be discussed later in Part III in the context of the assaults of 11 March 2004 in Madrid, and 7 July 2005 in London, which are not well understood in Europe. After 9/11 the Princeton professor Michael Duran contended in his essay on "Somebody Else's Civil War?"[26] that in September 2001 al-Qaeda primarily wanted to hit its enemies in the world of Islam via the United States. Analogically, one may say, the jihadists of Madrid and London wanted to hit their Islamic rulers indirectly. This view is wrong, however. Even though Duran's essay is very intelligent, it overlooks or confuses the order of the two levels in the strategic thinking of the Islamists: *First*, the replacement of secular regimes in the world of Islam itself by the *nizam*/system of *hakimiyyat Allah*/God's rule, and, on these grounds, *second*, the establishment of a global *Pax Islamica* via a *thawra alamiyya*/world revolution of jihad (Qutb) mapping the globe into *dar al-Islam*. Of course, this is a utopia, but it is also a mobilizatory ideology.

To read the Islamist mindset it is best to read their mentor Sayyid Qutb, who made it clear: the target is the world order and the goal to be achieved is a remaking of the world.[27] When Islamists hit Western targets in the West itself, one cannot speak of "somebody else's war." The strategy of jihadist Islamism combines the levels of the domestic (the world of Islam) and the global (world politics) in its internationalism. This internationalism is intrinsic to Islamism embodying a world-political concept of order, for it is not merely concerned with the world of Islam, but considers in its views the world at large, of course including Europe. Pro-Western Islamic rulers are viewed as a "proxy" of the West, and therefore toppling them is also a part of the "revolt against the West." In addition, there is a European dimension of the issue. It is heralded through the existence of a non-integrated second and third generation of no-future kids born in Europe but in no way European in their identity. As proven again and again, this Islamic youth of the Islamic diaspora is susceptible to Islamism.

Another dimension of the Europe connection of Islamism concerns the outlets of transnational religion. As stated, Islamists take refuge in Europe in order to make full use of Western democratic civil rights in establishing Islamist logistic networkings for the respective movements, as safe havens in Western Europe itself.[28] From this fact follows the need to enhance the study of the internationalism of Sunni jihadist Islamism as a security concern to include Europe itself in the scope of the analysis. In other words, the study of Islamic migration to Western Europe is part and parcel of the needed study of the internationalism of political Islam as an issue in security politics. This is the subject-matter of Part III of this book. At this point, I want to warn against any indiscriminate criticism of the Islamic diaspora in Europe and propose my concept of Euro-Islam as an alternative to jihadism, as will be explained in the final part of this book.

One of the major areas of Islamist indoctrination is comprised of some mosques and madrasas in Europe and in the world of Islam. Among the few Western commentators who understand that a "deadly idea" is at work one finds Roger Cohen. In a remarkable editorial published in the *International Herald Tribune* of 20 July 2005, he rejects simple interpretations and questions the view: "remove the repression or exclusion and the catalysts to kill in the name of faith would disappear." Truly, this is not the issue. At issue is a "bellicose idea whose time has come"; it constructs the narrative of an imagined Islamic *umma* under siege[29] in the context of an equally constructed "history of Western intrusion into the world of Islam" (ibid.). This story of politicization of religion for the restoration of Islamic supremacy is brought to Europe via Islamic immigration making full use of "democracy against itself"[30] in the war of ideas. It was not Huntington but Sayyid Qutb, in his *Mushkilat al-Hadarah* [The Problem of Civilization],[31] who established the rhetoric of a "clash of civilizations."

World order and the place of civilization in world politics: the return of the sacred in a political garb

The foregoing analysis of Sunni internationalism has propounded the jihadist idea of a world revolution aimed at a remaking of the world order in the context of an irregular war, and has revealed its religious legitimation. This is the Islamic variety of "terror in the mind of God"[32] as related to the birth of political Islam. As earlier shown, this process precedes the end of the Cold War. However, it is only in the course of post-bipolar developments that jihadist Islamism has become a mobilizatory ideology generating a great impact. At issue is an Islamic variety of the return of the sacred that can be phrased with Mark Juergensmeyer's idea of a competition between religious and secular orders already taking the shape of the "new Cold War" (note 25). In shedding light on this return of the sacred I continue the analysis still in its second step dealing further with the politicization of religion.

Despite the activities of Saudi Arabia in promoting Wahhabi Islam, there is a shift in Sunni Islam from the state to non-state actors as one of the sources of the "troubled peace" in the post-Cold-War era. In fact, this is the emerging "new world disorder" heralding the already addressed conflict between religious and secular views over what order should prevail. In my earlier book on Islamic fundamentalism I coined the term "new world disorder" to refer to a real threat of destabilization, but equally to point to the inability of the Islamists to create the envisaged order through a lack of needed capabilities. The core issue is the politicization of religion from which jihadism grows. However, it leads to nowhere, and not to the envisioned vague Islamic world order. The outcome is international destabilization. It is true, in a way, that the irregular war of jihad helps Islamists to compensate for the technological superiority of their enemy in an asymmetrical situation of power. Under the present conditions the most they can accomplish is to trigger destabilization. It is within the nature of jihadism to create disorder, and this would be a step in the direction of the new order of God's rule they envision. Therefore, the reference to the "world disorders" caused by a jihadist irregular war should not be belittling of its serious security challenge; it poses a great threat in that its nature is based on the concept of order. In this way Islamism provokes a civilizational competition of two concepts of order expressed by military means.

At this point a repeated reference to Huntington and to his view that the new process is a clash of civilizations is pertinent. I published a book on this subject a year ahead of Huntington's *Clash*.[33] I look at the issue in terms of an inter-civilizational conflict related to the return of the sacred, preferring to follow in the footsteps of Ibn Khaldun's "*ilm al-umran*/science of civilization,"[34] and not to deal with the issue in a superficial political way. Despite this clear dissociation I do not join those who demonize Huntington, even though he burdened the use of this approach. An effort at a synthesis was made in my contribution to the book of the former president of

Germany, Roman Herzog, published under the title *Preventing the Clash of Civilizations.*[35] There I take pains to pursue an analysis that seeks an accord without overlooking the conflict, but seeing a peaceful resolution to it. Despite all disagreement, I still acknowledge Huntington's seniority in the debate and also his success in introducing the theme into International Relations, but I do not refrain from making corrections to his views about Islam and its civilization, and the potential of conflict resolution.

In this continuation of the second step in the present inquiry into Sunni jihadist internationalism, it has by no means been a digression to refer to Western academia's way of handling these issues, as well as the tremendous obstacles limiting liberty of expression. I honestly hope that this book will see the light of day and will not become a victim of peer-group readers, who pretend to make a scholarly evaluation but in fact engage in censorship. The curtailment of the right of free speech in research is a troubling disservice to Western scholarship. If we forbid stating that global jihad is rooted in realities and the conflicts of the twenty-first century, and accept the propaganda that jihadism is "un-Islamic" and that denies its reality as an Islamic interpretation of jihad, then we deny ourselves the distinction between the spirit of Islamism and the spirit of Islam. At issue is the politicization of Islam to Islamism and the militarization of jihad to jihadism. There are ideas that connect to concrete realities underpinning the rise of Islamist internationalism in networks of transnational religion.

In an effort at conceptualization and in a confession of a major source of inspiration for my study of the politicization of Islam, I refer to the great multi-million dollar project for the study of religious fundamentalisms in all world religions, run at the American Academy of Arts and Sciences. It resulted in the publication of five seminal volumes on this subject (see note 9). In further reference to the stated intellectual impediments in scholarship, I emphasize how regrettable it is to face the fact that these findings are seldom quoted in Islamic studies and are even denied an appreciation. After 9/11, 11 March 2004 and 7 July 2005, it has become more than clear to what great extent we need to pursue an uncensored study of jihadist Islamism and international security. After the foiled plot of the Islamists in August 2006 to blow up ten US-bound planes, the Swiss *Neue Zuercher Zeitung* regretted, in the editorial of its weekend edition of 11–13 August, that one "barely finds the adjective 'Islamist' added to terror." This happens also in scholarship. It is sad to state that even many students of Islam and the Middle East ignore in their work these five seminal volumes on fundamentalism. It is only recently that some scholars have looked at religion and international politics in the post-bipolar age, to study the return of the sacred with an impact on world politics.[36] The contention is: Post-bipolar world politics is determined by the return of the sacred[37] expressed in a context of the religionization of politics as well as the politicization of religion; it results in a culturalization of conflict and also in the emergence of a "New Totalitarianism" not recognized by major political theorists.[38]

Among the exceptions in social science is a project by a group at the London School of Economics, which engaged in creating a team of experts for studying religion and International Relations. The result was a publication first presented, in an unprecedented way, at the annual meeting of the International Studies Association in Chicago (March 2001) in a panel devoted to "religion and International Relations."[39] Then followed 9/11 in the same year, displaying the lack of approaches for the study of politicized religion in terms of international security and the threat to the existing world order posed by internationalist jihadism. There are political implications to international politics in the developments since the end of the Cold War, embedded in the context of the "cultural turn" and the return of the sacred in a political shape. At issue is a cultural phenomenon in world politics characterized by a drive at de-Westernization as a challenge to the cultural impact of globalization. In the case of Islam, the revival of the *umma* identity connected to these developments is not properly understood in the West. One finds, for instance, the acclaimed political philosopher Jürgen Habermas contending that there is an emerging "post-secular society" while turning a blind eye to all political implications to a real phenomenon, of course with the exception of US- and West-bashing. Habermas fails to grasp non-Western civilizations and to see the competition between a secular and a divine order as a part of the war of ideas waged between two worldviews opposed to one another: neo-absolutism and relativism,[40] arising from the very same context. This war of ideas also takes place in the post-bipolar Islamic civilization resulting from a continued politicization of religion. Political Islam is among the prominent expressions of this neo-absolutism, but uniquely as a universalism. Therefore it appears in the garb of a political internationalism based on religion challenging the contemporary world order. In contrast to this revival, one sees a cultural relativism that has been addressed in Europe in terms of post-Christian developments. This currently emerging trend in Western Europe also results from a crisis of identity amounting to civilizational self-denial.[41] Leaders of European opinion fail to recognize the tensions between the described absolutism and democratic pluralism, and thus overlook the threat of Islamist internationalism to the inner peace of Europe if the conflict between the Muslim diaspora and European democracies is not peacefully resolved.

The irregular war of Sunni internationalist jihadism is not a war of liberation, nor does the movement that wages it resemble a civil rights movement, as some contend. The claim to de-center the West in order to replace its Westphalian secular order through a divine Islamic one, as shown in the analysis by Daniel Philpott and in my work (see note 1), makes the role of religion clear, although some – like Robert Pape – dispute this.[42] With the exception of Western civilization, almost all other world civilizations are related to and determined by a concept of religion and the corresponding worldview. In the case of Islam, an Islamist concept of order as an essential

part of political Islam is becoming a broadly accepted public choice determining the worldview of the people involved. The concept of *din-wa-dawla/*
unity of religion and state is viewed as essential for the *nizam Islami* that
challenges the validity of the secular nation-state for the world of Islam. In
a further step, the new ideology based on the return of the sacred enhances
its claim to world politics at large in envisioning a *dar al-Islam* mapping the
entire globe. This is what Sunni jihadism is all about. To reiterate: it is not
mere terrorism in an asymmetrical war of the oppressed, but rather a vision
of a new world order based on *Pax Islamica*.

This revitalization of religion in a political context is also related to
identity politics in international affairs. In the Islamic civilization, the outcome is Islamism as an expression of an Islamic revival being equally political, cultural and religious. One can refer to this issue in the case of
Palestine. The conflict is national and was earlier addressed in this manner
by the secular PLO. The issue was then religionized, which underpinned the
rise of Hamas to power and the emergence of the Islamist elite of Hamas.[43]

The world-political perspective for understanding internationalist jihadism requires going "beyond left and right" and equally, in the study of
International Relations (IR), overcoming inherited traditional boundaries
of a dividing discipline. In this pursuit, an IR-orientated study of religion
needs to be included. The assumption that the politicization of religion
results in the emergence of religious fundamentalisms, of which the Islamic
variety is only exceptional in the sense that it creates the new internationalism, put political Islam at the core of world politics. At issue is not
a phenomenon to be studied in terms of "fanaticism, hatred, terrorism and
extremism" or in terms of prejudice about Islam. This is not the business of
the IR discipline. However, it would be dishonest to refer to these deplorable images of Islam in the West in order to dismiss the study of the jihadist
threat of Islamism to world order as an expression of "Islamophobia." We
need to make it clear that what is at issue is internationalist jihadism as a
variety of a politicized transnational religion, and not Islam as such,
although this threat emerges from the politicization of Islam itself. The
Saidian book on "covering Islam"[44] addresses the deplorable coverage of
Islam by Western media, but instead of enlightening the subject of political
Islam it rather serves to dismiss any critical approach to it. In the Saidian
mindset, not only are academic books written and published by university
presses under titles such as *The New Crusaders*: there are also others, published by Islamist propagandists, contending that *"une vaste conspiration
judéo-chrétienne"*[45] is being spun against Islam.

Islamist internationalism draws on the fact that Islam is a transnational
religion. In this mindset the jihadists establish transnational networks on a
global level parallel to the politicization of religion. This is the unique
character of political Islam that can be shown in a comparative manner. For
example, one can state that in Hinduism the concept of order is restricted to
the territoriality of the imagined Hindu nation of Hindustan. It follows that

the Hindu-fundamentalist threat to security is regional, as confined to the territory of the Hindu civilization, i.e. it is exclusively regional and only pertinent to South Asia. In contrast, Islam is a universalist religion and its politicization results in an internationalism that touches upon the very secular nature of the international order. As repeatedly quoted, the intellectual father of political Islam, Sayyid Qutb, proposed that international peace can only be achieved on the grounds of establishing *hakimiyyat Allah*/ God's rule as a new world order. As repeatedly quoted, the implication of this view is that there can be no world peace without the global domination of Islam.[46] This is the very nature of the Islamist–jihadist internationalism with a bid for a related new international order. Such a transnational character of a politicized religion is reflected in movements like al-Qaeda, whose members believe they are acting *fi sabil Allah*/in the path of God to establish the Islamist order of *Pax Islamica*. To point at this jihadist ideology and the related practice is to refer to a threat that is neither a representation of a myth[47] nor an engagement in any kind of Islamophobia. Instead of acknowledging that cultural diversity is enriching for humanity and implied in the "heterogeneity of civilizations," the jihadists engage in lethal conflicts in which cultural diversity is transformed into dividing lines that separate humanity, not only among civilizations but also within them (e.g. Sunni jihadists killing Shi'ite Muslims in Iraq). The jihadists, not disputed scholars like Huntington, are those who ignite the "clash of civilizations" as a "jihad in the path of God."[48]

Sunni political Islam is based on the visions of Sayyid Qutb, the intellectual source of the new challenge for an Islamic world order.[49] Qutb maintained that a deep civilizational crisis of the West could be overcome only by re-establishing Islamic dominance. In his pamphlets, in particular "Signposts along the Road" and also "World Peace and Islam," he proposed that only Islam is in a position to overcome this crisis and to save humanity. At issue is neither a criminal gang nor an insignificant "un-Islamic" minority, but the public choice of jihadist internationalism. This is the virus of a deadly idea generated by bin Laden and his al-Qaeda jihad-fighters. The worldview expressed is clearly not restricted to these people. They are a minority, but the worldview is shared in the world of Islam. The target is the Westphalian order in world politics.[50] Qutb, who was an ideologue and not an IR scholar, presented his understanding of order for world politics and in substance shares with Huntington the view that "civilization matters."

Hedley Bull did not know of Qutb and of his views, but was aware of the fact that the stated civilizational "revolt against the West" is best "exemplified in Islamic fundamentalism,"[51] even though he was not aware of the "return of the sacred." It would be utterly wrong to disqualify the Bull statement in a Saidian manner as an expression of Islamophobic Orientalism. In the course of the post-bipolar crisis of international order these ideas (e.g. those of Qutb) of religionized politics became more pertinent. Gobal jihad transforms this potential into a "deadly idea" – based on the politicization of religion – in action. The reference to it reinforces political Islam's new role as well as its appeal as a public choice that assumes the nature of a mobilizatory ideology.

In summing up the preceding analysis of Islamist–jihadist internationalism resulting from the politicization of Islam in a "revolt against the West" it can safely be stated that the major target is the existing secular order and its Westphalian origins. In light of this knowledge, one may ask: Are we heading in a direction "beyond Westphalia"?[52] There is no doubt that the Westphalian order is not a sacred cow and cannot last forever, but what would follow? A divine order? And what about the need for more pluralism of cultures and religions, in particular in an age of the return of the sacred not restricted to the world of Islam? Would people of other religions accept the claims of jihadist transnational Islamism related to an order of *hakimiyyat Allah* as a divine rule for the world at large?

Humanity is characterized by religious diversity and needs common political concepts of order not grounded on one religion being imposed on others. This is the bottom line in answering these questions. For non-Muslims as well as for pro-democracy-minded Muslims, an Islamic system/ *nizam Islami*[53] is a totalitarian political system (see note 38) and can never be acceptable. In addition, there are inner-Islamic obstacles. The new or traditional concepts of order of the caliphate of the Sunna that one faction of the Sunni jihadists is yearning for are not acceptable to the Shi'a. The inner-Islamic conflict and the sectarian Sunni–Shi'ite violence emerging from it in post-Saddam Iraq is a sad case in point. While killing their Shi'ite rivals, the exponents of political Sunni Islam believe that in the long run they will prevail and will be in a position to materialize Qutb's vision of world peace under the banner of Islam. The Shi'ite militias retaliate. In short, the envisioned Islamist peace is a threat not only to non-Muslims, who according to the shari'a would be discriminated against as subdued *dhimmi*,[54] but also to Muslims themselves, in particular to those who prefer to live under democracy. It follows that the prescription of religious and cultural pluralism[55] in an age of Islamism is the only promising future prospect, not only for Islam and Europe, but also for Muslims themselves.

Like those Byzantine monks at the eve of the invasion of Constantinople, there are some European intellectuals who engage in fruitless debates and ridicule the jihadist call for an Islamic world order as practically irrelevant rhetorics and meaningless Islamist politics. Against these premature and even wrong views, the politicization of Islam in the context of the return of the sacred has been analyzed as a call for an Islamic shari'a state supported by a mobilizatory ideology enjoying a great appeal to the Muslim public. Jihadist leaders claim to speak in the name of the despised.[56] Their jihadist actions are contributing to the destabilizing and undermining of the legitimacy of the existing order, locally and globally. The political terrorist *action directe* of "jihad on the path of God" aims at establishing a *hakimiyyat Allah*/rule of God. This is much more than a romantic rhetoric of an envisioned order. The combination of terror and war of ideas is generating real disorder in world politics. To argue for a political failure and the end of Islamism as a passing phenomenon is not only a short-sighted view,[57] but proves simply wrong if confronted with the facts.

Ahead of moving to the third step of the analysis, i.e. to the political-military action of Sunni-jihadist internationalism conducted by Islamist movements, it is pertinent to point to the civilizational worldview[58] promoted by Islamists. This is a combination of civilizational politics and universalist religion. The Islamist is a political man of action, but he is also a "true believer." Jansen rightly addresses this fact as "the dual nature of Islamic fundamentalism."[59] In acknowledgement of the need for a civilizational approach to the study of religion in politics and society, I revive the tradition of Ibn Khaldun in placing civilizations within the study of history,[60] and cleanse the insertion of this approach from the damage done to it by Huntington. People with collective identity base this on an awareness of their civilizations and of their distinct worldviews. These are the grounds for constructing the new identity politics to underpin claims based on the return of history.[61] In this context, civilizations are referred to as providing substance for a new notion of order, war and peace. Civilizations are subdivided into local cultures. Along civilizational patterns, one may argue that local cultures (e.g. Indonesia and Senegal) and also states (e.g. the Organization of the Islamic Conference (OIC)) group to form civilizational entities in world politics. Therefore approaches to the study of religion and Islam in world civilizations and world politics can be linked to one another, particularly in our age of the return of the sacred and transnational religion in international affairs in general and in Western Europe in particular, as home to more than 20 million Muslim immigrants.

Transnational religion, jihadism and security: political Islam and the challenge of the new irregular war

The third step in the present analysis consists of dealing with the war waged by Sunni jihadist internationalism in a world time seemingly ending Clausewitzian inter-state war in favor of an irregular war by non-state actors. In the course of post-bipolar developments there has been a decline in inter-state warfare. The study of war and security is challenged to adjust to new perspectives. Earlier, Barry Buzan[62] presented a step in this direction at the beginning of what is a long road.

Even though the work done by Buzan was inspiring for security studies in going beyond the conventional military issues, the assaults of 11 September 2001 in the US and 11 March 2004 and 7 July 2005 in Europe pose a new challenge of great magnitude to traditional security studies, which are still dealing with issues now practically phased out. The jihadists as non-state actors are acting militarily, as cross-border warriors who simultaneously engage in a war of ideas based on a new interpretation of transnational religion as a political internationalism. In the needed new perspective, established traditional boundaries and related constraints must be overcome to allow thinking on military action beyond the force of the state. The inability of the Israeli Defense Force to subdue the 4,000 jihadists of Hezbullah in the Lebanon war of July/August 2006 has been a telling story.[63]

Islamist internationalism is militarily an irregular jihad war declared on Western civilization, and understood not only as a military action but also as a stand against European values. In fact, it is wrong to view this jihad as a guerilla war, for its irregular war involving non-state actors is a different kind of violence ignoring any prescribed rules. It is also a war of ideas. I reiterate the view that although the jihadists may be a minority in the *umma* community of Islam, this should not serve as an argument for belittling of the significance of the phenomenon. The power of the jihadists lies in their ability to mobilize politically in the style of Lenin's avant-garde party. This implies their potential to have a great impact, not to be downgraded by the reference to them as a minority in the Islamic *umma*. The jihadists of political Islam are well organized, with a global networking, and equipped to the extent that they cannot be ignored or belittled. Their numbers matter little, since these groups are very capable of destabilizing and creating disorder through their means of irregular warfare. One may ask: Why is the new jihad an irregular war? And what can we do to beware of confusing jihadism and Islam? And foremost: How can the jihadist war of ideas poisoning the relations between Islam and the West be stopped?

The reader is again reminded of the fact established in Chapter 1 that jihadism in the new shape of terrorism is no longer the classical jihad of Islam, subjected to clear rules of conduct and with limited targets. In the course of the second step of the analysis presented in the previous two section, light was shed on the politicization of religion in Islam which results in an "Islamism" being the Islamic variety of the global phenomenon of religious fundamentalism (see note 9). In contrast to the minority of Muslim fundamentalists, the Islamic civilization comprises one quarter of humanity and it manifests great cultural and religious diversity. As an example of this difference is the between Sunni and Shi'ite Muslims. Moreover, in Islam there exists a great variety of religious denominations and numerous sects. In addition to these sectarian distinctions, Islam is characterized by a great cultural diversity existing within the unity of the Islamic civilization. For example, African Islam is culturally very different from the Islam of Southeast Asia, or that of the Indian subcontinent. All of these varieties differ from the original Arab pattern of Islam. However, an Arab-centric concept of Islam determines the prevailing understanding of Islam. Once this diversity has been stated, any essentialization of Islam is pointless and has no foundations. It is not only Western Orientalists but most of all Islamists who overlook the addressed religious and cultural diversity.

Returning the focus to global jihad in its double meaning of an ideology and military practice of jihadist irregular war, two things are pertinent. At first, global jihad is reflected in multiple political Islamist movements that legitimize themselves through a reference to a monolithic religion for toppling existing orders. Second, despite their great diversity they can be addressed in general as a movement of politicized transnational religion. The new military interpretation of jihad as a war of irregulars, fighting without rules to accomplish an Islamic order combined with another war of ideas, is practiced by Sunni jihadists who do not represent a state. No state harbors them.

Among the fifty-seven nation-states united under the umbrella of the OIC which claim to represent the Islamic *umma* and its civilization, there are two Sunni states that – each in its own way – provide, however unwillingly, a kind of hinterland for jihadism. These are Saudi Arabia and Pakistan. Unlike this Sunni front, Iran on the Shi'ite side fully promotes its Shi'ite allies in Iraq and Lebanon. Unlike Iran, the Sunni states mentioned are considered to be allies of the United States and claim to participate in the war on terror; they therefore pay lip-service against terror – of course, without relating it to global jihad. There is nevertheless support for global jihad. In contrast to all three, Iraq under Saddam – once pronounced bully of the West – was truly a rogue state, but never a harbor for jihadist terrorism. Therefore, the justification of the Iraq war in terms of security was utterly wrong, and it was based on a severe strategic mistake that contributed to overlooking the real issue. The de-Saddamization of Iraq did not weaken jihadism but in contrast unwittingly strengthened it. The Iraqi Sunni jihadists fight what is mistakingly called "insurgency"[64] and the Shi'ite Islamists rule the country in the name of democracy, while their death squads engage in terror, as does the jihadist Mahdi Army of Muqtada Sadr that – despite being a terror militia – is represented in the parliament by thirty deputies and by five cabinet positions in the "democratic" government.[65] Similarly, Hezbullah in Lebanon has an irregular army and deputies in the parliament.

The jihadist war pursued by Islamist internationalism targeting "Jews and the crusaders" is one prominent source of "the new anti-Semitism."[66] In this regard, there is no distinction between Sunni and Shi'ite Islamism. The "war against the Jews" is a core issue in the new jihad war believed to be based on civilizational values. It is also a war of ideas in a competition between different concepts of world order. The conflict is viewed as revolving around the normatively different understanding of five issue areas: (1) the state; (2) law; (3) religion; (4) war/peace; and (5) knowledge. Civilizations have different standings on these issue areas. One may argue that value-related conflicts have nothing to do with military capabilities, but – if politicized – could nevertheless contribute to the emergence of real political conflicts that can be militarized (see note 10).

In my writings I use the term "war of civilizations," which could be looked at as a war of values and worldviews that directly affects conflict on all three levels: the domestic, the regional and the international. The thirty-three jihadist assaults that took place as an irregular kind of war between 1993 and 2005 placed jihadism in conflicts between civilizations. Against this, a security dialogue in the understanding of an instrument of conflict resolution is needed.

Europe faces the new warfare of jihadism, both as violence and as a mobilizatory idea, with a great uncertainty. I contend that the civilizational self-awareness among Westerners – particularly in Europe – is, in contrast to the image of the self among Muslims, not so reassuring. In fact, one can call this a civilizational weakness in Europe disproportionate to its political-military and economic power. In the language of Ibn Khaldun, this is an "*asabiyya*" in a state of a decaying civilization and this is the way in which Islamists view the West. The quest for a civic culture creating a common *asabiyya* to be shared by both Europeans and Muslim immigrants is an issue for Part III.

The challenge of new warfare of irregular jihad waged by the Islamists resembles the *action directe* (Georges Sorel) and is terrorism. The jihadists succeed in destabilizing and demoralizing, but do not win militarily. The conflict and the major targets are political. The over-arching issue is the order of the secular nation-state and, on a higher level, the international order. The jihadist irregular war aims to prevail over the enemy through demoralizing him and creating uncertainties about what lies ahead. In going beyond the casualties and fatalities caused by each jihadist *action directe*, the overall issue revolves around the claim of an alleged Islamic world order. The contestation of the existing is articulated by the jihadist terrorism of the Islamists. This irregular war, pursued to defeat the West and replace its political order by an Islamic one, leads us to a question asked by John Kelsay in his study *Islam and War*. As quoted in the introduction at length Kelsay states, "in encounters between the West and Islam, the struggle is about who will provide the primary definition of the world order." And then on the same page, he asks the seminal question: Who will lead the world in the future? In this reasoning, Kelsay asks further questions not to be repeated here.[67] In referring to Kelsay while refraining from engaging in speculation, I admit that the answer to these questions is not clear. In contrast, the jihadists believe they can foresee the future. They quote the spiritual father of their ideology, Sayyid Qutb. In his already mentioned booklet "Signs along the Road" (see note 12) Qutb believes that the decay of the West is sure and that only Islam is eligible to replace it and lead all humanity into a better future under its rule. It is clear that these questions and the answers given indicate the already stated competition between Western and Islamic concepts of world order on the level of public choices. This is one dimension in the war of ideas. When Islam – despite global jihad – is presented as a religion of peace, then at issue is a normatively different understanding of the notions of war and peace.[68]

In concluding this section, it is safe – despite all the limitations and differentiations undertaken – to engage in some generalizable statements concerning three central issues in the study of jihadism as an irregular war viewed in a broader meaning:

First: the problem of political order. Islamic fundamentalism as a powerful variety of the politicization of religion does not only bring existing cultural differences to expression. In this regard the revived worldviews touch upon a concept of order, with the implication of a conflict between existing civilizations. In terms of security, jihadists mobilize on religious grounds for their global jihad and are in this pursuit most appealing and subsequently successful. There is no doubt that military security measures are needed in facing actions of irregular war, but jihadists cannot be fought with armies alone, because they themselves also fight a war of ideas. In countering their activities, one needs a security approach that should be fixed neither on the state nor on the predominance of conventional military thinking and related traditional wisdoms.

Second: holy terror and irregular war. Among the Islamists there are those who fight for their goals peacefully within institutions and with political means. But others, like the jihadists, resort to violence within the framework of terrorism to enforce their concept of order. Jihadism is a variety of "terror in the mind of God" (Mark Juergensmeyer). This approach combines fundamentalism and the related worldviews about order, including the politicization of a conflict of values with terrorism (see note 1). In this understanding, "holy terror"[69] is an irregular war of non-state actors.

Third: is "Islamism" different from "Islamic fundamentalism"? In the present book, the terms "political Islam," "Islamism" and "Islamic fundamentalism" are used interchangeably. This is not common, because some dispute the application of the concept of fundamentalism to Islam, with the intention of combatting the spreading prejudice. However, this is utterly misleading. It is true that the term "fundamentalism" has been ill handled as a cliché, but it is – despite all odds – a scholarly and analytical concept for studying the politicization of religion. Some use the term "Islamism" as an alternative to the one referring to the global phenomenon of religious fundamentalism (see note 9). The scholars who do this are unwittingly contributing to the stereotyping of Islam by implicitly restricting the politicization of religion to it. In contrast, the term "Islamism" is used in this book only to address a specific depiction of a specific variety of the phenomenon of politicized religion – that is, the Islamic version of religious fundamentalism – with the implication that this phenomenon does not only occur in Islam. However, Sunni jihadism as the military dimension of this phenomenon is specifically Islamic, inasmuch as Islamist internationalism is based on the politicization of Islamic universalism. When it comes to war, an inquiry into Islamism in the field of security studies needs to engage in a reasoning addressed as "new frontiers of security,"[70] and to go beyond the traditional concept of security dominated by military thinking. A broadening of the scope and a deepening of the insights are needed to understand jihadism in its combination of the war of ideas and the violent war of the irregulars in their direct action towards establishing a new world order.

A few scholars in the field of international security have engaged in ground-breaking studies that unfortunately do not deal with Islam but are, however, pertinent to the understanding of the irregular war of Islamist jihadism. Leading among these scholars is Barry Buzan, followed by Martin van Creveld and Kalevi Holsti. They have contributed significant studies of security and war, going far beyond the fixation on institutionalized state armies.[71] Both the changed character of war, as one of the "new kind," and the non-military aspects of the conflict (ideas and worldviews) are to be emphasized. These are new subjects for security studies. In this sense, and only in this sense, I argue that religious fundamentalism in Islam and its jihadism are to be dealt with in the new security approach. Jihadism is both a propaganda fight (war of ideas) for a new order and also an irregular war against the political order of the infidels. Its manifestations on 11 September and the ensuing events in Madrid and Amsterdam in 2004 and in London in 2005 made the issue powerfully clear. Organized armies trained in conventional warfare are helpless against the terrorist acts of violent jihadists, in particular – but not only – against those of the suicide bombers. Iraq is a case which shows how weak and limited military might can be against the terror of suicide jihadists turning their bodies into bombs and into missiles. Prior to these post-11 September developments, there were earlier similar events in Algeria, Egypt, Israel and Afghanistan, as well as in Xinjiang, Kashmir, Kosovo and Macedonia; all of them make this issue clear. It follows that the West will not easily be able to come to terms with jihadism and the related challenges to security. The conventional forces of the North Atlantic Treaty Organization (NATO) were able to overpower the Serbian army as a regular armed force in 1999. The same applied when US and British troops toppled Saddam's regime in the Iraq war in March/April 2003. But neither the religious-ethnic acts of revenge by UÇK irregulars against the Christian Serbs, Macedonians or others, nor the irregular war against the coalition troops in Iraq, could be curtailed by the military power of regular troops. The most striking case is the inability of the Israeli Defense Force (IDF) to crack down on the jihadist second intifada, which has been taking place since September 2000. The IDF was victorious in all inter-state wars of the Middle East conflict between 1948 and 1982, but has been incapable of dealing with the war of irregulars "against the infidels" in the al-Aqsa intifada. This irregular war of jihadism dealt Israel another blow in the Lebanon war of July–August 2006. Despite a conventional well-orchestrated military action by its air force and ground troops, for thirty-four days the IDF was not able to beat 4,000 jihadists of Hezbullah fighting their irregular war worldwide in a networking of a transnational religion.[72]

The analysis presented here of Sunni jihadism as a direction within Islamist internationalism covering the world of Islam and the diaspora of Islam in Europe cannot be concluded without asking the question: Why do the jihadists establish their logistical bases in a transnational networking in the West? This recurrent question will be addressed in more detail in Part III on

Islam in Europe, but it is also posed here in the specific context of security and will therefore be addressed. Unlike the United States, Western Europe continues to fail to come to terms with global migration and has not been successful in integrating Muslims.[73] The result is a "gated diaspora,"[74] i.e. Islam in the West, but not of it. The denunciation of references to the conflict between political Islam and Europe as an indication of Islamophobia has been an effort pursued by Islamists themselves to obscure these issues.

Islamist internationalist jihadism as an issue area of the study of global migration and international security

Muslim immigration to Europe is a mixed bag. It enriches Europe through a cultural injection, but it also brings Islamist jihadists to the old continent. Europe has failed to engage itself in an integration of Muslims as European citizens. This failure is resulting in a new Western security concern. After all, there is a kind of political correctness that serves to camouflage jihadist fundamentalism in the name of tolerance. This contributes neither to the protection of Muslims nor to democracy. In a free spirit, the final section of this chapter addresses the abuse of the Islamic diaspora in Europe by Sunni jihadists of al-Qaeda in camouflaging their activities. I share Francis Fukuyama's view that "Europe has become and will continue to be a battlefront in the struggle between radical Islamism and liberal democracy."[75]

There should be no zero-sum game in the relationship between the protection of human rights and the countering of jihadist internationalism. Leaders of the Islamic diaspora in Europe are challenged to wholeheartedly join in countering jihadist terrorism to deny these soldiers of political Islam the use of the diaspora for jihadist networking on a transnational scale, as well as the Islamic legitimation. However, the behavior of these leaders after the failed plot of August 2006 to blow up ten US-bound planes was not reassuring. Instead of providing assistance they engaged in blame-games and accusations of Islamophobia, to an extent that led the British Home Secretary to turn the tables, confronting these leaders with the argument that the Iraq war should not be used as an excuse, and that they should look within their own communities to see what was wrong.

Instead of blame-games, Europe and its Muslim migrants need a Euro-Islam opposed to the gated diaspora ideology of Islamism that produces jihadists like those of Madrid, Amsterdam, Paris and London in 2004–6. The European diaspora of Muslim migrants should not become a home to al-Qaeda. In a research project at the University of California, Berkeley, this issue was addressed under the heading "Islam and the Changing Identity of Europe." The project was conducted by two major Berkeley centers and led to a publication under the title *Muslim Europe or Euro-Islam?*[76] If the alternative of a European Islam proves to be unfeasible, then the dream of "Muslim Europe" as envisioned by the Islamists will become a serious security threat. In another project at Cornell University, dealing with transnational religion with a focus on "Religion in an Expanding Europe," I outlined the options: Europeanizing Islam or the Islamization of Europe.[77]

In security terms, the German Islamic diaspora includes both Sunni and Shi'ite Islamism. The supporting systems of the jihadism of 9/11 were located in Western Europe, primarily in Germany.[78] These Islamist networks are powerful, not with regard to the number of jihadists (900 Hezbullah and 300 Hamas fighters in Germany) but in their capabilities. Germany hosts approximately 100,000 jihadists among 4 million Muslim immigrants. The real problem is that the Islamists in Europe are well organized, vocal and in control of major mosques and associations. Their power in the culture and the institution of mosques, and above all their richness in resources provided to them by transnational so-called Islamic welfare institutions, are awesome.[79] Why do they act in Western Europe? It is because most West European states provide the jihadists with a safe haven in the name of human rights.[80]

Until the assaults of 11 March 2004 in Madrid and 7 July 2005 in London, the public execution of van Gogh in Amsterdam (2 November 2005), the intifada of the *banlieues de l'Islam* 2005, the Copenhagen-turned-global conflict in early 2006 over the Mohammed cartoons, and last but not least the foiled plot of August 2006, some Europeans cultivated the misperception that they were not involved in 9/11 and that Osama bin Laden[81] was not popular in the Islamic diaspora. However, the language of political Islam has become popular in declaring the jihad-war on the West, even in Europe itself. The torching of some 12,000 cars and dozens of schools in the suburbs of Paris in October/November 2005 was an eye-opening event. Bin Laden's call for a war of *iman*/belief against *al-kufr al-alami*/international unbelief resonated well in many faith schools and other institutions in the Islamic diaspora, whether in Germany, the UK or Scandinavia. It is not the person of bin Laden, but rather the symbolic incorporation of this *global* jihad and its worldview, that renders this popularity its strength. Combine this with the fact that youngsters of the second and third generation of the Islamic diaspora are socially marginalized and susceptible to recruitment by Islamist movements acting between the worlds of Islam and Europe. Security and civilizational identity are the issues. This is an export of Sunni political Islam and its anti-Semitism to Europe. Fukuyama is right in stating that, in Europe, radical Islamism is "rather a manifestation of modern identity politics."[82]

Karl Popper's *The Open Society and its Enemies* is most pertinent for the pending issue in Europe. [83] It is argued that jihadist Islamism is the new totalitarianism of the twenty-first century. Tolerance in the name of cultural diversity is the wrong approach, because it is not the religion of Islam and its cultural system that are at issue, but rather the networking of Sunni jihadism in Europe itself. Karl Popper taught that we should not tolerate intolerance in the name of tolerance. This is a lesson not only for Europeans, but also for the leaders of the Islam diaspora; as well as making the distinction between Islam and Islamism, they need to learn to refrain from acts and pronouncements of false solidarity.

To date most European politicians and opinion leaders – despite the warnings of their security apparatus – pay little attention to the Islamists most active in Europe, even after the jihadist foiled plot of August 2006. It is sad to see many Europeans viewing it as improper and inappropriate, even politically incorrect, to relate Islamist jihadism to the study of civilizations as well as to the abuse of civil rights and of the Islamic diaspora by Islamists. This political silence has been an outcome of a questionable culture of political correctness, based on fears and self-censorship. In addressing the issue of Islamophobia, it is the right thing to do to curb prejudices against non-Western cultures, foremost those centered on Islam, and to combat all kinds of related racism, as well as xenophobia. However, there exists a constructed Islamophobia, often cultivated on purpose by Islamists to create taboos that prohibit free speech about them and their activities. In this context I refer to the authority of the late Myron Weiner and his book *The Global Migration Crisis* to justify looking at migration in security terms. To undermine such a debate, Islamic fundamentalists have been most successful in Europe's civil society in establishing an equation of the critique of jihadist Islamism with an ugly Islamophobia in the pursuit of censorship.

More acceptance, and even more impact than any liberal Muslim is enjoyed by one of the leaders of the Islamic diaspora in Europe, Tariq Ramadan, not only among Muslim youngsters of the *banlieues de l'Islam* but also among naïve Scandinavian multi-culturalists, who invite him to speak about "the mission of Islam in Europe." In contrast, well-informed authors like Robert Spencer in his *Onward Muslim Soldiers*[84] argue that Ramadan, the grandson of Hasan al-Banna, is an Islamist; Ramadan presents his grandfather in a disputed book[85] as a Muslim revivalist continuing the Islamic reform pursued by al-Afghani. This is, however, utterly wrong. Reformist Euro-Islam, as I present it, is not what Ramadan claims to be a European Islam. There are journalists, like Caroline Fourest, who have endeavored in investigative disclosures to uncover the double face of Islamists and expose this business.[86] In Germany, investigative journalists were taken to court by Islamists, accused in libel suits and then silenced.[87]

Conclusions

The best strategy for countering Islamist internationalism in the European diaspora of Islam is the integration of Muslim immigrants as true citizens of the heart.[88] I refrain from elaborating on this in this chapter, keeping this task for Chapter 6.

In drawing conclusions on a general level it can be stated that Islamism is embedded in a triangle: the world of Islam, the West as a civilization, and Muslims in Europe as a diaspora. In the area of the last issue things are not going well. Pro-democracy Muslims need to realize that the related challenge is also to them themselves. I believe in the potential of an enlightened Islam in the addressed triangle for shaping the world of Islam along of the wave of democratization. However, this hope can only materialize if these options become a public choice freely chosen by Muslims themselves in an Islamic approach against jihadist Islamism. The Islamic diaspora matters for the debate on supporting systems of global jihad, and the world of Islam, primarily its Arab core, matters most. The sad conditions in the Middle East described in the UNDP report in terms of lack of economic and political development underlain by a culture of repression allow no real democracy and no freedoms of basic human rights. In addition to the worldview of Islamism, these are the seeds of global jihad, given its roots in Islamic civilization, and a democratization by Muslims themselves is the only promising way out.[89]

In looking at jihad as a deadly idea and its related worldview, I do not overlook the structural roots of terrorism which ought not to be ignored and neglected. However, the repeated talk of poverty and Palestine as the alleged root causes is a distraction from the real root causes of history, ideology, religion and culture. The transmission of the global jihad-related worldview through madrasas is among the educational root causes to be dealt with in a concrete security approach.

This does not mean preserving the status quo, but defending freedom and democracy against the new totalitarianism. How can we prevent the enemies of the "open society" from abusing its freedom? Among the principles of civil society is securing it from the impact of the state. Sunni Islamist internationalists have been successful at this level by establishing themselves in Europe as part of civil society in a communitarian sense, and also in the world of Islam itself.

With regard to Europe as the focus of this book, one sees some basic differences between France, Germany and the United Kingdom. Despite the problems related to the uprising in the *banlieues de l'Islam* of Paris in October/November 2005, the French model has proved to be more promising than any model of multi-culturalism in facing the intrusion of jihadist Islamic fundamentalists into Europe. France has been successful in getting Imams at French mosques who express their loyalty to the constitution, to democracy and to the laïcité. This is not the case in the United Kingdom or in Germany. There were Muslim Britons and German citizens of the diaspora who were fighting in Afghanistan against the West. The British government seems to have needed the London assaults of 7 July 2005 to proceed in an unprecedented manner in requiring loyalty from Muslim migrants. Some Imams accused this measure not only of Islamophobia but also of using "right-wing policy" against Muslims. This is simply propaganda against an open society that protects itself. In contrast, multi-cultural tolerance can no longer be an "anything goes" after what happened in Europe in 2004–5. The Muslim community in Europe is challenged to commit itself to loyalty to the democratic polity. At this juncture, we should always remind ourselves of the difference between belief and its politicization to a jihadism as a pattern of irregular war which alienates Muslims from others.

Even though only one third of this book, i.e. the two chapters of Part III, deals directly with Europe, all chapters relate the pending issue to the Muslim diaspora community in Europe, which is also exposed to Sunni Islamist internationalism, particularly its jihadist terrorism. Those Muslims, foremost of the diaspora, who are committed to democracy and who are honestly geared to European citizenship should contribute, through a commitment to open society, to averting tensions between the world of Islam and Europe on a multifaceted level in order to replace the ideology of anti-Westernism taught at mosques and faith schools. The challenge posed by jihadist Islamist internationalism to Europe and to its international security is also a challenge to Muslims themselves, in particular those of Europe.

In my work during the past three decades on the crisis addressed, I have come to the conclusion that political Islam has grown from Islam's unsolved predicament with modernity. The solution for the world of Islam is not only democracy, and for Europe it is not only a Europeanization of Islam. For undermining the new totalitarism, the world of Islam itself needs to change and develop through reforms to facilitate a liberal Islam that smoothes the way for Muslims to join the rest of the world equally within the framework of democratic peace and of religious and cultural pluralism. As shall be shown in Chapter 7 an embracing of democracy in Islam combined with a cultural accommodation to modernity could help Muslims to come to terms with the rest of the world. Subsequently, existing illusions of an Islamization of the world through global jihad within an Islamist internationalism for mapping the globe into *dar al-Islam* would lead Muslims nowhere; such illusions need to be abandoned altogether. It is incumbent upon Europeans and pro-democracy Muslims to overcome the related impasse in an inter-civilizational dialogue based on a commitment to free speech and to the will to cooperate in resolving the issues to be identified in a free debate. This is the driving force for writing this book.

4 The Shi'ite option

Internationalism for an export of the
Islamic revolution of Iran. A failed effort!

The case of the Islamic Republic of Iran revives the classical question of
the national interest of the state. It also relates to the issue of nuclear
proliferation. With regard to the first question it is asked: how does
jihadist terrorism Shi'ite style, as combined with Iran's foreign policy,
reflect a national interest? Is this variety of state-sponsored jihadist
internationalism, run by non-state actors acting as irregular warriors,
incorporated into the national interest of the Iranian state? Well, the Shi'ite
variety of Islamist internationalism is based on a state policy.[1] Since its
"Islamic revolution" of 1979 Iran has viewed itself – like Russia after the
October Revolution of 1917 – as a stronghold of a transnational revolutionary movement. On these grounds, it can be safely argued, also in a
comparative manner, that Khomeini was a kind of Islamist revolutionary
Lenin. Whether this tradition ended after his death, as some contended, is
to be seen in the present analysis of a post-Khomeinism. Did this era of
revolutionary Islamist internationalism end? I argue that this assumption is
wrong. On the surface there were three different Islamic republics between
1979 and the end of the presidency of M. Khatami. In reality all three have
been rooted in the same political system of revolutionary Mullahcracy and
shared the same ideology of Islamist internationalism Shi'ite-style. All three
were equally committed to the bid of the revolution for the export of its
model. One of the most prominent experts on Iran, the exile Shahram
Chubin, states the issue succinctly in a way that deserves being quoted at
length:

> Since 1984 Iran has been labeled a state sponsor of terrorism, and in
> recent yeas it has been promoted to being the most active state sponsor
> of terrorism ... Iran's support of terrorism is in fact a mixed record.
> Although it is no longer used routinely as an instrument of state policy,
> Iran has by no means dispensed with terrorism completely ... Iran still
> actively supports Hezbullah and ... the crossover to Sunni Hamas and
> Islamic jihad ... Characteristically, the regime in Teheran seeks to have
> it both ways: to show that terrorism is a thing of the past, while keeping
> its options open.[2]

This statement applies to all three republics of Iran: Khomeini, Rafsanjani and the "reformist" President Khatami. The latter engaged in a rhetoric of "dialogue of civilizations" while Iran continued both its sponsorship of terrorism and its nuclear proliferation. The novelty – as Chubin states – "since the arrival of the Ahmadinejad presidency" is this: "the new team is more confrontational by nature and more prone to brinkmanship."[3] Therefore the novelty is the end of the rhetoric of dialogue, and not the return of revolutionary policies. These and the nuclear proliferation of Iran have never ceased. Both are a challenge and threat to Israel and Europe, as well as to the neighboring Sunni states. This is not news.

In an editorial published in the weekend edition of the *International Herald Tribune*, 10–11 December 2005, one reads: "Iran's hard-line president Mohammed Ahmadinejad has been conducting an ominous purge and a renewal of terrorist sponsorship abroad" (p. 6). The term "hard-line" employed in the report distorts the issue and is misleading. In fact, it stands for the term "religious fundamentalist." The other term, "terrorist sponsorship abroad," stands for Islamist internationalism. Journalists blur the issues in their sensational vocabulary and fail to see roots, as well as the overall context.

In dozens of other editorials one finds the false view that under the rule of the former so-called reformist Khatami – set in contrast to his successor, the so-called hard-liner Ahmadinejad – Iran had ceased to pursue its Islamist internationalism. Then it is inferred from this wrong view that in 2005 a resumption of former strategies, not continuity in policy, was at issue. In contrast, this chapter argues that the rhetoric of a "dialogue of civilizations" caused a blurring or even deception concerning the reality of a continuity existing in all "republics" of Iran based on "government of God,"[4] committed to the idea of an Islamic world revolution in the pursuit of establishing an Islamic world order. There are some "Iran experts" – like the German W. Buchta – who attack critics of the totalitarian views of the revolution by pointing at alleged "pluralism" and "elections" as part of the new system. These self-acclaimed "experts" reject the qualification of the Islamic Republic of Iran as a "fundamentalist state" with totalitarian rule. They seem to have been taken by surprise by the anti-Semitic and anti-Western pronouncements of Ahmadinejad. It is contended that a new era has begun. I dispute this and claim to see continuity.

Despite all the criticism of the Islamic revolution, no expert can escape acknowledging that a radical regime-change took place in Iran back in 1979. It was based on a revolution which – unlike Arab politics in the Sunni core of the Middle East characterized by numerous military *coups d'état* often legitimized as revolutions – was a real revolution, but it was not a world revolution. It is true that the Islamic revolution of Iran was carried out by the Mullahs, but in its beginning it was supported by the people giving it the shape of a revolutionary mass movement. A revolution is supposed to bring about a social transformation in state and society. The revolution in Iran failed to achieve such a goal. The Iranian state continues to be authoritarian and there is no sign of creating an open civil society. The new regime has failed to satisfy even some of the basic needs of the people who supported it with such expectations. Therefore, its model is at present neither promising nor appealing. Nevertheless, a real regime-change was without any doubt in place; it resulted in a new order claiming an overall Islamic internationalism, but in reality it has been divisive and a rival to the Sunni order. In continuity, it maintained the regional bid of Iran for hegemony, as pursued by the Shah, but in the shape of the Shi'ite model of revolution.

Regardless of all the obstacles in its way, the Shi'ite internationalism, rivaling the Sunni one – with a few modifications – has continued to give shape to the foreign policy of Iran for the past decades. With the rise of the Islamist al-Qaeda–Sunni internationalism, which presents a different, more competitive and more appealing model for an Islamic world revolution, the impact of the model of Iran has declined. Nevertheless it continues to be influential through its constituency among the Shi'a in Lebanon, Iraq and elsewhere. The revolution has been supportive for the Shi'a "reaching for power" in the Arab world[5] and thus intensifies, in particular since the Iraq war, the Sunni–Shi'ite rift. In this context, Iran's policy of nuclear proliferation also creates a bigger threat to the existing Sunni states. Add to this its cross-border terrorism. The Arab magazine *al-Watan al-Arabi* disclosed in its October 2005 issue a new

> offensive strategy designed by Iran for intruding the Arab Gulf states within the framework of an export of the [Islamic; B.T.] revolution ... This strategy goes far beyond the horizon of Iraq ... This strategic plan pursued for the export of the revolution via terror has been approved on the highest level of the state, that is by the office of the spiritual leader Khamenei, and also blessed by the council of guardians.[6]

Is this a "renewal" of the threat, or does it rather stand in continuity with the earlier politics of the Islamic Republic of Iran in past decades as the Shi'ite variety of Islamist-revolutionary internationalism? Is this Islamic revolution among the big world revolutions, as a Harvard scholar[7] contends?

Given the high priority of Iran to the economy and politics of the EU and in view of the existence of Shi'ite minorities and mosques among the Islamic diaspora throughout Europe, the internationalist approach of the Islamist policies of Iran matters greatly to Europe. This chapter is justified as a comparison to Sunni internationalism as well as with regard to the European Union and world politics.

By way of an introduction

In the early 1980s the image the Islamic revolution of Iran had of itself was a general Islamic one, not restricted to a Shi'ite event with a limited magnitude. In the beginning this claim seemed to be accepted by the people throughout the region of the Middle East, yearning for change and for alternatives to their current misery. However, the revolution never succeeded in passing the Sunna–Shi'a threshold, even though it gave hope for a light at the end of the very dark tunnel of Middle Eastern politics. Not only in its character as a revolution of the people, but also in its religion-based legitimation, the "Islamic revolution" of Iran seemed to mark a substantial change. The appeal was not restricted to the Middle East alone, in that it also applied to the world of Islam at large. With a view to the focus of this book, one may also add the diaspora of Islam in Europe.

The revolution was preceded by a legitimacy crisis of most secular regimes, felt throughout the world of Islam. Ruling secular elites came to power in the Middle East, though with no real structural secularization of society underpinning ideological secularism. The legitimacy crisis emerging from a superficial secularization amounted to a claim of de-secularization. The opposition, dominated by political Islam, was driven by this claim. Given the Islamic legitimation of this revolution, it must be noted that the politicization of Islam to an Islamism has also contributed to the reinterpretation of Islamic universalism in giving it a new political shape. Islamic universalism, transformed into a modern ideology of internationalism as dealt with in the preceding chapter, was in the beginning a Sunni phenomenon. Now, the Islamic internationalism of the Iranian revolution committed to the idea of a global jihad Shi'ite style is unique; however, it shares with its Sunni version a combination of religious fundamentalism and social populism.[8]

Another similarity with the Sunni version is the contestation not only of the political hegemony of the West, but also of its cultural values in a process of reversing Orientalism and with a mindset of a cultural schizophrenia[9] This contestation touches on the foundations of the Westphalian present world order. The Sunni and Shi'ite Islamist narratives are equally embedded into the worldview of the Islamic civilization despite the different legitimation underpinning each of them.

In the Shi'ite variety of Islamist internationalism, Khomeinism revives Iran's perception of itself as the "center of the universe"[10] which already existed under the Shah's regime. The novelty is, however, that the Islamic revolution brings an already stated resemblance of Iran to Soviet Russia under Lenin. Unlike the Iranian Shi'ite internationalism, based on a state as the Russian model was, the Sunni internationalism is a movement of non-state actors. The movement continues to be alive and kicking in its reliance on global networking despite the false prediction of Gilles Kepel of an end of Islamism. The irregular war and ideology of jihadism are expected to trouble the world for the foreseeable future. In Afghanistan – where, following 9/11, al-Qaeda's basis was destroyed – Sunni internationalism survives to date in its jihadist movement against Bush's "war on terror." Under these conditions Iran joins in as a state troubling the West, not only with its internationalism, but rather with its effort to unfold its nuclear capabilities through proliferation. The Iraq war strengthened the geopolitical position of Iran.

In fact, the Islamic revolution in Iran, which claims to unite the imagined *umma* of Islam, has been divisive, igniting more tensions between Sunna and Shi'a (e.g. Lebanon, Iraq) in the entire region of the Middle East. Therefore, this internationalism is hampered by the fact that it is legitimized as a rule in Shi'ite Islam that is utterly unacceptable to Sunni Arabs.[11] They were susceptible to an appeal, but not to the claim of leadership. The politics of a regional power in Iran under the Shah's regime is continued in an Islamic garb by the "republic" which makes reference to a universal Islam highly questionable through its commitment to a "national interest."

Viewed from the IR perspective, Iran is a state based on power that pursues its national interest. Against this background, it can be argued that there can be no such thing as a specific "Islamic foreign policy."[12] If, however, one concludes from this assumption that there cannot be any Islamic legitimation of power politics in international affairs, then this would be wrong. Any downgrading of the role of religion in contemporary post-bipolar world politics or in an expanding Europe[13] would be a refusal to acknowledge the combination of a religionization of politics and a politicization of religion. This happens throughout the world, and in the world of Islam as well. The use of religion in the ideology of Islamism is more than a pursuit of power. Therefore, the meaning of the Islamist revolution in Iran cannot be restricted to an expression of a bid for power. At issue is a new design for the role of religion in politics that leads to confrontation, both within the Islamic civilization and with regard to its neighborhood – that is, Europe. This is no myth, as some suggest, but rather a new world-political design![14]

For a proper understanding of the involvement of religion as a novelty in regional and world policies, and as a conceptual framework for dealing with the Shi'ite revolution that toppled an authoritarian secular regime in a geopolitical context, one needs a combined approach to grasp the perception of Iran's belief in itself as the "center of the universe" and the place of national interest. The world political impact of its internationalism is a necessary part of the story.[15]

The combination of a state-run variety of Islamist internationalism and the national interest of Iran in foreign policy needs also to be seen in the context of a country aiming to be a regional power in the Middle East and maybe also in the world of Islam at large. Despite all the cynicism of power, the reference to religion under issue displays a combination of belief with concrete policies of the state. At issue is a new cultural-religious factor in politics, with a global impact and therefore the need for a new approach.

Even though revolutionary Iran has failed in the competition to export its model[16] into other Islamic states it continues to be a challenge, in particular to still secular Turkey and to Wahhabi Saudi Arabia. After the toppling of Saddam's regime of pan-Arab Ba'thist Iraq, the position of Iran and of its internationalism in exporting its model to neighboring states has improved. It is ironic that the faulted US policies and the repercussions of the Iraq war have unwittingly contributed to giving Iran a boost, and even to pushing it to the center. The cultural determinants at work were not considered by the policy-makers.

A major assumption of this book is that religion is a cultural system which turns pertinent if politicized.[17] Under these conditions, politicized religion gives its shape to conflict. The outcome is "culturalized" and/or "religionized" politics. The fervor of anti-Westernism and its drive toward de-Westernization is to be placed in this overall context. In this environment of the arduous search for models alternative to the Western one, even Shi'i Islam, which is a particularism, dresses itself in a universal Islamic garb, giving it a powerful impact. This assumption was proven in the 1980s throughout the Arab Middle East in its severe crisis-ridden situation. The search for authentic, i.e. non-Western, alternatives for state and society received a boost through the Islamic revolution. Despite all disagreement with the unbalanced work of Francis Burgat, I have to endorse his observation that in the Arab Maghreb "the revolution of Khomeini breathed life into Islamist movements everywhere."[18] However, it can be added that none of the regimes there was successfully toppled, even though the destabilization worked well. Political Islam is the best recipe for a new world disorder;[19] it claims a new order, but it is restricted to delivering disorder.

The susceptibility of the Sunni Arab world to the appeal of the Islamic revolution is related to the overall background of the Arab defeat in the 1967 war. The de-legitimation of the secular regimes caused by the defeat was exploited by the Islamists. The revolution in Iran built upon this and materialized what the Muslim Brother sheykh and global mufti Yusuf al-Qaradawi prescribed with the term of the "Islamic solution/*al-hall al-Islami*" as a basic alternative to the existing regimes. Yet, Sunni Islamists were not able to implement this in their own countries. In contrast, the Shi'ite clergy of Iran proved able to promote its Islamist model as a remedy for the crisis of Islamic societies. At the outset a Sunni–Shi'ite reconciliation seemed to determine the agenda. After the revolution in Iran, the powerful Egyptian Sunni Islamist Mohammed Salim al-Awwa added to his book on the *nizam Islami*/Islamic system a chapter in which he calls for closing the Sunna–Shi'a gap and for a reconciliation ending the inherited tensions.[20] In considering all these favorable factors, one is inclined to ask why the efforts at exporting of the revolution did not bear fruit.

Parallel to the Islamic revolution in Iran, the Soviet Union invaded Afghanistan and unwittingly gave birth to new Sunni movements competitive with both the Islamic Shi'ite revolution and the global jihad of Shi'ite internationalism. Therefore the Soviet intervention in Afghanistan parallel to the revolution created another watershed.[21] Among the repercussions in question was al-Qaeda. It became more successful in its internationalism than Iran had ever been. Nevertheless, the "Islamic revolution in Iran"[22] and its Shi'ite internationalism continue to be pertinent. The rise in the price of oil combined with nuclear capabilities are factors contributing to some restoration of the power of the Islamic revolution. The historical roots of the Iranian Shi'ite jihadist internationalism and of its core state continue to affect the debate over the place of Islam in world politics at the level of the state.

The core state and the export of the revolution as a foreign policy

The Iranian perception of the self being "the center of the universe," mentioned earlier, reflects from the very outset the universal worldview of the Iranian clergy underpinning their thought of an Islamic world revolution based on their own model. Therefore, the watershed event of toppling the Shah's regime was never restricted to a domestic process, in that it is considered to be a world revolution based on an Islamic internationalism. This has been the result of the politicization of Islamic universalism recurrent in modern shape – no less than a claim of an "Islamic world order," as Ramazani put it.[23] Another expert points in this revolutionary setting at a duality of internationalism and national interest, arguing: "The Iranian Revolution was ... in a definite sense international ... Despite the revolutionary universalism ... it was felt to be a nationalist movement."[24] The conclusion is that this does not seem to stand in contradiction to the intriguing fact that "its universalism was more pronounced than that of the French or Russian revolution."[25] It may be this deceiving rhetoric that led a Harvard expert on European revolutions, although with a very poor knowledge on Islam, to place the Islamic revolution of Iran among the world revolutions.

In the course of looking for a persuasive explanation for the failure to export the Islamic revolution, the pointing at the Shi'ite character of Iran is meant neither to suggest that it was not generally appealing to non-Shi'ite Muslims nor to belittle its impact on the world of Islam at large. The appeal has been acknowledged and related to a real revolution with an international dimension – if not a world revolution – that took place in an environment determined by military rule of Arab *coup d'état* regimes.[26] Their populism – e.g. secular Nasserism – proved to be a great disappointment. As already stated, in this understanding the Islamic revolution in Iran has been in substance virtually the first revolution in the region. In the Arab world, a flawed development related to a structural crisis of the nation-state in the Middle East and combined with a de-legitimation of most of the existing regimes led to a legitimacy crisis.[27] These crises were visible particularly after the Arab defeat in the Six-Day War of 1967, as already mentioned. At the outset, the pronouncement of an alternative model for political change in the region by the Islamic revolution seemed to have filled an existing vacuum, and therefore its claims fell on fertile soil; however, this was only for a short period of time.

Why did the model fail? For an explanation of the failure, one needs to touch upon many issue areas. One is the fact that the revolution was constrained in its call for a jihad internationalism by its Shi'ite character. Except for Iraq after the toppling of Saddam Hussein, no Arab country would act along Iranian lines. The Iraqi Shi'a, mainly led by the Supreme Council for the Islamic revolution in Iraq (SCIRI), wishes to see an Islamic republic of Iraq,[28] but others certainly do not share this. Nevertheless, all religious groups of political Islam view the worldwide network based on a transnational religion under the impact of the Islamic revolution in Iran as a model and as evidence that Islamism could come to power. In this understanding, Iran was and continues to be a threat to the neighboring Arab states. This was openly articulated by Khomeini himself in his first Iranian New Year's speech, starting with the phrase: "(W)e should try hard to export our revolution to the world ... we shall confront the world."[29] The implication inherent in this phrasing relates not only a missionary belief, but also a strategy for the export of a religio-political revolution to the neighboring countries. It is underpinned by a worldview that legitimates an Islamic world order. As R.K. Ramazani argues, the notion of the revolution's export is "not well understood in relation to Khomeini's overarching concept of Islamic world order. The universalistic claim of this concept ... makes the export of the Islamic revolution a matter of international, rather than regional concern."[30]

For Khomeini this effort was all about global jihad understood as "self-defense of Islam" against Western intrusion. The pronouncement implies the right to defend Islamic principles, claiming universality and believed to be powerful enough to become victorious against the West. As Ramazani further argues: "Khomeini's concept is potentially even more troublesome; his concept of the Islamic world order basically rejects the validity of the very notion of the territorial state which is the principal subject of the modern law of nations" (ibid.).

Some Western critics of the nation-state believe they see in this political Islam an ally in their opposition to existing national boundaries. These critics, however, fail to realize that a religious neo-absolutism is at work. The same applies to the issue of anti-globalism. Western anti-globalists who unwittingly shoulder Islamism in the belief they share the same view are utterly mistaken: They do not know what they do and are not familiar with the Islamist claim for an Islamic globalization to replace the Western one.

At this juncture it is safe to state a commonality between the Sunni call by Sayyid Qutb for an Islamic world revolution and the Shi'ite call of Khomeini for an Islamic world order. The target is the same: to de-center the West for the benefit of Islam. Nevertheless, there are some sectarian differences between the Sunni and the Shi'ite visions. They diverge because they have deep roots in the history of the Islamic civilization. Yet, this has created no hindrance for the Iranian leadership in steering some Sunni Islamist movements which receive financial support from Iran (e.g. Algeria), although without acting as Teheran would dictate.

All in all and in view of the facts, it would be wrong to view the call for an Islamic world order simply as a fierce rhetoric and thus to play it down. It does pose a security threat. In both the Sunni and the Shi'ite case, the rhetoric has been combined with determined jihadist action throughout the world. For Europe, any commitment to this concept of order is an obstacle to the integration of Muslim migrants in making them European citizens. One cannot accept the political order of the European Union and at the same time adhere to a divine Islamic order. This is not a pluralism of order, but rather a severe contradiction and also a conflict.

The Iranian leadership never restricted itself to mere pronouncements. Iran sent its "revolutionary guards" to Arab countries like Lebanon and later to Sudan and it transferred funds to Islamist movements, such as the FIS in Algeria and Hezbullah in Lebanon. In addition, Iran has been involved in a great variety of covert actions and assassinations worldwide, including Europe. In all these cases terrorism has been legitimized as global jihad. Fred Halliday describes these activities in the following manner: The export of the revolution *sudur-i-inqilab*

> included the conventional means of exporting political radicalism –
> arms, financial support, training, international congresses, propaganda,
> and radio programs. Islamic tradition also provided specific elements
> that could be added to this process: ... in Islam there were no
> frontiers.[31]

With regard to the employed concept of communist internationalism applied to transnational religion for conceptualizing the described activities, in particular terrorism, the idea of global jihad is the Islamist articulation of this ideology. When implemented, it stands in the service of establishing the envisioned Islamic world order. This has been and continues to be the orientation of the Iranian foreign policy since the toppling of the Pahlavi state, even under the rule of the so-called reformer Mohammed Khatami and despite his rhetoric of a "dialogue between the civilizations." The continued failures of Iran's foreign policy combined with the maldevelopment of Iran itself led to the reverse, i.e. to the isolation of Iran. After the early positive response, the world of Islam was no longer open to the idea of the export of this revolution. Under the new hawk president Ahmadinejad, only Syria cooperates with Iran; other Arab and Islamic states keep aloof.

It came as no surprise that the already addressed overlapping of internationalist revolutionary claims of Khomeini with the national interest of the state of Iran continued to prevail in the post-Khomeini era. In his study *After Khomeini*, Ehteshami confirms that "the orientation of the Islamic Republic of Iran's foreign policy remains Islamist-based,"[32] but plays this down as mere "Islamic dressing" and believes he sees a change pursued by the Second Republic (1989–97) under Rafsanjani: "Iran's role in the region was based, not on Iran being primarily the hub of an expanding Islamic revolution ... but rather on regaining its position as a military power and politically influential player in the regional arena."[33]

As argued earlier along with Fred Halliday – despite the dissent over his alleged "myth of confrontation" – there is in fact no contradiction between the combined strategies of national interest and the foreign policy orientation of internationalism; some overlapping between both is even to be conceded. The export of the revolution did serve as a legitimating device for the claim for regional leadership in the pursuit of a role as a regional power. In fact, the jihadist internationalism Iranian-style existed consistently with the national interest of Iran. In this regard one can see only little difference between the rule of Rafsanjani and the rule of Khatami. The means employed to export the revolution were in continuity with the formative years. There were alliances with fundamentalist states – such as Sudan (e.g. Rafsanjani's state visit to Sudan and the related material support) – and cooperation with the proxies (foremost Hezbullah[34] in Lebanon). The related policies revolved around a double strategy: a state politics pursued as undercover activities (e.g. the Mykonos murder case in Berlin) combined with a novelty developed under the presidency of Khatami labeled as "a dialogue between the civilizations."[35] Even though the latter was meaningless, it successfully served as a deceiving device for non-dialogic policies. The Europeans bought the claim – I never did – and overlooked the ever-existing "Terror Central,"[36] as my columns and editorials in German newspapers document.[37] Along with this rhetoric Iran pursued its politics of nuclear proliferation, also under Khatami threatening the entire Middle East and Europe. In Iran, the Second Republic was believed to be "wholly at variance with the doctrines of the First Republic."[38] To be sure, in the Third Republic of Khatami the rhetoric was different, but the state and its order were the very same. In the study of the subject under issue the person of the president matters little, be it the pragmatist Rafsanjani or the alleged reformist Khatami, not to speak of the neo-Khomeinist Ahmadinejad, elected in 2005 with the support of the so-called hard-liners. What matters is the religious fundamentalism and the state of a "government of God" practicing it. The political system of Mullahcracy is in continuity with the established political structures for power distribution in Iran from its inception in 1979 to date. The earlier hopes for change pinned on the person of Mohammed Khatami and on his reformist outlooks faded. The divine order and its existing political institutions of a fundamentalist state survived what was claimed to be a reform.

The allocation of power and the Islamist legitimation of it are the real issue, not the persons who are in office. I had the opportunity to meet with President Khatami when he was still in office, at the invitation of the then German president Johannes Rau in Weimar on 12 July 2000. At first sight, I found him on the surface most impressive. However, I do not confuse this personal impression with the structure of power existing in Iran, nor do I identify rhetorical pronouncements with real policies. In Iran, the fundamentalist Mullahs have the power at their disposal and only they determine the politics of the state. The empty talk about elections, democracy and pluralism in Iran is laughable. The Council of Guardians above the clerics has always been committed to the politics of Islamist internationalism adjusted to the national interest of Iran, no more and no less. The overall frame for this is the totalitarian system of Mullahcracy as the hallmark of the fundamentalist state, which is based on an Islamist ideology. The talk about reformers and hard-liners makes no sense. In earlier Iranian parliaments the hard-liners were ready to concede the reformers a forum but no participation in the real decision-making. The reference in Iran to a so-called "Islamic democracy" to be accomplished by the powerless "reformers" was meant by some as a deception; by others it was based on illusions.

In returning to the Arab neighborhood, it can be stated that the Mullahs continue to ignore the repeated clear hints by Arab politicians and writers that they unequivocally reject Iran's claim to leadership. This rejection of a model of an Islamic state Iranian-style for the Arab part of the Islamic civilization has been expressed in a variety of ways at various events. Back in January 2004, I was in Abu Dhabi as an invited speaker, together with many Gulf state ministers. They were talking to the then deputy of President Khatami, who conspicuously ignored all hints made. Instead of listening, he rhetorically put the line of "Islamic identity" in terms of Islamic internationalism above national or ethnic identity, to advocate Iranian leadership regardless of the Arab leaders. I repeated this very experience in December 2006 at the Manama Dialogue of IISS in Bahrain. The foreign minister of Iran and his associates talked in general about Islam and were not willing to perceive the Iran related fears of the Arab Gulf politicians attending.

There are ethnic and sectarian Shi'ite-related fault-lines that have separated the Iranian revolution from other Muslims. Its legitimation through a reinterpreted Shi'ite concept of *"velayat-e-faqih*/guardianship of the jurisconsult"[39] is clearly not acceptable to Sunni Arabs. The claim by Khomeini to embody "true Islam" in contrast to what he despised as "American-style Islam" is in fact viewed by Sunni Arab leaders as a provocation. In March 1989 Ayatollah Khomeini voiced his aspiration in the following universalist phrasing: "Our revolution is not tied to Iran. The Iranian people's revolution was the starting point for the great revolution of the Islamic world."[40]

Clearly, Islamist Arab counter-elites[41] are receptive, however poised to establish an Islamic state, only in their own Sunni terms. Their understanding of an "Islamic state" is quite different from the Shi'ite one. The Iranian president of the Second Republic, Rafsanjani, had argued in 1993 along Khomeini's views that Iran and the alleged universal Islamic identity are the same in placing the Shi'ite-style Islamist internationalism above all: "Our people do not see national issues as being separate from Islamic issues ... We have become the mother country of Islam."[42] This phrase is reminiscent of Lenin's and Stalin's views that Russia is the "motherland of socialism." This mindset motivated Iran to engage repeatedly in unwanted and unwelcome intervention into the affairs of the neighboring Islamic countries. At the end of the day, this policy contributed to a regional isolation of Iran rather than to establishing its leadership. Rafsanjani put the quest to export the Islamic revolution in this manner:

> They [the Westerners; B.T.] accuse the Islamic Republic of terrorism and intending to export the revolution to the rest of the world ... [This; B.T.] is a baseless and meaningless allegation. A revolution is not a commodity which can be exported ... A revolution will export itself if it is justified, if it is rational and if it appears attractive to other nations. Yes, the revolution has been exported, but we did not export it. It exported itself.[43]

In Islamic terms it could be seen as a kind of heresy to translate the manmade political Islamist Shi'ite internationalism into the will of Allah. To interpret the phrase cited, it can be read as: Allah exported the revolution within the framework of global jihad. Foreign policy instruments like terrorism are no longer needed, because Allah's will dominates the universe, of which Iran builds up the center. Apart from this heretic thought, the conclusion is that failure is the outcome.

It can then be safely stated that spill-over effects of the revolution should not be confused with Iran's foreign policy itself. No well-informed scholar would seriously deny the impact of the Iranian revolution, but this statement does not translate into an endorsement of the foreign policy of the Islamic Republic of Iran as a "government of God" as being a successful one in its effort to export the revolution via terror. The politicization of religion does not unite Muslims, it separates them. Doctrines of Shi'a Islam are alien to Sunni Muslims.[44]

A significant distinction: spill-over effects are not yet an "export of the revolution"!

The appeal and its limits

In reiterating the fact that the contemporary phenomenon of jihadism and of its Islamist internationalism is related to political developments in Sunni

Islam and also predates the Islamic revolution of Iran, one is reminded how wrong it is to identify the idea of an Islamic state based on the shari'a with Khomeinism. As shown earlier, the concept of *hakimiyyat Allah*/God's rule is a Sunni concept first outlined as a novelty in the writings of Sayyid Qutb.

Political Islam is not rooted in Khomeinism, but rather in the political thought of the Muslim Brothers founded in 1928 in Egypt. It is the source and provides the overall framework[45] for Islamist internationalism. Viewed from this angle, the Iranian revolution can be characterized as a latecomer. It is just one – albeit important – variation in the contemporary history of political Islam. Despite the Sunni origins of Islamism it was Iran that succeeded in launching an Islamic revolution and in triggering spill-over effects throughout the world of Islam. We must beware of confusion between these spill-over effects and the model of the revolution itself. This confusion is caused not only by scholars but also by policy-makers, and above all on purpose by the Iranian leadership itself. The pronouncements and the spill-over effects of the "Islamic revolution" are confused in the service of the export of the revolution as a model for the world of Islam at large.

Khomeini's distinction between "true Islam" and "American-style Islam" is a political and not a religious thought. This distinction is aimed at de-legitimizing all regimes of neighboring Islamic foes as "un-Islamic," so laying the grounds for toppling them. This Shi'ite–Iranian variety of political Islam is described by some Sunni Salafists as itself "un-Islamic." In both cases, the reference to Islam is ideologically used to disarm one's own foes. The term is also used in domestic Iranian politics to deny the so-called reformists an Islamic legitimation by damning them as "un-Islamic." Islamic intellectuals and those who rhetorically claim to be reformers, such as Abdolkarim Soroush,[46] were targeted by Islamists in many ways. It is ridiculous to see some Western authors employing the same procedure in downplaying jihadist Islamism as "un-Islamic." In this study, I refrain from this thinking and accept any reference to Islam by any Muslim as Islamic, even if I do not share the related view. In contrast, the Iranian Mullahs see their own variety of Islam as the only true Islam. At issue here is in fact religion, but it is imbued with politics. Mallat points out,

> that the horizon of Iran is first and foremost Shi'ite, and that the Sunni world cannot intrinsically be part of the projection of the Iranian state as such. The physical basis for such a Sunni network simply does not exist. The absence of network is compounded by the absence of a satisfactory ideological model that Sunni political movements could follow.[47]

Mallat is right in referring to the limits of the appeal, but wrong in his statement about Sunni Islam. One sees al-Qaeda providing exactly what Mallat believes is missing. For a short historical period the Islamic revolution of Iran was appealing, but it could not be made acceptable to non-Shi'ite Muslims. The magic of salvation provided by the revolution did not last long. Today the impact is limited to Shi'ite minorities.

The Shi'ite minorities in the Arab world[48] compel continued cooperation with the political revolution in Iran and its impact in its environment, primarily in Iraq, Lebanon and Syria. As stated earlier, the very Iraq war unwittingly revived the significance of the Iranian model that most appeals to the empowered Shi'ite majority population of Iraq. The Iraqi Shi'ite clerics, as well as formerly secular Shi'ites (e.g. Chalabi) have successfully forged links with Iran. The irony is that while the Bush administration legitimized the sending of its troops to Iraq to topple Saddam with the introduction of democracy combined with "war on terror," the outcome has been the opposite. The implicit introduction of the shari'a into the Iraqi constitution is not a sign of democracy. An editorial in the *International Herald Tribune* asks:

> Did the United States wage a costly war in Iraq in order to introduce shari'a? Did the decision makers in Washington know that in post-Saddam Iraq there are divergent understandings of democracy and the rule of law – the Western secular and the shari'a-based?[49]

The Iraqi constitution is highly questionable.[50]

Even though the discourse of the Islamist revolution in Iran is intrinsically Islamic, the language of its pronouncements as an Islamist ideology bears resemblance to third-worldism in a broader context stated by Graham Fuller:

> This ideology must remain basically threatening ... Iran could seek to be the leader of the "South" against the "North" ... Iran will not necessarily have to export a revolution replete with violence, subversion, or terrorism ... The ideology will elicit forces for social change in the Islamic world. Iran would thus hope to be the guide, the beacon of Islam in politics. Cultural programs ... training in Iran – all would represent the stuff of Iran's export of the revolution.[51]

To be sure, this ideology of third-worldist Islamist internationalism revives the concept of the "third world"[52] phased out in post-bipolar politics. Nevertheless, the mindset of revolutionary *tiers mondisme* (F. Fanon) is not exactly in line with what is claimed by the "Iranian internationalism." One can hardly view the death squads of the late Musab al-Zarqawi[53] or their Shi'ite foes of the Mahdi Army within the framework of liberation ideology. At issue is a Sunni–Shi'ite cleavage within Islam. The fact that the Iranian leadership carries on its commitment to the "same universalist ambitions ... Iran still sees itself in its role in a global sense,"[54] a new power of the so-called "third world," is not third-worldism, it is a bid for power.

In concluding this section on the political record of Shi'ite internationalism, it can be argued that the issue is the state model implied in the projection of the Iranian revolution into the neighboring Sunni-Arab world. This model is placed in a power game that is being religionized.

In drawing a balance of the Iranian resort to terrorism and to subversion as instruments for the export of the revolution in an "Iranian connection," the Shi'ite minorities in the Arab world have been fully abused. The Lebanese case in point shows how Hezbullah acts on behalf of Iran. Iran has been successful in translating its position in Lebanon into a leverage in Lebanese politics and from there into the Middle East at large. The overall concern of Iran while using Hezbullah in Lebanon and the Shi'a in Iraq is – as the former Iranian minister of foreign affairs, Ali Welayati, once put it – to be entitled to participate in any shaping of Middle Eastern politics. The Iranian embassy in Damascus continues to be a center of the "Islamic revolution" of Iran. The pursuit of a new world order, despite the focus on the Arab world and the use of its Shi'a constituency, continues to be the global claim; as Ramazani aptly once put it: "Khomeini's overarching concept of Islamic world order ... makes the export of the Islamic revolution a matter of international, rather than regional, concern."[55] With this claim the Islamic revolution entered world politics, competing with Sunni internationalism, and continues to play this role during the presidency of Mahmoud Ahmadinejad.

Thus Khomeinism is still alive and kicking. Its mindset is documented in a speech delivered by Khomeini while addressing young Iranians going abroad, when he blatantly stated:

> We should try hard to export our revolution to the world ... Today we need to strengthen and export Islam everywhere. You need to export Islam to other places, and the same version of Islam which is currently in power in our country.[56]

This Khomeini vision of "true Islam," set in contrast to "American-style Islam," was thought to be a message for the entire Islamic *umma*. After the passing of Khomeini, this vision has never been abandoned, even though it was not publicly endorsed by the Second Republic of Rafsanjani nor by the Third of Khatami. Under the new president, Ahmadinejad, who perceives himself publicly as a Khomeinist, this vision is revived anew. To be sure, the change is in the pronouncements, not in the policies of Islamist internationalism which have never been abandoned.

The Sunni Arab world and the Shi'ite Iranian revolution

It is no contradiction to continue arguing that Khomeini's Shi'ite teachings – as revived by the new president of Iran, Ahmadinejad – had earlier succeeded in generating significant demonstrative spill-over effects on the neighborhood, while at the same time stating that the ideology of the Islamic revolution in Iran never affected the Arab-Sunni ideology of Islamism. There are, however, two exceptions concerning major issue areas of Shi'a Islam on Sunni Islamism. The first is Shi'ite clandestine action in the underground paired with "*taqiyya*/religious dissimulation." This Shi'ite religious doctrine of *taqiyya* was developed in early Islam to protect the Shi'a followers from a "brutally repressive campaign," as Moojan Momen informs us; he also adds that this deception "is considered lawful in Shi'ism."[57] Militant Sunni Islamic groups adopted this doctrine and the related practice of cunning. They gave the traditional Shi'ite practice of *taqiyya* the Sunni name "*iham*/deception of unbelievers." It is for this reason that honest Muslims avoid the industry of Islamic–Christian dialogue in which Islamists talk about tolerance and democracy while something else is on their minds. The second issue area of Shi'ite impact is the "*shahid*/martyrdom" death for legitimating terrorist actions of suicide bombing. These religious practices were hitherto alien to Sunni Islam and their very existence today heralds the impact of the Shi'ite revolution and of its mindset.

In looking at Egypt as a case in point for the described impact of the Iranian revolution, one can refer to the Egyptian political scientist Saad Eddin Ibrahim, who states in an authoritative article of 1980:

> The most regional effect on the future growth of Islamic militancy in Egypt and elsewhere is likely to come from the Iranian Revolution. Its success in dealing with the host of global, societal and individual issues ... would enhance Islamic militancy.[58]

Sixteen years later, S.E. Ibrahim published this article in his collection of essays aimed at drawing a balance based on earlier writings. Today, more than a quarter of a century later, the rightly predicted growth of Islamic militancy in Egypt,[59] spilling over to Algeria[60] and to elsewhere in the world of Islam following the Islamic revolution in Iran, proves to be only one aspect of a cross-sectarian Islamist internationalism. The ideology of discontent that bolsters the rise of political Islam also emerges from a development crisis and related problems. The Islamist education in the madrasas translates these concerns into an Islamist revolt against the existing order. These references do not support the view that the rise of political Islam is only – interpreted in a reductionist manner – a response to a pattern of social change related to an uneven economic development. It is rather argued that the internationalism of political Islam also reflects a civilizational project based on a worldview. In this capacity, it has much deeper-lying historical roots than a simple political ideology focused on the present discontent.

The revival of the Islamic civilizational project in an Islamist shape is coupled with the prevailing negative attitudes vis-à-vis the West and is embedded in a mix of the ills of disruptive development and increasing mobility. The spread of modern education and information systems is also among the factors that contribute to the ferment in Islamic societies as well as to exacerbating the legitimacy crisis of the existing secular political order. The rise of the West itself as a civilization – viewed in the Islamist narrative as a process that took place at the expense of the Islamic expansion – is also among the perceptual constraints.[61] Add to all of this the fact that the adoption of modernity did not work well. Under these conditions there was a need for an authentic promise, based on an Islamic dream of coping with the predicament. It was the Islamic revolution of Iran that pronounced such a promise. It failed to deliver, but the Islamic dream based on Islamist narrative continues to be alive as a challenge to world politics and to the existing world order.

The Islamic dream, embraced by a variety of Islamist movements but suppressed by the sophisticated security apparatus of the hated un-Islamic state, promises to do away with the disruptive effects of uneven development combined with the legitimacy crisis. All of the existing regimes in the Arab Sunni Middle East were challenged by the Islamic revolution in Iran. Ahead of it Michael Hudson published his work on this subject and stated: "Government by threat and coercion can temporarily hold people in check," but, as he further argues, "in the long run it probably exacerbates the basic grievances ... Arab political systems, whatever their ideology, have been singularly unsuccessful in developing the kind of institutionalized mass participation that social mobilization requires."[62]

This statement reflects Hudson's conclusions resulting from case studies of all Arab political systems and implicitly predicted an explosion. The prediction seemed to materialize in the aftermath of the Islamist revolution in Iran. The internationalism of Khomeini's "true Islam" that promised light at the end of the tunnel, combined with the ability to topple an authoritarian regime through an Islamic revolution, created under the described conditions a political earthquake throughout the Arab world and elsewhere in the Islamic civilization. Here again the reader is reminded of the fact that political Islam is much older than the variety "made in Iran." However, the Iranian revolution fueled the crisis situation in its articulation of an "Islamic dream" for uniting Sunni and Shi'ite Muslims in an "Islamic world revolution" based on an imagined Islamic *umma*. The Islamic diaspora in Europe has been included in this dream. The universal claim of "true Islam" has been based on:

a shared perception of one Islamic world revolution;
the belief in the existence of the unity of a cohesive Islamic *umma* under siege to be united against its Western oppressors through politicization and the direct action of jihad, while overlooking all ethnic and sectarian divisions and frictions within this imagined community;
a unique Islamic system of government, for both the state and the envisioned new world order to map the entire globe.

Clearly, this "true Islam" is conspicuously a political Islam, and is neither the Islamic faith itself nor a reflection of sectarian Shi'a Islam. Corresponding identity politics blurs the distinction between Islamism as political religion and the faith. The cultural meaning of Islam is translated into identity politics. At issue is basing the fault-lines of "us versus them." The identification of Iran with Islam in general as the "center of the universe" clashes herethrough, not only with the other, i.e. the West, but also with similar Arab claims to centrality in Islamic civilization. The application of the dichotomy "American-style Islam" versus "true Islam" proved to be most successful in the identity politics embedded into competing civilizational models. This happened long before Huntington invented his term for pointing at dreadful fault-lines.

What is identity politics and how does this concept – as used by the Islamist revolution of Iran – translate into the relations between Islam and the West, be it in the understanding of "Islam and the rest" or of "the West and the rest"?[63] In the article on identity politics added to the second edition of the *Routledge Encyclopedia of Government and Politics*, one reads:

> Makers of identity have always played a role in politics and have often been used as a device to create opposition to perceived oppression … The term identity politics is more commonly understood as a wave of political organization and contestations … Identities would serve … as the basis for producing new political agendas and social movements.[64]

Political Islam is the agenda of a civilizational project in the outlined understanding. At issue is an internationalism based on contemporary identity politics combined with transnational religion. In the perceptual confrontation with the West – which is also a political reality and not, as alleged by Halliday, a myth – Islamic identity serves as a platform for political agendas, as shown in the case of the revolution in Iran. In such a confrontation most Muslims take a stand against the West. Within the Islamic civilization, however, characterized as it is by great diversity, there are sectarian and ethnic divides that not only create other patterns of identity politics but also undermine any claim of being "the overall representative of one Islam." The Iranians and the Arabs, the Sunna and the Shi'a are paramount cases, not to speak of the great cultural diversity existing within Islam. The fragmentation of Iraq after the disastrous war is a case in point for a developing of sectarian tensions into hatred and bloody conflict.[65]

The use of identity politics as based on the allegation of an overall and, moreover, immutable Islamic identity, as the vehicle for mobilizing the world of Islam in the service of global jihad, is a double-edged sword. It serves the purpose of putting groups of jihadists, ready for action, into a better position. The case of Khomeinism, with its wishful thinking of mobilizing all Muslims under the leadership of Iran united by "true Islam," indicates the use of identity politics in a political concept for remaking the world. But this concept is undermined by the reality of ethnic and sectarian strife. The related distinctions are also coupled with identity patterns which the Khomeinist approach does not account for. Cultural patterns change with social transformation, and identity is no exception. The Iranian revolution has succeeded in changing the politico-cultural climate in the Middle East and even in the world of Islam at large, but it has failed to construct new collective identity patterns for uniting Sunni and Shi'ite Muslims, even though both share almost the same universalist worldview. However, the Iranian claims of leadership were not acceptable to Sunni Arabs. Having been accused of essentialism by some postmodern scholars known to be non-readers, I hasten to add to this statement that the allegation of an essential and immutable overall Islamic identity reflects an Islamist notion and is not my own position. In contrast, my thinking consistently relates religion and culture to change because both are always in flux. Those who read my books will know of this awareness. The accusation of essentialism is therefore baseless. A reference to my work at the "Culture Matters Project" of the Fletcher School is in place and the related research has resulted in the two volumes *Developing Cultures*.[66]

In short, identity politics which underpins commonalities in the service of the Shi'ite Iranian claim is based not only on an imagined *umma*-community, but also on shared resentments against the West. It is also articulated in a historical situation promoting defensive-cultural attitudes. However, the sharing of these attitudes does not imply the existence of a collective Islamic identity equally shared by Sunni Arabs and Shi'ite Iranians. In so arguing, I am contesting neither the idea of an Islamic civilizational identity nor that of a shared Islamic worldview.[67] However, this worldview is undermined by ethnic and sectarian divides as well as by the related local identities ever changing along with their environment. It follows that not only ill-devised Iranian policies but also the realities addressed have underpinned the failure of Iran to impose its views on all Muslims.

There also exists a constructed Arab political identity which stands in the way of the Iranian claims. Islam and nationalism, whether pan-Arab or local, are a framework for determining Arab identity.[68] Islam, by virtue of its claim to be a universal religion, maintains the belief that it is the absolute. In reality, there enter different Islamic societies with a great variety of cultures and identities. In this regard one may refer to Clifford Geertz's comparative analysis of Moroccan and Indonesian Islam[69] to reveal the unity and the diversity within the Islamic cultural system. In going beyond Geertz's appraisal by placing cultures in a broader context, I add to the term "culture" the other of "civilization" and do not use these interchangeably. The existence of an Islamic civilization is acknowledged, but the statement is made more specific by reference to the thousands of local cultures subdividing this civilization. In this regard I coined the term: "cultural diversity within civilizational unity." This notion also applies to other civilizations, such as the West. Identity politics in this understanding can be both civilizational and cultural: I am a Damascene Arab and a Muslim at the same time. Add to this the fact that people in the modern world are individual citizens of nation-states. Here the question arises of how the Islamic *umma* within the context of the Shi'ite Iranian call for an Islamist internationalism, once claimed by Khomeini, is in conflict with citizenship of the nation-state and with the cultural-political foundations of the Westphalian order of the international system of sovereign states. Ramazani states this conflict in the following context:

> Khomeini rejected ... the very idea of the nation-state on the ground that it is the creation of man's "weak mind." In other words, in Khomeini's ideal Islamic world order there would be no room for the modern secular post-Westphalia conception of the international system.[70]

In a traditional challenge to Iran's perception of itself as the "center of the universe," contemporary Sunni Arab Islamists like Mohammed Imara argue that Arabism and Islam are to be viewed as a unity. In a major book this Islamist states: "The universality of Islam as a religion does not deny local and domestic realities ... However, and despite its universal claims Islam asks its believers to arabize [*an yata'rrabu*] and this makes the specific Arab character of Islam."[71]

This Arab-centrism collides head-on with Khomeini's claim that Iran is the "center of the universe." Add to this inner-Islamic clash the realities of Islamic history. In contradiction to the provision of the Prophet that Arabs and non-Arabs/*ajam* are equals in Islam, historians are familiar with intentional or unintentional discrimination of non-Arab Muslims often related to an Arab-centric interpretation of Islam. The Shi'ite Iranians – earlier viewed as Mawali – were among the victims of this Arab-centrism and that is why they invented *taqiyya* to save their own lives. One also finds this Arab-centrism in the ideology of pan-Arab nationalism, which reduces universalist Islam to an Arabism, as is well known. Add to this the fact that neither universal Islam nor secular nationalism have ever succeeded in overcoming tribal identities and related loyalties.[72]

In summing up this section, it can be stated that the revival of Islamic universalism in the interpretation of an internationalism in a Shi'ite shape claimed by Iran is questionable. Iran is not the heart of the Islamic political revival and hence the justification for an "Iranian internationalism"[73] lacks firm foundation. The related claim of an overall Islamic identity politics clashes with the fact that Islam is in reality shaped by local cultures: African in Senegal, South Asian in Indonesia and Mediterranean in many Arab countries. Underlying this diversity is the fact that the production of meaning in different cultures takes place under socially different conditions and in socially different environments. There are "multiple identities in the Middle East."[74] It follows that the claim of Khomeinism to be accepted as an Islamic internationalism has no firm grounds and is in conflict with Arab and other local-cultural Islamic identities. It is also safe to conclude that in reality there is no unique, invariable Islamic identity that could be found in all Muslim countries. This allegation is an essentialism. Despite all diversity, there exists a common, if changing, Islamic worldview with some local-cultural variations. Although Islam is a religion based on precepts fixed in religious sources, the reality of the social production of meaning under historically diverse conditions and in geographically and culturally different regions prohibits any discussion of one Islam. Islamic realities are not a reflection of the scripture. All in all, the Iranian claim can be viewed as an ideological response to a specific historical situation, a politics of identity, but not Islam itself. The articulated claim may not be conducive to the realization of a united Islamic *umma*, but as a call to global jihad it could nonetheless lead to destabilizing the existing political regimes and threatening the status quo in the region, which in fact it did in the past. In the foreseeable future the competing Sunni internationalism presented in the preceding chapter is expected to capture the lead. Nevertheless, it is sadly acknowledged and repeated that the war in Iraq unwittingly brought Iran back to the fore after a seeming decline of Shi'ite internationalism. To what extent? This remains to be seen. Also, the Hezbullah war in Lebanon of July/August 2006, summarized by *The Economist* with the formula "Nasrallah Wins the War," contributed to boosting the legitimacy of Iran. Hezbullah acted as a proxy of Iran in a context of transnational religion and was even endorsed by the Sunni Muslim Brotherhood of Egypt.[75]

Conclusions and future prospects

The major conclusion can be stated in two steps, the first of which refers to the Islamic revolution in Iran as a source of change in the political development in the world of Islam at large and in particular in the Middle East. In its claim to be a world revolution in Islamic terms, it symbolizes the emergence of a state-run model of global jihad with Iran providing a hinterland. The Islamist world revolution breathed life into Islamist movements throughout the world of Islam and had also an impact on Europe.

The second step is related to qualifying the success of the revolution compared to its claims. It was a limited success because of the Shi'ite character of Iran. It constrained the impact to the extent that it could not become an accepted overall model to emulate. Therefore, the revolution as an Islamic upheaval against foreign dominance was successful in toppling its local proxy, the despotic government of the Shah. This was admired at the outset, but it was simultaneously rejected by Sunni Islamists in its claims to be an overall valid Islamic model. Both assessments are complementary to one another.

The conclusion of a limited impact has to be modified through a reference to the Shi'ite minorities in the world of Islam, be it in Lebanon, Iraq,

Saudi Arabia, Pakistan or the Gulf states. These communities have been more receptive to Iranian claims. In particular, in Iraq the Shi'ite majority has been able, as a special case, to establish its rule – even with US assistance – in the name of democracy. This fact increased Sunni resentment against the Shi'a and the USA as well. What are the general conclusions?

In the post-Khomeini era the rhetoric of the revolution has subsided, even though revived by Ahmadinejad. Under the rule of President Khatami the state divorced its outlook from Khomeinism in its rhetoric but not in its deeds. The ideology of global jihad as Shi'ite internationalism continues to be the major source of legitimacy for the Islamic state in Iran in the twenty-first century, in particular under the new president Ahmadinejad. In short, Khomeinism never ceased to prevail. This has been made abundantly clear with the so-called "election" of Ahmadinejad in 2005, who is – unlike his predecessor, masked with "dialogue" – an unmasked Khomeinist.

Iran is not only powerful in its revolutionary ideology. Iranian politics is also based on the power of oil and the unfolding of nuclear capabilities.

With hindsight, one is inclined to quote a statement made by a well-informed observer of militant Islam, the foreign policy editor of the *Financial Times*, Edward Mortimer, who later became an advisor of and speech-writer for Kofi Annan. He concluded from his observation in several Arab and non-Arab Islamic countries:

> The Iranian revolution may perhaps succeed in exporting itself, in the sense that it could help to inspire revolutionary change in some other Muslim countries. But it is impossible to imagine other Muslim countries adopting precisely the same laws and institutions as revolutionary Iran, for these reflect a specifically Iranian Islam, which is a product of Iranian history.[76]

This statement of Mortimer leads to another conclusion. The Iranian model has failed to be a revolution for export, although its spill-over effects have been taken and – despite all changes – should continue to be taken into serious consideration. Arab political counter-elites, committed to political Islam and consequently accepting the Iranian spirit of Islamic internationalism, are not willing to implement the Iranian model itself in the Sunni Arab world. Iranian jihadist internationalism has always been restricted to a limited impact. The Iraq war changed the situation to the benefit of Iran, to the extent that this country has resumed its involvement in international terrorism.

In a general conclusion to this Part II it can be stated that global jihad understood as a world revolution, be it in its Sunni or Shi'ite variety, claims to politically mobilize the Muslim *umma* in the pursuit of a new world order based on Islamic tenets. However, the fact that by and large there exists neither a cohesive Islamic political *umma* community nor an immutable and universal Islamic identity makes the limits of the claim clear. In the case of the Islamic revolution of Iran, the regime brought to power can no longer present itself as a model of upheaval against an oppressive regime. The ruling Mullahcracy in power has itself become more repressive than the political regime it overthrew, and its credibility has suffered accordingly. Now, even naïve observers are aware of the fact that no radical change, let alone a reformist transformation, ever took place. Instead, nuclear proliferation – parallel to the violation of human rights – has gone side by side with the deception of a dialogue between the civilizations.

The transition from the presidency of Mohammed Khatami, who had no real power, to that of Mahmud Ahmadinejad took place within the rule of Mullahs. Members of the Western-educated Iranian elite call for a reconciliation with the West. The Yale alumnus and former revolutionary Shahriar Rouhani wrote in *Time* magazine: "Iran has been evolving. Social, political and economic realities have caused the radicalism and revolutionary romanticism to subside. A new era of rationalism has dawned in our country ... It is now the time for peace and friendship."[77]

Certainly, the quoted call expresses more honesty than Khatami's dialogue of civilizations, but the question remains: How politically powerful are these segments of the Iranian elite? The issue is not the expression of goodwill, but rather the power of the Mullahcracy and the structure of the state. There is no democracy in Iran, period. Wishful thinking cannot be an adequate policy vis-à-vis Iran's political system of a "government of God," as this continues to prevail. The dialogue between civilizations proclaimed by Khatami was no more than a smokescreen ended by Ahmadinejad. Iran's threat to world politics is based on its development of nuclear capabilities. This nuclear proliferation in times of a continued growth of Sunni jihadism exacerbates the complex situation, but in one way also displays the isolation of Iran. The situation of a stand-off with the combined West – the USA and the EU – and the articulated will "to extinguish the state of Israel" (Ahmadinejad) expressed in a clear anti-Semitic jargon may contribute to some popularity in the world of Islam, but this popularity may make very little difference to the outcome described in this chapter. Shi'ite internationalism is much less significant to world politics than its Sunni competitor based on irregulars in a global connection of transnational religion. The question remains: Will this religionized challenge to the secular international system lead to a confrontation (this is real, not a myth), or would a successful reform Islam lead to secularization[78] that would end this confrontation? The conflict between the sacred and the secular has already entered world politics[79] and it affects both world politics and Europe. The rest of the book is focused on the impact of this process in Europe and on democracy, and the solution for the World of Islam for itself and for its relations to others.

Part III

Europe as a battlefield for the competing options

Islamization versus Europeanization resulting in Muslim Europe or Euro-Islam?

Introductory remarks

A never-ending series of challenges related to post 9/11 events taking place in Europe since 2004 seems to have convinced some politically interested Europeans, if not all, that their continent too has its own jihadist dilemma (see note 6 to Chapter 6). The intrusion of political Islam into Europe is contributing to turning it into a battlefield between the secular and the divine in the course of the return of the sacred. It is perplexing to watch the contradictory reality of Europeans abandoning their faith while the global religionization of politics and conflict enters Europe under conditions of Islamic immigration. At issue in the first place are values, worldviews and the understanding of political order. The integration of Muslim immigrants in European societies becomes a top priority. The alert has been the chain of events that stretch from the Madrid bombings on 11 March 2004, including the public execution of Theo van Gogh condemned as an unbeliever by the globally linked Islamist Mohammed Bouyeri in Amsterdam on 2 November 2004, and continuing the following year with the London assaults in July 2005. Some may not agree with including the uprising in the *banlieues de l'Islam* in Paris 2005 in this chain of events, nor with seeing the violent 2006 contestation of the *Jyllands-Posten* cartoons as a part of this conflict. Nevertheless, this is the case, and the facts on the ground compel us to acknowledge it as such. I am also convinced that the global outrage over Pope Benedict's call to dissociate religion in Islam from violent jihad is a part of this story. Intelligent Europeans have begun to grasp the issue: Islam matters to Europe in a situation of conflict. Multi-culturalists, however, continue not only to reject any reasoning on this issue, but also to prohibit others from engaging in such reasoning to any extent.

The relations between Europe and the Islamic civilization are determined by structural interconnectedness and in addition are deeply rooted in history.

The references made to the topicality of the issue dealt with in this part of the book, which was completed between 2003 and 2006, merely serve to underpin the argument that Europe is becoming the battlefield for a competition over the validity of European and Islamic or Islamist values within the EU itself. This is the new situation. On the grounds of my commitment against any Islamophobia and the rhetoric of a clash of civilizations, I take pains – as a Muslim reformist who with the former German president of Germany co-authored *Preventing the Clash of Civilizations* – to find a peaceful resolution of the conflict. A Muslim by faith and socialization, I have lived as an immigrant by status and a European by citizenship for the past four decades in Europe. This *conditio humana* compelled me to cope with the pending conflict, in bridging between the conflicting parties. It must be openly stated, in case the issues underpinning the conflict between Islam and the open society in Europe are overlooked, that no solution can be in sight. In this context, Fukuyama's Lipset Lecture is worth referring to, in view of the fact that Islamism has found a safe haven in the European democracies, contesting their values while simultaneously making full use of civil rights that the Islamist model of "God's rule" clearly despises. This ideology of Islamism, addressed in the context of Islamic immigration to Europe, indicates cultural differences that cannot be accommodated within the traditional wisdoms of multi-culturalism. In a conflict between European cultural relativism and Islamist neo-absolutism, it becomes clear that the Islamists are the winners of the ongoing war of ideas. It is legitimate to defend an open society against the enemy within, and to engage in this is not Islamophobia. I am both dismayed and amazed when Western atheists accuse me, a faithful Muslim, of this filth when I engage in critical thoughts about the issue and my own religion.

To make the issue clear: one is reminded of the fact that, after brutally killing the Dutch film-maker Theo van Gogh, the Islamist Mohammed Bouyeri used a knife to pin a letter to the body. Included in the letter was not only a threat to van Gogh's companion, Hirsi Ali, but also the warning phrase: "Europe! It is now your turn!"

Interestingly, this warning was not cited in the European press coverage on this issue, in line with the practiced rules of political correctness. This is clearly self-censorship. The source of this information is a public speech by the prime minister of the Netherlands, Jan Peter Balkenende, at a meeting of the project "Europe. A Beautiful Idea?" held in Rotterdam on 4 December 2004. I was there as a Muslim among the speakers. During his trial in 2005 Bouyeri showed no remorse and repeated his desire to kill "unbeliever Europeans" if he were to be released from prison. Clearly, this mindset precludes any rational communication and no multi-culturalism could ever accommodate such Islamists. Despite these facts, most European newspapers never stopped playing down the execution as an action committed by a loner, allegedly as a result of social marginalization. It is, however, a proven fact, evidenced both by the police and at court, that Bouyeri acted as a member of an Islamist connection in a network of transnational religion. This reference to the van-Gogh–Bouyeri story is made as an introductory note to ascertaining the real challenge. The following two chapters will endeavor to study both roots and constraints in an attempt to find a solution acceptable to Europeans and Muslim immigrants alike, as grounds for living in peace with one another.

This endeavor requires rational universal knowledge. In engaging in this analysis as a social scientist also trained in the sociology of religion and in history, I look at religion in the Durkheimian sense as a *fait social* embedded in a historical context.

With a view to history, authoritative historians suggest that Europe was founded by Charlemagne in the eighth century in the course of dealing with Islam. In the twenty-first century a similar challenge is on the agenda, and Europeans are asked to look at the historical roots of this conflict that go back to the early medieval Islamic expansion. Therefore, I refer to the classic by the Belgian historian Henri Pirenne, in which the phrase "*sans Mohammed, pas de Charlemagne*" was coined. Translated into a historical interpretation, this is to state that Europe was constituted in response to a challenge posed by the then expanding Islamic civilization. Since the authoritative Sayyid Qutb and his work, contemporary Islamists claim in their writings a return of history in terms of reviving collective memories for underpinning their related aspirations. Thus this book starts on the first page of its introduction with a questioning of the contention of an "end of history." The opposite, rather, is taking place. Unlike the jihad fighters of the earlier Islamic medieval *futuhat* expansion the bulk of today's Muslims are pouring into Europe peacefully within a massive Islamic *hijra*/migration, not as jihad warriors. Europe's jihadist cells are at present rather the exception, not the rule. In the course of a changing composition of the population, European values are being contested by the newcomers. The challenge to the identity of the continent is the pivotal issue that should not be silenced by political correctness, but it should equally not serve as grounds for fault-lines, as Huntington suggests it. Muslims and Europeans need common solutions and must engage in a dialogue of conflict resolution.

The increasing and intensifying Islamic migration to Europe is transforming this continent into a space heralding a new pattern of a Muslim–Western encounter. *The Economist*, in its report "Awkward Partners," describes the issue in this manner:

> Islam's fast rising profile in a continent ... [is creating] nervousness about Islam watering down Europe's Christian heritage ... Existential angst is nothing new for Europe's Christians ... Tensions are between a religion that in Europe is small but growing and one that is big but declining.

(12 February 2005)

In the same report the late prominent cardinal Jean-Marie Lustinger, a former bishop of Paris and an ex-Jew who converted to Christianity after surviving the Holocaust, is cited as stating: "There is a risk of Islam becoming a state-religion by the backdoor." I met Lustinger in Berlin in 2005 at Castle Hardenberg, debated with him, listened carefully to his concern about the Islamist new anti-Semitism spreading in France and shared his misgivings. Assaults on synagogues provide the evidence and should not be played down, but no general accusation is to be allowed. We need to remain rational and be balanced.

A part of the needed rationality is a research project linked to a workshop held in 1998 at the University of California Berkeley under the title "Islam and the Changing Identity in Europe." Back then, the pending issue was addressed and I was given the opportunity to present my concept of Euro-Islam designed to bridge Islam and Europe. In fact, the concept of Euro-Islam goes back to Paris, where it was first presented in 1992. It was taken up in Berkeley by the then directors of the Centers for Middle Eastern and European Studies Nezar AlSayyad and Manuel Castells, who published their edited volume *Muslim Europe or Euro-Islam?* (Lexington Books, 2002) reflecting the findings of the project mentioned. I claim the concept of Euro-Islam, first presented in Paris and published in French and German in 1992–5 before it was presented and published in the Berkeley context mentioned. Others use the notion "Euro-Islam" without a reference to its origin and often in a different, clearly distorted meaning. I prefer not to mention names, but nevertheless it is imperative to dissociate my reasoning on Euro-Islam from that of Tariq Ramadan, whom I consider a rival within Islam in Europe.

In contrast to any deceptive presentation, I state the issue plainly: Either Europe succeeds in the politics of integrating Muslim migrants as European "citizens of the heart," or the Islamist and Salafist leaders of this diaspora will manage to incrementally Islamize Europe while abusing the Islamic diaspora community, creating an "enclave" (John Kelsay) in Europe as a hinterland. This is taking place in a context of demographic change in Europe, combined with Islamic proselytization. The reasoning in Paris and Berkeley on this issue was continued at Cornell in a project chaired by Peter Katzenstein and Timothy Byrnes on "Religion in an Expanding Europe" (see the publication of the same title, Cambridge University Press, 2006). My contribution states the two competing options in its title: "Europeanization of Islam or the Islamization of Europe?" I continue this argument in this part of the book, clearly not in a rehash but in new line of thought. I contend that a challenge for a century's reasoning is at issue; it is not a matter for a single book or a lone scholar to engage with.

Unlike many of my fellow Muslims in the diaspora, I avoid the discourse of self-victimization combined with accusations aimed at others, whether of Islamophobia, Orientalism or racism. In fact, we Muslims do not constitute a so-called "race" but rather a transnational religious community. The application of a disputed concept of race, based in biology, to a religious community is not only misleading but also highly flawed. One cannot change one's assigned/attributed "race," but an African or a European or an Asian could indiscriminately share Islam and join its community by conversion. The Muslim community, comprising more than one and half a billion, and stretching from Asia to Africa and reaching out to Europe, does not constitute a "race." Members of the worldwide Islamic *umma*, as a transnational religious community, share values and worldview, but not biology. The self-victimizing discourse of some Muslims and the political correctness of some Europeans lead nowhere. Instead, we need common reasoning in the search for common solutions.

In this book I propose that my fellow Muslim immigrants and Europeans accept the religion-, ethnicity- and race-blind civilizational idea of Europe combined with a reform Islam as the grounds for bridging between one another. I embrace a multiple identity addressed in terms of a Euro-Islam. The substance of the notion of Euro-Islam is aimed at the incorporation of the European values of democracy, laïcité, civil society, pluralism, secular tolerance and individual human rights into Islamic thought. In doing this, identifying with the precedent of the Hellenization of Islam between the ninth and the twelfth centuries, which gave birth to medieval Islamic rationalism, is pertinent. The Muslims of today need to revive this tradition in their heritage to open their minds, thus insuring a better future against the claims of totalitarian political Islam.

Not only Muslims but also Europeans are challenged to do their homework. Cultural diversity is precious, but it also needs to have limits. In the *Economist* report on the Islamic jihadist assault in Amsterdam, one finds such ridiculing phrases as this: Those waging "an uncertain struggle to defend Western civilization ... to counter Islamist extremism [do this] by putting more emphasis on the rule of law and less on accommodating differences" ("Islam, Tolerance and the Dutch," *The Economist*, 2–8 April 2005, pp. 22–4). My chapter in the cited Cornell project carries the title "Democracy Against Difference." I acknowledge the acceptance of diversity wholeheartedly, but only on the foundation of accepting the basic rules of religious and cultural pluralism related to sharing civic core values. This is not a cultural relativism. Pluralism combines diversity with shared basic values.

In Europe, one needs a consensus between immigrants and Europeans over basic values. I maintain that Muslims living in Europe need to accept that an open society is a law-governed polity and that the related values are not negotiable for the sake of diversity. This is not a matter for ridiculing. The right to "individual choice, dissent or apostasy" needs to be defended. To use the phrasing of *The Economist*, this idea "might sound intolerant," but I do not share this sentiment. Some Europeans and *The Economist* seem to put a "respect for cultural diversity" and an indiscriminate "accommodating different values and faiths" above the idea of individual human rights, civil society and religious pluralism. In the Cornell project on "Religion in an Expanding Europe" I question this view and even reject it, as I continue to do here and throughout this book in a new line of reasoning.

Coming as a Muslim from Damascus to study in the Frankfurt School, I learned from my teacher Max Horkheimer, a Jewish Holocaust survivor, that the identity of Europe must be defended against any totalitarianism. Politicized shari'a and a jihadized Islam cannot be accommodated in a democratic Europe. The indifference of multi-culturalism distorts the issue. In addition to Horkheimer, I follow Sir Karl Popper's insight that intolerance cannot be admitted in the name of tolerance. From this point of view I contest reports like the one cited above, in which those who subscribe to the "idea that values are important" are being classified as "ideologues of the new right." To be sure, I'm not one of those. With my background in the Frankfurt School I was a "leftist" who grew as a Muslim under the intellectual influence of Jewish and Holocaust-survivor teachers. They established the Frankfurt School of Critical Theory from which I learned to appreciate Europe as "an island of freedom located in an ocean of despotic rule" (see note 15 to Chapter 6). Freedom needs to be defended against all totalitarianisms (Stalinism and Nazism). The cited Horkheimian phrasing is his legacy. It is not "new right" thinking to advocate defending Europe against undemocratic "foreigners." In my study of Islamism (to be distinguished from Islam) I come to the conclusion that it incorporates "the new totalitarianism" and therefore oppose it. In short, the problem is not only related to the Islamists in Europe, but also to those Europeans themselves plagued by their indifference.

Another authority for my reasoning is Ibn Khaldun, the great fourteenth-century Muslim philosopher. I refer to his *Muqaddina* [Prolegomena] for supporting my arguments. Ibn Khaldun founded the *ilm al-umran/* science of civilization and it is a pity that Huntington is not familiar with his work. For Ibn Khaldun an *asabiyya/esprit de corps* is the heart of any civilizational consciousness, therefore the strength or weakness of a civilization depends upon the commitment of its members to civilizational core values. In other words, *asabiyya* is the barometer for measuring and forecasting the condition of a civilizational identity. In short: it is not an indication of racism or nationalism if members of a civilization stand by their *asabiyya* as an awareness of self. In this regard, Europe should be no exception and it is entitled to a European *asabiyya*. It is incidental that the year 2006 (the 600th anniversary of Ibn Khaldun's death: 1406–2006) was commemorated on two pivotal occasions: in Granada, in the context of the "Alliance of Civilizations" (June) and in Tunis at the fourth Humanity Convention on "New Directions in the Humanities." I take the liberty – and ask for the tolerance of some readers – to mention that on both occasions I was given the honor of being a keynote speaker, and in both Granada and Tunis presented the ideas developed in this book, as based on Ibn Khaldun's thoughts. This is not "right-wing" but Enlightenment reasoning. I engage in a search for a Euro-Islamic *asabiyya* as a means of accommodation.

To be sure, neither in Islam nor in Europe is there a monolithic identity. In both civilizations there are always multiple identities that emerge from cultural diversity. These cultural and civilizational identities are historically related to different ages, as well as to local cultures. In the ensuing chapter I shall argue for the need to distinguish, with regard to Europe, between Christendom, stretching from Charlemagne to the Renaissance, and Western secular Europe, from the Renaissance onwards to the present day. Present-day Europe is characterized by uncertainty, oscillating between vanishing Christianity and crumbing secularity. From a dialogic Euro-Islamic perspective it is a healthy sign if a common European *asabiyya* can be shared. In contrast, a multi-culturalism that questions the identity of Europe and denies its values is doomed to decay. I believe that a cultural pluralism of binding core values combined with diversity is a better option than multi-culturalism. Europeans need to recognize that demanding Muslim immigrants embrace the idea of Europe requires its enhancement to what I term the "Euro-Islamic *asabiyya*." This is the right thing to do and creates the substance of the chapters of this Part III. It is highly important to note that the rejection of shari'a in Europe is not a "cultural racism." I take the liberty of mentioning that I descend from a centuries-old Muslim Damascene family of shari'a scholars and know that traditional shari'a is not the totalizing shari'a order envisioned by the Islamists against all historical facts.

In summing up these introductory remarks it can be stated with certainty that the Islamic and Islamist challenge to Europe create this century's core question. I am familiar with the objections and refer the objectors to the basic right of free speech and academic freedom. In my view, the recognition of ethical values of religion can be combined with laïcité, though in the limited understanding of a separation of politics from religion. Laïcité is a European idea, to be defended against Islamization jointly by pro-democracy Muslims and Europeans. In defense of the open society and of its principles, it needs to be spoken out candidly: Europe is not *dar al-Islam* (or, in the cover language of some, *dar al-shahada*), i.e. it is not an Islamic space but a civilization of its own, albeit an inclusive one that is open to others, including Muslims. These are, however, expected to become Europeans if they want to be part of Europe as their new home. It is acknowledged that Islamists and Salafists constitute a minority, but one that dominates the organized parts of the Islamic diaspora and thus is powerful. Islamists reject the idea of Europe and agitate in the ongoing war of ideas against the very democracy that is sheltering them and protecting them from prosecution in their Islamic countries of origin. It is sad to see these Islamists come to Europe but refuse to embrace its values of open society. The outcome is a conflict that reflects a possible scenario for the future of Europe in the late twenty-first century. I do not essentialize this conflict, but instead seek a peaceful solution to it. In concluding these introductory remarks, let it be said in passing and reiterated: freedom of speech is a basic individual human right to be taken at face value. Those academics, who undermine this right are challenged to reconsider! The story of the publication of this book is the background to the expression of this concern and for its repetition. I am sorry for this!

5   Political Islam and Europe in the twenty-first century

The return of history as the return of civilizations into world affairs

Often, even though wrongly, the rise of radical political Islam is viewed as an outcome of unbalanced US policies by some not so well-informed Europeans who are aiming at washing their hands of the matter in taking this attitude. Since the emergence of political Islam, however, Europe has been the traditional foe. The prophet of the ideology of third-worldism, Frantz Fanon, did not deal with this issue, but he wrote in his classic *The Wretched of the Earth* that Europe and the third world had long known each other equally as enemies and as friends. This very dichotomy of Europe and the third world is used at present by Islamists in their approach of historically rooted self-victimization; they translate this *tiers mondisme* into the new relationship between Europe and Islam and only then extend it to the West at large to include the USA. In fact, the USA is a latecomer on the fringes of this conflict. The Muslim outrage over the insensitive and offensive Mohammed cartoons published by the Danish newspaper *Jyllands Posten* extended to the entire European community and brought the conflict back to Europe. An editorialist of the German *Tagesspiegel* (Berlin), Bernd Ulrich, wrote in his column of 4 February 2006 that "the conflict comes back home, to Europe." Another editorialist of *International Herald Tribune*, John Vinocur, engaged in pondering how one is "Trying to Put Islam on Europe's Agenda" (21 September 2004, p. 2.)

Is Islamism a variety of third-worldism? I do not think so. It is a variety of religious fundamentalism inspired by the idea of a revival of a real Islamic-European history, even though enhanced and reshaped by an invention of tradition. It is something other than the "third world" bid for liberation. The relevance of the conflict over the Mohammed cartoons is the return of Europe in Islamic collective memory to the perception of a traditional "enemy of Islam," embedded in a war of ideas in an effort at a remaking of the world within the framework of the divine order of *Hakimiyyat Allah*, as Sayyid Qutb and his heirs envision the future.

The framework: preliminary notes and thoughts

Historically, the Mediterranean[1] was the boundary between the competing civilizations of Islam and of Europe. This is a fact presented by classical historians, who argue that the birth of Europe took place in the age of the Carolingians in a world-historical interaction with the still young but expanding Islamic civilization. The foundation of a European identity, which was by then basically Christian, as in the German term *"christliches Abendland,"* best describes the major characteristic of this epoch. This Western Christendom was, however, reshaped at the eve of the Renaissance. By then, Europe had changed under the impact of Hellenism, transferred to it via the Islamic civilization. In this context, Europe became secular and developed a new civilizational identity. Aside from the centuries-long episodes of Islamic presence in Europe, be it in *al-Andalus* or the Ottoman Balkans, the world of Islam was located beyond the southern and eastern Mediterranean boundaries. Contemporary Islamic migration to Europe has changed this feature: no Mediterranean boundary exists any more, because Islam is now within Europe itself. The weeklong Islamic uprising of October/November 2005 in the suburbs of Paris, much earlier described by Gilles Kepel as *"banlieues de l'Islam,"*[2] was an exemplary challenge to French society and reminded the Europeans of the fact that their boundary to Islam is no longer the Mediterranean border. The boundary is now within Europe in segregated cities. It is between the mainstream society and the Islamic enclaves of socially marginalized Muslim welfare-payment recipients.

One cannot deal properly with the Islamic parallel societies now existing throughout Europe and representing an ever-increasing community of a diasporic Islam. They comprised 20 million Muslims in the year 2006, living within most countries of the EU. The reminder of Paris was repeated through the global outrage over the Mohammed cartoons and the call for censorship of the press in Europe and, months later, of the Pope himself. A decade earlier, in my 1997 Global Village Lecture given at the traditional Ridder Husset of Stockholm under the title "Islam and Europe, Islam in Europe,"[3] I outlined the transition from an Islam at the southern and eastern Mediterranean boundaries to an Islam of diaspora existing within Europe itself. This is the subject-matter of the following analysis and deliberations.

The call by the diaspora leaders for a free space of Islam within Europe has been identified as a challenge to the validity of the identity of Europe within its own boundaries. This is a correct perception. Islam and Europe are two civilizations characterized by a historical relationship that has been described both positively, by a combination of intercultural borrowing and a cross-cultural fertilization, and negatively, by conflict and war. The latter assumed the historical shape of Islamic jihad, from the seventh century onwards, and in response to it the Christian crusades, characterized by historians as counter-jihad. The combination of jihad and crusade (see note 18) was a violent indication of a civilizational conflict translating ideas and worldviews into war in a medieval history of competition between two models of expansion. How can we alter this tradition in transforming the mindset of expansion into one of convergence?

In modern history the European expansion stretching from colonial conquests to the contemporary economic globalization has been accompanied by a vision of cultural Westernization. It first subdued the Islamic globalization model of *futuhat*[4] and then succeeded in mapping the world of Islam itself into the modern world intrinsically shaped by the design of Western civilization.[5] This has been a humiliation for Muslims, earlier subdued, but at present their rebellion goes beyond the call for more justice. At issue is a pursuit of a reversal of history. What does that mean? I contend most Europeans do not understand the nature of Islamic nostalgia and the related claims. A free debate on this issue is also suppressed.

In the introductory remarks to this Part III, the notion of collective memories has been introduced. At issue is the revival of the civilizational claim of Islam to return to dominance in the world. This "revolt against the West"[6] was articulated by Sayyid Qutb. The IR Oxford scholar Hedley Bull conceptualized it without knowing Qutb's work. At issue is not simply a revival of Islamic religious tenets or an expression of contestation of the hegemony of the West. The real issue is rather a competition over the order of the world in the twenty-first century. This is a fact, like it or not. Our present world time is determined by a new age of politicization of religion, of religionization of politics and of the culturalization of conflict.[7] This is the overall context in which secular Europe is challenged by the revival of Islam and becoming a battlefield[8] of an international conflict ignited by Islamism. Of course, a minority is acting for the mobilization of socially marginalized groups, but the issue is not restricted to this in that a combination of culture and religion is involved as mobilizatory ideology. At issue is a competition between two different understandings of the world at large envisioned for the twenty-first century.

While dissociating myself from Huntington's clash of civilizations, I do not deny the conflict and argue that one needs to grasp the return of history in the shape of a revival of historical collective memories. These are imbued by an invention of tradition and are also related to fantastic claims. To be sure, the history commemorated is not always the history that really happened. In this regard, two issues need to be clarified at the very outset and stated for the record. First, I reiterate that my relating of Islam and Europe to the revived debate on civilization is utterly free from the Huntingtonization of a "clash of civilizations" and equally from the bias of Orientalism. This dissociation has been made abundantly clear in the introductory remarks, but my critics compel me to reiterate endlessly. Second, the present analysis does not share the view of a sweeping globalization extended to shaping culture globally. Existing cultural diversity belies the contention of a global culture. Culture is meaning and global consumption is a different issue.

In going beyond the extremes of looking at culture either as a generator or as being generated, I view culture as a local production of meaning based on a worldview without denying an opening to cross-cultural civilizational values and norms. There is no essential culture: it is always changing in an interplay between structural and normative constraints.[9] Local cultures undermine the effects of globalization even though culture is always in a state of flux, but it does not mechanically reflect economic realities, as some reductionists believe. In fact, what is named "McCulture," allegedly presented as evidence for a cultural globalization, is nothing more than a spread of the American popular culture of consumption and the use of modern communications technology. To be sure, neither the eating of a hamburger nor the use of the internet by a Muslim or an Islamist affects his/her culture or worldview. The latter is related to values, norms, symbols and traditions which underpin a worldview of an imagined or real distinct *umma* community of Islam. Islamists drink Coca-Cola, wear jeans and make full use of computers/internet for their jihad. At the same time they hate the West and wage global jihad – with the assistance of Western technology – against the validity of its values. For them, this is no contradiction. To be sure, the anti-Western culture of the Islamic diaspora in Europe should not be equated with the native culture of the country of origin. The Turks of Berlin and the Maghrebian Arabs of the suburbs of Paris are culturally quite different from the native Turks of Turkey and the Algerians of Algeria. Nevertheless, their ethnicity serves as a basis for them to resist becoming Europeans, and culturally speaking they are not Europeans in their views. Culture is changeable, so how can this be changed? This is the concern of the argument in the final part of this book.

At the same time as these topical issues are addressed, the historical constraints related to the return of civilizations will be borne in mind. In inquiring into the return of history in collective memories, the following analysis takes as its source of inspiration not Huntington but Ibn Khaldun, who is the real authority in the study of civilizations, as acknowledged by the great twentieth-century historian Arnold Toynbee. In his *Muqaddima* [Prolegomena] Ibn Khaldun laid the foundations for what he labeled "*ilm al-umram*/science of civilization."[10] Following in his footsteps, Toynbee reconstructed the history of humankind in his six-volume *Study of History* as a history of civilizations. In addition to these two great authorities I also refer to Raymond Aron's book *Paix et guerre entre les nations*, published at the height of the Cold War. Aron argued that bipolarity is nothing but a "veil" that conceals the real divide within humanity, for which he coined the term "the heterogeneity of civilizations."[11] Despite his fame, Huntington is a newcomer to the study both of Islam and of civilizations, and therefore his work is not only biased, but also replete with scholarly flaws. For these reasons alone, any serious student of these issue needs to dissociate the argument concerning the return of civilizations from any Huntingtonization and related bias. Having stated these reservations, I hasten to add that I beware of any demonization of Huntington. I acknowledge his contribution in introducing the study of civilizations to IR, but we need to overcome his bias and go beyond him, as well as beyond the other extreme as expressed in the work of Albert Houranis and his peers in Middle Eastern and Islamic Studies. All of these moralists condemn the critics of Islam, accusing them of regarding "the enemy other" as imaginary and claiming that they have the truth of the matter while they in fact overlook the real issues. Europe and world disorder are issues that have nothing to do with any Orientalism or related moralistic bias. The Islamic presence in Europe is related to conflicts that have to be addressed if they are to be resolved by both parties in peace and mutual understanding.[12]

In our present world there is a "war of ideas" taking place in Europe. This has nothing to do with the idea of a clash of civilizations. It is true that the competing ideas and *Weltanschauungen* (worldviews related to ideologies) are based in concrete rival civilizations. That said, it must be added that civilizational entities are never monolithic in character. Throughout this third part of the book, which deals with Europe as a battlefield of inter-civilizational conflict between rival normative orientations, a vision of a Euro-Islam (see notes 46 and 47) is presented with the aim of bridging the divide between the competing and conflicting civilizational entities: for they can change in order to come to terms with one another. In this context one can state the conflict and beware of essentializing it.

To the dislike of most of the leaders of the organized part of the Islamic diaspora (they represent foremost no more than 10 per cent of it) I maintain that it is most important to acknowledge the existence of many Islams. Despite the ideological assertions to the contrary, there is *not* one essential Islam, in Europe or anywhere else. Therefore, in Europe there can be a specifically European variety of Islam, a Euro-Islam for which for decades I have been at pains to lay the needed foundations. I continue to be faithful to my profession of social science and thus refrain from indulging in any wishful thinking or any undue culturalist harmonization. As a scholar standing in the Durkheimian tradition of the study of religion, I look at Islam as a *fait social*. In so doing, I see a conflict at work, and not what Goody of today and Hourani of yesterday have claimed to see: cultural harmony, disturbed only by power, prejudice and some so-called misunderstandings. Political Islam is a reality and Euro-Islam is no more than a vision for a better future.

The point of departure and the core issue

Since the demise of the Cold War and its East–West conflict, one can no longer state with certainty the major traits of the present post-bipolar and post-9/11 crisis-ridden world order. It would seem to be foolish to share the views related to the opposite extremes of a militarily designed concept of "war on terrorism" US-style (George W. Bush), on the one hand, and the deception of a "dialogue between the civilizations" Iranian-style (Mohammed Khatami) on the other. An Islamic–Western dialogue that overlooks the challenges on both sides is deprived of honesty and leads nowhere in our time of disarray, turmoil and disorder. Of course, there are better examples for a promising dialogue.[13]

The core issue, as outlined in the introduction to this book, is political Islam's questioning of the secular foundations of the existing Westphalian world order. The point of departure for grasping the issue in an era of the cultural turn is dealing with the context of the related return of civilizations as just that – a return, not an "end of history." The revival of collective historical memories underpinning the war of ideas is accompanied by a religionization of these issues. From this emerges the Islamist challenge to the secular world order in a bid for an Islamic order. This is a general claim, but it touches on the European Union giving a home to 20 million Muslims, because it undermines the integration of Muslim immigrants as European "citizens of the heart." Islamists and Salafists teach even European-born Muslims that they are members of an imagined *umma*,[14] not a European citizenry.

Since the assaults of 11 March 2004 in Madrid, 2 November 2004 in Amsterdam and 7 July 2005 in London, the Paris uprising in October/ November 2005 and the cartoons conflict in 2006, Europe's opinion leaders and decision-makers have started to acknowledge the core issue, namely the Muslim contestation of the European secular order. Some seem to make a real effort to understand. However, there is a lack of the knowledge required for a better grasp of Islam and of its relationship to Europe within the history of civilizations in an age of Islamisms.

Some appreciate the alert and acknowledge the European ignorance of it: as one of the Danish cartoonists stated: "We Danes are naïve, we know nothing about Islam and its people." One is compelled to ask: "So why then this provocation with the cartoons?" This ignorance is as rigid as the belief by Salafist Muslims in an essential Islam. Fleming Rose, the editor of *Jyl-lands Posten*, the paper responsible for the publication of the Mohammed cartoons, acknowledges in an essay that Europe has opened its doors to an influx of Muslim immigrants, although without abandoning the concept of the ethnic European; the implication is that Muslims remain aliens in a pre-dominantly ethnic Europe. He also acknowledges that Europe supplies these immigrants with generous welfare-state payments, this without giving them any incentive to work for their living. This is correct, as is the conclusion that "[i]t is no longer the Middle East, but at present rather Europe becoming the major source of Islamist terrorism."[15] However, Fleming Rose fails to grasp the overall issue even though he rightly recommends that Europeans should de-ethnicize their conception of what is European and change the welfare state. One cannot at one and the same time endorse European values against the multi-culturalist approach of cultural relativism and ask Muslims – as Rose does – to accept the stupid defense of the Mohammed cartoons with the irrational argument that "The publication was an act of inclusion, not of exclusion." This pseudo-argument is, rather, evidence that those Europeans do not yet understand Islam and Muslims. They will therefore continue to be unable to deal with its challenge.

The European diaspora of Islam is embedded in the networking of a transnational religion that shapes the worldview and the action of the people. If this is not well understood as a major lesson of the cartoon conflict, then the civilizational challenge to the values of Europe will not be understood either. The outrage over these dreadful cartoons goes far beyond the contestation of distasteful European behavior. However, the cartoons themselves reveal the cultural conflict between Europe and its Islamic diaspora as an extension of *dar al-Islam* within the West itself. It is simply incredible how an act of cultural provocation becomes, in the European mind of Fleming Rose, an act of inclusion. This reveals not only an ignorance of Islam but also a decay of "human wisdom." Unlike Muslims, who in an invented tradition are at pains to rediscover their civilization as an imagined *umma* community, the people of Western Europe and Japan seem to disregard "revitalizing culture and intelligence."[16] People who lack this sentiment of the cultural self fail to realize that, for its survival, any civilization needs that sense of self-awareness for which Ibn Khaldun coined the term *asabiyya,* a kind of *esprit de corps*, a concept which is to be explained shortly. It follows that there is a growing gap in cultural attitudes between Muslims pouring into Europe as migrants/*muhajirun* (in the Islamic sense) and the ethnic Europeans, declining because of an extremely low birth rate. While Muslims, in a strong self-assertive sentiment, believe they know well who they are, most Europeans painfully engage in a self-distorting questioning of themselves, and some even deny the existence of an overall European civilizational identity altogether. For Ibn Khaldun (see note 10) each vivid civilization is based on a spirit of *asabiyya*, best translated with Montesquieu's term *"esprit de corps,"* as already mentioned. The rise and decline of civilizations is related by Ibn Khaldun to the state of *asabiyya*: if this is strong, then a civilization thrives; when it weakens, then the decay begins. As a Muslim immigrant living in Europe, I believe I can see a very weak European *asabiyya* facing the strong self-assertive sentiments of Muslim newcomers. It is intriguing to see those Europeans supporting the immigrants' strong cultural identity in the name of justice, while simultaneously dismissing the same notion with regard to Europe as a "racist" attitude and a "right-wing" orientation. These Europeans overlook the potential of an Islamization of Europe in the name of identity politics. Both multi-culturists and Islamists and equally Euro-centric Europeans fail to understand that the Europeanization of Islam is the best way to combat any exclusion of Muslims. In our age, described as a "cultural turn," one needs to avoid fault-lines and to enhance an *asabiyya* of Europe into a Euro-Islamic *asabiyya*. If no distinction between Islam and Islamism is made, alongside efforts to make Muslims in Europe European "citizens of the heart,"[17] then a European accommodation of both the core and the overall issue as a way out of the crisis will continue to be lacking, and the long-term implication will be the piecemeal Islamization of Europe.

The contemporary civilizational challenge to Europe has a precedent in history. In fact, the foundation of Europe as Western Christendom in the age of Charlemagne was related to a response to the rise of Islam, as one can learn from the already quoted work of the historian Henri Pirenne. In my 1999 book *Kreuzzug und Djihad* (see note 18), I revive the classical interpretation presented by Pirenne, not only for a better reading of the history of civilizations, but also for relating this precedent to the present day. Let me first outline my understanding of the terms employed. Civilizations are viewed as historical that is changable entities, being a grouping of local cultures related to one another through sharing similarities in norms, values and worldviews. In this understanding there is an *umma* civilization rooted in the history of Islam. One should be aware of the distinction between this fact of diversity and the contemporary "reimagining the *umma*." The Islamic civilization is not a construction, but rather a real cross-cultural entity. It is wrong to equate culture and civilizations, or to use the terms interchangeably, as is done by Huntington and many others. As stated, there exists an Islamic civilization – and of course a Western European one – which is united by a cross-cultural identity and by a shared worldview. Any civilizational entity is subdivided into a great variety of local cultures. Therefore in Islam, the notion and reality of cultural diversity do not stand in contradiction to this civilizational unity, be it in the past or at present. This is also reflected in the Islamic diaspora of Europe. Muslim immigrants claim to stand as one block of Islam vis-à-vis Europe, but this very same diaspora is subdivided along cultural, ethnic and even sectarian lines which at times develop into fault-lines and cause great tensions within the Islamic community itself. In their interaction with Europeans, Turkish Muslims claim an Islamic identity, without, however, abandoning ethnicity. A Turk would rarely go to a non-Turkish mosque in Berlin or Frankfurt. Existing mosques in Europe are divided along ethnic and sectarian lines. Nevertheless, the presentation of the European Islamic diaspora as one civilizational entity of *dar al-Islam* in Europe continues to be salient.

The assumption: political Islam and its contemporary challenge to the European civilization

In this chapter and throughout my work I subscribe to the view of the Belgian historian Henri Pirenne relating the birth of the civilization known as Christian Europe. This emerged in the Carolingian age in the late eighth century as a response to the challenge of expanding Islam. Charlemagne, "the founder of Europe," based this process on the worldview of Western Christianity. In the view of Pirenne, this formation of Europe took place in response to the challenge of rising Islam, which had succeeded in dominating the Mediterranean, weakening and even undermining the Roman Empire. These processes were launched with the transformation of the Mediterranean from the Roman *mare nostrum* into an Islamic sea, culminating in the jihad intrusion into Europe after the Muslim conquest of Spain in 711. In this context Henri Pirenne coined the term "*sans Mahomet, pas de Charlemagne*." Most historians agree – with some nuances and modifications – with the view that Charlemagne was the "founder of Europe," but some – like the German Horst Fuhrmann (see note 18) – completely overlook the role of Islam in a disturbingly Germanic and Euro-centric manner. Fuhrmann declines to even mention Islam. In passing, I should mention as a Muslim scholar working in Germany that there is no single chair of Islamic history in any department of history throughout that country. My Goettingen chair in International Relations (with a focus on Islamology) will be transferred to pedagogy upon my retirement. Some Europeans – in particular the Germans – close their eyes and think they do not need the study of Islam's impact on Europe.

In reviving the work of Henri Pirenne and in considering the shift to secular Europe in the Renaissance, we can divide the history of occidental Europe into two different entities: "Christendom" and the secular West.[18] I follow Pirenne in arguing that the first wave of jihad expansion led to a weakening of the Roman Empire and subsequently contributed to the end of its dominance over the Mediterranean. This historical context facilitated the rise of Charlemagne as founder of Europe. The challenge of jihad as an expression of Islamic expansion continues to be essential to the under-standing of the history of Western Europe.[19] Europe's reply to the Islamic conquests was the crusades, as one German historian of the crusades argues. However, the history of Islam and Europe is not restricted to the rivalry of jihad and crusade. There has been a mutual impact based on cross-civilizational fertilization. Medieval Islam was Hellenized, and Europe was fertilized by an interaction with the Islamic civilization, in the course of which Europeans adopted an Islamic version of Hellenism. This led to the Renaissance, as Leslie Lipson contends. Analogously to the European Renaissance[20] one can speak of the rise of the West – in distinction to European Christendom – as a new civilization with a secular worldview, inspired by Athens and no longer by Jerusalem. While I refer to Pirenne for understanding Carolingian Christendom, I draw on the theorist of civiliza-tions, Leslie Lipson, for grasping the nature of the Renaissance. In his work he addresses the issue in this manner:

> The chief reason why there was such a difference in the West before and after the Renaissance ... can be summarized in one sentence: the main source of Europe's inspiration shifted from Christianity back to Greece, from Jerusalem to Athens.[21]

and one page later he significantly notes: "Aristotle crept back into Europe by the side door. His return was due to the Arabs who had become acquainted with Greek thinkers" (ibid.).

It is deplorable that these positive facts and the related arguments of mutual cultural borrowing are not present at all in the collective memories of Muslims today, nor are they considered in Huntington's essentialist "clash" approach. On the basis of these facts it follows that the emergence of the new civilization of the West in Europe is also indebted to Islam, specifically to its tradition of Islamo-Aristotelian rationalism. The Islamic civilizational contribution is the passing of the great Greek legacy to the Europeans[22] in an Islamically designed new version. In both cases, i.e. that of Christian Europe and that of the secular West, the role of Islamic civilization was pivotal in determining the formation of Europe and of its identity. This applies to both the negative (threat) and positive (fertilization) aspects in inter-civilizational history. Islamic medieval jihad smoothed the way for Charlemagne, and the passing of Hellenism to Europe contributed to bolstering the Renaissance as a component in the rise of the West. What can we learn from this history in the context of the contemporary double challenge posed by Islam and Islamism to Europe?

Unlike in the past, contemporary Muslims do not come to Europe as jihad fighters, but peacefully, within the context of massive Islamic migration. Given the fact that they are not jihad warriors, why the talk of a challenge? At first, a distinction between Islam and Islamism is needed. Both generate challenges that are related but different from one another. Islam is a universal religion that includes a model of proselytization/*da'wa* revolving around one civilizational worldview. This is a challenge. The challenge of Islamism or political Islam is different. In reviving collective historical memories it refers to the early project jihad as the first effort of this kind in world history. Islamism claims the return of this history. The revival of collective memories propagates that model. It is true that Islamic jihad expansion failed to achieve the envisioned Islamic mapping of the world in comparison to global Westernization,[23] which did succeed in reaching this goal. Islamic jihad expansion led to establishing a world empire stretching from China to the Atlantic[24] but it failed to give birth to a global system covering the entire world. The rise of the West was not only indebted to what the Japanese professor Nemoto (see note 16) called "intelligence and culture" – as based on Hellenism – but also to inventions resulting in the new technology of war growing within the framework described by historian Geoffrey Parker as a "military revolution." Parker concludes: "If the dynamics of European overseas expansion are to be fully comprehended, a study of the changing military balance between the West and the rest is essential."[25] With the power of the new means of military technology employed for the expansion of Europe, the West was in a position first to halt Islamic jihad expansion, then to roll Muslims back, and finally to replace the civilizational primacy of Islam with its own. These are the roots of the present resentment of the West, which is not simply a backlash against flawed US policies but primarily a revolt against the Western globalization model as rooted in Europe. It is neither Palestine nor the Iraq war, but rather this world-historical context that determines the contemporary relationship between Islam and Europe.

Indeed, the contemporary "revolt against the West" envisions a de- Westernization of the world. The Islamists seek to re-establish Islamic rule and a competitive model of globalization. In short, the contemporary Salafist Islamic and Islamist challenges to Europe are not simply directed against Western hegemony: they herald a claim implying much more than that. This historical observation is stated by a Muslim educated in the scholarly, not apologetic, study of history. At issue is understanding what the return of the civilizations is all about – not defending or excusing it, but rather explaining world politics with a focus on Europe.

Under the presently prevailing conditions of self-censorship, with political correctness curtailing freedom of speech and of research, only a few Western scholars dare to address the real issue in question, even though it is most meaningful and even essential for the future of the European Union. Among the few scholars who do dare, one finds John Kelsay, who rejects the downplaying of the contemporary revival of Islamic collective memories in the contemporary ongoing war of ideas. The revived memories are both selective and based on an invention. They include the claim for an Islamic primacy. In the introduction to this book (see pp. 30–2) quoted

> the contemporary call for revival among Muslims is not a simple nostalgia at length for explaining that. As Kelsay continues, the mood of Islamist ideologies is not nostalgia, but outrage over the state of the world ... The call for renewal, then, relates to Islam and to its mission.[26]

In putting the blame for the downfall of Islam on Europe – and this, in the Muslim perception of history, is exactly what went wrong – Muslims are called upon in a mobilizatory manner to resume the *da'wa*/proselytization parallel to the pursuit of a de-Westernization. At this conjuncture the worldviews of Salafists and Islamists converge and their challenges resemble one another. This drive reaches Europe itself through migration and is articulated in some aspects of the political culture of the mosques in major European cities. At these mosques and also in faith schools, imported Imams teach the worldview summarized in Kelsay's statement as grounds for an educational socialization of young Muslims born in Europe in an Islamist mindset of incitement. Instead of a European competitive effort to win the hearts and minds of Muslims born in Europe (see note 17), multiculturists speak of tolerance, by which they mean their indifference and "anything goes" attitude. This, in Ibn Khaldun's terms, is an indication of a weak European *asabiyya*. The acceptance of diversity – if related to pluralism – is bound to rules.

The aspiration to de-center the West is directed by the will to re-establish the supremacy of Islam. The writers involved in this pattern of contemporary revivalism, like those to whom Kelsay refers, are mostly contemporaries of political Islam who share with Salafism the idea of *siyadet*/primacy of Islam. It is valid not only for the world of Islam itself, but globally. To understand this sentiment properly we need to grasp the role of civilizations in history, old and new. Why is the West civilizationally in crisis? It is economically and military still dominant, but in its *asabiyya/* civilizational awareness it is very weak. To explain this, a recourse to Ibn Khaldun, the great Islamic philosopher of the fourteenth century, seems to be most helpful.

As already stated, Ibn Khaldun measures the strength of a civilization by viewing the state of its morality, for which he coined the term *asabiyya*, i.e. its *esprit de corps*. In fact, *asabiyya* is a value system that underpins culture and the intelligence of its people. With this notion, Ibn Khaldun addresses the rise and fall of civilizations in terms of *asabiyya*.[27] As a Muslim living in Europe I observe how the European *asabiyya*, i.e. its value system, is rapidly declining. The decay is self-perceived as a progressive cultural relativism. Ernest Gellner calls for a revival of enlightenment against it.[28] The reasoning pursued in this chapter revolves around the challenge to the idea of Europe and to its cultural values undergoing a crisis. I am concerned about including Muslims living in Europe into the existing polity for overcoming an "other-ing" of Islam and of its believers. I am of the view that only a culturally healthy Europe, i.e. one with a stable identity, can accomplish this task. America is in a position to make Americans of Muslims living there, because of its inclusive strong identity. Europe fails in this venture. My life in Germany of more than four decades is an individual's evidence for this statement. The ethnic concept of "a German" precludes even Muslims born in Germany, as ethnic "non-Germans." Under these conditions Europe is not in a position to respond to the civilizational challenge to the West as a whole and to its European core. In this context, the idea of a return of history, as already mentioned, is most appealing to excluded Muslims in Europe, with their mosque indoctrination based on identity politics and a war of collective memories. This is the other side of the coin.

Europe and the hub of the world of Islam, located geographically around the Mediterranean,[29] are linked to one another in terms of both hostility and cross-cultural fertilization. A positioning of the Mediterranean as the center of the history of civilizations is required. In this context it is asked whether the Mediterranean has been and continues to be a *"Grenze oder Bruecke/borderline or bridge"* between Europe and the world of Islam (see note 1). As repeatedly stated, the inter-civilizational boundaries between Europe and Islam are blurry. It is clear that viewing the Mediterranean in the historical perspective of conflicting civilizations, i.e. of being "borderline or bridge," is not enough for understanding the present, when migration from the Islamic south of the Mediterranean to the European north of it is creating the major issue. At this point I reiterate my reference to the Berkeley and Cornell research done on Islamic migration and on the changing identity of Europe. In short, Islam exists not only in the south of the Mediterranean, but now within Europe itself.[30] It follows that migration and its cultural-demographic effects are at the center of the contemporary challenge incorporated into inter-civilizational history. A range of authors, in dealing with this issue, restrict their view to political Islam spreading to a focus on a specific ideological expression. They mostly overlook the fact that Islamism is directed against Western civilization and its concept of world order. Of course, there is a security concern, but the issue is broader.[31] In order to avoid the misconception of relating the conflictual civilizational issues to security in world politics, in 1999 I joined the then president of Germany Roman Herzog in his call to avert any potential for a clash. This effort does not deny existing threats – in stating that there is a need to prevent something that we do not like, we already concede that it exists. It is recognized that an inter-civilizational conflict exists and that mediation may contribute to what is needed for "preventing the clash of civilizations."[32] My contribution to this endeavor focuses on "cross-cultural bridging"[33] for mediating between Europe and Islam, as the parties of the inter-civilizational conflict. The policy recommendation is a problem-focused inter-civilizational dialogue as a means for conflict resolution. The first requirement for this endeavor is to acknowledge the conflict, and this has to be accompanied by a normative standing that it can be averted. In this spirit the orientation of this study on Europe and Islam is based on a normative position and is combined with a realism aimed at going beyond the two extremes of power, as contrasted with wishful thinking.

In determining the pending challenges and the conflicts ignited, in this context one can speak according to the revival of collective memories, simultaneity, globalization and fragmentation. This notion will be spelled out in the next section. The history-based inter-civilizational conflict between Islamic and European civilizations over power and values escalates in its present form as the dichotomy between structural globalization and cultural fragmentation creates more tensions. The intensifying conflict is embedded in transnational religion.

Transnational religion, universalization, globalization and fragmentation: scenarios for Islam and Europe?

With regard to Western Europe we need to ask the following questions: Do Islam and Europe as civilizations undergo a convergence under the impact of a globalization, which incorporates them into one global civilization? Is there such a thing as a techno-scientific civilization? Does the world, as a global village, unite Islam and Europe within the framework of migration? These are tough questions. Some established views and assumptions are challenged by hard facts pointing to a conflict. This is something different from the benign talk about an alleged misunderstanding between civilizations.

In a search for appropriate answers the best way to start is to clarify what the global village idea is all about. In citing Brzezinski, the late IR scholar Hedley Bull refers to the idea of "shrinking of the globe" as a result of the mutual awareness and interaction among culturally different societies. The question addressed by Bull is the premature conclusion that this "shrinking" has contributed to overcoming cultural differences. Bull is of the view that this shrinking "does not in itself create a unity of outlook and has not in fact done so ... the paradox of our time is that humanity is becoming more unified and more fragmented."[34]

In my work I combine the reference to Geertz's delineation of culture as "local production of meaning" with the quoted criticism forwarded by Bull. On this combination I rest my assumption, first, that the "globalization of culture" is wrong – there are no supporting realities – and second, that any effort at pursuing this goal of a cultural standardization of the world will fail. The notion of a cultural global village is nothing less than a constructed illusion. On these grounds I distinguish between the concept of globalization and that of universalization. Each refers to different issue areas. On these grounds I present my empirical observations of a cultural fragmentation rather than engaging in wrongly assumed standardization as the ideology of globalism.

In the following I shall outline the distinction between globalization and universalization, already reflected in the language itself. The term "globe" refers to the tangible, and globalization can therefore only be related to material structures. In contrast, value systems are intangible: they can only be universalized, definitely not globalized. Empirically one can ascertain a globalization of the structures that have originated and unfolded in Europe in the course of European expansion, be it in economy (world economy), politics (international system of states), transport or communication. However, there is no evidence for supporting the contention of a successful process of universalization of Western values parallel to globalization. It is a fact that the aspired-to universalization does not match with the globalization that has been accomplished. In particular, in today's cultural turn, the currently prevailing identity politics does not seem promising. There is no progress in the direction of more universalization. In Europe the Islamic diaspora presents its particularism with a claim for a universalism. And what about the USA?

A world historical novelty is the shift of centrality on almost all levels from Europe to the USA since 1945. And in the twenty-first century the center of Western civilization will continue – to the dislike of Europeans – to shift from Western Europe to North America. To be sure, American values – such as democracy, secularity and human rights – derive from Western European values, but they are not yet accepted worldwide. The failed democratization of Iraq, along with the unsuccessful introduction of Western values, is a prominent case in point. To be sure, Western values are a different concept from what is perceived to be the "American way of life" based on a perception of a popular US-American culture of consumerism. I believe the concept of McWorld is a construction, not a reality,[35] and it contributes to a diversion from the values debate to the extent of derailing it, distracting from the substance. I refrain here from addressing the US–

European value divide in order to keep the focus on Islam. I therefore restrict the reference to the contemporary pattern of consumption American-style, combined with what Max Horkheimer criticized as "instrumental reason,"[36] to argue that this is not an expression of culture, nor an expression of a cultural modernity. Technical communication is not tantamount to a cultural discourse, and technical rationality is not a culture-based reason. It is simply instrumental. The spread of instrumental reason is not yet a cultural globalization, but its globality leads to a loss of meaning and therefore to the crisis of meaning, be it in the West or in Islam. There are Muslims – even those who have studied in the West – who embrace science and technology, but vehemently reject the European cultural values underpinning them.

The described simultaneity of universalization, globalization and fragmentation – also related to the return of the sacred within the confines of transnational religion – is exacerbated and intercepted by global immigration of Muslims to Europe. This phenomenon has to be placed in the context of the "Global Migration Crisis."[37] A closer look at the issue shows that the shrinking of the world does bring people closer to one another physically, but not culturally. The generated physical closeness leads to cultural conflicts. The world of Islam exists in Europe in enclaves. This is no civilizational reconciliation. I allow myself a quote from the text of my published Bosch Lecture of 1994, which includes these phrases:

> The civilizational conflict between Islam and Europe takes place parallel to the drive toward de-Westernization of the world under circumstances of a simultaneity of structural globalization and cultural fragmentation ... In our age of global migration ... this conflict between the civilizations does not only occur on the external level, but within the West itself.[38]

The facts referred to in this statement underpin the position presented in this chapter, namely that Europe is becoming the battlefield for the competition between the concept of order of political Islam and the idea of Europe. Only an integration of incoming Muslim immigrants to a position of "citizens of the heart" seems to provide a way out of this impasse. The general phenomenon of cultural fragmentation growing from globalization is reflected in Europe itself through the mushrooming of Islamic parallel societies (*Parallelgesellschaften*). These can be described in the plain language of American scholar John Kelsay: "the increased presence of Muslims in Europe ... [is] a presence that makes for a more intense interaction ... than ever before."[39]

And then he adds that this presence is intensified by a "rapidity of Muslim immigration ... [which] suggests that we may soon be forced to speak not simply of Islam *and*, but Islam *in* the West ... Islamic communities form a sort of sectarian enclave ... in the West, but not of it."[40] Are we talking about the beginning of the mapping of Europe into *dar al-Islam*?

The existing alienation between Europeans and Muslims in Europe in the shadow of the conflict over the Mohammed cartoons of 2006, and earlier in the warlike fighting in the *banlieues de l'Islam* in Paris in October/November 2005 between Muslim teenage gangs and the police, illustrates a cultural fragmentation indicating the existence of two worlds within Europe. In an impartial report it was shown that outrage is not the only problem. At issue is this: "The rioters aim to turn neighborhoods into no-go zones for the French state so that underground ... can thrive."[41] This is the meaning of "parallel societies" as extraterritorial enclaves. If they are religionized then one may talk about an extension of *dar al-Islam* existing in Europe.

The historical mutual conquests in the shape of jihad and crusades are now taking place as wars of collective memories on European soil. The historical lines between the past and the present of a growing "Islamic enclave" are blurred in the dreams of the Salafists and Islamists of an Islamized Europe. To deter related fears, I coined the term "Europeanization of Islam" as a contrast strategy aimed at encouraging Muslim immigrants to embrace the idea of Europe. To be sure, the reference to the perceived threat of Islamization is no polemic. The statistical figures demonstrate the issue: the pattern of aging Europeans and young Muslims reflects a diminishing and a growing of two culturally distinct populations. Some speak of the "demographic suicide of Europe." After the end of the Second World War around 800,000 Muslims were living in Europe, mainly in France and Great Britain. By the end of the twentieth century the number had climbed to 15 million Muslims. By the completion of this book in 2006, the figure had increased to 20 million.

The majority of Muslim immigrants living in Europe are ordinary Muslims, not Islamists, but they are culturally not integrated and do not belong to the European polity.[42] Why so? In September 2002 I participated in a meeting of the cultural centers of the leading European Union member states in Brussels. The conference took place under the theme "*Penser l'Europe*" while being given the title "Islam en Europe." There, I was disturbed to hear Tariq Ramadan[43] speaking of Europe as *dar al-Shahada*, i.e. house of Islamic belief. The attending audience was alarmed, but did not get the message of the perception of Europe in an Islamist mindset as a part of house of Islam. If Europe is no longer perceived as *dar al-Harb*/house of war, but viewed as part of the peaceful house of Islam, then this is not a sign of moderation, as some wrongly assume: it is the mindset of an Islamization of Europe. Is this "changing the identity of Europe" (see the Berkeley formula, as referenced in note 46)? This issue refers to a taboo zone guarded by Islamists and multi-culturalists, both hating Europe. Those who dare to discuss the issue, and who ask whether the question is not simply one of numbers but relates to the very identity of Europe itself,[44] risk being accused of racism and Islamophobia. In German these words can be identified as *Kampfbegriffe* (notions of a war of ideas). Being myself both a Muslim and an immigrant, I prefer to remove myself from this war as I am engaged in mediation and reconciliation, an effort represented by my concept of Euro-Islam,[45] first developed in Paris. It was introduced in the USA back in 1998 in the Berkeley project "Islam and the Changing Identity of Europe"[46] and expressed a core concern related to the impact of Islamic migration on Europe. The formula suggests a challenge under which European identity is changing. In this context it is important to know that unreformed Islam is a religion strongly characterized by the obligation to the *da'wa*, i.e. to proselytize people of other faiths to Islam. This is not consonant with religious pluralism. In addition, the religious doctrine of relating *hijra*/migration to the obligation to spread the Islamic faith complicates the issue. If these facts are treated as taboos in Europe, no solution can be found. If *da'wa* and *hijra* combined continue to be at work, the envisioned "Islamization of Europe" will be the result in the long run. In a balanced manner these issues were addressed in a Cornell project without Islamophobia and instead with an alternative to the threat, namely in the Europeanization of Islam:[47] the result would be Euro-Islam, which could bridge between Europe and Muslim migrants, who need to abandon the determination to proselytize and instead embrace religious pluralism. The looming conflict can be averted if Muslims acknowledge the civilizational identity of Europe, which is not Islamic, and if the Europeans de-ethnicize Europe for a real and honest inclusion of Muslim immigrants. At present, both parties are failing.

Under these conditions and based on the facts, one may outline three scenarios, one of which is clearly stated by some enlightened Europeans and Muslims (Europeanization), while the second is not clearly and honestly declared by most political leaders of the Islamic diaspora in Europe (Islamization). The third is based on the neglect of the European civilizational identity and of the issue itself. In the following I reverse the order and start with the third scenario, i.e. multi-culturism, then continue with Islamization and conclude with the positive scenario of Europeanization.

The first option is multi-culturism.[48] This worldview is based on cultural relativism which allows the existence of Islamic entities within Europe in the framework of multi-cultural communitarism. Multi-culturalists do not bother about the result, be it "enclaves" or "parallel societies." The cultures of migrants coming from the world of Islam are put within Europe itself on an equal footing with European cultures. Multi-culturalists promote the collective rights of the migrants and deny European identity bashed as a hegemonial culture. In fact, the idea of Europe is based on the *principium individuationis* – i.e. the value system Habermas calls *das Subjektivitaetsprinzip*, the substance of cultural modernity.[49] According to this European worldview, men and women are seen as free individuals entitled to rights with an individual identity, as well as being European. Rights, in the sense of entitlements vis-à-vis state and society, are also individual, not collective, rights. This is the cultural underpinning of the human rights tradition adopted in the UNDHR as a distinctly individual rights understanding[50] in which there are no hegemonial implications. In contrast, the concept of collective rights – e.g. Islamic rights – supports ethnicity and the unfolding of ethnicized religious communities as a diaspora culture, and even the claim to Islamic superiority. If these religious grounds are accepted, then the consequence would be a conflict flaring between Europe and Islam within Europe. European cultural-relativists fail to grasp that ethno-nationalism and religious fundamentalism are an indication of a neo-absolutism promoted in the name of cultural relativism.

With a view to Muslim immigrants in Europe, the outlined multi-cultural option qualifies their diaspora community to collective rights as legal entitlements. On these grounds the Islamic enclave could develop into a communitarian setup of its own within the Western European civilization. Then we would no longer be in a position of talking about a free polity consisting of individuals entitled to individual human rights that override any collective cultural rights. At issue would be a fragmented and Balkanized society. It is sad to see critics of this option being defamed as "right-wing." The concern over the civilizational identity of Europe, of which individual human rights are part and parcel, is clearly not an expression of racism. Nevertheless, one sees those who are concerned about civil society and an individual human rights-focused identity often being attacked and, with no justification whatever, accused of "cultural racism." The underlying ideological concept is highly controversial and is a most dangerous and irresponsible approach in the ongoing war of ideas. The late Ernest Gellner deplored the fact that these cultural relativists direct

> their attacks only at ... non-relativists within their own enlightened tradition, but play down the disagreement which logically separates them from religious fundamentalism. Their attitude is, roughly, that absolutism is to be tolerated, if only it is sufficiently alien culturally. It is only at home that they do not put up with it.[51]

In returning the focus to the causes of the lack of integration of Muslim immigrants, the area of identity politics will be singled out as a major concern. On the one hand, one encounters a weak European identity facing a very assertive Islamic identity. This leads to a war of constructed identities in which there are losers and winners. On the other hand one cannot escape the contradiction concerning European identity: it is based on universal values, but Europeans have an exclusive ethnic image of the self and they consistently act along these lines. I have lived in Europe for forty-four years, long enough to be familiar with this. This very ethnic element in European identity, not so explicit, unwittingly promotes identity politics on the Muslim side, and on these grounds there can be no light at the end of the tunnel. Multi-culturalists do not understand this and are supportive of a diasporic identity while not knowing what it is all about, as well as ignoring the implications and consequences. In Chapter 4 on Iran identity politics was discussed at length regarding the construction of an overall Islamic identity. There is no need to resume the debate, despite the differences in the context of Iran and that of the diaspora. It suffices in this case to state that identity politics undermines the integration of Muslim immigrants to citizens of the respective European states. It has to be added that on the left one finds a double standard with regard to identity politics. The claim to universality of the values of European civilization is attacked, while the quest for an identity that is mostly based on a neo-absolutism of non-Western civilizations is admitted. There is the exception of one writer of the left, the French philosopher Alain Finkielkraut, who identifies this double standard as a *defait de la pensée*.[52]

The second option or scenario is an incremental process of an "Islamization of Europe," which is already in process. This option, pursued by Salafists and Islamists acting in the hijra diaspora, is based on the Islamic worldview that the enhancing of *dar al-Islam*/abode of Islam to a global structure is the ultimate religious duty of all Muslims, including those living in Europe. It is worth mentioning that orthodox Salafi Muslims and Islamists express this view almost exclusively within their community; they mostly refrain from pronouncing it in public. Publicly they pay lip-service to a "wishy-washy" unspecific inter-cultural dialogue implicitly based on deception. For them, dialogue is a cover for acting in the mind of proselytization. Most Europeans fail to understand this ambiguity and often take this lip-service at face value. The needed open dialogue is replaced by the one of dishonesty and deception. Orthodox Muslims and Islamists are not scrupulous and seem to have no problems with their double tongue, because – as they believe – they are *not* pursuing dialogue in the understanding of an intellectual exchange, but rather in their Islamic understanding of proselytization.

In fact, in Islam *da'wa* is considered to be a dialogue directed by an effort at proselytization. The Islamic term "*da'wa*" covers both meanings: dialogue and proselytization. Islamists talk to Europeans in the language of dialogue, but in fact practice proselytization. In short, in this case we have an example of the existing consequential difference in the cultural understanding of concepts. Another example is the rule of law. In Europe it is positive law, in Islam it is shari'a. These are conflicting concepts. These cultural differences constitute an obstacle to coming to terms with one another, because communication over substance does not take place. Dialogue is understood by one party (the Europeans) as an intellectual inter-cultural communication, while the other party (the Muslims) views dialogue as a means for proselytization. Is this the desired cultural diversity? In view of these facts, I put democracy above cultural difference and defend the open society against its enemies. I go for a liberal Islam of pluralism against Islamism and Salafism.

Conceptually the cultural differences in question indicate an existing simultaneity of structural globalization and cultural fragmentation, as addressed earlier. The assumption of cultural standardization is belied by the facts on the ground. There is no cultural globalization, but rather fragmentation. Without a proper understanding of these facts no effort at conflict resolution can bear fruit and avert the scenario of an Islamization of Europe. In addition, the established rules of political correctness impede any enlightenment about the conflict and are self-defeating.

In contrast to the supporters of the ideological multi-culturalism and the supporters of the vision of an Islamization of Europe – strange bedfellows indeed – the third scenario of a Europeanization of Islam could serve to bridge the Islamic diaspora and Europe. This scenario is based on the feasibility of transforming the vision or concept of a Euro-Islam into a European reality. It has become inflationary to speak of a European Islam, but in West European realities there is no such a thing, with the exception of a few enlightened individual Muslims who have been successful in putting their religious faith in harmony with an adopted European identity. In fact, multiple identity is feasible. The background to the concept of Euro-Islam, as first outlined by me in Paris back in 1992 (see note 45), was my first encounter with one non-Arab cultural variety of Islam in Senegal back in 1982. Islam practiced in Africa was strange to me as a Sunni Arab, but it was a home in a non-Arab environment. Africans had succeeded in Africanizing Islam by adapting it to their pre-Islamic local cultures. In contrast, Islam continues to be alien to Europe. While Europeans barely make efforts to make Muslims feel at home in Europe and therefore fail to integrate them, Muslim immigrants are in general not willing to integrate to European citizens of the heart (see note 17). The problem is not psychological and restricted to attitudes, it is – to put it plainly – a religious one. Without religious reforms in Islam, without a clear abandoning of concepts such as *da'wa*, *hijra* and shari'a, as well as jihad there can be no Europeanization of Islam. That is why the concept is not popular within the European diaspora of Islam.

These three scenarios for forecasting the future of the relationship of Islam and Europe in the twenty-first century under conditions of fragmentation and globalization of structures could serve as grounds for designing feasible policies. It is time to abandon the illusion that the dominant, tacitly Western-style globalization is in a position to give shape to one civilization all over the world. The study of culture and civilization[53] in relation to the history of humankind reveals enduring cultural and civilizational diversity. Religion is a cultural system determined by a social production of meaning[54] constrained by time and space. Therefore culture is always a local entity, and is ever changing. However, local cultures that are interrelated and resemble one another group along a worldview to a civilization. Local cultures in Europe and in the world of Islam are in each case very diverse; nevertheless, there exists one European and one Islamic civilization. In short, the facts allow us to speak of a great local-cultural diversity and simultaneously of a civilizational unity. Islam, as a religion, is a cultural system and in this capacity has a dual dimension: local and universal. When it comes to the religious civilization of Islam and the secular civilization of the West, one finds that both claim universality and are therefore in conflict with one another. Through migration Europe itself has become a battlefield of this conflict. Political Islam emerges in this context as a challenger to the civilizational identity of Europe and to the validity of its secular values, not only in the world at large but within the European territoriality as well. Islamists are at pains to mobilize the Islam diaspora for the vision of remaking the world. Can they succeed?

Political Islam and the drive toward de-Westernization: between the values of enlightenment and the instrumental reason of semi-modernity

Political Islam is neither the faith nor the culture of Islam: it is related to the challenges articulated in the famous booklet *Ma'alim fi al-tariq* [Signposts along the Road], the major source of contemporary fundamentalist thought written by Sayyid Qutb.[55] Among these signposts is instruction into the neo-Islamic system of *Hakimiyyat Allah*/God's rule.[56] Islamists believe that their *Pax Islamica* does not only apply to *dar al-Islam*, but also to Europe. Here, to protect myself against the invectives of Orientalism and Islamophobia, I reiterate not only the fact that I am a Muslim, but also that I descend from the Islamic Damascus-based nobility of Banu al-Tibi. My family enjoys a background going back to the thirteenth century[57] and provided the city of Damascus with its major shari'a-*qadis* (judges) and muftis. Nevertheless, I share the view that people of different religious communities, whether in Europe or in the rest of the world at large, could share basic secular values and one human reason and its wisdom based on logic. Together with my philosophy teacher Max Horkheimer, I beware of the "instrumental reason" of the West, but there must be other alternatives to challenging this "instrumental reason" than the one presented by political Islam and its fundamentalist varieties. Instrumental reason and computer literacy do not provide any proper answer to the value-based challenge of Islamic fundamentalism. Europe is exposed to this challenge and needs to determine its civilizational future together with Islam.

The need for inter-cultural communication and an accepted cross-cultural value-morality is underlined, while honoring cultural difference under conditions of globalization requires a standard of civilization not shared by Islamism. Islamists are favorable to Western modern science and technology[58] in their adoption of instrumental reason, but combine this with a rejection of the values of cultural modernity. Europe can no longer consider its cultural values as universal. European Westernization is being superseded by a de-Westernization. Does this also apply to Europe itself, given the demographic change taking place in the continent? In the view of Ibn Khaldun, civilizations rise and decline. Is the contemporary European civilization declining? Can a civilization survive if it does not defend and maintain its values? As argued earlier, Ibn Khaldun relates the state of a civilization to the state of its values, i.e. to its *asabiyya*. My Europeanization argument is not a universal one and is restricted to Islam within the boundaries of Europe. Only Europeans and Muslims living in Europe will achieve the outcome.

At present almost all civilizations, including those of Europe and the world of Islam, seem to share the new breed of human lost in the virtual space of computer literacy. This is an indication of a prevailing instrumental reason. In this atmosphere, semi-modern Islamists are committed to values and want to de-Westernize the globe, imposing their values not only against the instrumental reason of the West but also against its humanism. The Islamists firmly believe in their own particular religious values and reject the humanist man-centered view of the world. They argue that it is possible to combine their religious view of the world with modern technology in the pursuit of remaking the world along an Islamist order. In Western Europe this worldview, including the idea of jihad and its spirit of conquest, is becoming established but is not well understood by Europeans. In the Islamist worldview there is a splitting of modernity in cultural values (Western values) and instruments (modern science and technology); Islamists reject the European values, but adopt the instruments of modernity. For this "halving" of modernity I have coined the term "the Islamic dream of semi-modernity."[59] This dream envisions a de-Westernization of the world related to its Islamization. Europe is top priority on the agenda.

In comparing Islamic semi-modernists with the "new breed of humans" in Japan and Western Europe, we find that both are in full mastery of computer literacy, but with one significant difference. Unlike the Japanese and West Europeans, who today lack a commitment to binding values, or *asabiyya*, the fundamentalist Muslim semi-modernists are not lost "in the ever-growing virtual space" (see note 16). On the contrary, they are highly committed to the reinvented Islamist value system. This "invented tradition," i.e. developing tradition to new totalitarianism, provides the absolute terms in a claim for their value-orientation to universal validity. These Islamists despise cultural relativism and believe they can defeat the West with its own weapons: the instruments and the values of relativism. De-Westernizing the globe is the vision of an Islamic globalization which seeks to replace the realities of Western (and Japanese) globalization.

Semi-modern Islamists are aware of the loss of values in Europe and the related cultural crisis of meaning addressed in this chapter. For this reason Sayyid Qutb (1906–66) – the founder of political Islam – states on the very first page in his "Signposts along the Road" that "Humanity is on the brink ... the reason for this is the bankruptcy in the realm of values ... This is very clear in the West; it is no longer in a position to offer values for humanity."[60]

Two pages later he offers an alternative to Europe which is now unfortunately most popular throughout the world of Islam:

The "Western leadership" of humanity is about to subside ... The Western system no longer disposes of values that legitimate its leadership ... Now it is the turn of Islam and the Umma [community of Islam; B.T.] to take over ... This Umma will be reactivated to make Islam fulfill its expected role in again leading humanity.[61]

This is a program for a de-Westernization of the world, a reflection of the contemporarily prevailing Islamic worldview. The mind of Sayyid Qutb, the *rector spiritus* of Islamism, is also spread in the diaspora of Europe. Islamists acknowledge the still existing economic and political supremacy of the West, but they are aware of the moral crisis of Western civilization resulting from a loss of *asabiyya* as a value orientation. In contrast, a strong value commitment can be found among Muslims, morally superior to the West.

The politicization and the religionization of politics divide humanity, and Europe, into rival religious communities. This is the reality of multi-cultural diversity in which a religionization of politics is a salient feature. In fact, a fragmentation is at work that can only be countered by a cross-cultural morality shared by Europeans and Muslims, in particular on European soil. A de-Westernization of Europe in the name of tolerance and multi-culturalism would mean the end of it as a civilization. The message is unequivocal, but it falls upon deaf ears in Europe.

Conclusions: What future for Islam and Europe? What about Islam in Europe? Are there prospects of a cultural pluralism?

In the first decade of the twenty-first century, Europe finds itself undergoing a civilizational crisis while facing a great challenge related to Islam, both in its geopolitical neighborhood and within its own borders. How could Europe manage to maintain its civilizational identity while positively acknowledging the presence of Islam as a basic factor in European life? Can Europe and the people of Islam engage in a common process of changing of the self, holding an honest dialogue to find common solutions? In my view, Euro-Islam as European Islam and the idea of pluralism could provide possible options for peaceful coexistence. The indigenization of Islam in Europe is the alternative to the return of Islamic history and of the related claims amounting to a call for the Islamization of Europe.

To be sure, it is not only Europe that is undergoing a crisis of culture and identity. Despite all the self-congratulation and most assertive high self-esteem of Muslim intellectuals, they and their people are also in a severe crisis, amounting – as the Iranian Shayogan phrases it – to a "cultural schizophrenia."[62] Every expert on the Islamic Middle East is familiar with the related misery both of the self and of social life. It is not simply economic in its nature and merely restricted to poverty. As revealed by a study of the UNDP completed in 2002 by Arab scholars and experts working for the UN, unfilled basic needs and the extensive deterioration in the conditions of life are also combined with and underpinned by cultural constraints. This misery emerges from an overall development crisis. Long before this UN study was published, a well-known Moroccan philosopher, Mohammed Abed al-Jabri, was at pains to revive Islamic rationalism against the Islamic orthodoxy. In an effort at bringing new intellectual life to the medieval Islamic rationalist Averroës, the philosopher al-Jabri coined the phrase: "The future can only be Averroëist."[63] Averroëism is the term for Islamic rationalism. Twenty-first-century Islam is burdened with a home-made predicament with modernity. Unless the leaders of Muslim opinion, both religious and secular, come to terms with cultural modernity, the aggressive–defensive culture of self-assertion, heightened to a rhetoric of offensive claims comprising politics across the world and in Europe, will continue unabated, to the detriment of not only Islam but also all people who are obliged to live with Islam in the world at large. Not only is Europe no exception, it is precisely at the hub of the issue.

The malady addressed is growing from a crisis of Islam into one touching on Europe, which itself is in a crisis of its own. To come to terms with the real Islam existing in Europe, beyond mere wishful thinking a strategy is needed, but there is none in place. At issue is Islam, first that of the diaspora and second that in the world of Islam itself.

Islam is a transnational religion promoting great links and networks. In the world of Islam, politics is constrained. In the Islam diaspora in the European Union, Muslims enjoy all civil rights and all links are clearly reflected. It is not only for analytical reasons but also for policy concerns that different concepts for dealing with Islam are needed, and these on two different levels: first, Islam *in* Europe (diaspora) and second, Islam *and* Europe, that is the neighborhood of Europe – basically in the Mediterranean. For designing the future the following aspects seem to be most relevant:

1   In the present state of affairs European and Islamic states interact and coexist within the international system of nation-states. Contemporary Islamists want to topple existing regimes at home, but have to date failed to accomplish this. Prosecuted, they flee as asylum-seekers to Europe and try to hijack the diaspora.
2   In the long run, a Muslim promoting the Islamic dream of Islamizing Europe is demographically supported in transforming this dream into reality by the low birth rate of the Europeans combined with increased Muslim migration. A de-Westernization of Europe could result from this migration, if the failed integration of Muslim immigrants goes on. Identity politics, ethnicity on both sides and the exclusion enforce one another in an alarming context.

3 The implementation of the Kantian option of a democratic peace requires a democratization of the world of Islam not simply restricted to the introduction of voting procedures. The victories of Hamas in Palestine in 2006 and of the Islamist parties in the election of Iraq in December 2005 have not been signs of democratization. What is required is an Islamic acceptance of a cross-cultural morality that entails the culture of democracy, based on religious and cultural pluralism (see note 45). This culture of democracy cannot prevail if democratization is merely restricted to a voting procedure. A ballot does not make a democracy!

The twenty-first century is a crisis-ridden time in an increasingly destabilized world with all its disorders (see note 12). The still prevailing order of nation-states is no longer accepted in the world of Islam and it suffers a legitimacy crisis. Muslims also have a different understanding of peace which is not consonant with the Western idea of world peace based on the secular Kantian concept of *ewiger Friede*/perpetual peace.[64] According to the Kantian concept, peace is understood as the contrast to war, and republican orders can accomplish a democratic world order. These rival and competing views of world order lead to a war of ideas. In contrast, Kant foresees that democratic states are therefore expected to be a precondition for a lasting, i.e. "democratic" peace. The questions relating to the world of Islam are whether it would be democratized and become a safe neighborhood for Europe, and whether its Imams would accept the Kantian idea of democratic peace. These questions were asked in Part I of this volume and answers are given there. Our concern here is the pertinence of these issues to Europe.

Among the findings is the fact that political Islam is against the nation-state, not only in the world of Islam but also in Europe as well. As Huntington tells us in his book *The Third Wave*, the institution of the secular nation-state stands in a co-relation to democracy. "Modern democracy . . . is democracy of the nation-state and its emergence is associated with the development of the nation-state."[65] In recalling the argument presented in Part I, an enlightenment and a reform-Islam are required for bringing democracy into Islam,[66] be it in the Islamic world or in Europe. In contrast, the ideology of Islamism precludes any harmonization between Islam and democracy. Of course, not all Islamists agree with the pronouncement that "democracy is *kufr*/heresy." There are other Islamists who endorse democracy, but they do this – as is the case of AKP in Turkey[67] – simply for the sake of convenience and for instrumental reasons. The Shi'ite alliance in Iraq, Hamas in Palestine, the Hezbullah in Lebanon and the Muslim Brothers in Egypt, among others, play the game of democracy but definitely do not accept its political culture: above all, they do not renounce the idea of a shari'a-based Islamic state. The appeasement of Islamism is a dangerous European illusion. What are the conclusions of this Islamic challenge, in particular for Europe in an age of cultural turn and of Islamism?

Europe faces the challenge of an enhancing of *dar al-Islam* to map the entire globe, including Europe itself. To avert the development of migration into an Islamization, one needs first to be knowledgeable about the issue. It is ridiculous to read some so-called experts of traditional wisdom playing down the Islamization, stating that there is no united Islamic civilization with its own Islamic armed forces for conquering Europe. No one is stupid enough to consider such a scenario. At issue is a return of history in terms of revival and construction of collective memory, be it of the year 711, when Muslim Arabs invaded Spain, or of 1453 when Turkish Muslims invaded Constantinople.[68] Some scholars address this Islamic expansion as "Islamic imperialism" in history and relate it to political Islam at present.[69] I leave this to one side, without overlooking the fact that organized Islamists envision accomplishing their mission peacefully through the massive Muslim immigration to Europe accompanied by a war of ideas against European values. This would be based on the Islamic understanding of *hijra* in the Islamic traditional meaning of an Islamization.[70] In this context, rejected European values are used by Islamists to undermine Europe itself. Revel describes this as "democracy against itself."[71] In the already mentioned Berkeley and Cornell projects on this subject, the options were stated as "Islamic Europe or Euro-Islam" or "Europeanization of Islam versus the Islamization of Europe." These phrases reflect my standing as a freedom-loving liberal Muslim immigrant living in Europe. I say yes to a European Islam in Europe and reject all Islamization.

It can be observed that Europe is neither politically nor morally well equipped for coping with the challenge described in this chapter. As stated, Europe itself is undergoing a crisis of meaning, and lacks the clear moral orientation and a firm commitment to its own values, i.e. it lacks an *asabiyya*. A similar crisis in the world of Islam has led to the rise of religious fundamentalism with the reverse outcome: a strong *asabiyya*.

Islamism is spilling over to Europe. *Newsweek* asked in a special issue of 5 November 2001: "Why do Islamic terrorists like Europe?" The answer was given in an article with the title "Tolerating the Intolerable."[72] The missing distinction between tolerance and value-indifference is an indication of the cultural crisis of Europe that makes it incapable of unfolding a proper response to the pending challenges. In his column in the *International Herald Tribune* under the heading "Europe Needs to Decide How to Live with Islam" (*International Herald Tribune*, 26 July 2006) John Vinocur stated that Europe does not know how to deal with Islam. If this does not change, some Muslim opinion leaders in Europe – such as Tariq Ramadan, the grandson of Hasan al-Banna, the founder of the Muslim Brotherhood and of jihadism – will receive a boost in their transmission of "the Muslim mission in Europe."[73] This grandson of Hasan al-Banna constructs a line of an "Islamic renewal"[74] that started in the nineteenth century with al-Afghani and was continued by his own grandfather. As a liberal Muslim and as a student of Islam over four decades, I cannot support this reading of history and continue to view al-Banna as the founder of jihadist political Islam.[75] At issue is a challenge to Europe. In this conflict situation I proposed, in my Paris paper "Les Conditions d'un Euro-Islam" (see note 45), a Europeanization of Islam as a strategy for bridging. Today, others are using the term "Euro-Islam" while ignoring the original proposition. I restrict myself to stating that my Euro-Islam is not the Euro-Islam of Tariq Ramadan and emphasize my firm belief in Islam as a most flexible faith and cultural system. There is no essential Islam, and Islam is always what people make of it. It could be interpreted as jihadism,[76] as is done by Hasan al-Banna, or it could become European in the way I see it, if reformed by overcoming its predicament with democratic pluralism.[77]

6 The European diaspora of Muslim migrants and the idea of Europe

Could they become Europeans by choice?

Euro-Islam, legal citizenship and "citizens of the heart"

In a historical long-term perspective Europe faces two competing options in the future. The first is the Europeanization of Islam in its European diaspora. This also requires that Europeans and Muslims living in Europe share a European identity as a sense of belonging to the same polity. The other option is the Islamization of Europe,[1] i.e. viewing it as a part of *dar al-Islam*, as some Muslims already do. This statement is neither a polemic nor is it a panic – let alone an expression of Islamophobia, as some contend. This is a realistic perspective based on the demographic growth of the Muslim diaspora community combined with self-assertive expansionist attitudes of leaders of the Islamic mosques, occurring simultaneously with a shrinking of European population – due to the low birth rate – and the spread of postmodern and self-denying fashions among European intellectuals. Those Europeans and Muslims engaged in identity politics in favor of immigrants are asked: Are you dealing with a Europe with no identity?[2] Migration is making Europe a battlefront[3] between these competing options. My stand is against "clash" and I claim to be a mediator.

Introduction

The frame of reference employed here relates to the fourteenth-century Muslim philosopher Ibn Khaldun, who – as repeatedly stated – places the self-consciousness, i.e. the *asabiyya/esprit de corps*, of a civilization as a criterion for its flourishing or decline.[4] Europe's image of itself seems, at the beginning of the twenty-first century, not to be a promising one. After having lived as a Muslim immigrant for four and a half decades in Europe, I claim to see a very weak European *asabiyya* replacing the earlier ugly Euro-centrism. This is a shift from one extreme to the other. I translate *asabiyya* as civilizational self-awareness. As a Muslim who is committed to freedom and rationality, and who fled the despotism and authoritarianism that is currently not only prevailing but spreading in the world of Islam, I do not like to see the political culture of Islamism establishing itself in the Islamic diaspora in

Europe. This is happening through the espousal of the indiscriminate mindset of multi-culturalism. I see an Islamist neo-absolutism embracing a cultural relativism in order to put it to use. For the Islamic diaspora in Europe, I present Euro-Islam as an alternative to the vision of Islamization. This is based on the assumption that a Europeanization of Islam is a feasible project. To be sure, it can only be accomplished if change and religious reforms are admitted by Muslims.[5]

In Europe, anti-Americanism reinforces the popular perception that the Muslim contestation of the West, as articulated by violent actions inspired by the new Islamist jihadism,[6] is a revolt against US unilateralism and the *Pax Americana*. The facts of thriving self-ethnicization and the unfolding of an Islamic enclave within Europe are overlooked, as are the realities on the ground of Europe as a battlefront (see note 3). To put it succinctly and plainly: Europe faces equal challenges, both Islamic and Islamist. One is related to Islamic universalism and its proselytization, the other to political Islam and its jihadism, which is already established within the Islamic diaspora of Europe.[7] In this context, I argue against polarization and suggest a Euro-Islam as a strategy for peace within Europe, to replace the exclusion which is inflicted by Europeans on Muslims and which contributes to their defensive response of self-ethnicization. The issue is wrongly presented in terms of a conflict between "communitarian multi-culturalism" and its critics, viewed as enemies. It is no such thing: it is a fight over the shape of Europe in the decades to come – Europeanization or Islamization.[8]

The rioting in the French suburbs, labeled *banlieues de l'Islam*,[9] in October/ November 2005 was a warning which was not well taken either by the European Union, as a reminder of existing problems, or by the Islamic community, which was itself challenged. At issue was not only a revolt against exclusion, but also rebellion with a religionized character. It was a French intifada. After the rioting died down, for the French state and society it was business as usual, as if nothing had happened. Other Europeans remarked, in a self-congratulatory manner, that it was a French affair. However, well-informed experts were of the view that the Islam-based uprising of Paris, spilling over to other cities, showed challenging realities which cannot be managed within a security approach, as the then French minister Nicolas Sarkozy, then later elected into the office of president, repeatedly suggested. A policy based on the consequences of what is taking place on European soil needs to be much more than that.

If we take the idea of Europe at face value, i.e. as being based on a religion- and ethnicity-blind secular civilizational identity, then a Europeanization of Islam should by no means be an adjustment to Christian values, as some German politicians repeatedly argue, with consequent damage to the integration of Muslims. Euro-Islam, institutionalized through educational channels and incorporated into a policy for integration endorsed by both civil society and the European Islamic diaspora, is in no way a copy of distorted Christianity in a Europe that fails to distinguish between secularization and profaneness – and this is not to speak of Europeans as "religious illiterates," as a prominent German Jew, Michael Wolffsohn, has rightly suggested.

To understand those Muslim youngsters of the *banlieues* who torched some 12,000 cars while calling *"Allahu Akbar,"* thus clearly thinking of themselves as warriors waging jihad, Europeans need more knowledge of real existing Islam. The related allegation that the uprising was socially determined and has nothing to do with Islam is useless for any strategy attempting to deal with the religionization of politics. Of course, in a short-term perspective concrete measures are needed. But in order to make clear that jihad and shari'a are no alternatives to European law, a policy seems to be more promising than a policing – yet there is none in place. A surveillance of 20 million Muslim migrants living in Europe is neither possible nor recommendable. In the long term the message has to be both conciliatory and determined to maintain the identity of Europe. My concept of Euro-Islam as a value orientation for the Muslim diaspora claims to provide the strategic guidelines for integration.

The concept was first presented in Paris, where I coined the term "Euro-Islam." I propose to specify its content and dissociate my understanding of Euro-Islam from the one propagated by Tariq Ramadan, the proud grandson of Hasan al-Banna. My own understanding has been well covered in the following quote from *Time* magazine of 24 December 2001. On page 49 of that issue one reads:

> Bassam Tibi … who coined the term Euro-Islam, insists that the integration of Europe's Muslims depends on the adoption of a form of Islam that embraces Western political values … "The options for Muslims are unequivocal," says Tibi. "There is no middle way between Euro-Islam and a ghettoization of Muslim minorities."

The concept goes back to 1992, when the French were about to abandon the illusion that the assimilation of immigrants could be achieved by drawing on a concept of integration restricted to an acceptance of the civic values of the republic. In this context I presented my paper "Les Conditions d'un Euro-Islam"[10] at the Institut du Monde Arabe; it was also published in Paris to provide a framework for integration. In terms of documentation, this is the origin of the concept, which has been elaborated upon in my writings ever since in both German and English.

The idea of Europe, Euro-Islam, legal citizenship and "citizens of the heart"

The starting point is the changing composition of the European population; the demographic growth of Muslim immigrants is skyrocketing throughout Europe in comparison to migrations from other parts of the world. This is also related to the fact that these immigrants are mostly an ethnic underclass. The rioting of the *banlieues de Paris* in 2005 compels Europeans to see that they are under pressure to deal with this new Islamic element in their societies, as well as with the related social problems. One adds to this the Islamic claims that affect the identity of Europe itself. At issue is the question of whether the idea of Europe can be made compatible with Islam in a cultural synthesis here called Euro-Islam.

In the present situation one encounters two extremes: the populist, unacceptable Islamophobic view on the one hand, and indiscriminate multi-culturalism, based on the cultural-relativist understanding of "anything goes," on the other. In big European cities the realities reflect the emergence of parallel societies creating an Islamic enclave within the old continent. The assaults in a series of events stretching from Madrid to Amsterdam in 2004 and from London to Paris in 2005 clearly illustrate the relevance of Islam for the future of Europe. In line with this is also the conflict over the Mohammed cartoons in early 2006, followed by another dispute the same year over a lecture by the Pope calling for a dissociation of religion from violence. The lecture was viewed as offensive.

Throughout this chapter it is argued that a politics of integration that differs from both multi-culturalism and assimilation is the most pertinent strategy. In this pursuit, there is a need to combine civics with economics in order to make integration happen. By this I mean accomplishing a sharing of basic values by Europeans and Muslim immigrants, combined with integration in the workplace. The ongoing migration into the welfare system is not only deadly for Europe, it also precludes Muslim immigrants becoming true European "citizens of the heart," i.e. sharing the civilizational identity of Europe.

It is most dismaying to see those Islamists and Salafist leaders of the Muslim community claiming "a place for Islam in Western society" (this is an aspect that European multi-culturalists fail to understand) while at the same time rejecting the call to embrace the "idea of Europe." The mushrooming Islamic enclaves within Europe are challenged by the bid to make Muslims living in Europe true European "citizens of the heart." Citizenship is much more than a passport: it is membership of a polity based on a culture of democracy and individual human rights.

It has to be candidly stated that the integration needed for Muslim immigrants to become European citizens cannot take place alongside claims that run counter to secular civil and open society. The related absolutist vision of Islamizing Europe, which for tactical reasons is not spelled out by Salafists and Islamists, is a strange bedfellow for a multi-culturalism based on the cultural relativism of "anything goes." In contrast to this communitarianism, as well as to assimilation, an integration limited to civic values, shared identity and the workplace can be made compatible with a reformist interpretation of Islam through embracing the core principles of cultural modernity.[11]

The background to the concept of Euro-Islam comes from my observations of customary – i.e. lived – Islam in Western Africa. There, Islam – though an Arab culture by origin – is basically African, just as in Indonesia it is Indonesian, accommodated to *adat*/traditions of local cultures. In non-Arab traditions of Islam, one encounters varieties of cultural accommodation. There one may ask: Why cannot Islam be European in Europe, along similar lines? If Muslim immigrants are willing to leave their culturally gated enclaves in order to become European "citizens of the heart," then they must be challenged to open themselves instead of being aliens and *muhajirun* – frankly speaking, migrants in the Islamic meaning of a proselytizing diaspora in the process of extending *dar al-Islam*.

To be sure, Europeans themselves are the other obstacle to the project in question. If they were honestly politically and socially inclusive – of course, beyond hubris and rhetoric: in other words, in practice – then integration could be accomplished. I lived as a Muslim in Europe for four decades, and this lived experience denies Europeans that honesty. The idea of Europe based on values of secular democracy, individual human rights, pluralism, civil society and the enlightenment culture of tolerance could be accommodated in a Euro-Islam consonant with cultural modernity. In the present situation, there can be no half-solutions for the competing options: either a "citizenship of the heart" or citizens by passport; not real members of civil society, but rather nominal Europeans living in enclaves, "in the West, but not of it,"[12] not only because of the lack of a will to integrate, but also because they are denied equality and membership in the polity – even if they cross the threshold related to Islam.

The existing obstacles related to Europeans by Muslims contribute to a thriving of an Islam diaspora existing in Europe, but not of it. The Islamic rioting in France back in fall 2005 could become the model for sidelined Muslim youth throughout Europe. On the occasion of the first anniversary of the assassination of Theo van Gogh by a jihadist Islamist, this threat was addressed by the political Dutch elite in dialogue with some enlightened Muslims under the heading "One Year On: Radicalization and Society's Response." There, as a keynote speaker, I again presented my concept of Euro-Islam, in which the starting point has been both normative and factual. The murderer of Theo van Gogh, the well-connected Islamist Mohammed Bouyeri, regarded his crime as the fulfilling of a religious duty against *kufr*/unbelief. After the execution of this jihadist duty, Bouyeri reiterated and reconfirmed this view throughout the trial, assuring the court that he had no remorse and would do the same again if he were to leave prison. To be sure, this is also the mindset of those who were torching cars in France in October/November 2005. The letter Bouyeri pinned to van Gogh's body included the phrase: "Europe! It is now your turn."

A deeper problem is related to tensions related to identity politics and based in a religionization of the conflict.[13] Both Islam and Europe need to acknowledge the challenge, to accommodate and to change. It is wrong to put the blame either on Muslim immigrants or on Europeans; both are responsible for the existing state of affairs. There are Muslims who are willing to participate in the defense of civil society, but there is a price Europeans must pay for this if they really want Muslim allies. For paving the way for Euro-Islam from a vision to reality, Europeans need to be inclusive, while Muslims in return need to be willing to become Europeans. If integration fails, then the radicalization taking place in the world of Islam will spill over to Europe. In fact, this process is already in place. Regrettably, time is running out for Europe and Europeans to continue to be blind and to turn deaf ears to burning issues. Europe needs a double-track strategy for dealing with Islam and Islamism: in general, on the one hand a dialogue with pro-democracy Muslims who are willing to abandon the jihadization and shari'atization of Islam in order to promote a Euro-Islam; and on the other hand, a security approach for dealing with Islamism and its jihadist branch.

For many reasons Europe attracts people from the world of Islam/*dar al-Islam*, who are currently pouring in. They come as legal and illegal alike, be it as asylum-seekers, refugees or simply guest workers. Among the attractions is prosperity, promising a better life. Others seek refuge for themselves on the continent, a home where they can be assured of human rights and the benefits of democracy, both lacking to varying degrees throughout the world of Islam. The question asked here is: Could these Muslims also be attracted by the idea of Europe and consequently become true Europeans? That is, can they become true "citizens of the heart" (Charles Maier of Harvard, see note 17 to Chapter 5) and not merely holders of European passports or people living at the fringe of society in their enclaves?

Throughout this chapter I criticize Europe but also defend its ideals, as I learned them from one of the major sources of inspiration, my late teacher Max Horkheimer. This great Jewish philosopher and social scientist established the Frankfurt School of thought, but was forced in 1933 to flee Germany in order to save his own life.[14] He found refuge in the USA but in 1950 returned to Europe, remaining grateful to America until his dying day. For Horkheimer both Europe and the US constitute the pillars of Western civilization. The Jewish Horkheimer's plight in Nazi Germany and his legacy are highly pertinent to pro-democracy Muslims, who share with such Jews the suffering of exclusion and a love of the idea of Europe.

Shortly before his death in 1973, Horkheimer wrote, in the preface to his collected essays, what would remain an intellectual legacy of the Frankfurt School: "in terms of time and space Europe remains an island of freedom surrounded by an ocean of despotic rule/*Gewaltherrschaft*."[15] He continued that it is "an obligation on those who subscribe to critical theory" to be committed to Europe as the West, and to defend it against all varieties of totalitarianism (ibid.). Indeed, this legacy should become a civilizational creed for all Europeans, if they wish their civilization well and want the idea of Europe to survive the present great challenges posed by Islam and Islamism;

however, they need to make sure that those Muslims who accept democracy share it too. In my view, as a pro-democracy Muslim and a European by choice, the contemporary jihadist Islamism, and its call for a world revolution to remake the world in a "revolt against the West," incorporates the most recent variety of totalitarianism[16] to be countered by all who are committed to the open society. Here, there can be no tolerance in the name of cultural diversity and multi-culturalism.

The vision of a Europeanization of Islam presented in this chapter has been introduced with this reference to Horkheimer, my university teacher, to express my commitment to this *Vermächtnis*/legacy of a European Jew who suffered the exclusion of Nazi Germany; in the same way, we Muslims living in Europe suffer exclusion from a democratic Europe, but are not quite open to the idea of Europe. In the present civilizational crisis there are Muslims and postmodern challenges to cultural modernity to be taken seriously. To be sure, I stand against civilizational fault-lines[17] as much as I do against a postmodern, indifferent Europe. Self-congratulatory attitudes are not promising while dealing with Muslims and the related challenges.

The starting point for the following reasoning is the reality that the combination in Europe of low birth rates, leading to demographic decline, and high migration rates, of people from non-European cultures, is clearly affecting European identity.[18] But who can – and who will – change whom? Will Europe prove able to shape the incoming migration through the strength of its own identity – in Ibn Khaldunian terms, its *asabiyya*, albeit enhanced by inclusiveness – or will it be the migrants who shape Europe by imposing their own identity upon it? To reiterate the option expressed earlier: will we see their Europeanization or an Islamization of Europe?

Between Islamization and Europeanization

Is Islam changing the identity of Europe? A project at Berkeley, University of California, was suggested by the title "Islam and the Changing Identity of Europe." Is this appropriate for dealing with the issue? Statistically one can state that more than 50 per cent of the non-Europeans currently heading to Europe come from the world of Islam. Between 1950 and 2000, the number of Muslims in Western Europe rose from 800,000 to 15 million. It is now 20 million. German figures acknowledge that 20 per cent of the German population are people with *Migrationshintergrund* – they are not ethnic Germans. Can harmony be established between the immigrants and the Europeans, or will tensions be the outcome, with a religionized fight over the future shape of Europe? This will depend on the potential for an unfolding of a European Islam, or Euro-Islam. Of course, Muslims have the right to freedom of religion, but they have no right to an Islamization of Europe, for Europe – even though it has become home to 20 million Muslims – has its own European identity and is not a subject for remapping in a global *dar al-Islam*. Europeanization of Islam is the antithesis to the

Islamization of Europe. Muslims living in Europe and Europeans themselves are exposed to these options.

Lawrence Harrison, who spent decades studying poverty in Latin America, coined the phrase "underdevelopment is a state of mind" to refer to a cultural attitude, and concluded that "culture matters."[19] In a similar vein I argue that belonging to a particular civilization is also a state of mind. Some civilizations have been able to develop a modernity, like Europe, and therefore Europe is "a beautiful idea"[20] even though corresponding realities in European societies are not fully in line with this civilizational project. Others, like the Islamic civilization, continue to have difficulties with modernity. The politicization of Islam is an expression of this predicament.[21]

The term "a beautiful idea" as used to refer to Europe was coined during the Dutch presidency of the European Union in 2004. A related project turned the slogan into a question: "Europe – A Beautiful Idea?" In a meeting that took place in Rotterdam, none of the participating Europeans was publicly ready to profess willingness to sacrifice for Europe. This is the prevailing European mindset. So, how could one expect Muslims living in Europe to agree to Europeanization as consent to the civilizational identity of Europe?

On these grounds one sees a Moroccan Islamist killing an "infidel" in the name of Islamic law/shari'a as an act of jihad and issuing a warning for Europe, while Europeans either talk about a "clash of civilizations" or belittle the issue in a mindset of appeasement. In going beyond this impasse it is possible to contribute to "preventing the clash of civilizations" by establishing a cross-cultural international morality inspired by the pluralist idea of Europe. However, it would be foolish to overlook the existing conflict. It is possible to address the conflict, and not to be silent about it in the name of a political correctness of cultural-relativist multi-culturalism, while equally subscribing to "the sound of Europe." This is the Mozart theme coined at a subsequent EU presidency, that of Austria in 2006. I was sad to see, at the celebration in Salzburg, that only a few politicians were honestly willing to acknowledge the place of Islam in their project. Is the conclusion that there is no hope for Europe? No hope for the Europeanization of Islam on European soil – that is, its integration within an inter-civilizational dialogue? And of course, an honest dialogue, not like Khatami's camouflaging of global jihad into European civilization. In the present conflict, Europeans are challenged to engage in defending Western civilization by taking a stand.[22]

The contemporary predicament of Islam to come to terms with modernity stands in contrast to the rationalism of Islamic heritage. An unfolding of guidelines for a combination of Europe and Islam within a Euro-Islamic identity is a model of Europeanization that could contribute to making the increasing Muslim population of Europe accept the "idea of Europe" in an age of global migration combined with a "cultural turn." Collective identity politics is leading to entrenching communities as separate from one another, not only globally but also within Europe. Europeanization does not contradict cultural diversity, which is precious, but it needs to be addressed – as in a famous Amsterdam debate a decade ago – within the framework of "the limits of pluralism." In the framework of the controversy that developed between relativism and neo-absolutism,[23] Islam, in its radical forms of Salafist orthodoxy and totalitarian Islamism, was addressed as an anti-pluralist ideology. If those spokesmen for the Islamic diaspora in Europe who control most of the mosques and are either Salafists or radical Islamists embrace this anti-pluralist ideology in the name of cultural diversity, as they do, then one must have the right to say "No!"

The envisioned mapping of Europe into the *dar al-Islam* is, in other words, the Islamization of Europe. This is not only done through proselytization, but also through the spreading of a worldview among the Muslim diaspora that is in contrast to the idea of Europe. There is clearly a conflict between this worldview of neo-absolutism and the pluralist idea of Europe, often phrased in politically correct language as a cultural misunderstanding. It is most disturbing to see this orthodox Salafist and Islamist challenge facing up to a European worldview of cultural relativism which denies Europe the very civilizational identity it needs to try and stay alive. To argue in a relativist manner that European culture is – on European soil – merely one among others is self-defeating. Yes, the migrants have their own culture, but in this case it is not a valid one for Europe. Collective identity politics becomes an instrument against the civilizational identity of Europe itself. In this context, relativism, when exposed to neo-absolutism, is certain to be the worldview of the loser, because it does not defend itself against challenges and threats. The French scholar Raymond Aron was among the very few who foresaw that the era of "bipolarity" in world affairs concealed the reality of a world consisting of a "heterogeneity of civilizations."[24] He rightly predicted that bipolarity would end and that this true vision would be revealed. Aron did not live long enough to see the materialization of his prediction, which we are currently witnessing.

It is clear that, today, peace means a peace among civilizations, not only in the world at large but also within Europe, with its emerging cultural diversity. How can such a peace be achieved while the idea of Europe is still maintained, and what is the necessary framework? In earlier times, there were obvious civilizational boundaries, e.g. between Europe and Islam, and in those days the Mediterranean[25] marked such a boundary. However, global migration is blurring these territorial boundaries.[26] As John Kelsay put it, one is "forced to speak not simply of Islam and the West, but of Islam in the West."[27] It matters, therefore, that we make it clear which Islam we are talking about. Is it a European Islam, an indigenous version of Islam such as those that have evolved in Senegal or the many varieties existing in Indonesia, like the one in Java? No. Kelsay tells us that at issue here – as already quoted – are sectarian "enclaves in Western culture, but not of it"[28] – in other words, parallel societies.[29] To conceptualize the change, in the

Global Village Lecture held in Stockholm 1997, I coined the slogan: "Islam *and* Europe – Islam *in* Europe." This is not playing with words, but rather a way of maintaining that these are two different issues. The interaction between these civilizations is in our case no longer restricted to an activity spanning the Mediterranean; rather, it exists under conditions of Islamic migration within Europe itself. What are the implications for Europe? What policies are needed? Should we conduct a dialogue in the name of multi-cultural tolerance at the expense of European identity? If we talk about cross-civilizational bridges, what should they look like?

To be sure, any dialogue can only be successful if the needed requirements are fulfilled and it has its limits and constraints. It seems clear that one cannot carry out a dialogue with individuals like Mohammed Bouyeri and similarly minded Islamists, who – as well as their movements – only understand the language of jihad. Their understanding of the politics of the "sacred" is neo-absolutist in nature. They envision the Islamization of Europe.

In contrast, a moderate Islam open to change and also open to Europe could help achieve the dual goal of being inclusive while preserving Europe's identity. Here, we have to set clear terms and they need to spell out what is European. At stake is a stark choice: either the Europeanization of Islam or the Islamization of Europe (see note 1). The middle road of multi-culturalism, a vision of two different worlds expected to live peacefully side by side in Europe, is a deception. For Islamists and their allies, multi-cultural communitarianism is only one transitory step on the road to Islamization. This is not my view, but rather the way neo-absolutists themselves view the issue. It is a state of mind that relativists fail to understand.

Let us refer to the Netherlands as a case in point. In his "Dutch Diary," published as a series in *Die Welt*, the Dutch writer Leon de Winter first cites Recep Tayyip Erdogan: "Europe has no other option, than either opening itself freely to Islam, i.e. through accession of Turkey under AKP-rule to EU, or involuntarily through exposure to extremist jihadist violence."[30] Leon de Winter then goes on to state that we need to have the courage

> to educate our Muslim fellow citizens in tolerance, individualism and the rights and duties of modern citizenry. But instead of fulfilling this task, we succumb to illusions of multi-culturalism, which paralyzes Europe ... In the Netherlands, as well as throughout Europe, the pressure of intolerance on our tolerance is increasing ... we must ask ourselves what we want to be and what we are willing to sacrifice for this end.
>
> (ibid.)

In fact, Leon de Winter speaks – of course unwittingly – in the language of the great Muslim fourteenth-century philosopher Ibn Khaldun, the first theorist in the history of humankind to write on civilization/*umran*.[31] In his science of civilization/*ilm al-umran* Ibn Khaldun argues that the civilizational awareness of the self is expressed in *asabiyya*. This Arabic term can be translated as "*esprit de corps*," summarized in a system of values and norms and the related worldview: *asabiyya* is thus the identity of each civilization. Ibn Khaldun argues that civilizations are strong when they are based on a strong *asabiyya* and weaken in general alongside the weakening of their *asabiyya*. In reviving this Ibn Khaldunian understanding, I view the idea of Europe as the *asabiyya* of the European civilization. Can it be extended to and shared by Muslim migrants, or is it so weak that it will succumb to Islamization? On an individual level I can say that many Muslims have succeeded in becoming Europeans by choice. I believe myself to be one of these, while experiencing the fact that European societies do not appreciate this move and continue to lack the ability to be inclusive. In fact, this is in contrast to the idea of Europe and cannot be the basis for a Euro-Islamic *asabiyya*.[32] It is not only Muslims but also Europeans who need to change if the conflict is to be solved peacefully to make a shared polity possible.

I conclude this section with a reference to the great philosopher Ernst Bloch's book on Islamic rationalism based on an enlightenment in Hellenized Islam, *Avicenna und die Aristotelische Linke*. In doing so, I argue that the "idea of Europe" can be incorporated into the concept of Euro-Islam in an effort to bridge two civilizationally different worlds. The identity of Europe – which, despite ugly European attitudes, I see as also my own identity, as a citizen of Europe by choice and a "citizen of the heart" – is based on freedom and democracy and individual human rights. Therefore, the idea of citizenship/*citoyenneté* is not restricted to a legal status, and as such it must include the demand for commitment. One cannot be Arab or Turk by choice, because this is an ethnic identity. But a Muslim, Turk or Arab could, by embracing the idea of Europe, become a true European citizen. This is an assumption which I state without any sense of naïvité: I know that the idea of Europe is not in line with everyday life in European societies. If Europeans do not change, they risk the Islamization of Europe.

The pending issues

To state it plainly: the basic issue is the fact that Islamic migration is changing the identity of Europe, and not only in a positive way. I contrast two options, a vision of Euro-Islam and a communitarian ghettoization expanding in parallel societies. The assumption that Islamic migration is changing the identity of Europe is based on Islamic claims that are not consonant with the idea of Europe. Islamists and Salafists have another vision for Europe. As a Muslim migrant myself, though a European citizen by value-orientation, I seek a compromise between the competing assertions of a European identity and of an Islamic identity. The idea of a multiple identity determines the concept of Euro-Islam, inspired both by the idea of Europe and by the historical experience of the Hellenization of Islam in the better days of Islamic civilization. This normative orientation takes as a starting point the reality that Islamic migrants are caught between those Islamists who abuse them in an effort to confront the secular state and those Islamophobic Europeans who do not give Islam a chance to become European. This conflict is also reflected in the French debate following the release of the report on church–state relations with a focus on the Islamic head-scarf issue in France. This report makes clear that accepting *laïcité* is the bottom line for the integration of Muslim migrants in France. At issue, therefore, is the idea of a Europe in which *laïcité* is part and parcel, and not simply a way of clothing oneself. The controversy highlights – as Elaine Sciolino phrases the issue in the *New York Times* – "the challenges that secular France – like much of Europe – faces in coming to grips with Islam ... organized groups are testing the secular French state."[33]

This test is also a test of the idea of Europe and of the strength of the European *asabiyya*. Clearly, a civilization conflict is at issue. As Nilüfer Göle puts it, "the contemporary veiling of Muslim women underscores the insurmountability of boundaries between Islamic and Western civilization ... as a contemporary emblem for the Islamicization ... the conflictual encounter between civilizations."[34] But I reiterate my own standpoint that I do not subscribe to a Huntingtonian point of view, and refer to my contribution to *Preventing the Clash of Civilizations*.[35] In this chapter I therefore renew my proposition of Euro-Islam presented in Paris a decade and half ago, but do so by incorporating it into the venture of "Europe: A Beautiful Idea?" without overlooking the ugly part of it.

In their dealings with Islam and Europe in the age of mass migration, Europeans resent having to acknowledge the basic issue with both civilizations, namely the values-related conflicts, while Muslims stress their basing of "values" in Islamic culture, often viewed as an essentialized civilizational monolithic identity. Again, in my discourse I emphasize the need for opening an inter-civilizational dialogue beyond essentialization as means of conflict resolution. The rhetoric of a clash between Islam and Europe is not helpful for Europeans or for Muslims in dealing with this issue. Islam's difficulty with cultural modernity, of which pluralism[36] is part and parcel, is a basic issue. There is a lack of willingness on the Islamic side to be involved in such a discourse, going beyond the cult of self-victimization. On the European side there is in fact very little beyond the rhetoric of dialogue endorsed as a substitute for the alternative rhetoric of "clash." Neither sentiment is helpful in the pursuit of a cross-cultural consensus over values of the political culture of democracy. I respect "difference," but – unlike Seyla Ben-Habib[37] – I unequivocally put political democracy above it in my concept of pluralism (see note 36). It is, however, unacceptable to stop short at acknowledging that there are entrenched differences. Clearly, cultural relativists who essentialize "difference" fail to provide any prescriptions for dealing with the conflict. In this case the conflict arising from this difference is between *laïcité* and shari'a and it can be resolved in a concept of Euro-Islam.[38] However, if this cannot be accomplished, the two parties cannot exist side by side in Europe if European identity is to be maintained and Muslims insist on shari'a.

In this regard I share the view of Ernest Gellner in his criticism on cultural relativism, which I will return to later. It suffices to note here that cultural relativists conspicuously accept cultural differences without any limitations, and in so doing even admit neo-absolutisms (see note 23). Yet they apply their cultural relativism only to Western values and stop short of proceeding in a similar manner with non-Western cultures. The winners in the game are the absolutists aiming at shari'a. Moreover, any critique of these mostly pre-modern cultures[39] is often misconceived and qualified as a "cultural racism." Such an accusation is of course belied by the fact that Muslims are not a race but an *umma*/religious community, multi-racial and, characterized by tremendous diversity.

Interestingly, the rampant drive to employ relativist concepts does not halt even in those cases in which such a critique comes from people belonging to these very cultures – e.g. Islamic reformers and secularists. As a Muslim scholar who – according to the authoritative history of Damascus – descends from a centuries-old Muslim–Damascene notable family (Banu al-Tibi) but who lives as a migrant in Europe, I maintain that the present attitudes of self-victimization and accusation on the Islamic side and self-accusation and self-denial on the European side are inappropriate ways for dealing with "difference" as related to Islamic migration to Europe. One must ask, then, whether Europe and Islam could come to terms with one another while maintaining a European-inclusive *asabiyya* that can be shared by Muslim migrants. The context of the Muslim– European encounter is the time and space set by Europe itself. It follows that Europe itself is exposed to the effects of globalization, i.e. to the process Europe itself has set in motion through European expansion.[40] In our age, migration to Europe has unwittingly become a component of this very globalization.

In facing the challenges related to "difference," the idea of "remaking the club" has emerged. The phrase refers to needed changes in the identity of the hitherto exclusive "Club of Europe." Even though I agree with this demand, I strongly feel the need to add that the "remaking" encompasses the need for all members of the club, old and new, i.e. including the migrants, to change their identity. I find this insight missing in some of the pleas for attitudinal change.[41] The call for a de-ethnicization of European identity must equally apply to the identity of the migrants, lest we find ourselves dealing with both a "one-way change" and a "one-way tolerance." I share the view expressed in a French report of December 2003 that France has "no other choice" than prevention when facing "groups seeking to test and undermine core values" (*International Herald Tribune*, 12 December 2003). Likewise, the idea of Europe should be the bottom line in finding a solution for the future of Europe itself. Europe is changing in the light of migration, so why shouldn't Muslims also accommodate to the civilization giving them home?

In embracing the typology of Manuel Castells concerning identity-building, I would like to single out his ideal type of "project identity," by which he means that identity is not primordial but determinable. This pattern explores the idea that social actors need to "build a new identity that redefines their position in society ... No identity can be an essence."[42] Among the basic issues is the call upon Europeans to de-ethnicize and de-essentialize their identity to allow the newcomers to become Europeans too. To the same extent, Muslim migrants are requested to redefine their identity in the diaspora by adding a European component to it, in approaching a multiple identity. There is no such thing as an essential identity, be it European or Islamic.

One cannot escape the observation that Islamists and Salafists claim to live in Europe but with the firm belief that they do not want and do not have to change. This attitude is not reconcilable with the idea of Europe if European civilization is to survive in an age of global migration. Moreover, the cited Muslim belief demonizes and deprives Europe of its own identity. To be sure, despite its Muslim population, Europe is not *dar al-Islam*.

In the age of migration, Europe needs to overcome its Euro-arrogance, while Muslim migrants must engage themselves in the unfolding patterns of a Euro-Islamic identity by abandoning their universalist absolutism. In so doing, they could establish a commonality between themselves and European civilization while recognizing the idea of Europe, in order to become citizens of the heart. As a starting point, I view the de-ethnicization of Europe on the European side and religious-cultural reforms on the Muslim side as basic requirements for the feasibility of the Euro-Islam project. The idea of Europe provides an opening for this venture. Are Muslims willing to adjust their cultural identity in a more flexible manner along these lines?

In short, the requirement of change and the challenge to both to redefine identity are the pending issues. As much as one should overcome stereotypes about Islam, one must recognize that it is equally wrong to essentialize Europe as "racist," "genocidal," etc. To essentialize Islam in an Islamophobic manner is as wrong as doing the same to the West. Europe and the world of Islam are two established civilizations with centuries-old records that equally encompass enmity and cordiality.[43] In this regard the dichotomies built up on this legacy – such as those of East versus West – are based on "artificial categories," as Nezar Al-Sayyad rightly argues. He adds that "societies are constructed in relation to one another and are ... perceived through the ideologies and narratives of situated discourse."[44] When it comes to the construction of identities – as based on the production of meaning – academics need to free themselves from their "preoccupation with globalization" in acknowledging that "each individual belongs to many cultures and people have multiple cultural identities ... Identity is always under construction and in constant evolution."[45] My vision of a Euro-Islamic multiple identity as a new *asabiyya* for Muslim migrants in Europe is developed along lines that question constructed dichotomies – however, without overlooking existing value conflicts related to the entrenched differences and, of course, subsequent limits. It cannot be reiterated enough that if Muslims are really willing to become Europeans by embracing the idea of Europe, they need to disconnect their understanding of Islam from jihad and shari'a and also abandon the *da'wa*/proselytization. Moreover, this disconnecting should not only be *stated* unequivocally but also *practiced*, as these concepts are unacceptable in Europe.

Living across cultures produces cross-cultural meanings and affects identity patterns. In the context of Islamic migration to Europe, I envisage an identity affected by the concept of Euro-Islam. This concept was first introduced at the Institut du Monde Arabe in Paris and I have since developed it on various occasions at several European and international institutions from Stockholm to Sydney to Berkeley. Euro-Islam also applies to Euro-Turkish relations, and in this regard the integration of Turkish migrants to Europe[46] is a case in point. To be sure, I strongly differentiate between integration and assimilation, and thus these concepts constitute the prescriptive part of my analysis of the Islamic presence in Europe as creating a basic challenge to the idea of Europe.

The term "New Islamic Presence"[47] has been coined to describe the increasing contemporary migration from Muslim countries to Western Europe. By the end of the Second World War there were fewer than one million Muslim people living in Western Europe, with the majority in France and the United Kingdom. By 2000 the figure had risen to 15 million, in 2006 to 20 million, and it is expected to reach 40 million by 2035. Muslim migrants now live in virtually all European societies, from Scandinavia in the north to Italy in the south, and with their increasing numbers and presence they are beginning to make demands that touch on European core values. People like Bernard Lewis predict that Europe will become a part of the Arab-Muslim Maghreb by the end of this century. I contradicted this view,[48] arguing that the problem is not whether a majority of immigrants pouring to Europe believe in Islam as a religion. Rather, what is important is the question of what kind of Islam they adhere to. If European Islam were to be accepted by Muslims living in Europe, then their presence in Europe would not pose a problem, because a Euro-Islam would be in line with the idea of Europe.

In discussing these issues one should also not forget that there are native European Muslims[49] who live predominantly in southeast Europe and number around 10 to 12 million. In view of the focus of the present analysis on Western Europe, I shall set aside this native Muslim-European community and concentrate on Muslim immigrants to EU countries from the Middle East, Asia and Africa. It may sound strange to Americans to see Muslims born in France, the United Kingdom or in Germany addressed in this analysis as immigrants rather than natives. The reason for doing this is the fact that second and even third generations of Muslim migrants to Europe are still not accepted as belonging to the existing polity. In stating this unfortunate reality, I acknowledge and reiterate that Europeans are also responsible for this lack of integration.[50] The issue is not simply related to Muslim problems with the idea of Europe.

Now we need first to deconstruct the phrase "Muslims in Europe" by looking at the migrant community in a dis-aggregative manner – that is, as a community that is both ethnically multifaceted and also divided along sectarian lines. Only on the surface can one speak of one Muslim diaspora in Europe. Muslims living in France were and still are predominantly migrants from the Maghreb,[51] whereas those living in the United Kingdom remain largely from South Asia (Pakistan, India and Bangladesh). Until the early 1960s, the Muslim presence in these European states was almost exclusively related to French colonial rule in North Africa and to British colonial rule on the Indian subcontinent. In addition, the sectarian divide among these Muslims is decisive: The Muslim Sunni community in the German state of Hessen, for instance, in its application for recognition as an institution refuses to view Shi'ites, Alevis, Ahmadis and others as Muslims, i.e. members of their community of faith. This attitude discloses a rejection of diversity and pluralism even within Islam. So how can one expect such people to recognize other faiths within a broader concept of religious pluralism?

In 1950 fewer than one million Muslims lived in Europe. Since the 1960s, Islamic migration has been growing ever more significantly, due to labor migration linked to the once booming European economies. West European countries are today home to about 20 million Muslims. Due to the low birth rates and the related demographic growth, West European countries other than France and the United Kingdom (e.g. Germany) started to encourage people from the Mediterranean region to come to Western Europe to earn their living. This process received a further boost from the loosening of border controls after the end of the Cold War. Despite its magnitude, this new migration did not change traditional European attitudes. In Germany, for example, the majority of workers – not only the Turks, but also South and South-East Europeans working in German factories – were perceived as *Gastarbeiter*/guest workers, i.e. people coming for a limited stay that would end when the need for their work no longer existed. Germany has been a country of reluctant immigration,[52] even after the legislation of a new law admitting migration. It has become common for critically minded Germans to state, with equal parts prudence and repentance: "We have imported labor and have overlooked the fact that we were importing human beings." But by then, sarcastic and cynical jokes were already being tossed around, and accusing fingers pointed at the Germans as stingy people who would invite people as *Gäste*/guests but would make them *Gastarbeiter*/guest workers, thereby neglecting accepted manners of hospitality according to which hosts do not require their guests to work, let alone carry out unskilled, physical "*Drecksarbeit*/dirty work." To be sure, there were and still are academic *Gastarbeiter*, like me. My life in German academia reflects this unpleasant experience of discrimination.[53] Indeed, were Germany the sole criterion for the idea of Europe, I would never embrace it. Sadly, this background promotes the growth of political Islam in the German Muslim community of about 4 million (2.5 million of whom are Turks and Kurds). Among its powerful representatives we find largely Islamists and other extremists,[54] although they play a double game of pretending to be moderate, at least in their rhetoric.

The earlier social-democratic/green German coalition government expressed its open-mindedness in legislating the new citizenship law in 2000. However, in their politics almost all German parties intrinsically continue to confuse the complex understanding of integration with the simple granting of a German passport. Theo van Gogh's slaying by a Moroccan Islamist with a Dutch passport has served as a wake-up call in the Netherlands, but not in Germany. Citizenship/*citoyenneté* means more than receiving a passport: it must resemble membership of a special club, one with rules. These rules should be based on the idea of Europe and inclusiveness. Accordingly, becoming a European requires above all the willingness to be a "citizen of the heart" and, in return, to be accepted as such by fellow Europeans.

Among the pending issues to be seriously taken into account is the one of the imposed Imams. These either come from within Islamist groups or are appointed by Muslim governments like those of Turkey and Morocco. Even Saudi Arabia is having considerable impact through providing petrodollar funds for appointing Imams in Germany in Saudi-funded mosques, despite the fact that there are no Saudi migrants in the country. In this regard, Germany is the most extreme case. For instance, the Saudi-funded Fahd Academy in Bonn has over the years educated some 500 young Muslims in Wahhabi Islam and thus serves to directly undermine any efforts at integration. Despite powerful press coverage about calls for jihad against the West stemming from this "academy" (*Der Spiegel*, 13 October 2003) there was not enough concern to get this madrasa on European soil closed down. It is clear, though, that if the Imams preaching in European mosques continue to be powerful, the vision of a European Islam will never flourish. An abandonment of the "anything goes" mentality of multi- culturalism is needed as much as an end of Saudi Wahhabi poison in Europe.

Does Europe respond to the Islamist challenge beyond security? Does it engage in embracing Euro-Islam?

Among the migrants coming as asylum-seekers to Europe we find those militant Muslims who relate migration to the religious obligation of *hijra*, to be discussed below. This is in contrast to most of the first-generation Muslims, who, like the Europeans themselves, did not view the "presence of Muslims in Europe" as a lasting phenomenon related to migration. Ultimately, however, their continuing long stay and the fact that a second and, by now, third generation of Muslims have been born, are changing not only attitudes but also perceptions. What is the identity of these Muslims, born in Europe but not committed to the idea of Europe? Should it be admissible to acquire European citizenship without accepting the identity that comes along with it? I have observed that Turks born in Germany are disliked in Turkey as *allemanci* (meaning something negative, like "Germanized"), but are at the same time not considered to be Germans in the country where they were born and where they live permanently. Thus they are torn between Turkey and Germany. This notion applies also to others. The complexities of this type of inner conflict were addressed at an international conference on migration held in Sydney, Australia, in July/August 1998 under the heading, "Adventures of Identity."[55] Given the fact that the interrelation of identity and migration has been dealt with elsewhere, the focus of this chapter will be on the competing options for future strategies concerning the risks and the opportunities related to Muslim migration to Western Europe as it increasingly poses a challenge to the idea of Europe.

In honoring the fact that Muslims living in Europe[56] are there to stay and thus are not temporary residents, my first question concerns the status of the current 20 million Muslim immigrants living in Europe. At the outset it is important to know that there are basically three major and comparable groups among them. The first of these are the Muslim Turks and Kurds, who number around four million, with 2.5 million living in Germany alone. The second group are the Maghrebians, with more than ten million in Europe, about eight million of whom are in France. A study on this second group carries the appropriate title "Algeria in France." The final group is made up of the South Asians, who are found predominantly in the United Kingdom, where their number is around two million, but a total of a few million can be found in all other European countries. It is most interesting and profitable to engage in comparative studies on this subject.[57] The figures show that Muslim immigrants to Europe come from all over the world of Islam. In the city of Frankfurt, 30 per cent of the city dwellers are foreigners who carry the passports of 165 different states. Among them, representatives from virtually every Muslim country worldwide can be found.

The Muslim diaspora in Europe is characterized by two traits. On the one hand there is an ethnicized Islam vis-à-vis European societies, claiming unity; on the other hand, however, ethnic and sectarian divides among Muslim migrants are most clearly reflected in the structures of the mosques. In Germany religious associations (*Moscheevereine*) are not purely Islamic, but rather Sunni or Shi'ite, Turkish, Bosnian, Arab or Pakistani, or perhaps divided between Ahmadi and Sunni, but almost always divided along ethnic and sectarian lines. Apart from the rhetoric of an overall Islam ethnicized in confrontation with Europe, one very rarely finds comprehensive Islamic mosques or associations. Most worrying is the politicization of this divide and the inter-Islamic violence involved. What is the European response? In the Netherlands, after van Gogh's death the Dutch people and a few others have started to look at the *Innenleben der Moscheen*[58] and have begun to see them as representing something not just in contrast to the idea of Europe but vehemently opposed to it. However, in Scandinavia and in Germany people continue to carry on as usual. Among the few exceptions is the German journalist Udo Ulfkotte, who published a book on the German Islamic diaspora entitled *Der Krieg in unseren Staedten* – "The War in Our Cities"[59] – in which he describes Islamist activities. He paid a high price for his disclosures. He was taken to court by supposed Islamists (who were mostly living on welfare payments; the German welfare state paid most of the legal expenses) and as a result his life was ruined. Those he exposed in his investigations remain active and thriving. What are the prospects for a Euro-Islam under these unfavorable conditions? Sadly, not promising!

Though I am respectful of Islam's capacity to adjust to a variety of divergent cultures and I remain hopeful, I acknowledge that the identity of culturally different people of Islam who nevertheless share the very same religious faith creates some obstacles. We may talk therefore about the simultaneity of unity and diversity in Islam. However, in considering the fact of existing Afro-Islam for African Muslims and Indo-Islam for Indian Muslims, I ask why we can't talk about the feasibility of a Euro-Islam in the context of the migration of Muslims to Western Europe.

What exactly would such a concept comprise? In Euro-Islam I address the effort of devising a liberal variety of Islam acceptable both to Muslim migrants and to European societies, thus an Islam that can accommodate the ideas of Europe, ideas including secularism and individual citizenship along the lines of a modern secular democracy. Yet I reiterate that Euro-Islam is the very same religion of Islam as exists anywhere. In the case of Europe, however, it is culturally adjusted to the civic culture of modernity.[60] In European civil societies an "open Islam" could be as much at home as – for instance – Islam in Africa (Afro-Islam), which is adjusted to coexist with domestic African cultures. The major features of the concept of Euro-Islam would include *laïcité*, cultural modernity, and an understanding of tolerance that goes beyond the Islamic tolerance restricted to Abrahamitic believers (*ahl al-kitab*). In addition, Euro-Islam acknowledges cultural and religious pluralism and thus gives up on the claim of Islamic dominance, which is, in any case, out of touch with reality. In sum, Euro-Islam is compatible with liberal democracy, individual human rights and the requirements of a civil society. Therefore, Euro-Islam departs from *citoyennité* and thus represents a contrast to communitarian politics that result in ghettoization. It is important to note that the politics of unfolding patterns of Euro-Islam should in no way be equated with assimilation. The integration is limited to the adoption of the civic culture of civil society, resulting in a variety of Islam addressed here as Euro-Islam. Thus I am speaking out in favor of an enlightened and open-minded Islamic identity that would be compatible with European civic culture. In line with this thinking, it is pleasing to see that the French are now using the term "integration" and no longer "assimilation"; in other words, they are limiting the understanding of Europeanization to meaning the acceptance of civic rights for becoming European "citizens of the heart."

As a student of Europe and the potential of Europeanization by choice, I am aware of the fact that the "beautiful idea" of Europe is much more than a civic culture. Art too is a part of *das Schoene*/the beautiful. Acceptance of the European civic culture that determines a person as an individual is the bottom line. This civic culture is not negotiable and not compatible with the Islamic law of shari'a.[61] Here lies the "challenge," both to Muslims and to Europeans. Mohammed Bouyeri killed Theo van Gogh because he was a *kafir*/unbeliever. Years ago, Salman Rushdie was denied basic human rights in the name of the shari'a and some Europeans asked for tolerance. Euro-Islam is simply a proposition for a response driven by a commitment to individual human rights, to be demanded of Muslims living in Europe as a kind of a Euro-Islamic *asabiyya* shared by Europeans and Islamic immigrants.

In light of the demographically increasing Muslim community in Europe, the option of Euro-Islamic political integration as a response to this challenge should be taken seriously. The proposition here is that Muslims become members of the European body politic they live in, without giving up their Islamic identity or rejecting the identity of Europe. To be sure, the Islamic identity of Muslim migrants needs first to be compatible with a European identity related to the idea of Europe. The reader is reminded of the earlier debate and of the fact that both identities, European and Muslim, are changable and not to be essentialized. Citizenship issues ought to be placed within this framework. Enlightened Islamic education is a means of maintaining an Islamic identity, but not if it serves segregationist ends. Neither imported Salafist and Islamist Imams nor the cultural relativists of multi-culturalism are friends to the idea of Europe. I repeat the reference to Ernest Gellner who puts it this way:

> Logically, the religious fundamentalists are of course also in conflict with the relativists … In practice this confrontation is not so very much in evidence … The relativists direct their attacks only at those within their own enlightened tradition, but play down … religious fundamentalism.[62]

It follows that not only the totalitarian Islamists, but also those European cultural-relativist multi-culturalists are no friends of the open society or the idea of Europe related to it.

Back to Islam and the idea of Europe: commonalities and disagreements in a historical perspective

Euro-Mediterranean relations reveal a centuries-long history of all kinds of civilizational interaction. Migration is now changing this pattern in a way that has led a prominent American student of Islam, John Kelsay, to raise the following question: "The rapidity of Muslim immigration … suggests that we may soon be forced to speak not simply of Islam and, but of Islam in the West. What difference will this make?"[63] It is sad to see that the differences between Muslims and Europeans based on cultural divergences are becoming an inter-European issue of conflict, while earlier commonalities are sidelined. Basically, migration as a basic concern is bringing these differences in worldviews to the fore within the framework of gated communities in Europe. In public speech, these conflicts are often obscured and even denied, often presented as a misunderstanding. It is important that, in going beyond the censorship of dictatorial political correctness to address impending and real issues, we lean towards reconciliation, aiming not to antagonize divergent views but to talk about them clearly and without concealing them. Only in this manner can we put ourselves in a position where we realize how foolish it is to deny the existing cultural differences and the conflicts they engender.

In Europe, Islam's importance for the West lies in its being a close neighbor. In this regard, there is a shift through migration from Islam to the West and also to Europe. In this new situation there is a need to deal with persistent commonalities between both civilizations in a new manner. As John Kelsay puts it:

> Perhaps such commonalties serve, in the main, to indicate the nature of disagreement between the West and Islam ... But there should be no doubt that in certain contexts, the common discourse about ethics ... has the potential for creative and cooperative endeavor. Given the increased presence of Muslims in Europe and North America – a presence that makes for a more than intense interaction between the two traditions than ever before – it is important to see this.[64]

Even though conflict is the core issue in this book, I argue for a common discourse about inter-cultural ethics and link this to the migration debate. The outcome could be a civic culture based on the idea of Europe to be shared by all. With this concern in mind, dealing with Islam in Europe leads us to ask what our choices are. To do this rationally we need a common discourse and there is a precedent for this in the history of Islamic and European civilizations, to which I shall return in more detail.

At this point, I shall focus on two European extremes at work: Euro-arrogant exclusiveness on the one hand, and, on the other, European attitudes of self-denial being presented in a distorted manner as a self-opening to other cultures. These two attitudes are mutually exclusive and both have an impulse to dominate, i.e. not to tolerate or even consider other positions. The French response to migration to date has been "*intégration ou insertion communautaire.*" In reviewing the French response I would argue that "integrated Muslims," i.e. those who accept the beautiful idea of Europe, are a part of the polity, whereas "communitarian ghettos" are a threat both to the civilizational idea of Europe and to the security of European societies, because civic values are not accepted in these ghettos. In this regard, the Ibn Khaldunian notion of *asabiyya* – a kind of *esprit de corps*, or civilization-awareness – is highly pertinent in the process of opening oneself to others without self-denial. Some see in this issue signs of a phenomenon of decline in the West, concealed as open-mindedness. It is a misperception of Europeans that they can earn respect through self-denial. It is exactly the other way around. It is very important that Europeans grasp the idea that a low degree of *asabiyya* is not the alternative to their Euro-arrogance and racism. Similarly, as much as philo-Semitism does not represent an overcoming of anti-Semitism, cultural relativist self-denial is only the other side of the coin of Euro-centric exclusiveness.

For a cooperation between the two strange bedfellows in the context of "Islam in Europe" for the sake of a better European and Muslim future, the two parties involved need to cultivate an ability to dialogue with one another in order to develop common responses to the pending challenges, and thereby solve the conflict on the grounds of a consensus on the idea of Europe. I repeat my contention that there is no such thing as an essentialist Islam – much as there is no such thing as an essentialist Europe – in order to argue against a constant pattern of exclusive Islamic or European identity. Islam will always be an ever-changing cultural system designed by Muslims themselves, and similarly, Europe can be an open society in which there is a place for the "other," like Muslims, as equal citizens. In short, both need to change.

My reference to the European extremes discussed focused on dominant inclinations among Europeans, i.e. the exclusivist and the self-denying attitudes, and is meant as a reference to great obstacles to an inter-cultural dialogue based on reason. A real inter-civilizational dialogue aimed at establishing multiple identities, a cross-cultural consensus – for instance over individual human rights[65] – is required.

It would be dishonest to limit the talk about obstacles to European exclusiveness undermining the integration of Muslim immigrants. I am equally concerned about the maintenance of certain orthodox Islamic views among parts of the European Muslim community. It is especially worrying to see those views in the Islamic *hijra* doctrine according to which migration is related to the *da'wa*, i.e. the call to Islam as a proselytization, spreading in the Islam diaspora. It is alarming to see the neo-absolutists pursuing their *un*compromising proselytization in the name of religious freedom. Salafist Muslims in Europe refer to the meaning of *hijra* and view themselves as an outpost for the spread of Islam in Europe.[66] This belief – and, of course, the voicing of its rhetoric – can only contribute to the growth of anti-Islamic attitudes among Europeans and to the bolstering of existing prejudices. Among the exile groups of Islamists in London was the one led by Sheikh Omar Bakri before he returned to the Middle East. That group, named the Movement of the Muhajirun, supported the terrorist attacks on the US embassies in Africa and celebrated the 9/11 assaults as "heroic acts of

Islam." Bakri clearly links the status of migrants Muhajitum to the doctrine of *hijra* in the pursuit of the *da'wa*/call to Islam. Like his predecessor, the late fundamentalist Kalim Siddiqi, who established the Islamic Counter-Parliament in London, the Syrian preacher Bakri has become most prominent through the British media. In a BBC interview held after the blasts at the US embassies in Africa and the retaliation by the United States on Sudan and Afghanistan, Bakri described Muslims in Europe by saying "We are all Osama Ibn Laden." Slogans like this are of the greatest disservice not only to Islam but also to all Muslims living in Europe. More peaceful Imams, like Zaki Badawi of London or the Swiss-born Tariq Ramadan, present themselves as moderates, but the fact that they label Europe as a part of *dar al-Islam*/abode of Islam is an offense to the idea of Europe. Cultural-relativist multi-culturalism accepts these offenses as examples of cultural communitarianism and fails to see the religious imperialism that is included within this neo-absolutist universalism. In this context one is inclined not only to recall the judgment made by the late Ernest Gellner, cited above, but also to seriously consider the attempt at an "Islamization of Europe"[67] a recent variety of "Islamic imperialism."[68]

In the search for alternatives and commonalities I propose to draw lessons from history. These are culturally enriching European–Muslim encounters which were reason-based. The reference is basically to the traditions of medieval Islamic rationalism and its impact on the Renaissance leading to European Enlightenment.

The current cross-cultural search for an acceptance of a political culture of democracy and human rights may benefit from history. One can draw much from the words of the Prince of Jordan, Hassan Ibn Talal, who attended the crucial Nexus project during the Dutch presidency of the EU in 2004 and an earlier speech held in 1996 argued that "Muslims and Europeans have been at their worst when they sought to dominate each other and at their best when they looked to learn from each other."[69]

My own research on Muslim–Western relations supports this very profound insight. In my view, the opening of the Islamic mind to Hellenism and the ensuing Hellenization of Islam in the medieval period led to the heights of Islamic civilization. In return, European adoptions from Islamic rationalism on the eve of the European Renaissance contributed to processes of rationalization in European civilization. As Berkeley scholar Leslie Lipson wrote in his work on civilizations,

> Aristotle crept back into Europe by the side door. His return was due to the Arabs, who had become acquainted with Greek thinkers ... Both Avicenna and Averroës were influenced by him ... Aristotle was introduced from Cordoba. Aristotle was significant not only for what he taught but more for his method and spirit.[70]

Muslim thinkers in medieval Islam had combined this method and spirit with their Islamic minds and identities. In learning from Aristotle they were in a position to give the Greek philosopher the status of "*mu'alim al-awwall* the first teacher.*"* That was the height of Islamic tolerance. The great Islamic philosopher al-Farabi was only second to Aristotle in the ranking by the Islamic medieval rationalists.[71]

This reference to historical records must admit that history cannot repeat itself in our age of migration, but in the shadow of looming Christian–Muslim encounters, perceptions and misperceptions are still at work. Therefore, the reference to positive traditions remains both topical and relevant for Euro-Mediterranean dialogue. As Arab Muslims and Europeans in the past engaged in positive encounters with one another on the grounds of a spirit based on *aql*/reason, it must be equally possible to revive this tradition and its spirit as a framework for the needed dialogue in our own age, rather than engaging in new varieties of jihad and crusades.

In the pursuit of a revival of the heritage of Islamic rationalism, the Harvard Iraqi-born Muslim philosopher Muhsin Mahdi believes that al-Farabi was the greatest thinker in Islamic political philosophy. In fact, al-Farabi was by origin a Turk, but his cultural language was Arabic and his commitment was to the Islamic civilization, not to his ethnicity. The Farabian Islamic *aql*-based philosophy is a lasting indication of a Euro-Islamic encounter at its very best. In my view this encounter continues to be of great importance and relevance, and could even provide the framework for Western–Muslim common ground in the age of migration. But instead of referring to al-Farabi, many Turkish mosques in Europe are named after Sultan Fatih, who conquered European soil. This is not an indication of cultural pluralism but an abuse of multi-culturalism! To be sure, cultural pluralism is not the relativism of multi-culturalism. The commitment to a European civic culture that is shared by all stands in opposition to a cultural relativism that negates common values. Multi-culturalism is based on cultural relativism; European multi-culturalists look at other cultures with a sense of romantic-eccentric mystification, following in the Euro-centric tradition of viewing aliens as *bons sauvages*. There are multi-culturalists who look at Cordoba as an example of multi-culturalism, while in fact lacking profound knowledge about the subject. I want to refer to this mystification to underscore my urgent and important distinction between cultural pluralism and multi-culturalism. In this pursuit I need to come back to the question regarding the choices: Do Muslims living in Europe want to belong to a peripheral minority with respective minority rights, or do they want to be full members of the European polity itself, with the respective rights and duties that this entails? I see no contradiction between being a European and being a Muslim. But in contrast to this position, there are Islamist groups in Europe which are not interested in the role of Muslim migrants as a bridge between the civilizations. They are, rather, interested in using the Muslim diaspora for a political confrontation.

The repeated references in this chapter to the Hellenization of Islam in the past serve to present an Islamic model for European–Islamic commonalities in the present day, in order to underpin an acceptance of Europeanization by Muslim migrants in Europe. If this enlightened Muslim position should now fail in favor of a multi-cultural communitarianism that admits different laws and different treatment for people from different cultural communities, then Islamization will doubtless be the future of Europe. There are blind Europeans who fail to see that such an Islamization would result from their idea of "multi-cultural discourse," a romantic ideology directed against cultural pluralism that combines cultural diversity with a consensus over core values. The link of "Islamization" to "communitarianism," as in the vision of some leaders of the Islamic community with the aim that their minority will become the majority in Europe in the future, is the opposite strategy.

Aside from this vision of an Islamic Europe, one should look to Muslim minorities in non-European countries for comparison. In looking to the experiences of others, India,[72] with its considerable Islamic minority, is a significant case in point. In a study completed for the project of the University of Leiden on the Islamic presence in Western Europe, I have for comparative purposes dealt with the status of Muslims in India. Despite the fact that the constitution of India prescribes one secular personal law for all religious communities, the early Congress government, for political expediency in luring Muslim votes, allowed the practice of a "Muslim Personal Law." One result has been the rise of Hindu fundamentalism, of which the elections of 1996 and 1998 were just an alarming sign. This rise is related to resentment over privileges being given to minorities. Pointing to these privileges, Hindu fundamentalists call for the de-secularization of India and infringe on even the physical existence of Indian Muslims. Based on my study of the Indian case[73] my conclusion for the case of Muslim migrants in Europe is that, given the already existing evidence of a growing hatred toward foreigners and the dreadful right-wing radicalism, we should be very cautious in discussions on collective minority rights and also need to discern the Muslim hatred ignited in some mosques against "Jews and crusaders." I have misgivings that any granting of minority privileges and special collective rights to cultural and religious groups would be counter-productive, leading to similar results as in the case of India. Most worryingly, such measures would not only contribute, I fear, to impeding the political integration of these groups, but moreover would encourage the growth of right-wing radicalism on both sides. Some Muslim speakers view themselves in a propagandist manner as the "new Jews" of European anti-Semitism.[74] The hypocrisy comes to the light when, at the same time, they are completely silent about Islamist anti-Semitism,[75] if not openly in favor of it.

Conclusions: what lies ahead?

There is an Islamic and Islamist challenge to Europe. One response to both is multi-culturalism, the other is cultural pluralism. We must keep in mind that political integration does not have to mean assimilation. Muslim migrants can become Europeans, accepting both the individual citizenship rights and duties that would smooth the way for their membership of the club, without ceasing to be Muslims. However, it is appropriate to demand from them loyalty to the democratic polity in which they live, i.e. to the "idea of Europe," a formula which covers the core values of European civil society such as those related to secular European laws and above all the secular constitutions separating religion from politics. This loyalty and the acceptance of corresponding values is in conflict to the loyalty to an imagined *umma* as well as to the Islamic concept of the legitimacy of the Imam. Cultural reforms would enable a Muslim migrant to live under the governance of a non-Muslim *imam*/ruler. On the part of the Europeans, religious reforms are no longer needed, although a change in their cultural attitudes is imperative if society is to become really inclusive, as the idea of Europe suggests. Only such cultural changes could lead to the acceptance of Muslims as citizens. In Europe, the rules of the club and of the game have to be European, inspired by the true idea of Europe. In short, success depends on the willingness of both sides to change and to deliver.

The vision of a Euro-Muslim is based on the assumption that multiple identities are feasible within the framework of cultural pluralism and political integration. In my own life I have lived migration in a context of adventures of identity. In considering this adventure and conceptualizing this multiple identity, it seems appropriate to draw on the idea of "project identity" that has been cited for combining different civilizational patterns.

Again, it will not be possible to promote and defend the idea of Europe within the framework of multi-cultural communitarianism as pursued equally by Muslim segregationists and European cultural relativists. I continue referring to Gellner, who has described these groups as strange bedfellows that, however, end up becoming allies. My criticism of multi-culturalism departs not only from my commitment to sharing a civic culture, but also from my opposition to rampant universalisms. As a Muslim committed to European Enlightenment I oppose all varieties of hegemonic universalisms, be they Western or Islamic. I also believe I find in multi-culturalism just another universalist variety. This is shown by David Gress in his overall study of Western civilization as he states:

> Although multi-culturalism might seem to contradict universalism, the two were compatible; indeed, multi-culturalism was simply universalism applied to cultural politics ... Universalism ... never solved its fundamental dilemma of being both a Western idea ... and an anti-Western idea.[76]

This is a rigorous criticism pointing to the fact that cultural relativism is in fact a rampant universalism. The ethical integrity and the relationship of cultural relativists is also questioned by the late Ernest Gellner in the following argument, which I share:

> Three principal options are available in our intellectual climate: religious fundamentalism, relativism, and Enlightenment rationalism ... Logically, the religious fundamentalists are of course also in conflict with the relativists ... In practice, this confrontation is not very much in evidence.[77]

The reason for this is that both share an enmity to Western civilization; even though this is for different reasons and motivations, the result is the same.

The commitment to Enlightenment rationalism is based not only on its substance, but also on the fact that it succeeded in building bridges between Islam and Europe over the course of two fundamental encounters. The rationalism of medieval Islamic philosophy constituted the seeds of an Islamic Enlightenment that was ultimately prevented from unfolding by the Islamic *fiqh*-orthodoxy. This rationalism resulted from the Hellenization of Islam, and was the result of the first positive Euro-Islamic encounter. The impact of Islamic rationalism on the European Renaissance was the second. According to Habermas the Renaissance is one of the sources of cultural modernity. In a reversal of that second positive encounter, the Islamic fundamentalism[78] of our age could succeed in fulfilling the wrongful prophecy, creating a "clash of civilizations" rather than building bridges to prevent this clash. Therefore, the expansion in the European diaspora of Islamism is detrimental, both for Muslim migrants and for the European societies that shelter them. Political Islam hinders these migrants from an embracing of the idea of Europe, and the result is that they are isolated in a dreadful ghetto.

Ethnic identities are exclusive in character. If cultivated in the diaspora they lead to a kind of neo-absolutism and subsequent related social but ethnicized conflicts. An all-inclusive civil identity based on cultural pluralism is the alternative. In contrast, fundamentalism is a modern variety of neo-absolutism. Pluralism in turn refers to the European concept of people representing different views while at the same time being strongly committed to shared cross-cultural rules and values, above all to mutual tolerance and mutual respect. Tolerance can never mean that only one party has the right to maintain its views at the expense of the other. This would be the opposite of pluralism. For this reason I look at the fairly exclusivist bias of multi-cultural communitarianism as standing in contrast to a polity of citizens based on cultural pluralism and tolerance. One-way tolerance is the tolerance of the loser. Truly, Muslim migrants cannot deny others what they require for themselves. When in the majority they oppress others;

however, when a minority they make victims of themselves if their will is questioned.

The granting of multi-cultural minority privileges to Muslim migrants in Europe could prove to be a double-edged sword with far-reaching harmful consequences. On the one hand it could facilitate the unwanted interference of Islamic-Mediterranean, mostly undemocratic governments in the affairs of Muslim migrants in Europe, which happens already. On the other, it could also lead to the minorities in Europe being used as the ghetto, hijacked by the self-proclaimed representatives of political Islam acting in exile and operating as a transnational movement. These Islamists are by no means democrats.[79] In their hearts they consider democracy as *kufr*/unbelief,[80] while in public they pay lip-service to it and abuse it in their actions. In contrast, a Euro-Islamic interpretation of Islam is in a position to smooth the way for an Islamic Enlightenment that would contribute to an embracing of the idea of Europe as grounds for Muslim immigrants to become European citizens of heart. The necessary rethinking of Islam would lay the groundwork for introducing *"démocratie et democratisation"* into Islam.[81]

In sum, the Euro-Islamic view that Muslim immigrants could act as a bridge between Islam and Europe leads to opposing the politics of making Europe a refuge for Islamic fundamentalists. These new totalitarianists are not interested in the integration of Muslim migrants because they flatly reject the idea of Europe, so why should the open society shelter those who want to undermine it? The concept of civic culture for all, on grounds of cultural pluralism, stands in contrast to the multi-culturalists and to their cultural relativism. I argue that the bottom line for a pluri-cultural – not a multi-cultural – platform is the unequivocal and binding acceptance of the core European values of secular democracy, individual human rights of men and women, secular tolerance and civil society. In my understanding this is the basis for Euro-Islam, and contrasting options of ghetto-Islam or fundamentalist Islam are anti-European. At the beginning of the century, Muslim migrants in Europe face the challenge of having to choose a destiny for themselves and for their children; will they continue to be alien or will they join a changing club on the grounds of embracing the idea of Europe?

Let it be said without ambiguity: It is not an exaggeration to state that the future of Europe will be determined by the ability of both Europeans and Muslim immigrants to establish peace between themselves. They need to forge a pattern of Euro-Islamic identity based on the core values of Europe, described as the idea of Europe endorsed by a liberal and reformed Islam. A polity for people of different religions can only be a secular one, and the idea of Europe is secular, not Christian.[82] The value-conflict between Islamism and the idea of Europe is not a conflict between Islam and Christianity, nor is it a clash of civilization.[83]

7 Political Islam and democracy's decline to a voting procedure

The political culture of democracy is the solution for Islamic civilization

The fact that books are written by humans, who incorporate their selves and their work into their writings, also applies with academic books such as this. It is a fallacy to think otherwise. Some readers who lack philosophical education may not be familiar with the distinction between subjectivism and subjectivity. According to Jürgen Habermas "the principle of subjectivity" – that is, the awareness of the human self as a thinking individual – is the hallmark of cultural modernity.[1] Being a Muslim who grew up in a pre-modern culture[2] in Damascus and then received his academic education in the thoughts of the Frankfurt School,[3] I am familiar with the two divergent worlds and with the related conflicts between both entities on all levels. An indication of these conflicts should never be confused with the rhetoric of a clash of civilizations. As one of the co-founders of the Arab Organization of Human Rights and as a writer of the early Arab left, I have always believed not only that democracy is the solution for the Arab-Muslim world, but also that democratization and cross- cultural morality are the bridges that could help solve the value-related conflicts between both civilizations. This is my creed that directs my scholarly work and it lies at the core of my reasoning.

Introduction

Essentialism has never been my thing. Despite this accusation by some foes of essentialism, those who read my work know very well that the opposite is true and are familiar with my commitment to the opposite, i.e. to cultural change. The recognition of an "interplay between social and cultural change"[4] lies at the center of my work. I was a member of the "Culture Matters Research Project" (CMRP) at the Fletcher School and co-authored its two volumes on *Developing Cultures.*[5] That project was dedicated to the promotion of cultural change, thus belying any cultural essentialism. The views developed in the CMRP research were related to the need for reform, for instance in Gulf societies to ensure the capability of survival beyond the age of oil. This can only be managed through change,[6] and this commitment to change through reforms applies foremost to societies of Islamic civilization. At the top of this agenda is a Muslim embracing of democracy. In an earlier book, *Islam and the Cultural Accommodation of Social Change* (Boulder, CO: Westview, 1990), I argued for a cultural change to match the ongoing social change and criticized those of my fellow Muslims who essentialize Islam; for them, Muslims may change but not Islam itself, as it is believed to be divine and perfect, existing beyond change and therefore allegedly immutable. For me as a social scientist, religion is to be viewed in line with the sociology of Emile Durkheim as a *fait social*, that is, as a social fact, always subject to change. It is pertinent to note that the book mentioned was praised by some as a post-Orientalist contribution while others defamed it as having falling into Orientalism. The discrepancy between the two qualifications is related not to my work but to the way some "non-executive readers" among scholars deal with books, judging without looking at the arguments presented and instead insisting on their own bias and preconceptions. This sad state of affairs shapes ongoing debates as an outcome of the politicization of scholarship. This is not the subject-matter of this chapter; nevertheless, my deliberations in this concluding chapter start with these comments, which are not a digression. The underlying reason for this reference is the fact that there are some readers who disagree – and they have the right to do so, and to engage in criticism, but they confuse defamation and critique. Dealing civilly with disagreement is an essential part of scholarship. Defamation indicates a lack of civility. I always state, with reference to the principle of *ijma'* – the consensus of Islamic shari'a – that there can be no *ijma'* in scholarly debates based on critical reasoning. The outcome is disagreement, and therefore the need to deal with it democratically, with civility and above all with rationality. I claim this democratic culture of debate for this book.

That being said, it is now possible to move on to the core argument of this concluding chapter, namely that democracy is not only needed but also possible in the world of Islam in its present crisis. However, democracy is much more than just a voting procedure. Without the political culture that is related to it, there can be no democracy. There are prerequisites for this democratization that can only be fulfilled by Muslims themselves. In operating on this assumption – proven by the sad experience of unsuccessful democratization in Iraq, Lebanon and Palestine – the restriction of democracy to a voting procedure is rejected. The political culture of democracy is not in line with the agenda of political Islam. Therefore, Islamism is not eligible for the task of democratization. One of the underlying reasons is that religious reforms in Islam, a basic requirement for moving towards embracing the related values of the culture of democracy, are not on the agenda of political Islam which is based on an essentialism that rejects cultural change. I know the text of the Qur'an very well, and I am familiar with the two very short verses (virtually two phrases) on *shura*-consultation, but fail to see a culture of democracy in these few words. Religious reforms and scripturalism are two different issues. Now, Islam is always what Muslims make of it; it is changeable, and it could embrace the culture of democracy, but this is conditional on accomplishing the religious reforms required.[7] In this understanding, Islam is a "developing culture" (see note 5) inasmuch as most Islamic countries are developing societies. In fact, one explanation for the rise of political Islam is a reference to the unsolved developmental problems that underpin the legitimacy crisis. What applies to social and political structures also applies to cultures: all can change.

Current research shows that Islamic fundamentalism is a semi-modern response to modernity.[8] In response to the need to change Islamists' claim that the only exit strategy is to be articulated in the formula *al-Islam huwa al-hall* (i.e. Islam – read Islamism – is the only solution), I firmly distinguish between Islam as a cultural system and Islamism as a political ideology. During my Bosch Fellowship 1998–2000 at Harvard, I wrote *Islam between Culture and Politics* in this spirit. On the basis of this research I do not buy into Esposito and Voll's contention that political Islam is compatible with democracy: it is not. On the basis of the distinction presented, I argue in contrast that the culture of Islam could embrace democracy, but that this is conditional on religious reforms being successfully accomplished by Muslims. The fact that the Islamist-jihadist ideology is totalitarian in its character precludes such an accomplishment.

After having presented my core argument and ahead of moving to the central analysis, it needs to be stated that some of my foes – again they are not critics, as part of scholarship – propound their disagreement in a defamatory manner, contending that I dig trenches between Islam and democracy in order to establish an argument of incompatibility. This is utterly wrong, as an honest and careful reading of Part I of this book reveals. There, I present two competing options, democratization and the jihadization of Islam, and support the first. In this context I present culture as a developing entity in order to view it as a power for innovation in a process of interplay with society, politics and economics (see notes 4 to 6). I do not go for any essentialism or for any culturalism. I also oppose all varieties of Orientalism, of course, including the "Orientalism in reverse" criticized by Sadik Jalal al-Azm.[9] Even though I share this criticism I have never been a foe of Edward Said. I pride myself in having made my very first English presentation under his chairmanship during my very first visit to the USA; he edited my lecture and published it in one of his books.[10] Another personal note is justified: being a Damascene by ethnicity and a Muslim by belief and socialization, I grew up in the cultural environment of an Arab Islam which shaped my personality. How can I be trapped in Orientalism? In my adult scholarly years I went beyond the narrow confines of the Arab world and Europe, and I was fascinated by non-Arab varieties of Islam, be they in West Africa (e.g. Senegal) or in Southeast Asia (e.g. Indonesia), as really developing cultures open to change. In African Islam and in the civil Islam of Indonesia, it is most impressive to see not only the capability to change, but also a cultural flexibility in a combination of pre-Islamic cultural patterns espoused with the religious creed of an Arab Islam. In their Arab-centric views of Islam, many Arab scriptural Salafist-Muslims dislike what they see in Western Africa or in Southeast Asia. In contrast, I find this not only fascinating but equally a model for cultural change in the Arab world itself, to facilitate bridging between Islam and democracy. It is sad that the impetus does not come from Indonesia, but from the Arab world. I have watched Wahhabis decrying Southeast Asians as not being true Muslims, but I have never met an Indonesian preaching civil Islam to Arabs.[11]

In returning to the more general level, it can be stated that this book's analysis of political Islam in world politics and in Europe suggests that Muslims are confronted with competing choices and are squeezed by Islamists into conflicts not favorable to their well-being. Therefore the need to change for the better through making the right choice compels pro-democracy Muslims to come to terms with the self in a crisis-ridden situation, to face political Islam and to stop their "other-ing"[12] of non-Muslims. It is neither the religion nor the culture of Islam that create these obstacles for Muslims, but rather the way Islamists use both in an essentialized manner to undermine a cultural accommodation to be achieved by Muslims themselves. In this environment, Islamists of political Islam spread the Islamic narrative of "Islam under siege"[13] and religionize conflicts. The tensions created by the Islamists on the grounds of politicizing Islam to a religious fundamentalism are the grounds of what can be labeled as "conflict, culture, globalization." This is the title of an international research project.[14]

From the standpoint outlined in this introduction, in the remainder of this concluding chapter I shall discuss avenues for introducing the values of the culture of democracy into an Islamic environment open to change. I do not overlook how daunting and difficult this undertaking is and will continue to be under conditions of a prevailing Islamism with its competing agenda. An alliance between Islamists and Salafists should be countered by an alliance with Muslim democrats. In Europe this is a part of making Muslim immigrants European citizens. I pride myself on standing alongside enlightened Muslim thinkers such as Hamid Abu Zaid and Abdullahi An-Na'im, who are among those promoting the Muslim Democrats of Denmark – a group poised to be the counterweight to those Copenhagen Imams who ignited the conflict over the distasteful cartoons, using them as a pretext to mobilize worldwide against Europe. It is to be hoped that the left-liberal Europeans catch up with this Danish model and stop supporting Islamists, who are in fact the new totalitarianists,[15] not the alleged anti-globalization movement.

Democratization is the solution

The 2003 war in Iraq took place with the promise of democratization in a so-called "wind of change." However, democracy was limited to a voting procedure devoid of the related culture of open civil society and pluralism. The outcome has been that Saddam's "republic of fear" was replaced by a republic of horror. Past-Saddam Iraq is ruled by Shi'ite-Islamists ranging from "the Supreme Council of the Islamic Revolution of Iraq SCIR" with its militias of the Badr Brigade to the terrorist Mahdi Army, purging Iraq of its Sunni population. What a democratization without a culture of democracy!

The reference to the sad Iraqi experience, combined with those of fundamentalist Hamas in Palestine and Hezbolla in Lebanon, supports the idea of the unfeasibility of a genuine democratization under political Islam. To establish a culture of democracy one needs new education in values and cross-cultural morality in an age of civilizational self-awareness and against the odds of Islamism. One cannot talk about introducing democracy and about installing an agenda for the entire Middle East without studying the culture that underpins patriarchical patterns. Kanan Makiya who – under the pseudonym Samir al-Khalil – published the classic *The Republic of Fear*[16] promised President George W. Bush an easy undertaking prior to the entry of US troops to Bagdad on 9 April 2003; he forgot about the culture that underpins the "republic of fear." By the end of March 2003 Bush was addressing the people of Iraq from Philadelphia as "Iraqi citizens," promising them freedom, just like Napoleon Bonaparte in 1798 when he claimed he was "liberating" Cairo from the despotic rule of the Mamlukes. Napoleon too addressed Egyptians as *citoyens*, promising them *liberté* of the French Revolution.[17] Plunder aside, both Napoleon and George W. Bush had to face the disappointment that the spell of democracy did not enthrall the Muslim people, as they had expected. Why not? The answer is quite simple: Democracy cannot be introduced from outside, least of all by force. There is a need to educate the people in democracy. The UNDP report *Arab Human Development Report 2002*[18] links lack of development in the Arab world with the lack of democracy and human rights. Why did democracy fail to "conquer" the hearts of Arab Muslims? The lessons to be learned from the historical records of the world of Islam are also highly pertinent for the education of Europe's Muslim diaspora in democracy.

In arguing that democracy is the solution while stating the absence of a culture of democracy, we need to relate the lack of education in democracy to a historical perspective. In talking about change in the world of Islam in general, and in the Arab world in particular, it has to be acknowledged that education has been the key to cultural change. In the past, Islamic orthodoxy has succeeded in preventing the spread and establishment of the worldview of Islamic rationalism through keeping it out of the madrasa.[19] At present, the revival of orthodox Islam is based on the spread of the madrasa pattern of education. On the example of Turkey[20] we can see that the conflict over the primacy of religious or secular education taking place between Kemalists and the AKP Islamists has been revolving around the Imam Hatip schools educating young Turks. These schools have contributed to the disseminating of orthodox i.e. non-reformed Salafi Islamic ways of learning and related values among the more than one million students who attend. In this context, new Islamist counter-elites are emerging, contesting the secular elites. Elsewhere in countries of the Islamic civilization the traditional madrasa or high school has been revived with Saudi funding to sow the seeds of jihadi Islamism. These educational institutions are currently being screened in light of 11 September and the ensuing assaults in Europe. The key to what is called "Wahhabi International"[21] are Saudi funds to promote Salafist education. This observation applies to Europe as much as it does to Western Africa and Southeast Asia.

The view that democratization is the solution for the world of Islam in its present crisis for coping with pending challenges and for overcoming its misery is combined with highlighting the obstacles to this end. Among them is the flourishing of political Islam as a variety of religious fundamentalisms emerging from the crisis of Islamic societies. It follows that there are competing solutions: democratization vs Islamization. Indeed, both have different answers to the existing crisis and pursue different agendas. To promote the needed change, a new education is required to be put in the service of democracy. In most Islamic countries the issue is *not* like that in Turkey, i.e. a radical choice between religious or secular education. It is rather the way "religion" is being thought of in schools and what Islamic students are taught. In the Salafi-orthodox madrasas in the world of Islam, and in many faith schools in Europe, one encounters the teaching of interpretations of Islam that are not consonant with basic democratic values. In fundamentalist institutions of learning the case is even worse: In their drive to remake the world, Islamists put education in the service of their political goals.[22] The educational indoctrination in the values of Islamism along with the shari'atization of Islam[23] are the political instruments employed for Islamist ends. I fail to share the concept of "Islamism without fear" put forward by some pundits.

For countering the Islamist indoctrination in a war of ideas I contend that there is a need for a new education based on enlightened, i.e. reformed, Islam to promote the global aspiration of liberal democracy. The envisioned "wind of change" in Iraq has not been a success story, but rather a case for arguing that external interference combined with a lack of education in democracy would result in a failure in promoting democratic political culture. On general grounds one needs to relate cultural change in Islam to cultural modernity through religious reforms. It is not a sin to readdress the accusation of "Orientalism" and imposing "Western-style democracy" when democratization of non-Western societies is at issue. There is truth in the fact that democracy can be traced back to classical Greek roots, but it is also intrinsically part of a universal cultural modernity (see note 1). Yet, the norms and values of this very cultural modernity are intrinsically secular, as is the democratic and rational worldview related to them. It is also true that modern democracy is a product of Western civilization. The Saidist critics of Orientalism and the Islamists share an engagement in polemics aimed at disqualifying such cultural adoptions from Western culture. Islamists go a step further and associate such adoptions with *kufr*/heresy. They relate democracy to Christianity and disqualify it by labeling it a *"hall mustawrad/* imported solution" to be replaced by a *hall al-Islami*, as the global mufti Yusuf al-Qaradawi prescribes.[24]

The propaganda of *al-hall al-Islami*/Islamic solution pursued by the Islamists as *da'wa* in a political shape at times embraces democracy for instrumental reasons, but only as a voting procedure. In the anti-European propaganda war Western Christendom[25] and the West[26] are put on equal footing. It is true that the Western civilization has Christian roots, but it is secular. When it comes to democracy the Greek roots would suggest a close relationship between the Western and Islamic rational heritage rather than the opposite, propagated by the Islamists. Leslie Lipson is right in arguing that the rise of the Western civilization can be summarized in one sentence that, though oversimplified, stresses the essential: "The main source of Europe's inspiration shifted from Christianity back to Greece, from Jerusalem to Athens. Socrates, not Jesus, has been the mentor of the civilization that in modern times has influenced or dominated the planet."[27] One page further on, Lipson refers to the historical fact of the Hellenization of medieval Islam as the background for the passing of the Islamic Hellenized heritage to Europe. Due to its great significance I reiterate the quotation:

> Aristotle crept back into Europe by the side door. His return was due to the Arabs, who had become acquainted with Greek thinkers ... Both Avicenna and Averroës were influenced by him. When the university of Paris was organized, Aristotle was introduced there from Cordoba.[28]

The reference to these historical facts and to the related interpretation can serve as grounds for establishing a cross-cultural underpinning for the introduction of democracy into the Islamic civilization. In referring to the classical Greek sources of the democratic tradition in the West and in drawing on the worldview of classical Islamic rationalism, one can repudiate the Islamist rejection of the introduction of modern democracy, and this legitimates itself with the argument of authenticity. The Hellenization[29] process in the Islamic civilization helped it to prosper and to develop an Islamic rationalism with authentic roots. The cultural change in Hellenized Islam is a model for contemporary Islamic societies in their mechanisms for overcoming their present backwardness. I base my arguments on the findings of the already quoted UNDP's *Arab Human Development Report* of 2002 (note 18) which attributes this backwardness to the lack of democracy and of proper education. I unfold my reasoning on the grounds of the following three arguments:

First: Democracy is not simply a procedure of voting, but basically a political culture.[30] This culture can be transmitted and practiced in institutions. Education is basic among them. Religion could provide the needed ethical grounds, but the political culture of democracy is utterly secular. In other words: Religion can both promote and hinder democracy. Democracy cannot thrive without an established religious pluralism, putting all religions on an equal footing, and thus is by definition secular. A part of any religious faith is what each religion claims to be, namely the absolute. In contrast, pluralism without discrimination or othet 'ing denies all religions the claim of superiority over others.

Second: We are living in an age of a "cultural turn" in which those local cultures and regional civilizations defined in terms of religion indulge themselves in cultivating a civilizational self-awareness. This is expressed in defensive-cultural self-assertions. In this context, religion comes to the fore and culture to prevalence. At issue is a revolt against efforts of cultural globalization; it assumes the shape of a "revolt against the West."[31] In the Islamic civilization the outcome is the rise of Islamism, being the result of a politicization of Islam.[32]

Third: I contest the notion of Islamic *shura*-democracy and see in it a disguise for the effort of political Islam to create obstacles in the way of introducing a real culture of democracy.[33]

These three arguments are based on realism positioned to avoid wishful thinking. An argument for democracy as the solution must also be attached to a proper understanding of religion in relation to democracy in contemporary Islamic societies. A conflict can be observed in the realm of education. In coping with this conflict there are different dimensions we need to understand.

The first dimension refers to the gap between globalization and universalization. In his already quoted work, Lipson refers to the Greek and Arab-Muslim reason-based (i.e. secular) sources of the inspiration of Europe as the core of the modern civilization that "has influenced or dominated the planet." On these grounds it can be asked whether these cross-cultural sources can be revived to create a promising scenario for a better future. A contemporary Moroccan philosopher, Mohammed Abed al-Jabri,[34] emphasizes that a better perspective for Arabs can only be based on the revival of their rationalist heritage based on the tradition of Hellenization. The conclusion is that secular rationalism is not alien to Islam,[35] and nor is it imported, as Islamists contend. The values of cultural modernity based on rationalism can be universalized and can also be shared by Muslims just as their ancestors shared the legacy of Hellenism.

In asking whether worldwide democratization is feasible or the global aspiration of liberal democracy an illusion, we need to enquire about possible matchings of structural globalization with universalization of values. I claim to see a gap existing between both processes. Values do not emerge out of global structures. They are transmitted through education. Can values claiming universality be transmitted through education in an age of the "return of the sacred"[36] characterized by the values of political religion?

The second dimension of the issue which needs to be cleared up is culture and its place in development. Culture is never marginal and therefore it is a fact that cultural patterns can promote or impede change: If we follow Clifford Geertz's interpretation of culture, we may adopt the idea that cultures are always local, in that they are based on "social production of meaning"[37] always taking place in a local situation. In further developing this concept, I argue that the cultures related to one another (e.g. by Islamic meaning and the related worldview) group into regional civilizations, as is the case with Islam. In this understanding I have coined the term "Islamic civilizational unity in a cultural diversity." Relating these insights to the subject-matter under issue raises the questions: Can education in Islamic values be employed to promote the culture of democracy? Could universal secular values be established by a civilization which is defined by religion?

These questions relate to the return of the sacred in the guise of political religion and civilizational self-awareness coupled with exclusive self-assertion. At issue is the rise of a civilizational conflict over values and worldviews.[38] Political Islam is a variety of neo-absolutism that belies the premise of cultural relativism. In contrast, pluralism could accommodate diversity in a better way. There is yet another problem with this form of relativism over values, to which Gellner refers:

> The relativists ... direct their attack only at those they castigate ... within their own Enlightened tradition, but play down the disagreement which logically separates them from religious fundamentalism. Their attitude is roughly that absolutism is to be tolerated, if only it is sufficiently alien culturally. It is only at home that they do not put up with it.[39]

The conflict between absolutism and relativism touches on another civilizational conflict, i.e. the conflict over values that underpin democracy. Is there a universal claim of culturally based democracy also valid for the people of Islamic civilization? It is true that Islamists pledge to subscribe exclusively to Islamic values, but nevertheless they do not reject modernity fully. They split modernity in two segments: first, instruments of science and technology and, second, the values of cultural modernity. They consent to adopting the instruments, which are believed to be "neutral," while rejecting the Western values as "opposed to Islam." They envision a de-Westernization of knowledge[40] on the way to a *Pax Islamica*, an order based on Islamic values. With regard to education Islamists accept an instrumental education in science and technology, but vehemently reject education that is in line with liberal democratic values. As quoted earlier, Islamists despise liberal democracy as a *"hall mustawrad/imported solution"*.[41] Does this notion mean Huntington is right? I believe not, for democracy is not uniquely Western.

Unlike Huntington I distinguish between Islam as a religion in the sense of faith, and Islamism as the Islamic form of religious fundamentalism, i.e.

political religion (see note 15). In my contribution to the book *Preventing the Clash of Civilizations*, edited by the former German president Roman Herzog, I outlined my concept of "cross-cultural morality"[42] for bridging the gap between civilizations. If we succeeded in educating Muslims in cross-cultural morality, we would manage to establish a cultural under-pinning for liberal democracy in the Islamic civilization and thus open their minds and hearts to the spell of democracy. In short: there are cultural grounds for underpinning the quest for democracy presented as the solution for the people of Islamic civilization, and they could claim authenticity.

In terms of moral philosophy and education as well as in terms of politics, there exists a conflict between the call for a new pro-democracy education in values and cross-cultural morality and the civilizational self-awareness of Islamism that runs counter to "liberal democracy" being despised as *kufr*/heresy. I believe that there can be no world peace without cross-cultural bridging contributing to the global aspiration for liberal democracy. After the end of the East–West conflict and its bipolar split of the globe into dichotomic political blocks, Islamism should be denied a reviving of this split on religious-political grounds. The conclusion is: "democratic peace"[43] is the solution.

Education in democracy in the age of the "revolt against the West" and the Islamic call for a return of history

The reader is reminded of the debate concerning the end or return of history described in the introduction of this book. This debate can be incorporated into Hedley Bull's contribution, who as early as 1984 described the new "revolt against the West" as one based on values. Unlike the anti-hegemonic earlier anti-colonial revolt, the new rebellion "has been conducted ... in the name of ... values, that are themselves Western," as Hedley Bull states. He continues,

> [this] re-assertion by ... non-Western peoples of their traditional and indigenous cultures, as exemplified in Islamic fundamentalism ... is ... a revolt against Western values as such ... It has become clear that in matters of values the distance between non-Western peoples and Wes-tern societies is greater than in the early years of ... decolonization.[44]

Political Islam as analyzed in this book is an expression of this Islamic fun-damentalism as the Islamist version of a general and global phenomenon (see note 8). The agenda of re-Islamization is an effort at the de-Westernization of all realms of life including education in liberal democratic values. Thus it contributes to a further deterioration in a situation of cultural polarization. In this context a commitment to universal values has suffered a blow yet continues to be a feasible option. Muslim children are now being educated in the spirit of cultural self-assertion which serves the dichotomy between "them" and "us" and ends up in a mentality of "other-ing non-Muslims" (see note 12). This results in an ethnic-religious identity incorporated in identity politics of exclusion and conflict.[45] In Egypt, Turkey and North Africa I came across such conflicts between elites and counter-elites, that is, between ruling elites and Islamist opposition in the Islamic civilization, over the values to be recognized.[46]

Islamists revive madrasa education to unfold re-assertive sentiments and pursue defensive-cultural attitudes. They also use the veil for women, which is one of the symbols employed for establishing civilizational divides.[47] Education in Islamic history serves the revival of constructed collective memories in underpinning the call for a return to the history of Islamic glory. This is not the "restoration of the caliphate" as some would-be pundits like to maintain. Clearly, the agenda of a return of imperial Islamic history[48] is not in line with universal values of liberal democracy. There would be nothing wrong with opposing global Westernization in Islamic civilization if this was reduced to a rejection of the use of Western values to establish dominance over Muslim people. However, the anti-Westernism employed by some Saudi professors in the shape of anti-Americanism uses Westernization as a cover for essentializing existing differences in values and world views.[49]

In contrast to the strategy of "other-ing" practiced by the Islamists and in the pursuit of living with one another peacefully, an enlightenment-oriented education is the proper means for transmitting this intercultural consensus presented as cross-cultural morality (see note 42). Education in cross-cultural, universally valid values is the very basis of democratic peace. This goal stands in conflict with political Islam, which promotes civilizational self-awareness to uphold the call for a return of history while contesting international morality. In fact, this is a call for a "clash of civilizations" that uses the assertion of a cultural identity vis-à-vis the others to undermine democratization and reject pluralism. The pitfalls of cultural self-assertion leading to "other-ing the others"[50] in the world of Islam and to establishing "gated communities" in the Islamic diaspora of Islam in Europe[51] are horrible to contemplate for the future of humanity. Instead, the commitment to universal values is a contribution to democratic peace. This understanding is in conflict not only with the neo-absolutism of the Islamists, but also with the cultural relativism of some trends by contemporary left-liberals.[52]

Throughout this book I argue that overlooking the fact of existing different civilizations would prove to be counter-productive. The acknowledging of the differences has to be linked to bridging through a cross-cultural underpinning of values to be shared and transmitted via education. In again referring to the gap between structural globalization and universalization of values, I point at a simultaneity: It is the one of structural globalization and cultural fragmentation existing side by side. Is this an impasse? My answer is no: a search for a moral philosophy, and an education in cross-cultural values for underpinning the aspiration for liberal democracy under the conditions of value-change, is a feasible strategy. It is impeded by an increasing civilizational self-awareness standing in the way of cross-cultural bridging. In this context one needs an alternative way of looking at the interrelation between culture/civilization, development and globalization. This is the appropriate framework within which we can develop a new moral philosophy for dealing with civilizational conflict in the new century.

Earlier Western approaches of modernization were preoccupied with the dichotomy of tradition/modernity and the related evolutionist view on uni-linear progress. In a Eurocentric manner, they saw in the European expansion an effort at shaping a new world along the lines of Western civilization and its standards. Nowadays, the backlash of the penetration of the modernization–acculturation–Westernization project assumes the shape of a reversal: a re-traditionalization, a counter-acculturation and a de-Westernization. This backlash also affects the quest for democracy in our time. In a real or perceived confrontation of the "West and the rest"[53] in the context of glo-balization, democracy is censured as a *hall-mustawrad*/imported solution (see note 24) by the Islamists.

Under these conditions, how could one contribute to an establishing of the values of the culture of democracy? Is it possible to accommodate this quest with the need of Muslims for authenticity/*asalah*? Is orthodox Islamic learn-ing, based on studying the Qur'an and the tradition of the Prophet, the *hadith*, an expression of this *asalah*?[54] It is well known that Mohammed as the Muslim messenger of God asked his community to "seek for knowledge, even as far as China/*utlubu al-ilm wa law fi al-sen*," yet Islamic scribes, the *ulema*, instituted a contrary tradition of closed-minded education, exclusive and restricted to learning the scripture. The latter established the authority of the *text* that replaces the authority of the *reason*.[55] In classical Islam there was a tradition of learning from others promoted by the tradition of Muslim travelers.[56] New reason-based disciplines of knowledge were introduced, but they could not reach the madrasa institution of learning.[57] Thus, no institu-tionalization of rational sciences could take place in Islam. In cultural studies the insight has been established that the institutionalization of new knowl-edge is conditional to its impact on cultural change.[58]

The exposure of Islamic countries to cultural modernity in the course of the expansion of Europe[59] led to the introduction of modern education from outside, and this created a crisis in Muslim education. A Muslim-Bangladeshi scholar, arguing in Saudi-Wahhabi manner, describes the crisis thus:

> Modern Western education places an exaggerated emphasis upon reason and rationality and underestimates the value of the spirit. It encourages scientific enquiry at the expense of faith; it promotes indi-vidualism; it breeds scepticism; it refuses to accept that which is not demonstrable; it is anthropocentric rather than theocentric ... The Muslim World too has been invaded by this Western form of civilization.

This feeling of rootlessness has already entered Muslim society because our intellectuals are now being educated in the West, being brainwashed and returning to their own countries after reading text-books which are all filled with ideas in conflict with their traditional assumptions. Even in Muslim countries the traditional Islamic education system has been superseded by a modern one which has been borrowed from the West.[60]

In promoting the reintroduction of the madrasa Saudi Wahhabism aims at reversing this trend of rationalization and democratization. It is a fact that Saudi oil money has succeeded in such a reversal through funding the reintroduction of thoughtless learning by rote, using the authority of the text as the basis for a cultural promotion of Wahhabi Islam.[61] This revival of madrasa education under conditions of prevailing orthodox and political Islam is dismissed here, though without falling into the trap of a Euro-centric bias of Westernization[62] or that of ignoring the tensions between the *global* and the *local*.[63]

In concluding this section it can be stated that respect for the values of discrete cultures cannot and should not be equated with the identity politics of self-exclusion that leads to a conflict in the context of the politicization of civilizational worldviews. Ideologies of religious fundamentalism, such as political Islam, undermine cross-cultural bridging. A quest for a convergence of values is the alternative to conflict. In arguing for an education in democracy, I state the conflict and outline a solution for it. Clearly, if the traditional Islamic education were to prevail in the service of an Islamist revolt against the West in the meaning outlined, then there could be no scenario for cross-cultural bridging. The "revolt against the West" debate, and the collective memories revived with such a claim are in contrast to universal value systems and are not beneficial for the promotion of democracy, human rights and civil society. My fellow reform Muslim Abdullahi An-Na'im and I have engaged in projects establishing cross-cultural foundations for universal values and in reasoning about shari'a reforms.[64] At issue is democratic value-change to overcome exclusive self-assertion through establishing cross-cultural, universally minded standards of cultural change. At issue also is dealing with the gap between the globalization of structures and the universalization of values, creating a simultaneity of the unsimultaneous that determines our age.[65]

Cultural change and democratization in Islam

The world of Islamic civilization is exposed to the processes of structural globalization and to the universalization of values of cultural modernity, even though these do not match up with one another. In dealing with the related challenges, the altered historical context compels us to reconsider the inherited concepts, overcome their limited frameworks and bid farewell to traditional wisdoms. Issues of cultures and civilizations are becoming more pivotal. In this context, cultural change as a change of values is needed for overcoming self-assertive attitudes creating obstacles in the way of global democracy. Self-assertive education is detrimental to the spread of values needed to underpin liberal democracy in a process of cultural change.

The dichotomy of tradition and modernity and the assumption of a transition from traditional to modern societies once dominated reasoning in moral philosophy, but are now considered to have been phased out. Thus, values earlier considered either traditional or modern have to be defined anew and related to civilizations. Of course, there have been earlier challenges to the evolutionist paradigm of modernization, for instance that posed by the critical theory of the Frankfurt School. However, the challengers were no less Eurocentric in their views than those who were supposed to be challenged. The social philosopher Raymond Aron was among the very few scholars who went beyond such confines in challenging traditional wisdoms and acknowledging the social fact of "heterogeneity of civilizations"[66] resisting the standardization effects in a globalizing world. Another scholar of the same mode, Hedley Bull, criticized the view that globalization would lead to a "shrinking of the globe" to the extent of becoming a "global village" with only one set of values.[67] Are democratic peace and democratization possible in Islamic civilization[68] under these circumstances, within the context of a cultural change of values?

Given that democracy is based on political culture, we need to acknowledge that there is no global culture in sight paralleling structural globalization. In our new century we are witnessing the return of history to center-stage in the return of civilizations, yet in different varieties and, of course, under radically different conditions. As already stated, cultures and civilizations are different settings and therefore diverge from one another. I contend that each civilization has its own sets of worldviews that determine the values of the people belonging to it. Thus, the issue is to be able to address pivotal issues of moral philosophy with the assistance of general concepts and theories, addressing questions of cultural change that facilitate cultural divergence. It is imperative, however, to honor the fact that in each case cultural and civilizational sets of values are involved. To reiterate: It is wrong to reduce values to a formula according to which they are either "modern" or "traditional" in a mechanistic manner. There is also an interplay between cultural, socio-economic and political change. Men and women are embedded in these intricate processes while they have their culturally determined perceptions based on differing values. These perceptions are not always mechanistic reflections of an objective reality, inasmuch as humans themselves can shape existing realities and are simultaneously affected by them. For this reason the moral-philosophical study of values in the process of change in developing cultures needs to be disentangled from approaches that do not acknowledge these realities, as well as from those which ignore the potential of humanity to give shape to social conditions. Change and values lie at the core of a cultural change that will create the grounds needed to underpin the establishment of liberal democracy.

The study of change and values from the point of view of moral philosophy and its educational links also needs to consider the fact that our century could be described as an "age of extremes," to borrow the term coined by Eric Hobsbawm and used as the title of one of his significant books. This view is pertinent to the present analysis, in that the European expansion has not only been an expansion of modern economic structures, but also entails the claim to Westernize the world in the name of a sweeping modernization. From this situation extremes have emerged. In the non-Western parts of the world, developing cultures are muddling through a process that might be described as "a transition from tradition to modernity." In this context they are becoming highly self-assertive. The reverse is taking place in a Europe which has fallen into a series of postmodern doubts about its civilizational self.

No doubt, from a moral-philosophical perspective all people belong to one humanity, yet given their divergent values they are at the same time parts of varying cultures and civilizations. The processes of modernization inherent in the ongoing globalization cannot undo the existence of cultural and civilizational diversity. In fact, the shrinking of the world to a "global village" has led to an unprecedented mutual awareness and interaction among people of different cultures and civilizations, but it could not "in itself create a unity of outlook and has not in fact done so," as Hedley Bull put it (see note 67). Mutual awareness on global grounds has not led to more standardization, but rather to the opposite: an awareness of being distinctly different; and thus an assertive civilizational self-awareness has been growing. The revival of the asserted values of one's own civilization as directed against the West is among the outcomes of this development. In my study of the civilizational conflict, I focus, unlike Huntington, on worldviews and related values. In view of the fact of a "war of ideas" and of conflicting worldviews, some competing concepts claim universality for themselves. In the case of Islam and the West we are dealing with competing universalisms which contest the claim of others to the same. On the grounds of these worldviews, the tensions escalating to a conflict could contribute to a perceptual war of civilizations.[69] To avert this, one needs a globally valid consensus over values that could facilitate a peaceful conflict resolution. The concept of an international – i.e. cross-cultural – morality would be a contribution to establishing an inter-civilizational consensus based on core values of the culture of democracy. The needed democratization in the world of Islam could lead in this direction. In pursuit of this end, one needs to establish new values and transmit them through education in a process of cultural change. The Islamic madrasa is not the right place for this task. Therefore, its current spread is an impediment to education in the culture of democracy and runs counter to the needed cultural change.

The vision of establishing universally accepted core values of a culture of democracy may prove to be wishful thinking if we fail to accommodate this goal to the revival of local cultures and the civilizations around which they revolve. In this regard I would like to put forward two basic views:

First, the awakening of pre-modern cultures, believed to be parochial (see note 2), and of the religion-based civilizations such as those of Islam, Hinduism or Confucianism is embedded in the same context. It is a context of "world-time" and of "global village." In other words, the revival is articulated as a call for tradition, but the context is intrinsically a modern one. It is the *simultaneity* of the old and the new, the local and the global, which results in conflicting values. In short: at issue is an invention of tradition.

Second, the structures developed by Western civilization are globalizing within the framework of the centuries-old European expansion, but at the same time the underlying values of the very same civilization have not yet been universalized. On the contrary, they are more widely rejected than ever.

The outcome is the earlier mentioned *simultaneity of structural globalization and cultural fragmentation*, i.e. the co-existence of global structures and dissent over related values. This gap between universalization of values and globalization is among the major findings of my work in the past decades. It creates obstacles in the way of educating in a culture of democracy in the world of Islam, which impede cultural change as a process that touches on the social production of meaning affecting values and attitudes.

The debate over cultural change, as smoothing the way for the acceptance of the values of democracy, could be dismissed altogether with a reference to cultural diversity in general as well as within an Islamic civilization subdivided into a great number of local cultures. In my study of Islam I have addressed this problem in terms of arguing for a civilizational unity while acknowledging cultural diversity. Islamic values in Indonesia, for instance, are not the same as Islamic values among Muslim Palestinians. With regard to the prevailing worldview, however, the different peoples of Islamic civilization share the very same patterns vis-à-vis the West, even though they are quite different in terms of local cultures. Nevertheless, their values, even though they may differ, are closer to one another than to the values of the West and other civilizations. When it comes to the problem of the acceptance of democracy in the world of Islam, we encounter almost the very same issues, be it in Indonesia or elsewhere in the Islamic part of Asia. The ongoing globalization generates processes of change in which values are embedded but not universalized. In this context I identify three different levels of analysis: the local-cultural, the regional-civilizational and the global. A mediation between these three levels, aiming to link them to one another in the analysis of cultural change and democracy in the pursuit of a democratic peace, is a political and analytical necessity. The change in values is also a theme of cultural dialogue in the search for value commonalities, i.e. for a shared international morality. Lessons from Iraq show that one civilization imposing universalism on another is no less harmful to the acceptance of democracy than any Islamist particularist identity could ever be. This insight leads to the core argument of this concluding chapter.

Political Islam, institutional Islamism, voting procedures and the culture of democracy

Among the findings of this book is the understanding of political Islam (Islamism) as a totalitarian ideology based in a movement incorporated in global networks of transnational religion. The result is a religionized conflict over a remaking of the world. Islamists envision accomplishing this remaking in two steps: first, establishing an Islamic state for the world of Islam, and then establishing a world order to replace what is termed as the "Westphalian Synthesis," as the basis of the present international system. Those who perceive Islamism as an expression of extremism, fanaticism or radicalism fail to understand the rationale and strategy of political Islam. And those who look at it as a passing phenomenon that has reached its end, or who see it as simply an act of desperation – even if globalized – as some French scholars do, are no less mistaken.[70]

The new movement is the paramount example of the entry of religion into post-bipolar world politics.[71] Islamism is a political internationalism, with two varieties analyzed in this book. The first is state-backed (Iran), while the second is carried out by non-state actors fighting as irregular warriors. However, it is made clear in the first part of this book, where jihadism and democracy are contrasted – as well as in the introduction – that it would be wrong to equate Islamism with Islamic civilization even though it grows from it. Therefore, the idea of a clash of civilizations is dismissed. It is also a mistake to equate political Islam with jihadism. Islamism is subdivided into institutional (peaceful) and jihadist branches; both pursue the same goal but disagree on the strategy for achieving it. While jihadism is committed to the idea of "Islamic world revolution" (Qutb) institutional Islamism (e.g. AKP of Turkey) embraces democracy, although only as a procedure. Going to the ballot instead of shooting bullets does not make a democracy. In short, these Islamists agree to democracy as a voting procedure and abandon jihad. Until recent years this distinction was valid, but contemporary developments have blurred it. The Sunni jihadists of Hamas[72] participate in elections and were able to come to power peacefully, but they maintain their jihadist warfare. In a similar vein Hezbolla built up an electorate, it sends its combatants to parliament and has ministers in the elected government. At the same time Hezbolla disposes an irregular army that was able to win a war against Israel in 2006, for the first time in the Middle East conflict. And in Iraq the Mahdi Army of al-Sadr and SCIRI (plus its Badr Brigade) are both not only in parliament but also have militias on the street. Is this the pursuit of democratization we have yearned for as the solution?

Repeated authoritative reports in the press on Hamas, Hezbollah and the Shi'ite militias in Iraq are not reassuring with regard to their commitment to democracy. All three of them are now engaging in a double strategy. On the one hand they act as institutional Islamists in democratic institutions. On the other, they practice jihadism in dealing with political groups and parties that disagree with them. This is evidence for a lack of acceptance of the political culture of democracy. Added to this anomaly is the fact that, on a local level, tensions between the cultures and civilizations continue to be promoted by all of these Islamists, who aim to upgrade them to a "clash of civilizations" dismissed in this study.

The imperative of honoring the subdivision of humanity into local cultures and regional civilizations is the insight needed for the acceptance of diversity in moral philosophy. One ought to view women and men as equals, without overlooking their civilizational context and setting within related communities. To accept diversity is, however, not to overlook the tensions between Western and Islamic values underpinning conflicts. The solution is the establishment of an inter-cultural and inter-civilizational agreement on core values, i.e. international morality based on cross-cultural and mutual, unimposed universalist grounds. The formula for this combination of diversity and consensus over core values is religious and cultural pluralism. Such pluralism is not consonant with the values and the attitude of Islamists, i.e. representatives of political Islam. The vision of democratic peace is not for them. Therefore, the challenge of fundamentalism is a challenge to the values of the culture of democracy and human rights.[73] The ideology of political Islam is an obstacle to educating in the values of democracy, which is a civic culture and not just a voting procedure. It would be a distortion to downgrade democracy to a ballot.

Years ahead of the revival of the Kantian idea of democratic peace, a group of scholars at the Woodrow Wilson Center in Washington, DC, and at the Norwegian Institute for Human Rights in Oslo engaged in promoting the idea of establishing a cross-cultural, instead of a universalistic, underpinning of democratic values. Among these scholars there were reform Muslims committed to the concept of international morality (see note 64). At issue was not only a reasoning on the potential of a cultural underpinning for the introduction of democracy to the world of Islam, but also efforts at cross-cultural bridging between the civilizations based on an agreement on common core values. Fears of "Westernization" in the guise of universalism can be defused. Among the instruments of such a strategy is a cross-cultural education in values of democracy and human rights. This is a most promising vehicle for promoting our moral-philosophical concerns of reconciliation. Beyond this new education there can be no democratization and democratic peace if self-assertive attitudes prevail. This insight applies – if in different ways – both to the world of Islam and to its diaspora in Europe. In Europe itself the strategy needs to be a different and adjusted one. In an Islamic–Western dialogue, Muslims need in general to learn how to deal with differences and, beyond acknowledging the differ-ences, to agree to a Europeanizing of Islam in Europe, as the concept of Euro-Islam suggests.

The final conclusion relates to the knowledge transmitted in this book about different worldviews and values. If these are politicized – as has been done in Islamism, as a case in point – they result in a political religion that hampers democratic peace. A war of ideas involving rival and conflicting worldviews can even be militarized, as has already been done by the jihadist branch of political Islam. The alternative scenario is that differences can be addressed within the framework of an inter-cultural bridging as a first step to enable differences to be resolved peacefully. Global democracy is the only real framework for materializing such a scenario, and it can only materialize if its culture can be shared on the grounds of mutual cross-cultural values.

In summing up, I maintain that the great challenge of the twenty-first century is a challenge to rethink old wisdoms, to develop new insights and then to do what can be done to achieve a global democratization, which cannot be imposed. We need a moral cross-cultural philosophy to underpin cultural change and the acceptance of universal values. Values are related to ever-changing cultures and civilizations. I distinguish between universality as a state of affairs and universalism as an ideology under conditions of structural globalization, which is a more intrinsic and complicated issue than is suggested by the belief some have in a "McWorld." The idea of a "jihad vs McWorld" is a misconception.[74] The "heterogeneity of civiliza-tions" (Raymond Aron) underpins the heterogeneity of values and could lead to a civilizational conflict. To state this is not to agree to a self-fulfilling prophecy of a "clash of civilizations." A democracy based on a cross-cul-tural international morality, as presented in this concluding chapter, could help to avert such a development.

In relating this general reasoning to Islam and Europe, I argue for a new education based on democratization and its related values in the European diaspora of Islam. If Muslims living in Europe want to join this endeavor, they need to rethink Islam,[75] accommodate it to changed conditions and dissociate themselves from the political ideology of Islamism, as well as from the movement it represents. In short, Islam is compatible with democracy, human rights and civil society if Muslims want this. Islam is always what Muslims make of it. The heritage of Islamic medieval ration-alism provides us with precedents and is a model for embracing the values of cultural modernity in a revival of the tradition of Averroëist Islamic rationalism. In contrast, Islamism is the worst option for the acceptance of democracy. Those Muslims who argue that Islam and civil society are not compatible[76] are mistaken. Those Muslims who engage in questionable identity politics, and not in democratization in the world of Islam and its diaspora in Europe, do harm both to Islam and to Muslims.[77]

Notes

Introduction

1 On Westphalia and the birth of the modern international system of states see Adam Watson, *The Evolution of the International Society* (London: Routledge, 1992), chapter 17; on the pre-Westphalian Islamic system, see chapter 11.

2 On the Mediterranean as a civilizational unity see the seminal work of Fernand Braudel, *The Mediterranean*, 2 vols (Berkeley, CA: University of California Press, 1995). The Pirenne thesis on the creation of the Mediterranean under the impact of the emergence of Islamic Civilization will be discussed in Part III. For a reference see note 13.

3 See Maxime Rodinson, *Mahomet* (Paris: Éditions du Seuil, 1975). In this book Rodinson also coins the term *"idéologie mobilisatrice*/mobilizatory ideology," employed in the present book for understanding the impact of "political Islam."

4 See Fred Donner, *The Early Islamic Conquests* (Princeton, NJ: Princeton University Press, 1981).

5 The interpretation of the Islamic *futuhat*-expansion (from the seventh to the seventeenth centuries) as the first model for an (albeit) incomplete globalization is unfolded in the comprehensive structural history of Islam by B. Tibi, *Kreuzzug und Djihad. Der Islam und die christliche Welt* (Munich: Bertelsmann, 1999).

6 Hasan Hanafi made this statement in a public panel during the European summit on "Safe Democracy, Terrorism and Security," held in Madrid in March 2005 in commemoration of 11 March 2004. On Hanafi see also note 16. On Islamic Spain as *al-Andalus*, see Roger Collins, *The Arab Conquest of Spain 710–797* (Oxford: Blackwell, 1989, reprinted 1994). This Islamic rule is viewed as "colonization" by Efraim Karsh, *Islamic Imperialism. A History* (New Haven, CT: Yale University Press, 2006), pp. 56–68.

7 On this classical *hijra* see Fred Donner, *The Early Islamic Conquests* (referenced in note 4) and the book by Khalid Yahya Blankinship, *The End of the Jihad State. The Reign of Hisham Ibn Abd al-Malik and the Collapse of the Umayyads* (Albany, NY: State University of New York Press, 1994). On Islamic migration to Europe viewed by Islamists as a modern *hijra* pursued by quasi settlers, see B. Tibi, *Islamische Zuwanderung. Die gescheiterte Integration* (Munich: DVA, 2002), chapter 6.

8 Francis Fukuyama, *The End of History and the Last Man* (New York: Avon Books, 1992).

9 See Fernand Braudel, *History of Civilizations* (New York: Penguin Books, 1994).

10 Samuel P. Huntington, *Clash of Civilizations* (New York: Simon and Schuster, 1996); and in contrast the book by the former president of Germany, Roman Herzog *et al.*, *Preventing the Clash of Civilizations. A Peace Strategy for the Twenty-First Century* (New York: St Martin's Press, 1999), co-authored among others (chapter 10) by B. Tibi.

11 Ibn Khaldun, *al-Muqaddima* (Prolegomena), Arabic reprints (Cairo: al-Maktaba al-Tijariyya, with no date), English translation by Franz Rosenthal, *The Muqaddimah: An Introduction to History*, 3 vols (Princeton, NJ: Princeton University Press, 1958). For a survey and on the scholarly debates, see chapter 8 in the comprehensive intellectual history of Islam by B. Tibi, *Der wahre Imam. Der Islam von Mohammed bis zur Gegenwart* (Munich: Piper, 1996), pp. 179–209.

12 Arnold J. Toynbee, *A Study of History*, vols 1–12 (London: Oxford University Press, 1951–61).

13 Henri Pirenne, *Mahomet et Charlemagne* (Paris: Presses Universitaires de France, 1937, reprint 1992), English translation: *Mohammed and Charlemagne* (London: Dover, 1939, reprint 2001).

14 Raymond Aron, *Paix et guerre entre les nations* (Paris: Calmann-Lévy, 1962).

15 See Mohammed Imara, *al-sahwa al-Islamiyya* [The Islamic Awakening] (Cairo: Dar al-Shuruq, 1991).

16 Hasan Hanafi (see note 6) engaged during the East–West conflict in an analogy to the historical situation of the birth of Islam, by then facing two decaying empires, making the following claim: today, "the two superpowers are degenerating, Islam is the power of the future, inheriting the two superpowers of the present," quoted by Martin Kramer, *Arab Awakening and Islamic Revival* (New Brunswick, NY: Transaction, 1996), p. 156.

17 See B. Tibi, "Europeanizing Islam or the Islamization of Europe," in Peter Katzenstein and Timothy Byrnes (eds) *Religion in an Expanding Europe* (Cambridge: Cambridge University Press, 2006), chapter 8.

18 Mark Juergensmeyer, *Terror in the Mind of God. The Global Rise of Religious Violence* (Berkeley, CA: University of California Press, 2000); chapter 4, pp. 60–83, is on the Islamic variety of this phenomenon.

19 See the introduction by Hobsbawm in Terence Ranger and Eric Hobsbawm (eds) *The Invention of Tradition* (Cambridge: Cambridge University Press, 1999, reprint), pp. 1–14; and my article "The Roots of Jihadism in Political Islam," *International Herald Tribune*, 30 August 2005, p. 6.

20 The variety of a "civil Islam" compatible with democracy and civil society is described by Robert Hefner in his excellent study *Civil Islam. Muslims and Democratization in Indonesia* (Princeton, NJ: Princeton University Press, 2000). In contrast, John Esposito and John Voll confuse Islam with Islamism in their questionable book *Islam and Democracy* (New York: Oxford University Press, 1996). See my critical review in *Journal of Religion*, vol. 74, 4 (1998), pp. 667–9; on the needed distinction see Peter Demant, *Islam vs Islamism. The Dilemma of the Muslim World* (Westport, CT: Praeger, 2006).

21 Hedley Bull, "The Revolt against the West," in Hedley Bull and Adam Watson (eds) *The Expansion of International Society* (Oxford: Clarendon Press, 1984), pp. 217–28. Unlike early decolonization as a political revolt, the new contestation is civilizational. On the place of civilizations in world history see notes 9 to 12 above.

22 Hasan al-Banna's *Risalat al-jihad* [Essay on jihad] is included in *Majmu'at rasa'il al-imam al-shahid* [Collected Writings] (Cairo: Dar al-Da'wa, legal edition, 1990), pp. 271–90.

23 Sayyid Qutb, *al-salam al-alami wa al-Islam* [World Peace and Islam] (Cairo: Dar al-Shuruq, 1992, legal edition, new printing), pp. 169–77 on jihad as a "Islamic world revolution."

24 See the sections on "Remaking Politics" and "Remaking the World" in Martin E. Marty and R. Scott Appleby (eds) *The Fundamentalism Project, Vol. Three: Fundamentalisms and the State. Remaking Polities, Economies and Militance* (Chicago, IL: University of Chicago Press, 1993), here Part 1 and Part 3; on the idea of the West challenged in the present day, see David Gress, *From Plato to NATO. The Idea of the West and its Opponents* (New York: The Free Press, 1998).

25 See Richard P. Mitchell, *The Society of the Muslim Brothers* (Oxford: Oxford University Press, 1969).

26 On Arab post-1967 thinking, see Fouad Ajami, *The Arab Predicament. Arab Political Thought and Practice since 1967* (Cambridge: Cambridge University Press, 1981); and on the 1967 war itself, as well as on its impact, see B. Tibi, *Conflict and War in the Middle East. From Interstate War to New Security* (New York: St Martin's Press, 1998, second enlarged edition), chapter 3, and on its repercussions, chapter 4.

27 See Nazih Ayubi, *Political Islam* (London: Routledge, 1991); and B. Tibi, *The Challenge of Fundamentalism. Political Islam and the New World Disorder* (Berkeley, CA: University of California Press, 1998, updated edition 2002), in particular chapters 1 and 5.

28 On this contemporary crisis see B. Tibi, *The Crisis of Modern Islam* (Salt Lake City, UT: Utah University Press, 1988). This book was also published in Bahasa Indonesia,

the national language of the Republic of Indonesia. After 9/11, Bernard Lewis used the same title for a book on this subject (New York: Norton, 2003), unfortunately without acknowledging the earlier use of this formula in the book cited.

29 See the papers of the EU think-tank Center for European Policy Studies (CEPS), edited by Michael Emerson, *Democratization in the European Neighborhood* (Brussels: CEPS, 2005), wherein my chapter "Islam, Freedom and Democracy in the Arab World," pp. 93–116. In contrast, Sayyid Qutb, *al-Salam* (referenced in note 23), p. 169, calls for an "Islamic world revolution" leading to the totalitarian order of *Hakimiyyat Allah*/God's rule.

30 For an authoritative civilizational history of the Islamicate see Marshall Hodgson, *The Venture of Islam. Conscience and History in a World Civilization*, 3 vols (Chicago, IL: Chicago University Press, 1974; paperback 1977).

31 See Geoffrey Parker, *The Military Revolution. Military Innovation and the Rise of the West, 1500–1800* (Cambridge: Cambridge University Press, 1988).

32 See Philip D. Curtin, *The World and the West. The European Challenge* (Cambridge: Cambridge University Press, 2000).

33 See the selected writings of Jamal ad-Din al-Afghani, translated and edited by Nikki Keddie, *An Islamic Response to Imperialism. Political and Religious Writings of al-Afghani* (Berkeley, CA: University of California Press, 1968); see also Rudolph Peters, *Islam and Colonialism. The Doctrine of Jihad* (The Hague: Mouton, 1979). It is utterly wrong to set al-Banna in a historical line with al-Afghani, as the grandson of al-Banna, the Swiss-born Tariq Ramadan, suggests in his highly disputed book *Aux Sources du Renouveau Musulman. D'al Afghani à Hassan al-Banna. Un Siècle de Réformisme Islamique* (Paris: Bayard, 1998).

34 See Tariq Ramadan, *Aux Sources du Renouveau Musulman* (see note 33) and the disclosure of his agenda by Robert Spencer, *Onward Muslim Soldiers. How Jihad Still Threatens America and the West* (Washington, DC: Regenery, 2003), pp. 64–9. See also Caroline Fourest, *Frère Tariq* (Paris: Grasset, 2004).

35 The Dutch Nexus Institute conducted the project "Europe. A Beautiful Idea?" during the Dutch EU presidency in 2004. Based on this project, the journal of the Nexus Institute published a special issue: see B. Tibi, "Euro-Islam, juridisch burgerschap en burgers van het hart," *Nexus*, no. 41 (2005), pp. 173–203.

36 See Anthony Arnold, *The Fateful Pebble. Afghanistan's Role in the Fall of the Soviet Empire* (Novato, CA: Presido, 1993), p. ix. For the role of bin Laden see Yossef Bodansky, *Bin Laden. The Man Who Declared War on America* (Rocklin, CA: Forum, 1999).

37 For more details on this argument see the publication of the "Culture Matters Research Project" (CMRP), directed by Lawrence Harrison at the Fletcher School of Tufts University, in two volumes: Lawrence E. Harrison and Jerome Kagan (eds) *Volume One. Developing Cultures: Essays on Cultural Change* and *Volume Two. Case Studies* (London: Routledge 2006). I was a member of this CMP and co-authored both volumes.

38 On this debate see the contributions in Erasmus Foundation (ed.) *The Limits of Pluralism. Relativism and Neo-Absolutisms* (Amsterdam: Praemium Erasmianum Foundation, 1994) with contributions by Ernest Gellner and Clifford Geertz, wherein my chapter "Political Islam as an Expression of Fundamentalism," pp. 29–35.

39 B. Tibi, "The Pertinence of Islam's Predicament with Democratic Pluralism," *Religion-Staat-Gesellschaft: Journal for the Study of Beliefs and Worldviews*, vol. 7, 1 (2006), pp. 83–117. See also Bat Ye'or, *Islam and Dhimmitude. Where Civilizations Collide* (Cranbury, NJ: Associated University Presses, 2002). In her subsequent book *Eurabia. The Euro-Arab Axis* (Cranbury, NJ: Associated University Presses, 2005), Bat Ye'or engages in overstretched polemics.

40 See: J. Millard Burr and Robert Collins, *Alms for Jihad. Charity and Terrorism in the Islamic World* (New York: Cambridge University Press, 2006), in particular chapter 10 on the "Islamization of Europe."

41 The early essay by Stanley Hoffmann, "An American Social Science: International Relations," reprinted in his collection of essays *Janus and Minerva. Essays in the Theory and Practice of International Politics* (Boulder, CO: Westview Press, 1987) continues to be worth reading. Hoffmann himself proves in a later book that he is not free from this sentiment. See Stanley Hoffmann, *World Disorders* (Lanham, MD:

Rowman & Littlefield, 1998). Other US scholars have started to acknowledge the place of religion in world politics. See Eric O. Hanson, *Religion and Politics in the International System Today* (New York: Cambridge University Press, 2006).

42 Daniel Philpott, "The Challenge of September 11 to Secularism in International Relations," *World Politics*, vol. 55, 1 (2002), pp. 66–95, here p. 67. Philpott addresses the Islamist threat to the secular Westphalian foundations of world order. On this debate see the new Part V completed after 9/11 for the second edition of B. Tibi, *Islam between Culture and Politics* (New York: Palgrave, 2005) in which the new chapter 11, pp. 234–72, deals with the "return of the sacred" to world politics.

43 Hedley Bull, *The Anarchical Society. A Study of Order in World Politics* (New York: Columbia University Press, 1977); regarding the difference between *system* and *society* in international politics, see pp. 13–14. On Bull see the essay by Stanley Hoffman in his collection of articles *World Disorders* (referenced in note 41), pp. 13–34.

44 John Kelsay, *Islam and War. A Study in Comparative Ethics* (Louisville, KY: John Knox Press, 1993), p. 117.

45 Jürgen Habermas, *The Philosophical Discourse of Modernity. Twelve Lectures* (Cambridge, MA: MIT Press, 1987), here pp. 1–22.

46 See B. Tibi, "Culture and Knowledge: The Politics of the Islamization of Knowledge. The Fundamentalist Claim to De-Westernization," *Theory, Culture & Society*, vol. 12, 1 (1995), pp. 1–24; and also Roxanne L. Euben, *Enemy in the Mirror. Islamic Fundamentalism and the Limits of Modern Rationalism. A Work of Comparative Political Theory* (Princeton, NJ: Princeton University Press, 1999), pp. 164–7.

47 On this see Ernest Gellner, *Postmodernism, Reason and Religion* (London: Routledge, 1992); see also the reference in note 38 which includes Gellner's contribution to the debate on this issue.

48 See the most influential expression of this theory in the work of David E. Apter, *The Politics of Modernization* (Chicago, IL: University of Chicago Press, 1965).

49 Samuel P. Huntington, *The Third Wave. Democratization in the Late Twentieth Century* (Norman, OK: University of Oklahoma Press, 1991); and Francis Fukuyama, *The End of History* (referenced in note 8).

50 This is the contention of Şerif Mardin in his chapter on civil society included in John Hall (ed.) *Civil Society* (Cambridge: Polity Press, 1995), p. 279; in contrast to this see Mary Kaldor, *Global Civil Society* (Cambridge: Polity Press, 2003). See also B. Tibi, "The Cultural Underpinning of Civil Society in Islamic Civilization," in Elisabeth Ozdalga and Sune Person (eds) *Civil Society, Democracy and the Muslim World* (Istanbul: Swedish Research Institute, 1997), pp. 23–32.

51 See B. Tibi, *Der Neue Totalitarismus. Heiliger Krieg und westliche Sicherheit* (Darmstadt: Primus, 2004). In a lecture given in November 2004 at Princeton University, the then German Minister of Foreign Affairs, Joschka Fischer, adopted my argument that Islamism is the "new totalitarianism," however with no reference. See the report "Fischer bezeichnet den islamischen Terror als neuen Totalitarismus" in *Financial Times Deutschland*, 20 November 2003, p. 16. In my commentary on the same subject and in the same newspaper, 22 December 2004, p. 26, I referred to this unreferenced adoption.

52 See Fred Halliday, *Nation and Religion in the Middle East* (London: Saqi Books, 2000); and B. Tibi, "From Islamist Jihadism to Democratic Peace? Islam at the Crossroads in Post-Bipolar International Politics," *Ankara Paper 16* (London: Taylor and Francis 2005), pp. 1–41.

53 For more details see B. Tibi, "War and Peace in Islam," in Terry Nardin (ed.) *The Ethics of War and Peace* (Princeton, NJ: Princeton University Press, 1996 and 1998).

54 On the tensions between secular and religious order see Mark Juergensmeyer, *The New Cold War? Religious Nationalism Confronts the Secular State* (Berkeley, CA: University of California Press, 1993). This tension is overlooked in the flawed book by James Piscatori, *Islam in the World of Nation-States* (Cambridge: Cambridge University Press, 1986) criticized by B. Tibi, *Arab Nationalism. Between Islam and the Nation-State* (New York: Macmillan, third edition 1997), pp. 222–3.

55 Sayyid Qutb, *al-salam* (referenced in note 23), p. 169.

56 Ibid., p. 171.

57 See Roman Herzog *et al.*, *Preventing the Clash of Civilizations* (referenced in note 10).

58 See Jürgen Habermas, *Glauben und Wissen* (Frankfurt am Main: Suhrkamp Verlag, 2001). For a critique see B. Tibi, "Habermas and the Return of the Sacred. Is it a Religious Renaissance, a Pronouncement of a 'Post-Secular Society,' or the Emergence of Political Religion as a New Totalitarianism?" *Religion-Staat-Gesellschaft*, vol. 3, 2 (2002), pp. 265–96; see also note 42.

59 Abdullahi An-Na'im, *Toward an Islamic Reformation. Civil Liberties, Human Rights and International Law* (Syracuse, NY: Syracuse University Press, 1990).

60 The concept is outlined by the *rector spiritus* of political Islam, Sayyid Qutb, *Ma'alim fi al-tariq* [Signposts along the Road] (Cairo: Dar al-Shuruq, thirteenth legal edition 1989). See also Qutb in note 23.

61 See B. Tibi, "Secularization and De-Secularization in Islam," *Religion-Staat-Gesellschaft*, vol. 1, 1 (2000), pp. 95–117.

62 The views of the French scholars Olivier Roy, *The Failure of Political Islam* (Cambridge, MA: Harvard University Press, 1994) and Gilles Kepel, *Jihad, expansion et déclin de l'Islamisme* (Paris: Gallimard, 2000) proved to be utterly wrong. More authentic and academic is the study on this overall phenomenon by Mohammed Dharif, *al-Islam al-siyasi fi al-watan al-Arabi* [Political Islam in the Arab World] (Casablanca: al-Ma'arif, 1992). In order to grasp this issue, one needs to consult Arabic sources and not the Western press coverage, unlike some of the US experts on these movements.

63 See the proceedings published by the Jakarta Center for Languages and Cultures/UIN (ed.) *Islam and the West. Obstacles and Solutions in Search for a New World Civilization* (Jakarta: UIN and Adenauer Foundation, 2003). My contributions to this volume are: "Islamism, Democracy and the Clash of Civilizations," pp. 3–13 and "Obstacles and Solutions," pp. 196–200. This dialogue was continued a year later, see Karlina Helmanita *et al.* (eds) *Dialogue in the World Disorder. A Response to Threat of Unilateralism and World Terrorism* (Jakarta: UIN Hidayatullah University, 2004). For my contribution on the quest of pluralism, see pp. 159–203.

64 More on this in Stephen Schwarz, *The Two Faces of Islam. The House of Sa'ud from Tradition to Terror* (New York: Doubleday, 2002).

65 On Euro-Islam see the references in note 17 and the debate in Part III in the present book.

66 On this in Egypt see Raymond Baker, *Islam without Fear* (Cambridge, MA: Harvard University Press, 2003); Carrie Rosefsky Wickham, *Mobilizing Islam. Religion, Activism and Political Change in Egypt* (New York: Columbia University Press, 2002); on Turkey see Marvine Howe, *Turkey Today. A Nation Divided over Islam's Revival* (Boulder, CO: Westview Press, 2000) and B. Tibi, *Mit dem Kopftuch nach Europa? Die Türkei auf dem Weg zur Europäischen Union* (Darmstadt: Primus, 2005).

67 On cultural fragmentation on global grounds see B. Tibi, *Islam between Culture and Politics* (referenced in note 42), chapter 4. I acknowledge that Aron, *Paix et Guerre entre les Nations* (referenced in note 14) coined the term "heterogeneity of civilizations" meaning cultural fragmentation.

68 This is the flaw in the book by Jack Goody, *Islam in Europe* (Cambridge: Polity, 2004).

69 See Peter Neumann, "Europe's Jihadist Dilemma," *Survival*, vol. 48, 2 (2006), pp. 71–84, and B. Tibi, "Gibt es eine islamische bzw. islamistische Herausforderung an die Identität Europas? Ein Plädoyer für eine euro-islamische Asabiyya," *Religion-Staat-Gesellschaft*, vol. 6, 1 (2005), pp. 19–62.

70 For more than two decades books on this subject have been mushrooming, but only a few among them meet professional expectations. Worth mentioning is Rouhollah K. Ramazani, *Revolutionary Iran. Challenge and Response in the Middle East* (Baltimore, MD: Johns Hopkins University Press, 1987).

71 On this see B. Tibi, "The Iranian Revolution and the Arabs," *Arab Studies Quarterly*, vol. 8, 1 (1986), pp. 29–44 (first presented at MESA, Chicago 1983); see also Graham E. Fuller, *The Center of the Universe. The Geopolitics of Iran* (Boulder, CO: Westview Press, 1991).

72 See Udo Ulfkotte, *Der Krieg in unseren Städten. Wie Islamisten Deutschland unterwandern* (Frankfurt am Main: Eschborn, 2003). This author was silenced by law-suits.

73 On this see Maxime Rodinson, *La Fascination de l'Islam* (Paris: Maspero, 1980); see also Franz Rosenthal, *The Classical Heritage of Islam* (London: Routledge, 1975).

74 On Turkey and Europe see B. Tibi, *Mit dem Kopftuch nach Europa* (referenced in note 66) and on the new meaning of the Islamic veil as civilizational fault-line see Nilüfer Göle, *The Forbidden Modern. Civilization and Veiling* (Ann Arbor, MI: University of Michigan Press, 1996), in particular p. 3.

75 John Kelsay, *Islam and War* (referenced in note 44), p. 25.

76 See Myron Weiner, *The Global Migration Crisis. Challenge to States and to Human Rights* (New York: HarperCollins, 1995), chapter 6; see also my book on this subject referenced in note 7 above in which I elaborate further on Weiner's approach.

77 On Islamic rationalism see Herbert A. Davidson, *Alfarabi, Avicenna and Averroes on Intellect. Their Cosmologies, Theories of the Active Mind, and Theories of Human Intellect* (New York: Oxford University Press, 1992); and B. Tibi, *Der wahre Imam. Der Islam von Mohammed bis zur Gegenwart* (Munich: Piper, 1996), Part Two.

78 Leslie Lipson, *The Ethical Crises of Civilizations. Moral Meltdown or Advance?* (London: Sage, 1993), on Islam's impact on Europe, pp. 60–1.

79 Franz Rosenthal, *The Classical Heritage of Islam* (referenced in note 73).

80 Mohammed Abed al-Jabri, *Arab Islamic Philosophy* (Austin, TX: University of Texas Press, 1999), pp. 120–30.

81 For more on this argument of institutionalization see Robert Wuthnow, *Meaning and Moral Order. Explorations in Cultural Analysis* (Berkeley, CA: University of California Press, 1987), in particular chapter 8.

82 For more details B. Tibi, *Islam between Culture and Politics* (note 42), here chapter 8.

83 John Kelsay, *Islam and War* (referenced in note 44), p. 117, see also pp. 26–7. See also the new book by Kelsay, *Arguing for just War* (Cambridge, MA: Harvard University Press, 2007).

84 For more on this issue see Niyazi Berkes, *The Development of Secularism in Turkey* (New York: Routledge, 1998, new edition).

85 Hasan al-Sharqawi, *al-Muslimun, ulama wa hukama* [Muslims as Ulema and Wise Men] (Cairo: Mu'ssasat Mukhtar, 1987), p. 12.

86 On this Islamic semi-modernity see B. Tibi, "The Attitudes of Sunni-Arabic Fundamentalism: Attitudes Towards Modern Science and Technology," in Martin Marty and R. Scott Appleby (eds) *Fundamentalisms and Society* (Chicago, IL: Chicago University Press, 1993), pp. 73–102.

87 John Kelsay, *Islam and War* (referenced in note 44), p. 25.

88 See Fred Dallmayr, *Dialogue among Civilizations* (New York: Palgrave, 2002), on my views, pp. 50–63; and Naika Foroutan, *Kulturdialoge zwischen dem Westen und der islamischen Welt* (Wiesbaden: DUV, 2004).

89 On this see Franz Rosenthal, *The Classical Heritage of Islam* (referenced in note 73).

90 Al-Farabi, *al-madina al-fadila*, English translation by M. Walzer, *The Perfect State* (Oxford: Clarendon Press, 1985) including the Arabic text.

91 Darfur in 2004–5 displays how bloodshed between Muslims and non-Muslims is a recurrent issue in the Sudan. See the contributions in M.W. Daly and Ahmad A. Sikainga (eds) *Civil War in the Sudan* (London: British Academic Press, 1993).

92 On Sudan see Dan Petterson, *Inside Sudan. Political Islam. Conflict and Catastrophe* (Boulder, CO: Westview, 2003).

93 See the chapter on Yusuf al-Qaradawi "The Global Mufti," in Birgit Schaebler and Leif Stenberg (eds) *Globalization and the Muslim World* (Syracuse, NY: Syracuse University Press, 2004), pp. 153–65.

94 See the contributions in Robert Hefner, *Remaking Muslim Politics. Pluralism, Contestation, Democratization* (Princeton, NJ: Princeton University Press, 2005).

95 See United Nations, *Arab Human Development Report 2002. Creating Opportunities for Future Generations* (New York: United Nations, 2002).

96 Mohammed Abed al-Jabri, *Takwin al-aql al-Arabi* [The Creation of the Arab Mind] (Beirut: al-Talia, 1984); see also Abdulhadi Abdulrahman, *Sultat al-nas* [The Authority of the Text] (Beirut: al-Markas al-Thaqafi, 1993).

97 See Mohammed Shahrur, *al-dawla wa al-mujtama* [State and Society] (Damascus: al-Ahali, 1994), p. 16.

98 See B. Tibi, "Between Islam and Islamism: A Dialogue with Islam and a Security Approach vis-à-vis Islamism," in Tami A. Jacoby and Brent E. Sasley (eds) *Redefining Security in the Middle East* (Manchester: Manchester University Press, 2002), pp. 62–82.

99 See B. Tibi, "A Migration Story. From Muslim Immigrants to European Citizens of the Heart," in: *The Fletcher Forum for World Affairs*, vol. 31, 1 (Winter 2007) pp. 147–168.

1 From classical jihad to global jihadism in an invention of tradition for mapping the world into Dar al-Islam

1 Among the popular writings on jihad is Paul Fregosi, *Jihad in the West* (Amherst, NY: Prometheus Books, 1998). Books on this subject have been mushrooming in the aftermath of 11 September 2001. For a more serious introduction see Reuven Firestone, *Jihad. The Origins of Holy War in Islam* (New York: Oxford University Press, 1999).

2 See my article on jihad in Roger Powers and William Vogle (eds) *Protest, Power and Change. An Encyclopedia of Non-Violent Action* (New York: Garland, 1997), pp. 277–81.

3 For more details see B. Tibi, "From Islamist Jihadism to Democratic Peace? Islam at the Crossroads in Post-Bipolar International Politics," *Ankara Paper 16* (London: Taylor and Francis 2005), pp. 1–41. For scholarly Western publications on jihad see first the reader edited by Rudolph Peters, *Jihad in Classical and Modern Islam* (Princeton, NJ: Markus Wiener, 1996) and for a comparative perspective the books by Peter Partner, *God of Battles. Holy Wars in Christianity and Islam* (Princeton, NJ: Princeton University Press, 1997) and James Turner Johnson, *The Holy War Idea in Western and Islamic Traditions* (University Park, PA: Pennsylvania State University Press, 2001). The book edited by Terry Nardin, *The Ethics of War and Peace* (Princeton, NJ: Princeton University Press, 1998) includes a chapter by B. Tibi on jihad on pp. 128–45.

4 On the first Islamic century of jihad-wars see Khalid Yahya Blankinship, *The End of the Jihad State. The Reign of Hisham Ibn Abd al-Malik and the Collapse of the Umayyads* (Albany, NY: State University of New York Press, 1994). These formative jihad-wars were essential to the history of the first Islamic empire of the Umayyads. This classical jihad was continued by the Ottomans until the seventeenth century; it was only halted through the rise of the West in the course of its "military revolution" (see note 12).

5 In my historical study *Kreuzzug und Djihad. Der Islam und die christliche Welt* (Munich: Bertelsmann, 1999; paperback edition: Goldmann Press, 2001) I argue that the jihad-expansion of the Islamic order from the seventh through the seventeenth century (chapter I on Arab jihad and chapter IV on Ottoman jihad) was the first globalization project in world history. In the referenced book I suggest that at present Islamists are trying to revive this project within the framework of their neo-jihad (chapter VIII). Their anti-globalism is not directed against globalization in general, but rather against the one of the West, intended to be replaced by the envisioned Islamist globalization of the twenty-first century.

6 For more details on the Islamic universalist worldview see B. Tibi, *Islam between Culture and Politics* (New York: Palgrave 2001, new expanded edition 2005 with a new Part V), chapter 2.

7 See the book by one of the late sheykhs of al-Azhar, Abdulhalim Mahmud, *al-jihad wa al-nasr* [Jihad to Victory] (Cairo: Dar al-Kitab al-Arabi, 1968). This work is an authoritative one; for other Islamic sources published in Arabic on jihad, see notes 10, 42, 46 below.

8 Maxime Rodinson, *Mohammed*, second edition (London: Allen Lane, 1971).

9 See Abdullahi Ahmed An-Na'im, *Towards an Islamic Reformation. Civil Liberties, Human Rights and International Law* (Syracuse, NY: Syracuse University Press, 1990). As An-Na'im rightly argues, the shari'a views on non-Muslims are incompatible with the idea of human rights. See also Ann E. Mayer, *Islam and Human Rights. Tradition and Politics* (Boulder, CO: Westview Press, 1991) and B. Tibi, "Universality of Human Rights and Authenticity of non-Western Cultures. Islam and the Western Concept of Human Rights" (review article on Mayer), *Harvard Human Rights Journal*, vol. 5 (1992), pp. 221–6.

10 This is the argument of Mohammed Shadid, *al-jihad fi al-Islam* [Jihad in Islam], seventh edition (Cairo: Dar al-tawzi al-Islamiyya, 1989) which is the most widely known and

authoritative study in Arabic on this topic. The early publication by Majid Khadduri, *War and Peace in the Law of Islam* (Baltimore: Johns Hopkins University Press, 1955) also suggests, though from different points of view, that a consistent concept of jihad can be found in the Qur'an. In contrast, I believe such a consistent concept is only constructed through interpretation, as outlined in this chapter.

11 Throughout this book, Qur'anic references are related to the Arabic text in the undated Tunis edition published by Mu'assasat Abdulkarim bin Abdullah. I have checked my own translations against the authoritative German translation by Rudi Paret (Stuttgart: Kohlhammer Verlag, 1979), and the following one by Adel Th. Khoury (Guetersloh: Gerd Mohn Verlag, 1987). In addition, I looked at the sometimes inadequate English translation by N.J. Dawood, fourth edition (London and New York: Penguin, 1974). On the Qur'an, see *Bell's Introduction to the Qur'an*, completely revised and enlarged by W. Montgomery Watt (Edinburgh: University Press, 1994).

12 See Geoffrey Parker, *The Military Revolution. Military Innovation and the Rise of the West, 1500–1800*, second edition (Cambridge: Cambridge University Press, 1996).

13 See Hedley Bull and Adam Watson (eds) *The Expansion of International Society* (Oxford: Clarendon Press, 1984); and Phillip D. Curtin, *The World and the West. The European Challenge* (New York: Cambridge University Press, 2000).

14 See Adam Watson, *The Evolution of International Society. A Comparative Historical Analysis* (London: Routledge, 1992), chapter 11 on the Islamic system and chapter 17 on Westphalia.

15 Bernard Lewis, "Politics and War," in Joseph Schacht and Clifford E. Bosworth, (eds) *The Legacy of Islam*, second edition (Oxford: Clarendon Press, 1974), p. 173 and p. 176; see also Marshall G.S. Hodgson, *The Venture of Islam. Conscience and History in a World Civilization*, 3 vols (Chicago, IL: University of Chicago Press, 1974).

16 See Najib al-Armanazi, *al-Sharii' al-duwali fi al-Islam* [International Law in Islam], reprint of the 1930 Damascus edition (London: Riad El-Rayyes Books, 1990), originally in French as a PhD dissertation. See also the historical documents and texts included in the edited volumes by Bernard Lewis, *Islam*, 2 vols (New York: Oxford University Press, 1987), Volume One: *Politics and War*.

17 See Bernard Lewis, *What Went Wrong? Western Impact and Middle Eastern Response* (Oxford: Oxford University Press, 2002).

18 See David B. Ralston, *Importing the European Army. The Introduction of European Army Techniques into the Extra-European World 1600–1914* (Chicago, IL: University of Chicago Press, 1990), especially chapters 3 and 4.

19 See Sabir Tu'aymah, *al-shari'a fi asr al-ilm* [Islamic Shari'a in the Age of Science], (Beirut: Dar al-Jil, 1979), p. 217, pp. 223ff.

20 Michael Walzer, *Just and Unjust Wars. A Moral Argument with Historical Illustrations*, third edition (New York: Basic Books, 2003); with regard to Islam see John Kelsay, *Arguing for Just War* (Cambridge, MA: Harvard University Press, 2007).

21 Majid Khadduri, *War and Peace* (referenced in note 10), pp. 63–4.

22 Ibid., p. 295.

23 Sayyid Qutb, *al-salam al-alami wa al-Islam* [World Peace and Islam] reprint (Cairo: Dar al-Shuruq, tenth reprint 1992), legal edition.

24 In those times Islamic jihad had been interpreted in Western terms as a war of liberation grounded in the right of self-determination against colonial rule. On this topic, see Rudolph Peters, *Islam and Colonialism. The Doctrine of Jihad and Modern History* (The Hague: Mouton, 1979); B. Tibi, "Politische Ideen in der 'Dritten Welt' waehrend der Dekolonisation," in Iring Fetscher and Herfried Muenkler (eds) *Pipers Handbuch der politischen Ideen* (Munich: Piper Verlag, 1987), pp. 363–402; and Jean-Paul Charney, *L'Islam et la guerre. De la guerre juste à la révolution sainte* (Paris: Fayard, 1986).

25 *An Islamic Response to Imperialism* is the title of the book with the selected writings of al-Afghani, edited by Nikki Keddie (Berkeley, CA: University of California Press, new edition 1968).

26 In this context I refer to Georges Sorel's formula *"action directe"* for describing the totalitarian resort to violence as terror by the jihadists. See the new printing of Georges Sorel, *Réflexions sur la violence* (Paris: Edition du Trident, 1987); English translation, Jeremy Jennings (ed.) *Reflections on Violence* (Cambridge: Cambridge University Press, 1999).

27 On the case of Egypt, see Nabil Abdulfattah, *al-mashaf wa al saif* [The Holy Book of the Sword] (Cairo: Madbuli, 1984) and Nu'mat-Allah Janinah, *tanzim al-jihad* [The Organization of Jihad] (Cairo: Dar al-Huriyya, 1988); on Lebanon, see Martin Kramer, "Hizbullah: The Calculus of Jihad," in Martin Marty and Scott Appleby (eds) *The Fundamentalism Project, Vol. Three: Fundamentalisms and the State. Remaking Polities, Economies, and Militance* (Chicago, IL: University of Chicago Press, 1993); and on Sudan, Edgar O'Ballance, *Sudan, Civil War and Terrorism (1956–1999)* (New York: St Martin's Press, 2000).

28 Mark Juergensmeyer, *Terror in the Mind of God* (Berkeley, CA: University of California Press, 2000); and Bruce Lincoln, *Holy Terrors. Thinking about Religion after September 11* (Chicago, IL: University of Chicago Press, 2003).

29 On the industrialization of warfare see Anthony Giddens, *Nation State and Violence* (Berkeley, CA: University of California Press, 1987), chapter 9, pp. 222–54.

30 The work of al-Nasiri was republished in nine volumes: Ahmed bin Khalid al-Nasiri, *al-istiqsa fi akhbar al-Maghreb al-aqsa* [Inquiry into the History of Maghreb] (Casablanca: Dar al-Kitab, 1955). I rely on the comprehensive study by Abdullatif Husni, *al-Islam wa al-alaqat al-duwaliyya. Namudhaj Ahmed bin Khalid al-Nasiri* [Islam and International Relations] (Casablanca: Afriqya al-Sharq, 1991).

31 Quoted in the book by Husni (referenced in note 30), here p. 141, examines al-Nasiri's work in its entirety. On al-Nasiri see also Kenneth Brown, "Profile of a Nineteenth-Century Moroccan Scholar," in Nikki Keddie (ed.) *Scholars, Saints and Sufis. Muslim Religious Institutions in the Middle East since 1500* (Berkeley and Los Angeles, CA: University of California Press, 1972), pp. 127–48.

32 Quoted by Abdullatif Husni (referenced in note 30), p. 149 and p. 150.

33 See Philip Khoury and Josef Kostiner (eds) *The Formation of States in the Middle East* (Berkeley, CA: University of California Press, 1990). This book includes my chapter on the simultaneity of tribes and nation-states.

34 Mahmud Shaltut, *al-Islam aqidah wa shari'a* [Islam as Religious Belief and Law], tenth printing. (Cairo: Dar al-Shuruq, 1980).

35 Ibid., p. 404.

36 Ibid., p. 409.

37 Jadul-haq Ali Jadulhaq (ed.) *al-Azhar, Bayan ila al-nas* [Declaration to Humanity], 2 vols (Cairo: al-Azhar, 1984–8). The page references to this work will be referenced in the text.

38 See Richard P. Mitchell, *The Society of Muslim Brothers* (Oxford: Oxford University Press, 1969).

39 For more on Qutb see the introduction to this book and the references given there for further reading.

40 The essay by Hasan Al-Banna, *risalat al-jihad* [Essay on Jihad], is included in his collected works, *Majmu'at Rasa'il al-Imam al-Shahid Hasan al-Banna* [Collected Writings], new legal edition (Cairo: Dar al-Da'wa, 1990), pp. 271–92. References in the text are to this source.

41 For the contrast between this understanding of "others" as *dhimmi* and the requirement of religious pluralism see Bat Ye'or, *Islam and Dhimmitude* (Cranbury: Associated University Press, 2002).

42 See Sayyid Qutb, *Ma'alim fi al-tariq* [Signposts along the Road], thirteenth legal edition (Cairo: Dar al-Shuruq, 1989), p.10; and also Qutb, *al-jihad fi sabil Allah* [Jihad on the Path of Allah] (Cairo: Dar al-Isma, reprint 1992).

43 Sayyid Qutb, *Ma'alim* (referenced in note 42), p. 201.

44 Sayyid Qutb, *al-Islam wa mushiklat al-hadarah* [Islam and the Problems of Civilizations] ninth legal edition (Cairo: Dar al-Shuruq, 1988); and Sayyid Qutb, *al-mustaqbal li hadha al-din* [The Future Belongs to this Religion] (Cairo: Dar al-Shuruq, 1981).

45 Sayyid Qutb, *Ma'alim* (referenced in note 42), p. 72.

46 Muhammad Na'im Yasin, *al-jihad. Mayadinahu wa asalibahu* [The Fields and Methods of Jihad] (Algiers: Dar al-Irschad, 1990), p. 76.

47 Ibid., p. 77 and p. 81.

48 Colonel (al-Muqaddam) Ahmad al-Mu'mini, *al-ta'bi'a al-jihadiyya fi al-Islam* [The Jihadist Mobilization for Islam] (Constantine, Algeria: Mu'asasat al-Isra, 1991).

49 For an interpretation of shari'a see B. Tibi, *Islam between Culture and Politics* (New York: Palgrave, 2001), chapter 7, and Ann E. Mayer, "The Shari'a: A Methodology or a Body of Substantive Rules?" in Nicholas Heer (ed.) *Islamic Law and Jurisprudence* (Seattle, WA: University of Washington Press, 1990), pp. 177–98.

50 Mohammed Said al-Ashmawi, *Usul al-shari'a* [The Origins of Shari'a] (Cairo: Madbuli, 1983).

51 Among these authors is James Piscatori, *Islam in the World of Nation States* (Cambridge: Cambridge University Press, 1986). The constructed concept of an "Islamic state/*dawla islamiyya*" is a recent Islamist addition to Islamic thought; it does not exist in the classical sources of Islam; the recent call for it is an indication of the ideology of Islamic fundamentalism. See, among others, Muhammad Hamidullah, *The Muslim Conduct of State* (Lahore: Sh. Muhammad Ashraf, 1977); Abdulrahman A. Kurdi, *The Islamic State* (London: Mansell, 1984); and for a critical evaluation B. Tibi, *The Challenge of Fundamentalism. Political Islam and the New World Disorder* (Berkeley, CA: University of California Press 1998, updated edition 2002), chapters 7 and 8.

52 Najib al-Armanazi (referenced in note 16); the page references in the following are given in the text.

53 See B. Tibi, *Islam and the Cultural Accommodation of Social Change* (Boulder, CO: Westview, 1990).

54 Ann E. Mayer, *War and Peace in the Islamic Tradition: International Law, mimeograph, ref. no. 141* (Philadelphia, PA: University of Pennsylvania, Wharton School, Department of Legal Studies, no date), p. 45.

55 See B. Tibi, *Conflict and War in the Middle East. From Interstate War to New Security*, second edition (New York: St Martin's Press, 1998); and also the third edition of my book, *Arab Nationalism. Between Islam and the Nation State* (London: Macmillan, 1997).

56 Abdullatif Husni, *al-Islam* (referenced in note 30), p. 59.

57 Charles Tilly, *The Formation of National States in Western Europe* (Princeton, NJ: Princeton University Press, 1985), p. 45.

58 On pre-modern societies see Patricia Crone, *Pre-Industrial Societies. Anatomy of the Pre-Modern World* (Oxford: Oneworld, new printing, 2003).

59 See Fazlur Rahman, *Islam and Modernity. Transformation of an Intellectual Tradition* (Chicago, IL: University of Chicago Press, 1982); W. Montgomery Watt, *Islamic Fundamentalism and Modernity* (London: Routledge, 1988); and B. Tibi, *The Crisis of Modern Islam. A Preindustrial Culture in the Scientific-Technological Age* (Salt Lake City, UT: University of Utah Press, 1988).

2 Polity and rule: the Islamic quest for civil society and for democracy against Hakimiyyat Allah as the Islamist system of totalitarian government

1 On this issue see the contributions to the volume edited by Larry Diamond *et al.*, *Islam and Democracy in the Middle East* (Baltimore, MD: Johns Hopkins University Press, 2003) and also Noah Feldman, *After Jihad. America and the Struggle for Islamic Democracy* (New York: Farrar and Straus, 2004).

2 Şerif Mardin, "Civil Society in Islam," in John Hall (ed.) *Civil Society. Theory, History, Comparison* (Cambridge: Polity Press, 1995), pp. 278–9.

3 The fallacy of an "Islamization of democracy" parallel to the missing distinction between Islam and Islamism is among the flaws in the highly contestable book by John Esposito and John Voll, *Islam and Democracy* (New York: Oxford University Press, 1996); see my critique in *Journal of Religion*, vol. 78, 4 (1998), pp. 667–9.

4 See Mohammed Arkoun, *Rethinking Islam* (Boulder, CO: Westview, 1994).

5 The allegation of the Christian roots of the idea of Europe is made by the Oxford scholar Larry Siedentop, *Democracy in Europe* (London: Penguin Books, 2000), in particular chapter 10. This view is contested in Part III of the present book.

6 The Muslim reformer Abdullahi An-Na'im argues in a similar manner with regard to human rights and their introduction into Islam: He dismisses the notion of their Christian roots in highlighting their secular character; see his book, *Toward an Islamic Reformation* (Syracuse, NY: Syracuse University Press, 1990) and his other volume,

edited together with Francis Deng, *Human Rights in Africa. Cross-Cultural Perspectives* (Washington, DC: Brookings, 1990), wherein also my contribution "The European Tradition of Human Rights and the Culture of Islam," pp. 104–32.

7 See Samuel P. Huntington, *Clash of Civilizations* (New York: Simon and Schuster, 1996); and in contrast, B. Tibi, "International Morality and Cross-Cultural Bridging," in Roman Herzog *et al.*, *Preventing the Clash of Civilizations. A Peace Strategy for the Twenty-First Century* (New York: St Martin's Press, 1999), pp. 107–26.

8 See Hisham Sharabi, *Neopatriarchy. A Theory of Distorted Change in Arab Society* (New York: Oxford University Press, 1992).

9 Sayyid Qutb, *al-jihad fi sabil Allah* [Jihad on the Path of God] (Cairo: Dar al-Isma, 1992, reprint) and also the reprint of Qutb, *al-salam al-alami wa al-Islam* [World Peace and Islam] (Cairo: al-Shuruq, 1992).

10 For more details see B. Tibi*, The Challenge of Fundamentalism. Political Islam and the New World Disorder* (Berkeley, CA: University of California Press, 1998, enlarged and updated edition 2002).

11 Daniel Philpott, "The Challenge of September 11 to Secularism in International Relations," *World Politics*, vol. 55, 1 (October 2002), pp. 66–95.

12 The literature on this subject is mushrooming. Worth mentioning are the books by Shireen Tahmasseb Hunter, *The Future of Islam and the West. Clash of Civilizations or Peaceful Coexistence?* (London: Praeger, 1998); Fawaz Gerges, *America and Political Islam. Clash of Cultures or Clash of Interests?* (Cambridge: Cambridge University Press, 1999); Graham E. Fuller and Ian Lesser, *A Sense of Siege. The Geopolitics of Islam and the West* (Boulder, CO: Westview Press, 1995). For an inter-civilizational dialogue perspective see chapter 10 in the Harvard book by B. Tibi, *Islam between Culture and Politics* (New York: Palgrave, 2001, enlarged edition, 2005), pp. 210–30.

13 B. Tibi, "Democracy and Democratization in Islam," in Michèle Schmiegelow (ed.) *Democracy in Asia* (New York: St Martin's Press, 1997), pp. 127–46; and chapter 9 in B. Tibi, *The Challenge of Fundamentalism* (referenced in note 10).

14 Robert Hefner, *Civil Islam. Muslims and Democratization in Indonesia* (Princeton, NJ: Princeton University Press, 2000). While writing this book in Jakarta, Indonesia, I found that location made it possible to engage in this reasoning; see my contributions to Chaider Bamualin (ed.) *Islam and the West* (Jakarta: UIN Hidayatullah University, 2003); and to Karlina Helmanita *et al.* (eds) *Dialogue in the World Disorder. A Response to Threat of Unilateralism and World Terrorism* (Jakarta: UIN Hidayatullah University, 2004).

15 Robert Hefner, *Civil Islam* (referenced in note 14), p. 20.

16 Masykuri Abdillah, *Responses of Indonesian Muslim Intellectuals to the Concept of Democracy* (Hamburg: Abera Verlag, 1997).

17 On popular sovereignty see David Held, *Democracy and the Global Order. From the Modern State to Cosmopolitan Governance* (Stanford, CA: Stanford University Press, 1995), pp. 31–47; and F.H. Hinsley, *Sovereignty* (Cambridge: Cambridge University Press, second edition 1986).

18 Masykuri Abdillah, *Responses* (referenced in note 16), p. 250.

19 Bruce Russett, *Grasping the Democratic Peace. Principles for a Post-Cold War World* (Princeton, NJ: Princeton University Press, 1993), p. 11.

20 Ibid., p. 135.

21 See Chapter 1 of this book and also B. Tibi, "War and Peace in Islam," in Terry Nardin (ed.) *The Ethics of War and Peace* (Princeton, NJ: Princeton University Press, 1996, also 1998), pp. 128–45; and on the status of minorities of non-Muslims in Islam see Bat Ye'or, *Islam and Dhimmitude* (Cranbury, NJ: Associated University Press, 2002).

22 Martin Marty and Scott Appleby (eds) *The Fundamentalism Project*, 5 vols, (Chicago, IL: University of Chicago Press, 1991–5), wherein see B. Tibi, "The Worldview of Sunni Arab Fundamentalists," vol. 2, *Fundamentalisms and Society* (1993), and also parts I and III in vol. 3, *Fundamentalisms and the State* on remaking polities.

23 Mark Juergensmeyer, *The New Cold War? Religious Nationalism Confronts the Secular State* (Berkeley, CA: University of California Press, 1993); and the subsequent volume by the same author: *Terror in the Mind of God* (Berkeley, CA: University of California Press, 2000).

24 On this argument see Ernest Gellner, "Expiation through Subjectivism," in Erasmus Foundation (ed.) *The Limits of Pluralism. Relativism and Neo-Absolutisms* (Amsterdam: Praemium Erasmianum Foundation, 1994), pp. 163–5.
25 See Mary Kaldor, *Global Civil Society* (Cambridge: Polity Press, 2003).
26 Abu al-A'la al-Mawdudi, *al-Islam wa al-madaniyya al-haditha* [Islam and Modern Civilization] (Cairo: reprint, no date). On these views of Mawdudi see also Muhammad Dharif, *al-Islam al-siyasi fi al-watan al-arabi* [Political Islam in the Arab World] (Casablanca: Maktabat al-Umma and al-Ma'arif, 1992), pp. 98–9; and Youssef M. Choueiri, *Islamic Fundamentalism* (Boston, MA: Twayne, 1990), pp. 93ff.
27 Jean François Revel, *Democracy Against Itself* (New York: Free Press, 1993), p. 200.
28 Ibid., p. 211.
29 Ibid., p. 217.
30 See B. Tibi, *Islamische Zuwanderung. Die gescheiterte Integration* (Munich: Deutsche Verlagsanstalt, 2002), on parallel societies as Islamic enclaves, chapters 3 and 4.
31 John Ehrenburg, *The Idea of Civil Society. The Critical History of an Idea* (New York: New York University Press, 1999).
32 Michael Walzer (ed. and transl.) *Al-Farabi on the Perfect State* (Oxford: Oxford University Press, 1985).
33 See chapter 2 in B. Tibi, *Islam between Culture and Politics* (referenced in note 12), pp. 53–68.
34 For views of liberal Islam see Mohammed Said al-Ashmawi, *Jauhar al-Islam* [The Core of Islam] (Cairo: Sinah, 1992); Mohammed al-Jabri, *al-turath wa al-hadatha* [Heritage and Modernity] (Beirut: al-Markaz al-Thaqafi, 1991) and Mohammed Arkoun, *Rethinking Islam* (Boulder, CO: Westview, 1994). It is most disturbing and ill-informing to see texts by fundamentalists (e.g. al-Qaradawi *et al.*) being listed in the disinforming and misleading reader edited by Charles Kurzman, *Liberal Islam* (New York: Oxford University Press, 1998).
35 See Hasan Hanafi, *al-din wa al-thaura* [Religion and Revolution], 8 vols (Cairo: Madbuli, 1977–88); Mohammed Shahrur, *al-kitab wa al-Qur'an, qira'a mu'asira* [The Book of the Qur'an. A Modern Reasoning] (Beirut: Sharikat al-Matbu'at, sixth edition 2000).
36 See B. Tibi, *Der wahre Imam. Der Islam von Mohammed bis zur Gegenwart* (Munich: Piper, 1996, several editions). This is a comprehensive intellectual history of Islam.
37 On the first and second wave of Hellenization in classical Islam see W.M. Watt, *Islamic Philosophy and Theology* (Edinburgh: Edinburgh University Press, 1962, reprinted last 1979), pp. 37ff, 91ff. The magnitude of intellectual indebtedness of Islamic political philosophy to Hellenism is shown in the contributions published in Charles Butterworth (ed.) *The Political Aspects of Islamic Philosophy. Essays in Honor of Muhsin S. Mahdi*, Harvard Middle Eastern Monographs (Cambridge, MA: Harvard University Press, 1992). Mahdi was the source of intellectual inspiration for me while I was writing my history of ideas of Islam, *Der wahre Imam* (referenced in note 36), wherein part II on Islamic rationalism and Hellenization (and on the impact of Mahdi on my thinking see the acknowledgement in that book on p. 13).
38 See note 32 above, and further on al-Farabi, T.J. de Boer, *Geschichte der Philosophie im Islam* (Stuttgart: Fromann, 1901), pp. 98–116; on al-Farabi as second master see p. 100.
39 Abu al-A'la al-Mawdudi, *al-Islam wa al-madaniyya al-haditha* (referenced in note 26).
40 Huntington, *The Third Wave. Democratization in the Late Twentieth Century* (Norman, OK: University of Oklahoma Press, 1991).
41 The authoritative history of Islamic civilization is Marshall Hodgson, *The Venture of Islam, Conscience and History in a World Civilization*, 3 vols (Chicago, IL: University of Chicago Press, 1974).
42 See John Esposito and John Voll, *Islam and Democracy* (referenced in note 3).
43 See the authoritative criticism of political Islam by a leading enlightened Muslim, Mohammed Said al-Ashmawi, *al-Islam al-siyasi* [Political Islam] (Cairo: Sinah, 1987), French translation: *L'Islamisme contre L'Islam* (Paris: La Decouverte, 1989), pp. 667–9.
44 See John Kelsay, *Islam and War. A Study in Comparative Ethics* (Louisville, KY: John Knox Press, 1993), p. 117.
45 See Bassam Tibi, "Islamic Law/Shari'a, Human Rights, Universal Morality and International Relations," *Human Rights Quarterly*, vol. 16, 2 (May 1994), pp. 277–99.

46 See the proceedings of the Erasmus Ascension Symposium (referenced in note 24).
47 On this see Ernest Gellner, *Postmodernism, Reason and Religion* (London: Routledge, 1992), in particular pp. 84f. (see also note 24).
48 B. Tibi, *Der neue Totalitarismus. Heiliger Krieg und westliche Sicherheit* (Darmstadt: Primus, 2004).
49 Robert Kaplan, *The Coming Anarchy. Shuttering the Dreams of Post Cold War* (New York: Random House, 2000).
50 For a historical background see M.C. Ricklefs, *A History of Modern Indonesia*, second edition (Stanford, CA: Stanford University Press, 1993), here part VI, pp. 237ff. See also Robert Hefner, *Civil Islam* (referenced in note 14).
51 Fred von der Mehden, *Two Worlds of Islam. Interaction between Southeast Asia and the Middle East* (Miami-Jacksonville, FL: University of Florida Press, 1993), p. 97.
52 Hamid Enayat, *Modern Islamic Political Thought* (Austin, TX: University of Texas Press, 1982), pp. 125–38.
53 On these encounters in the nineteenth century see William M. Watt, *Muslim–Christian Encounters* (London: Routledge, 1991).
54 Rifa'a Rafi al-Tahtawi, *Takhlis al-ibriz ila talkis Paris* [Paris Diary] (Beirut: Ibn Zaidun, reprint, no date). See the German translation of Tahtawi's Paris diary, completed and ed. by Karl Stowasser, *Ein Muslim entdeckt Europa* (Munich: C.H. Beck Verlag, 1989), p. 223.
55 See Leonard Binder, *Islamic Liberalism. A Critique of Development Ideologies* (Chicago, IL: University of Chicago Press, 1988). Despite deep respect for Binder's scholarship I have, however, had a hard time swallowing the chapter in his book on the intellectual father of Islamic fundamentalism Sayyid Qutb (labeled as a "religious aesthetic") being incorporated as a part of deliberations on Islamic liberalism (sic!). An even worse case is the anthology of Charles Kurzman (ed.) *Liberal Islam* (New York: Oxford University Press, 1998), in which leading fundamentalists are presented as "liberals."
56 Abbas Mahmud al-Aqqad, *al-demoqratiyya fi al-Islam* [Democracy in Islam] (Cairo: 1952, many reprints).
57 See W.M. Watt, *Islamic Philosophy and Theology* (Edinburgh: Edinburgh University Press, 1962).
58 Leslie Lipson, *The Ethical Crises of Civilization: Moral Meltdown or Advance?* (London: Sage, 1993), p. 63. For a detailed record of the cultural influence of Islamic civilization upon the European Renaissance see also Bassam Tibi, *Kreuzzug und Djihad. Der Islam und die christliche Welt* (Munich: Bertelsmann, 1999), chapter V.
59 This formula is coined in accordance with Ernst Bloch, *Avicenna und die aristotelische Linke* (Frankfurt am Main: Suhrkamp, 1963).
60 At the top of them we find Mohammed Abed al-Jabri, *Arab Islamic Philosophy* (Austin, TX: University of Texas, 1999).
61 See George Makdisi, *The Rise of Colleges. Institutions of Learning in Islam and the West* (Edinburgh: Edinburgh University Press, 1981), pp. 77–80.
62 For an elaboration of the two rival traditions in Islamic intellectual history, i.e. *fiqh* versus *falsafa*, see B. Tibi, "Politisches Denken im klassischen und mittelalterlichen Islam zwischen Fiqh und Falsafa," in Iring Fetscher and Herfried Muenkler (eds) *Pipers Handbuch der politischen Ideen: Das Mittelalter*, vol. II (Munich: Piper Verlag, 1993) pp. 87–140. See also part II in B. Tibi, *Der wahre Imam* (referenced in note 36).
63 On this issue see Robert Wuthnow, *Meaning and Moral Order* (Berkeley, CA: University of California Press, 1987), chapter 8.
64 For more details see Anke von Kuegelgen, *Averroës und die arabische Moderne. Ansaetze zu einer Neugruendung des Rationalismus im Islam* (Leiden: Brill Press, 1994).
65 See Albert Hourani, *Arabic Thought in the Liberal Age, 1798–1939* (Oxford: Oxford University Press, 1962).
66 Hamid Enayat, *Modern Islamic Political Thought* (referenced in note 52), pp. 138f.
67 See the overview of Adeed Dawisha, *Arab Nationalism. From Triumph to Despair* (Princeton, NJ: Princeton University Press, 2003) and also B. Tibi, *Arab Nationalism. Between Islam and the Nation-State* (New York and London: Macmillan and St Martin's Press, third enlarged edition 1997).

68 On this war see the two chapters of part II in B. Tibi, *Conflict and War in the Middle East, From Interstate War to New Security* (New York: St Martin's Press, second edition 1998) and Adeed Dawisha, *Arab Nationalism* (referenced in note 67), chapter 10 on "1967 and after."

69 In Raymond W. Baker, *Islam without Fear. Egypt and the New Islamists* (Cambridge, MA: Harvard University Press, 2003) political Islam is presented in a very distorted manner.

70 Therefore, I strongly disagree with John Esposito and John Voll, *Islam and Democracy* (referenced in note 3). Similarly I see great shortcomings in Esposito's *The Islamic Threat. Myth or Reality* (New York: Oxford University Press, 1992). Certainly Islam is no threat; however, it is highly misleading to confuse Islam and Islamism.

71 Ellis Goldberg *et al.* (eds) *Rules and Rights in the Middle East: Democracy, Law, and Society* (Seattle, WA: University of Washington Press, 1993), p. 8.

72 See the article "Fundamentalism" by B. Tibi, in S.M. Lipset (ed.) *The Encyclopedia of Democracy*, 4 vols (Washington, DC: The Congressional Quarterly, 1995), vol. 2, pp. 507–10; and also my recent chapter on "Islamic Fundamentalism," in Mary Hawkesworth and Maurice Kogan (eds) *Encyclopedia of Government*, 2 vols, second edition (London: Routledge, 2004), vol. 1, chapter 13, pp. 184–204.

73 Sayyid Qutb, *Ma'alim fi al-tariq* [Signposts along the Road], thirteenth legal printing (Cairo: al-Shuruq, 1989). For an interesting Qutb interpretation see Roxanne Euben, *Enemy in the Mirror* (Princeton, NJ: Princeton University Press, 1999), chapter 3.

74 Yusuf al-Qaradawi, *Hatmiyyat al-hall al-Islami wa al-hulul al-mustawradah* [The Islamic Solution and the Imported Solutions], new printing (Cairo: Mu'assat al-Risalah, 1980), p. 50f. Qaradawi is the leading Islamist – not a liberal, as Charles Kurzman (see note 34) contends.

75 On this misconception of al-Qaradawi in US publications see note 34 above.

76 Hamid Enayat, *Modern Islamic Political Thought* (referenced in note 52), p. 131.

77 On Islamic law see chapter 7 in B. Tibi, *Islam between Culture and Politics* (referenced in note 12), pp. 148–66. See also the book by Mohammed Said al-Ashmawi, *Usul al-shari'a* [The Origins of the Shari'a] (Cairo: Madbuli, 1983).

78 Joseph Schacht, *An Introduction to Islamic Law* (Oxford: Clarendon Press, 1964), p. 54.

79 Hamid Enayat, *Modern Islamic Political Thought* (referenced in note 52), p. 131.

80 Ibid., p. 126.

81 Mohammed Arkoun, *Rethinking Islam* (referenced in note 4).

82 B. Tibi, *Islam and the Cultural Accommodation of Social Change* (Boulder, CO: Westview Press, second printing 1991).

83 Hamid Enayat, *Modern Islamic Political Thought* (referenced in note 52), p. 135. In his book on Egypt, Nadav Safran presents examples of these evasions which resulted in the failure of Islamic liberalism: Nadav Safran, *Egypt in the Search for Political Community* (Cambridge, MA: Harvard University Press, 1961), p. 85 and pp. 96f., 120f.

84 Hamid Enayat, *Modern Islamic Political Thought* (referenced in note 52), p. 135.

85 Therefore it is not by accident but by conviction that I am among the authors of the book *Islamic Political Ethics*, ed. by Sahail Hashmi (Princeton, NY: Princeton University Press, 2002).

86 Robert Hefner, *Civil Islam* (referenced in note 14), p. 215.

87 Institute for Arab Unity Studies (ed.) *Azmat al-demoqratiyya fi al-watan al-Arabi* [Crisis of Democracy in the Arab World] (Beirut: Institute for Arab Unity Studies, 1984).

88 B. Tibi, "al-bina' al-iqtisadi-al-ijtima'i lil-demoqratiyya" [The political and social underpinning of democracy] in *Azmat al-demoqratiyya* (referenced in note 87), pp. 73–87.

89 See for instance United Nations, *Arab Human Development Report 2002. Creating Opportunities for Future Generations* (New York: United Nations, 2002).

90 The persistence of such tribal and clan or religious loyalties/identities is one of the major obstacles to democratization in the Middle East. See B. Tibi, "The Simultaneity of the Unsimultaneous. Old Tribes and Imposed Nation-States in the Middle East," in Philip Khoury and Joseph Kostiner (eds) *Tribes and State Formation in the Middle East* (Berkeley, CA: University of California Press, 1990), pp. 127–52.

91 The reference here is to the concept of a low degree of institutionalization, in Samuel P. Huntington, *Political Order in Changing Societies* (New Haven: Yale University

Press, 1968). This approach is adopted as a framework for the analysis of the contemporary Arab state. For more details see B. Tibi, *Das arabische Staatensystem* (Mannheim: Bibliographisches Institut, 1996), chapter 1.

92 See the UNDP report of 2002, accused by the followers of Edward Said of "Orientalism."

93 See Bassam Tibi, "Zwischen islamischem Erbe und kultureller Erneuerung: Die Chancen der Demokratisierung im Nahen Osten nach dem Golfkrieg," in Herfried Muenkler (ed.) *Die Chancen der Freiheit. Grundprobleme der Demokratie, Festschrift fuer Professor Iring Fetscher* (Munich: Piper Verlag, 1992), pp. 199–223. The English version of the quoted chapter was presented at the Harvard/MIT joint seminar on development in a paper (not published) in March 1991.

94 Among these Arab debates is the one pursued in November 1983 and published in a book (referenced in note 88).

95 For more details see Amatzia Baram, *Culture, History and Ideology in the Formation of Ba'thist Iraq 1968–1989* (New York: St Martin's Press, 1991); on Iraqi history see Phebe Marr, *The Modern History of Iraq* (Boulder, CO: Westview Press, 1985, reprinted after the war in Iraq).

96 See the important chapter on ethno-politics by Gabriel Ben-Dor in Milton Esman and Itamar Rabinovich (eds) *Ethnicity, Pluralism and the State in the Middle East* (Ithaca, NY and London: Cornell University Press, 1988), pp. 71–92.

97 Among the numerous publications of the Ibn Khaldun Center on minorities, it is worth mentioning Saad Eddin Ibrahim (ed.) *Humum al-aqaliyyat fi al-watan al-Arabi* [The Concerns of Minorities in the Arab World] (Cairo: Ibn Khaldun Center, second printing, 1994) and the annual yearbook of the Center.

3 The world-political Sunni fallacy: jihadist internationalism as a cosmic war of irregulars for remaking the world

1 See Daniel Philpott, "The Challenge of September 11 to Secularism in International Relations," *World Politics*, vol. 55, 1 (October 2002), pp. 66–95; and also B. Tibi, "From Islamist Jihadism to Democratic Peace?" *Ankara Paper 16* (London: Taylor and Francis, 2005), pp. 1–41.

2 The related three books are: Martin van Creveld, *The Transformation of War* (New York: The Free Press, 1991), Kalevi J. Holsti, *The State, War and the State of War* (Cambridge: Cambridge University Press, 1996), and B. Tibi, *Conflict and War in the Middle East. From Interstate War to New Security*, second enlarged edition (New York: St Martin's Press, 1998), chapter 12.

3 Myron Weiner, *The Global Migration Crisis* (New York: HarperCollins, 1995), chapter 6 on security; and B. Tibi, *Islamische Zuwanderung. Die gescheiterte Integration* (Munich: DVA, 2002), implementing Weiner's approach.

4 See an earlier contribution to the study of terrorism: Grant Wordlaw, *Political Terrorism* (Cambridge: Cambridge University Press, 1982, second edition 1989), where one finds no reference to jihadist Islamism. In contrast, political Islam and its jihad are abundantly present in recent books like the one by Bruce Hoffman, *Inside Terrorism* (New York: Columbia University Press, 1998). Ever since 9/11 there has been a mushrooming literature on jihad. See the reader by David J. Whittacker (ed.) *The Terrorism Reader* (London: Routledge, 2001). Among useful contributions are the monograph by Jean B. Elshtain, *Just War against Terror* (New York: Basic Books, 2003), the book by Mark Sageman, *Understanding Terror Networks* (Philadelphia, PA: University of Pennsylvania Press, 2004) and the contributions included in Martin van Creveld, *Countering Modern Terrorism*, referenced in note 16 below.

5 Hedley Bull forcefully places the study of order at the center of reasoning on International Relations. See his classic, *The Anarchical Society. A Study of Order in World Politics* (New York: Columbia University Press, 1977), in particular Part One. For an appreciation of Bull and his work see the essay "Bull and the Contribution to International Relations," by Stanley Hoffmann in his book *World Disorders. Troubled Peace in the Post-Cold War Era* (New York: Rowman & Littlefield, 1998), pp. 13–34.

6 However, books in these studies such as the one by Jack Goody, *Islam in Europe* (Cambridge: Polity, 2004) are neither helpful nor promising, because the major issue, i.e. the

conflict, is evaded. For a contrast in European studies see B. Tibi, *Europe and the Challenge of Jihadist Islamism*, published by The Hellenic Center for European Studies as EKEM-Paper 9, Athens 2007.

7 Raymond Aron, *Paix et guerre entre les nations* (Paris: Calmann-Lévy, 1962).

8 See Robert H. Jackson, *Quasi-States: Sovereignty, International Relations, and the Third World* (Cambridge: Cambridge University Press, 1990). On the concept of "the nominal nation-state" see B. Tibi, "Old Tribes and Imposed Nation-States," in Philip Khoury and Josef Kostiner (eds) *Tribes and State Formation in the Middle East* (Berkeley, CA: University of California Press, 1990), pp. 127–52; see also the new Part V to the new third edition of B. Tibi, *Arab Nationalism. Between Islam and the Nation-State* (New York: St Martin's Press, third edition 1997), pp. 199–233.

9 The publications that grew from these three projects are: (1) *The Fundamentalism Project*/American Academy of Arts and Sciences, published in five volumes (Chicago, IL: Chicago University Press, 1991–5) edited by Martin Marty and Scott Appleby. Volume 2 of this research project (*Fundamentalisms and Society*, 1993) includes B. Tibi, "The Worldview of Sunni-Arab Fundamentalists: Attitudes towards Modern Science and Technology," pp. 73–102; (2) the findings of the "Culture Matters Project" were published in two volumes by Lawrence E. Harrison (ed.) *Developing Cultures* (New York: Routledge, 2006), Vol. One: *Essays on Cultural Change* (Tibi on Islam, chapter 14); Vol. Two, *Case Studies* (Tibi on Egypt chapter 9); (3) the findings of the Cornell project on transnational religion are published in Timothy Byrnes and Peter Katzenstein (eds) *Religion in an Expanding Europe* (New York: Cambridge University Press, 2006). It includes the chapter by B. Tibi on "Europeanizing Islam," pp. 204–24, see also next note.

10 All three issues were studied in a UCLA project; the contributions are included in a volume edited by Helmut Anheier and Raj Isar, *Culture, Conflict, Globalization* (London: Sage, 2007); the volume includes my chapter on Islam and identity politics.

11 See the respective chapters in the section "Remaking the World through Militancy," in Marty and Appleby (eds) *The Fundamentalism Project, Vol. Three: Fundamentalisms and the State* (Chicago, IL: Chicago University Press, 1993), see also note 9 above on this project.

12 The origin of the concept of "*hakimiyyat Allah*/God's rule" is Sayyid Qutb, *Ma'alim fi al-tariq* [Signposts along the Road], published in millions of copies in Arabic as well as in diverse translations into other Islamic languages. It enjoys a tremendous circulation, not only throughout the world of Islam but also in the diaspora of Europe. Here I use the thirteenth legal edition (Cairo: Dar al-Shuruq, 1989).

13 B. Tibi, "The Pertinence of Islam's Predicament with Democratic Pluralism," *Religion-Staat-Gesellschaft*, vol. 7, 1 (2006), pp. 83–117; and on the difference between Islam and Islamism from a systematic perspective of security studies see B. Tibi, "Between Islam and Islamism: A Dialogue with Islam and a Security Approach vis-à-vis Islamism," in Tamy A. Jacoby and Brent Sasley (eds) *Redefining Security in the Middle East* (Manchester: Manchester University Press, 2002), pp. 62–82. See also Peter Demant, *Islam vs Islamism* (Westport, CO: Praeger, 2006).

14 Eric Hobsbawm and Terence Ranger (eds) *The Invention of Tradition* (Cambridge: Cambridge University Press, reprint 1996), introduction, pp. 1–14. For an example of this invention see the article "Jihad" by B. Tibi, in Roger Powers and William B. Vogele (eds) *Protest, Power and Change. An Encyclopedia of Nonviolent Action* (New York: Garland, 1997), pp. 277–81.

15 Eric Hoffer, *The True Believer. Thoughts on the Nature of Mass Movements* (New York: Perennial Library, 2002, reprint of the original of 1951).

16 See the contributions in Martin van Creveld and Katherina von Knop (eds) *Countering Modern Terrorism. History, Current Issues and Future Threats* (Bielefeld: Bertelsmann, 2005), including the chapter by B. Tibi on "Countering Terrorism as War of Ideas and Worldviews," pp. 131–72, and also the references in note 4 above.

17 Hedley Bull, "The Revolt against the West," in Hedley Bull and Adam Watson (eds) *The Expansion of International Society* (Oxford: Clarendon, 1984), pp. 217–28; on Bull see also note 5.

18 Hedley Bull, *The Anarchical Society* (referenced in note 5), p. 273. For more details on the concept of the simultaneity of globalization and fragmentation see B. Tibi, *The Challenge of Fundamentalism. Political Islam and the New World Disorder* (Berkeley,

CA: University of California Press, 1998, updated edition 2002), chapters 1 and 5. On political Islam see further Nazih Ayubi, *Political Islam, Religion and Politics in the Arab World* (London: Routledge, 1991).

19 On the European expansion see Philip Curtin, *The World and the West. The European Challenge* (Cambridge: Cambridge University Press, 2000); see also Roger Scruton, *The West and the Rest. Globalization and the Terrorist Threat* (Wilmington, DE: ISI-books, 2002). On the unfolding, the claims and on the failure as well as on the future of the universalism of Western civilization see David Gress, *From Plato to NATO. The Idea of the West and its Opponents* (New York: The Free Press, 1998), chapter 12. On Westernization see Theodore H. von Laue, *The World Revolution of Westernization* (New York: Oxford University Press, 1987).

20 See B. Tibi, "Culture and Knowledge. The Fundamentalist Claim of de-Westernization," *Theory, Culture and Society*, vol. 12, 1 (1995), pp. 1–24.

21 B. Tibi, "Secularization and De-secularization in Islam," *Religion-Staat-Gesellschaft*, vol. 1, 1 (2000), pp. 95–117; on education in the context of the spread of desecular-izing political Islam see chapter 8 in B. Tibi, *Islam Between Culture and Politics* (New York: Palgrave, 2001, new expanded edition, 2005), pp. 167–87 and by the same author "Education and Democratization in an Age of Islamism," in Alan Olson *et al.* (eds) *Educating for Democracy* (Lanham, MA: Rowman & Littlefield, 2005), pp. 203–19. For more details on this issue see the concluding Chapter 7 below.

22 See Peter Mandaville, *Transnational Muslim Politics, Reimagining the Umma* (New York: Routledge, 2004).

23 See Richard Mitchell, *The Society of the Muslim Brothers* (London: Oxford University Press, 1969).

24 See Hasan al-Banna, "Risalat al-jihad" [Essay on jihad], in the collected writings of al-Banna, *Majmu'at rasail al-Banna* (Cairo: Dar al-Da'wa, 1990), pp. 271–92.

25 See the reference in note 1, and Mark Juergensmeyer, *The New Cold War? Religious Nationalism Confronts the Secular State* (Berkeley, CA: University of California Press, 1993).

26 See the article – influential at the time of its publication – by Michael Duran, "Somebody Else's Civil War," *Foreign Affairs*, vol. 82, 1 (2002), pp. 22–42. In 2005, Duran joined the Bush administration.

27 Sayyid Qutb, *al-salam al-alami wa al-Islam* [World Peace and Islam] (Cairo: al-Shuruq, 1992), p. 172.

28 For this reason the weekly *Newsweek* asked on the cover of its issue of 5 November 2001 "Why Do Islamists Like Europe?" The answer was given in the article on Germany in its headline: "Tolerating the Intolerable." One reads in that article: "Bassam Tibi ... has warned for years ... no one wanted to hear that" (p. 46). European politicians, and scholars as well, are reluctant to acknowledge the link between migration and security, and I was silenced in a society that claims to allow free debate.

29 Graham E. Fuller and Ian Lesser, *A Sense of Siege. The Geopolitics of Islam and the West* (Boulder, CO: Westview Press, 1995).

30 Jean-François Revel, *Democracy against Itself* (New York: Free Press, 1993), chapter 12; and Michael Teitelbaum and Jay Winter, *A Question of Numbers. High Migration, Low Fertility and the Politics of National Identity* (New York: Hill and Wang, 1998), pp. 221–39.

31 Sayyid Qutb, *al-Islam wa-Mushkilat al-Hadarah* [Islam and the Problem of Civilization] (Cairo: al-Shuruq, reprint 1988).

32 See Mark Juergensmeyer, *Terror in the Mind of God. The Global Rise of Religious Violence* (Berkeley, CA: University of California Press, 2000); and also Bruce Lincoln, *Holy Terrors. Thinking about Religion after September 11* (Chicago, IL: University of Chicago Press, 2003), wherein on jihad chapter 3; and B. Tibi, "Islamism, National and International Security after September 11," in Guenther Baechler and Andreas Wenger (eds) *Conflict and Cooperation* (Zurich: Neue Zuercher Zeitung, 2002), pp. 127–52.

33 Ahead of his book, *Clash of Civilizations and the Framing of World Order* (New York: Simon and Schuster, 1996), Samuel P. Huntington published a related article in *Foreign Affairs* (1993). In my book on this subject-matter, *Krieg der Zivilisationen* (Hamburg: Hoffmann and Campe, 1995), I make a reference to Huntington's *Foreign Affairs* article, but despite sharing the idea of civilizational conflict, I not only clearly

reject his policy implications and his "clash"-rhetoric, but also avoid his flaws. Later on, in 1998 I added a new chapter 7 to the second edition of the referenced book, to identify the differences and to dissociate myself from a "Huntingtonization" of the conflict under issue. Despite our communications at Harvard on these issues, Huntington has remained completely silent about all of my work.

34 Ibn Khaldun's *Prolegomena/al-Maqaddima* exists in many editions and languages. On this classical work see chapter VI in B. Tibi, *Der wahre Imam. Der Islam von Mohammed bis zur Gegenwart* (Munich: Piper, 1996, new 2001), pp. 179–209; and the seminal work on Ibn Khaldun by Muhsen Mahdi, *Ibn Khaldun's Philosophy of History. A Study in the Philosophic Foundations of the Science of Culture* (London: George Allen and Unwin, 1957).

35 Roman Herzog *et al.*, *Preventing the Clash of Civilizations* (New York: St Martin's Press, 1999). This book includes B. Tibi, "International Morality and Cross-Cultural Bridging," pp. 107–26, contradicting Huntington.

36 See the introduction of this book, and Pippa Norris and Ronald Inglehart, *Sacred and Secular. Religion and Politics Worldwide* (New York: Cambridge University Press, 2004) as well as Eric O. Hanson, *Religion and Politics in the International System Today* (New York: Cambridge University Press, 2006).

37 On the debate on the return of the sacred see the many references to the earlier debate (Daniel Bell) in conjunction with the post 9/11 developments in the new Part V added to the updated and expanded new 2005 edition of my book, *Islam between Culture and Politics* (referenced in note 21), published in association with Harvard's WCFIA; see pp. 231–72.

38 Among those high-ranking Western intellectuals who fail to understand this, one finds Jürgen Habermas, *Glauben und Wissen* (Frankfurt aim Main: Suhrkamp, 2001). For a critique see B. Tibi, "Habermas and the Return of the Sacred. Is it a Religious Renaissance? Political Religion as a New Totalitaranism," *Religion–Staat–Gesellschaft*, vol. 3, 2 (2002), pp. 265–96. On Islamism as a new totalitarianism see B. Tibi, *Der neue Totalitarismus. "Heiliger Krieg" und westliche Sicherheit* (Darmstadt: Primus-Verlag, 2004), reviving Hannah Arendt's concept and applying it to the ideological totalitarian views of political Islam.

39 On this link see the contributions to the special issue of *Millennium, Journal of International Affairs*, vol. 29, 3 (2000), published under the title *Religion and International Relations*. The issue includes B. Tibi, "Post-Bipolar Order in Crisis: The Challenge of Politicized Islam," pp. 843–59. See also Jeff Haynes, *Religion in Global Politics* (London: Longman, 1998), in particular chapter 7 on the Middle East.

40 See the proceedings of the Dutch Erasmus Foundation, *The Limits of Pluralism. Neo-Absolutisms and Relativism* (Amsterdam: Praemium Erasmianum, 1994).

41 On this see B. Tibi, *Europa ohne Identitaet?* (Munich: Bertelsmann, 1998), many subsequent editions.

42 Robert Pape, *Dying to Win. The Strategic Logic of Suicide Terrorism* (New York: Random House, 2005). This is a flawed study that fails to understand jihadism.

43 For more details see Amal Jamal, *The Palestinian National Movement. Politics and Contention 1967–2005* (Bloomington, IN: Indiana University Press, 2005), chapter 5; and earlier Beverley Milton-Edwards, *Islamic Politics in Palestine* (London: Tauris, 1996). On Hamas see Matthew Levitt, *Hamas. Politics, Charity and Terrorism in the Service of Jihad* (New Haven, CT: Yale University Press, 2006).

44 See Edward Said, *Covering Islam* (New York: Pantheon, 1981) reprinted many times.

45 The Arab-Islamist allegation of "*une vaste conspiration judeo-chrétienne*" can be found among others in Mohammed Y. Kassab, *L'Islam face au nouvel ordre mondial* (Algiers: Editions Salama, 1991), pp. 75–93, and it reflects a view widespread in the Arab world.

46 See Sayyid Qutb, *al-salam al-alami wa al-Islam* (referenced in note 27), pp. 167–99.

47 See John Esposito, *The Islamic Threat: Myth or Reality?* (New York: Oxford University Press, 1992), who confuses Islam and Islamism.

48 Mary Habeck, *Knowing the Enemy. Jihadist Ideology and the War on Terror* (New Haven, CT: Yale University Press, 2006).

49 Roxanne E. Euben, *Enemy in the Mirror. Islamic Fundamentalism and the Limits of Modern Nationalism* (Princeton, NJ: Princeton University Press, 1999), on Qutb chapter 3.

50 See the reference to Daniel Philpott in note 1; and Lynn H. Miller, *Global Order. Values and Power in International Politics* (Boulder, CO: Westview, 1990), chapter 2 on the Westphalian system.

51 Hedley Bull, "The Revolt against the West" (referenced in note 17), p. 223.

52 See the contributions in the volume *Beyond Westphalia*, ed. by Gene M. Lyons and Michael Mastanduno (Baltimore, MD: Johns Hopkins University Press, 1995).

53 On this Islamist vision for the world of Islam see Mohammed Salim al-Awwa, *Fi al-nizam al-siyasi li al-dawla al-Islamiyya* [On the Political System of the Islamic State] (Cairo: al-Maktab al-Masri, 1975, sixth reprinting 1983).

54 On the discrimination of non-Muslims as *dhimmi* (protected minorities subjected to Islamic rule) in the shari'a misinterpreted as tolerance, see the work of the Muslim reformist Abdullahi A. An-Na'im, *Toward an Islamic Reformation* (Syracuse, NY: Syracuse University Press, 1990), chapter 7. See also the outcry of the Egyptian-Jewish writer publishing under the pseudonym Bat Ye'or, *Islam and Dhimmitude* (Cranbury, NJ: Associated University Presses, 2002). In short: Islamic shari'a contradicts individual human rights on all counts, as argued by B. Tibi, "Islamic Law/Shari'a, Human Rights, Universal Morality and International Relations," *Human Rights Quarterly*, vol. 16, 2 (1994), pp. 277–99.

55 See my Singapore (NUS/ARI) research paper on pluralism in Islam, referenced in note 13.

56 On this see Scott Appleby (ed.) *Spokesmen for the Despised* (Chicago, IL: University of Chicago Press, 1997).

57 Therefore, I question the controversial French studies by Olivier Roy, *The Failure of Political Islam* (Cambridge, MA: Harvard University Press, 1994); and by Gilles Kepel, *Jihad, expansion et le déclin de l'Islamisme* (Paris: Gallimard, 2000); for a contrast to Kepel see my introduction to the updated 2002 edition of *The Challenge of Fundamentalism* (referenced in note 18).

58 B. Tibi, "The Worldview of Sunni-Arab Fundamentalists" (referenced in note 9).

59 Johannes Jansen, *The Dual Nature of Islamic Fundamentalism* (Ithaca and New York: Cornell University Press, 1997).

60 The reference to the return of the history of civilizations compels a reference to leading historians such as Arnold Toynbee, *The Study of History* (New York: Oxford University Press, 1947) and Will Durant, *The Story of Civilization*, 11 volumes (New York: Simon and Schuster, 1953–67). Among books which revive this classical subject ahead of Huntington one finds Leslie Lipson, *The Ethical Crisis of Civilizations* (London: Sage, 1993). The work of Samuel P. Huntington has negatively charged the study of civilizations; it is characterized by lack of sensibility towards other cultures and thus has done disservice to the field. For a professional study of the civilization of Islam see the work of Sir Hamilton A.R. Gibb, *Studies on the Civilization of Islam* (Princeton, NJ: Princeton University Press, 1962, reprint 1982); and Marshall G. Hodgson, *The Venture of Islam: Conscience and History in a World Civilization*, 3 volumes (Chicago, IL: University of Chicago Press, 1974).

61 B. Tibi, *Einladung in die islamische Geschichte* (Darmstadt: Primus, 2001).

62 See Barry Buzan, *People, States and Fear. An Agenda for International Security Studies in the Post-Cold War Era* (Boulder, CO: Lynne Rienner, 1991).

63 See the cover story of *The Economist*: "Nasrallah Wins the War," 19–25 August 2006. Next to the Shi'a terror is Saudi Arabia's tacit promotion of the jihad terror culture discussed by Stephen Schwarz in *The Two Faces of Islam. The House of Sa'ud from Tradition to Terror* (New York: Doubleday, 2002), chapters 7 and 8; on the Pakistani case see Husain Haqqani, *Pakistan between Mosque and Military* (Washington, DC: Carnegie Endowment, 2005).

64 See Jean Charles Brisard, *Zarqawi. The New Face of al-Qaida* (New York: Other Press, 2005).

65 See Frank Rich, "The Disappearance of the War in Iraq," *International Herald Tribune*, 31 July 2006, p. 7.

66 Phyllis Chesler, *The New Antisemitism* (San Francisco, CA: Jossey Bass, 2003). See also B. Tibi, "Die Maer des Islamismus von der juedischen und kreuzzueglerischen Weltverschwoerung gegen den Islam," in Julius Schoeps *et al.* (eds) *Alter-neuer Judenhass. Antisemitismus, arabisch-israelischer Konflikt und europaeische Politik* (Berlin: Verlag Berlin-Brandenburg, 2006), pp. 179–202.

67 See the quote in full length on pp. 30–1 in the introduction to this book and John Kelsay, *Islam and War* (Louisville, KY: John Knox Press, 1993), p. 117.

68 On this see B. Tibi, "War and Peace in Islam," in Terry Nardin (ed.) *The Ethics of War and Peace* (Princeton, NJ: Princeton University Press, 1996 and 1998), pp. 128–45. These concepts were never revised by Muslims; see Najib Armanazi, *ald-Shar' al-duwali, fi al-Islam* [International Law in Islam] (London: El-Rayyes, reprint 1990, first published in Damascus 1930).

69 See Bruce Lincoln, *Holy Terrors* (referenced in note 32).

70 See Leonore Martin (ed.) *New Frontiers in Middle Eastern Security* (New York: St Martin's Press, 1999), introduction.

71 See Barry Buzan, *People, States and Fear* (referenced in note 62). On the "state of war" in post-bipolarity see the references in note 2 above.

72 The analysis of Hezbollah in the book by Magnus Ranstorp, *Hizb'Allah in Lebanon* (London: Macmillan, 1997) is still topical and worth reading.

73 See my book on Islamic migration to Europe, referenced in note 3, and my article "A Migration Story" referenced in note 99 to the Introduction.

74 The term "gated diaspora" is borrowed from Nikos Papastergiadis, *The Turbulence of Migration* (Cambridge: Polity Press, 2000) and is developed to a security-related concept in my book on Islamic migration to Europe, referenced in note 3.

75 Francis Fukuyama, "Identity, Immigration and Liberal Democracy," *Journal of Democracy*, vol. 17, 2 (2006), pp. 5–20, here p. 6.

76 B. Tibi, "Muslim Migrants in Europe: Between Euro-Islam and Ghettoization," in Nezar AlSayyad and Manuel Castells (eds) *Muslim Europe or Euro-Islam: Politics, Culture, and Citizenship in the Age of Globalization* (Lanham, MD and Berkeley, CA: Lexington Books with UC Berkeley, 2002), pp. 31–52.

77 See the Cornell project, published by Katzenstein (referenced in note 9).

78 See the documentary on 11 September: Stefan Aust and Cord Schnibben, *11 September. Geschichte eines Terrorangriffs* (Munich: Deutsche Verlagsanstalt, 2002), chapter 4 on the Hamburg cell.

79 On the abuse of welfare institutions see J. Millard Burr and Robert Collins, *Alms for Jihad. Charity and Terrorism in the Islamic World* (New York: Cambridge University Press, 2006), chapter 2 on the role of Saudi Arabia, chapter 3 on the banks and chapter 10 on "the Islamization of Europe."

80 See chapter VI, "The Fundamentalist Abuse of the Islam-Diaspora: Western Europe as a Safe Haven," in the new edition of my book, *Die fundamentalistische Herausforderung* (Munich: C.H. Beck, fourth edition 2003), pp. 184–214.

81 See Yossef Bodansky, *Bin Laden. The Man Who Declared War on America* (Rocklin, CA: Forum/Prima, 1999).

82 Fukuyama (see note 75), p. 6. See also the reference in note 10.

83 See my article, "The Open Society and its Enemies within," *Wall Street Journal*, 17 March 2004, p. A10, referring to Karl Popper, *The Open Society and its Enemies*, 2 vols (London: Routledge and Paul Kegan, 1945).

84 Robert Spencer, *Onward Muslim Soldiers. How Jihad still Threatens America and the West* (Washington, DC: Regenery Publishers, 2003), on Europe and Ramadan, pp. 63–70; see also the book by Fourest in note 86.

85 Tariq Ramadan draws a false line between the Islamic anti-colonial revivalist al-Afghani and his grandfather Hasan al-Banna in his most controversial book: *Aux Sources du Renouveau Musulman. D'al-Afghani à al-Banna* (Paris: Bayard, 1998). In fact, al-Banna was the founder of Islamist jihadism (for more details see B. Tibi, *Der neue Totalitarismus* (referenced in note 38), there chapter 3. To be sure, al-Banna never provided any cultural innovation to Islam; he was a man of political action.

86 Caroline Fourest, *Frère Tariq. Discours, stratégie et méthode de Tariq Ramadan* (Paris: Grasset, 2004) and also Ralph Ghadban, *Tariq Ramadan und die Islamisierung Europas* (Berlin: Schiler Verlag, 2006). Against Ramadan I claim the concept of Euro-Islam confirmed by *Time* magazine in its issue of 24 December 2001: "Bassam Tibi … who coined the term Euro-Islam insists on the integration of Europe's Muslims," p. 49. For me, Euro-Islam is a secular concept orientated towards European values of cultural modernity and thus quite different from what Tariq Ramadan preaches.

87 The most prominent case is the former *F.A.Z.* journalist Udo Ulfkotte, *Der Krieg in unseren Staedten* (Frankfurt aim Main: Eichborn, 2003). He was sued, then he

lost his job and his life was ruined by the Islamists with the assistance of the German legal system. This case served as a warning by Islamists to other journalists to think twice before acting, and as such it was most successful.

88 See B. Tibi on the concept of integration to "Citizens of Heart" in the Fletcher–Forum article referenced in note 99 to the Introduction of the present book.

89 B. Tibi, "Islam, Freedom and Democracy in the Arab World," in Michael Emerson (ed.) *Democratization in the European Neighborhood* (Brussels: CEPS, 2005), pp. 93–116; see also the reference in note 21 on secular democracy and Islamism.

4 The Shi'ite option: internationalism for an export of the Islamic revolution of Iran. A failed effort!

1 Edgar O'Ballance, *Islamic Fundamentalist Terrorism. 1979–95. The Iranian Connection* (New York: New York University Press, 1997).

2 Shahram Chubin, *Iran's Nuclear Ambition* (Washington, DC: Carnegie Endowment for Peace, 2006), p. 51.

3 Ibid., p. 135.

4 See the informative book by Cheryl Bernard and Zalmay Khalilzad, *The Government of God. Iran's Islamic Republic* (New York: Columbia University Press, 1984). The Muslim scholar Khalilzad later turned senior US diplomat in Afghanistan and was promoted to US Ambassador to Iraq and later to the US-Ambassador to the UN-Security council. See also the other significant contribution by the Iranian – American R.K. Ramazani, *Revolutionary Iran. Challenge and Response in the Middle East* (Baltimore, MD: Johns Hopkins University Press, 1988).

5 See Yizhak Nakash, *Reaching for Power. The Shi'a in the Modern Arab World* (Princeton, NJ: Princeton University Press, 2006) and the contributions in the earlier volume edited by Graham E. Fuller and Rend Rahim Francke, *The Arab Shi'a. The Forgotten Muslims* (New York: St Martin's Press, 1999).

6 Said al-Qaisi, "An Iranian Plan for the Export of Terror into the Gulf" (in Arabic), *al-Watan al-Arabi*, no. 1494 (21 October 2005), p. 21.

7 A Harvard expert on the comparative study of revolutions, the sociologist Theda Skocpol, bases her authority on her book, *States and Social Revolutions* (Cambridge: Cambridge University Press, reprint 1987). However, she published many questionable articles based on poor knowledge of Islam and equally of the Iranian "Islamic revolution," as a result ranking it among the major world events in this category. For an analysis based on better knowledge see Said Amir Arjomand, *The Turban for the Crown. The Islamic Revolution in Iran* (New York: Oxford University Press, 1989).

8 See Ervand Abrahamian, *Khomeinism. Essays on the Islamic Republic* (Berkeley: University of California Press, 1993), pp. 13–38; and on the practice of this ideology see R.K. Ramazani, referenced in note 4.

9 See the work by the Iranian scholars Daryush Shayegan, *Cultural Schizophrenia. Islamic Societies Confronting the West* (London: Saqi Books, 1992) and Mehrzad Boroujerdi, *Iranian Intellectuals and the West. The Tormented Triumph of Nativism* (Syracuse, NY: Syracuse University Press, 1996), in particular pp. 10–14 on the reversal of Orientalism by people who claim to overcome it.

10 Graham E. Fuller, *The Center of the Universe. The Geopolitics of Iran* (Boulder, CO: Westview Press, 1991).

11 As early as 1983, in a paper presented to MESA's Chicago meeting on "The Iranian Revolution and the Arabs. The Search for Islamic Identity and the Search for an Islamic Government," I expressed my doubts about Arab Sunni receptivity to the basically Shi'ite Iranian claims. The paper was published under the same title in *Arab Studies Quarterly*, vol. 8, 1 (1986), pp. 29–44. A more mature and comprehensive analysis of the Iranian setup is included in the chapter on Iran in B. Tibi, *Islam and the Cultural Accommodation of Social Change* (Boulder, CO: Westview Press, 1990), pp. 147–59; see also note 16.

12 See the contributions in Adeed I. Dawisha (ed.) *Islam in Foreign Policy* (Cambridge: Cambridge University Press, 1983).

13 Eric O. Hanson, *Religion and Politics in the International System Today* (New York: Cambridge University Press, 2006); Pippa Norris and Ronald Inglehart, *Sacred and*

Secular. Religion and Politics Worldwide (New York: Cambridge University Press, 2004); and on Europe, Peter Katzenstein and Timothy Byrnes (eds) *Religion in an Expanding Europe* (New York: Cambridge University Press, 2006).

14 It is a contradiction in the otherwise well-informed analysis of Fred Halliday that he uses this fashionable but misleading formula in the title of his book *Islam and the Myth of Confrontation. Religion and Politics in the Middle East* (London: Tauris, 1995), while stating facts of confrontation that run counter to it. Left-wing authors dismiss the fact of religionized politics and the way it leads to conflict and confrontation. For another view, see Shahrough Akhavi, *Religion and Politics in Contemporary Iran* (Albany, NY: State University of New York Press, 1980).

15 For more details see Shireen Hunter, *Iran and the World. Continuity in a Revolutionary Decade* (Bloomington, IN: Indiana University Press, 1990) and John Esposito (ed.) *The Iranian Revolution. Its Global Impact* (Miami, FL: Florida International University Press, 1990).

16 An evaluation of twenty years of attempting to export the "Islamic revolution" into the Arab world is provided by B. Tibi: "The Failed Export of the Islamic Revolution," in Frédéric Grare (ed.) *Islamism and Security* (Geneva: Programme for Strategic and International Security Studies, 1999), pp. 63–102. See also the reference in note 11.

17 On this assumption, see the reasoning in chapters 1 and 2 of B. Tibi, *Islam between Culture and Politics* (New York: Palgrave, 2001, second expanded edition 2005).

18 François Burgat in cooperation with William Dowell, *The Islamic Movement in North Africa* (Austin, TX: Center for Middle Eastern Studies, University of Texas at Austin, 1993), p. 185.

19 B. Tibi, *The Challenge of Fundamentalism. Political Islam and the New World Disorder* (Berkeley, CA: University of California Press, 1998, updated 2002).

20 Mohammed Salim al-Awwa, *Fi al-nizam al-siyasi lil-dawla al-Islamiyya* [On the Political System of the Islamic State] (Cairo: al-Maktab al-Masri, sixth edition 1983); on Iran, see pp. 253–99.

21 For more details see Barnett Rubin, *The Fragmentation of Afghanistan* (New Haven: Yale University Press, 1995) and Ahmed Rashid, *Taliban. Militant Islam* (New Haven, CT: Yale University Press, 2000).

22 On this see Nikki Keddie, *Roots of Revolution. An Interpretative History of Modern Iran* (New Haven, CT: Yale University Press, 1981), as well as her book edited together with Eric Hooglund, *The Iranian Revolution and the Islamic Republic* (Syracuse, NY: Syracuse University Press, 1986).

23 On Khomeini's worldview and his understanding of world order see Ramazani, *Revolutionary Iran* (referenced in note 4), chapter 2.

24 Halliday, *Islam and the Myth of Confrontation* (referenced in note 14), p. 64.

25 Ibid., p. 44.

26 On this issue see Eliezer Be'eri, *Army Officers in Arab Politics and Society* (New York: Praeger, 1970); and also B. Tibi, *Militaer und Sozialismus in der Dritten Welt* (Frankfurt am Main: Suhrkamp, 1973). At that time army officers were believed to act as modernizers: that is, as a kind of substitute for modernizing civil elites.

27 See Michael C. Hudson, *Arab Politics. The Search for Legitimacy* (New Haven, CT: Yale University Press, 1977); and on the repercussions of the Six-Day War as a source of the legitimacy crisis see B. Tibi, *Conflict and War in the Middle East. From Interstate War to New Security* (New York: St Martin's Press, second edition 1998), chapters 3 and 4.

28 On the Iraqi Shi'a and its bid for power, see note 5. On SAIRI, also addressed as SCIRI, see Faleh Jabar, *The Shi'ite Movement in Iraq* (London: Saqi, 2003), in particular chapter 14 on its Badr Army (Failaq Badr). More impartial is the study by Yitzhak Nakash, *The Shi'is of Iraq* (Princeton, NJ: Princeton University Press, 1994). Similar to SCIRI is the militia of the Mahdi Army led by Muqtada al-Sadr, based in Iraq's Shi'a but hostile to its Badr Brigade. The backbone of the security apparatus of post-Saddam Iraq, the so-called "democratic Iraq," is under the influence of Iran: it is composed of these Shi'ite militias trained in Iran fighting not only against US occupation but also against the irregular Sunni-jihadists. The Iraq war of 2003 replaced Saddam's "republic of fear" with a new republic of jihadist horror.

29 Quoted by Anoushiravan Ehteshami, *After Khomeini. The Iranian Second Republic* (London: Routledge, 1995), p. 131.

30 Ramazani, *Revolutionary Iran* (referenced in note 4), pp. 24 and 25.

31 Fred Halliday, *Islam and the Myth of Confrontation* (referenced in note 14), p. 44.

32 Ehteshami, *After Khomeini* (referenced in note 29), p. 165.

33 Ibid.

34 On Hezbullah, established in 1982 in Iran's embassy in Damascus, see Hala Jaber, *Hezbollah. Born with a Vengeance* (New York: Columbia University Press, 1997); and also the more important book by Magnus Ranstorp, *Hizb'Allah in Lebanon. The Politics of the Western Hostage Crisis* (New York: St Martin's Press, 1997). On Hezbullah's links to Iran see Edgar O'Ballance (referenced in note 1), chapter 4.

35 Mohammed Khatami's call for dialogue was taken at face value by Fred Dallmayr, *Dialogue among Civilizations* (New York: Palgrave, 2002), preface.

36 The cover story "Terror Central. How Iran's Mullahs Run their Secret Assassination Network," in *Time* magazine, 11 November 1996, pp. 82–9, suggests that Iran never ceased using the promotion of terrorism as an instrument of its foreign policy. This is also confirmed by Chubin (note 2).

37 See my German *Financial Times* commentary against Khatami: "Keine Demokratie in Iran, kein Dialog mit dem Westen. Echte Reformen gibt es mit Praesident Khatami nicht," *Financial Times Deutschland*, 15 May 2000, "Agenda" section.

38 Ehteshami, *After Khomeini* (referenced in note 29), p. 165.

39 On Khomeini's reinterpretation of *velayat-e-faqih* for the legitimation of seizing power see the chapter by Hamid Enayat, "Iran. Khumayni's Concept of the 'Guardianship of the Jurisconsult'" in James P. Piscatori (ed.) *Islam in the Political Process* (Cambridge: Cambridge University Press, 1983), pp. 160–80.

40 This is Khomeini's message to war refugees as quoted by Fuller, *The Center of the Universe* (referenced in note 10), p. 271.

41 On the concept of counter-elites see chapter 5, and B. Tibi, "The Fundamentalist Challenge to Secular Order in the Middle East," *Fletcher Forum of World Affairs*, vol. 23, 1 (1999), pp. 191–210.

42 Rafsanjani quoted by Chibli Mallat, *The Middle East into the 21st Century* (Reading: Ithaca Press, 1996), pp. 161–2.

43 Ibid., p. 162.

44 On the religious dogma of Shi'a Islam see Moojan Momen, *An Introduction to Shi'i Islam: The History and Doctrines of Twelver Shi'ism* (New Haven, CT: Yale University Press, 1983), here pp. 39 and 183, see also p. 193.

45 On this subject see the authoritative work by Richard Mitchell, *The Society of the Muslim Brothers* (London: Oxford University Press, 1969), in particular pp. 234ff., 245ff.

46 The highly acclaimed so-called Abdolkarim Soroush, *Reason, Freedom and Democracy in Islam* (New York: Oxford University Press, 2000), lost his legitimacy through political maneuvering.

47 Chibli Mallat, *The Middle East into the 21st Century* (referenced in note 42), p. 154.

48 See the references in notes 5 and 28 on the Shi'a in Iraq: on the Shi'a in Lebanon see note 34 and Fouad Ajami, *The Vanished Imam Musa Sadr and the Shia of Lebanon* (Ithaca, NY: Cornell University Press, 1986).

49 B. Tibi, "The Clash of Shariah and Democracy," *International Herald Tribune*, 17–18 September 2005, p. 6.

50 See the editorial "The Iraq Constitution Goes off Course," *International Herald Tribune*, 22 July 2005. See also the report: "The Islamists Who Police Basra Streets," *International Herald Tribune*, 1 August 2005. The US journalist who made the disclosures in this report was later assassinated by Shi'ite militia, setting a further precedent.

51 Graham E. Fuller, *The Center of the Universe* (referenced in note 10), p. 271.

52 See Peter Worsley, *The Third World* (Chicago, IL: Chicago University Press, second edition, 1967); and regarding Islam, see W.M. Watt, "Muslims and the Third World," in *Third World Affairs 1986, Yearbook* (London: Third World Foundation, 1986), pp. 207–14.

53 See Jean-Charles Brisard, *Zarqawi. The New Face of al-Qaeda* (New York: Other Press, 2005).

54 Fuller, *The Center of the Universe* (referenced in note 10), p. 246.

55 Ramazani, *Revolutionary Iran* (referenced in note 4), p. 24. See also Shireen Hunter, *Iran and the World* (see note 15), chapter 12, pp. 174–83.

56 Khomeini cited in R.K. Ramazani, "Khumayni's Islam in Iran's Foreign Policy," in Dawisha (ed.) *Islam in Foreign Policy* (referenced in note 12), p. 19.

57 M. Momen (referenced in note 44), p. 39, see also pp. 183–93.

58 Saad Eddin Ibrahim, "Anatomy of Egypt's Militant Islamic Groups," *International Journal of Middle East Studies*, vol. 12 (1980), p. 449. This article is reprinted in Ibrahim's collection of essays: *Egypt, Islam and Democracy* (Cairo: AUC Press, 1996), pp. 1–33.

59 See Mohammed Mahfuz, *al-lathin zulimu. al-tanzimat al-Islamiyya fi misr* [The Oppressed. Islamist Organizations in Egypt] (London: el-Rayyes Books, 1988); Barry Rubin, *Islamic Fundamentalism in Egyptian Politics* (London: Macmillan, 1990); and more recently Carrie Rosefsky Wickham, *Mobilizing Islam. Religion, Activism and Political Change in Egypt* (New York: Columbia University Press, 2002).

60 On the impact of Iran on Algerian events see Michael Willis, *The Islamist Challenge in Algeria. A Political History* (New York: New York University Press, 1997), in particular pp. 89–92, 202–3.

61 For some it may not be popular, but it is in line with scholarly rules to also quote Bernard Lewis' defamed book on this issue, which asks in its title *What Went Wrong? The Clash between Islam and Modernity in the Middle East* (New York: Oxford University Press, 2002). However, giving the reference is not tantamount to agreement.

62 Michael C. Hudson, *Arab Politics. The Search for Legitimacy* (referenced in note 27), p. 162, see also pp. 126ff.

63 See Roger Scruton, *The West and the Rest. Globalization and the Terrorist Threat* (Wilmington, DE: Intercollegiate Studies Institute, 2002), in particular chapters 2 (on loyalty) and 3 (on jihad).

64 See the detailed entry "Identity Politics" by Gary Lehring in M. Hawkesworth and M. Kagan (eds) *Routledge Encyclopedia of Government and Politics*, 2 volumes (London: Routledge, 2004), vol. 1, pp. 576–86; and my chapter on identity politics in Islam in Helmut Anheier and Raj Isar (eds) *Culture, Conflict, Globalization* (London: Sage, 2007).

65 On the increasing fragmentation of Iraq after the 2003 war see Liam Anderson and Gareth Stansfield, *The Future of Iraq* (New York: Palgrave, 2004).

66 See Lawrence E. Harrison *et al.* (eds) *Developing Cultures* (New York: Routledge, 2006); in vol. 1, *Essays*, see chapter 14, my chapter on Islam; and in vol. 2, *Case Studies*, see chapter 9, pp. 163–80, my chapter on Egypt, and on the impact of Iran see pp. 171–4. On this Culture Matters Research Project see the acknowledgements in this volume.

67 On this issue see B. Tibi, "The Worldview of Sunni Arab Fundamentalists," in Martin Marty and Scott Appleby (eds) *Fundamentalisms and Society* (Chicago, IL: Chicago University Press, 1993), pp. 73–102; and the chapter on the Islamic "worldview" in B. Tibi, *Islam between Culture and Politics* (referenced in note 14), pp. 53–68.

68 On this see B. Tibi, *Arab Nationalism. Between Islam and the Nation-State* (New York: Macmillan, third edition 1997).

69 See Clifford Geertz, *Islam Observed. Religious Development in Morocco and Indonesia* (Chicago, IL: University of Chicago Press, 1989).

70 Ramazani, *Revolutionary Iran* (referenced in note 4), p. 20.

71 Mohammed Imara, *al-Islam wa al-uruba* [Islam and Arabism] (Cairo: Dar al-Wihda, 1981), p. 9.

72 See B. Tibi, "The Simultaneity of the Unsimultaneous: Old Tribes and Imposed Nation-States in the Modern Middle East," in Philip Khoury and Joseph Kostiner (eds) *Tribes and State Formation in the Middle East* (Berkeley, CA: University of California Press, 1990), pp. 127–52.

73 See Mallat on Shi'ite internationalism in his book *The Middle East into the 21st Century* (referenced in note 42), pp. 147–9.

74 See Bernard Lewis, *Multiple Identities in the Middle East* (New York: Shocken Books, 1998).

75 On the Lebanon war of 2006 see *The Economist's* cover story, "Nasrallah Wins the War" (issue of 19–25 August 2006) and on its regional impact see the report: "In Mideast a Wave of Political Islam," *International Herald Tribune*, 19–20 August 2006, front page, continued p. 6.

76 Edward Mortimer, *Faith and Power. The Politics of Islam* (New York: Vintage, 1982), p. 405.

77 Shahriar Rouhani, "When Will We Meet Again?" *Time* magazine, 17 August 1998, p. 15. A decade later, following Iran's role in the Lebanon war of 2006 and the detaining of leading Iranian intellectuals, this question seems to be out of place.

78 The following two articles, written more than twenty years apart, document the continued reasoning on this highly sensitive issue in Islam: B. Tibi, "Secularization and the Functional Differentiation of the Social System," *Archives for the Philosophy of Law and Social Philosophy*, vol. LXVI (1982), pp. 207–22; and two decades later, B. Tibi, "Secularization and De-Secularization in Islam," *Religion-Staat-Gesellschaft*, vol. 1, 1 (2000), pp. 95–117.

79 On the new place of religion in world politics see the references in note 13 above; an earlier view is Mark Juergensmeyer, *New Cold War? Religious Nationalism Confronts the Secular State* (Berkeley, CA: University of California Press, 1993).

5 Political Islam and Europe in the twenty-first century: the return of history as the return of civilizations into world affairs

1 The arguments presented are based on the seminal work by Henri Pirenne, *Mahomet et Charlemagne* (Paris, 1937), German translation, *Die Geburt des Abendlandes* (Leipzig, 1937), and on Fernand Braudel, *The Mediterranean and the Mediterranean World in the Age of Philip II* (Berkeley, CA: University of California Press, 1995). For a contemporary perspective on the Mediterranean see my *Bosch Memorial Lecture* published as *Das Mittelmeer als Grenze oder als Bruecke Europas zur Welt des Islam?* (Stuttgart: Bosch Foundation, 1994), p. 30. The recent book edited by Emmanuel Adler and Beverly Crawford, *The Convergence of Civilizations. Constructing a Mediterranean Region* (Toronto: University of Toronto Press, 2006) is flawed, however, by overlooking the conflictual historical background outlined by the work of Pirenne and Braudel, among others in the past and recently by Alan G. Jamieson, *Faith and Sword. A Short History of Christian–Muslim Conflict* (London: Reaktion Books, 2006).

2 Gilles Kepel, *Les Banlieus de l'Islam. Naissance d'une réligion en France* (Paris: Seuil, 1987).

3 This Stockholm Global Village Lecture is incorporated in my book *Europa ohne Identitaet?* (Munich: Bertelsmann, 1998), as chapter 3, pp. 109–33.

4 Fred M. Donner, *The Early Islamic Conquests* (Princeton, NJ: Princeton University Press, 1981).

5 On the European expansion that undermined the Islamic globalization of *dar al-Islam* see Philip D. Curtin, *The World and the West* (Cambridge: Cambridge University Press, 2000), see also the reference in note 25.

6 See the chapter by Hedley Bull on "The Revolt against the West," included in Hedley Bull and Adam Watson (eds) *The Expansion of International Society* (Oxford: Clarendon Press, 1984), pp. 217–28.

7 B. Tibi, *Islam Between Culture and Politics* (New York: Palgrave 2001, second expanded edition, 2005). The new edition includes the new Part V on the overall context of post 9/11 developments. This is also the framework employed in the volume that grew from a UCLA research project on *Culture, Conflict and Globalization*, edited by Helmut Anheier and Raj Isar (New York: Sage, 2007) that includes my chapter: "Islam: Between Religious Cultural Practice and Identity Politics."

8 See Francis Fukuyama, "Identity, Immigration and Democracy," *Journal of Democracy*, vol. 17, 2 (2006), pp. 5–20.

9 Lawrence E. Harrison (ed.) *Developing Cultures*, 2 vols (New York: Routledge, 2006), Vol. 1, *Essays* (includes Chapter 14 by B. Tibi on Islam), Vol. 2, *Case Studies* (includes Chapter 9 by B. Tibi on Egypt).

10 See the excellent and authoritative monograph by Muhsen Mahdi, *Ibn Khaldun's Philosophy of History* (London: George Allen and Unwin, 1957). See also the comprehensive chapter on Ibn Khaldun in my book on the intellectual history of Islam referenced in note 27 below, there chapter 6, pp. 179–209.

11 Raymond Aron, *Paix et guerre entre les nations* (Paris: Colmann-Levy, 1962).

12 The related conflicts are fully overlooked in the highly flawed work of Jytte Klausen, *The Islamic Challenge in Politics and Religion in Western Europe* (Oxford: Oxford University Press, 2005) as well as in the book by Jack Goody, *Islam in Europe* (Cambridge: Polity, 2004). The same applies to scholars of the earlier school of thought, like Albert Hourani, *Europe and the Middle East* (Berkeley: University of California Press, 1980). They present only nice stories and evade any addressing of the burning issues. The realities of the world-political framework are in contrast outlined by Zbigniew Brzezinski, *Out of Control. Global Turmoil on the Eve of the 21ˢᵗ Century* (New York: Charles Scribner's Sons, 1993) and by Stanley Hoffmann, *World Disorders. Troubled, Peace in the Post-Cold War Era* (Lanham, MD: Rowman & Littlefield, 1998). See also B. Tibi, *The Challenge of Fundamentalism. Political Islam and the New World Disorder* (Berkeley, CA: University of California Press, 1998, updated and enlarged edition 2002).

13 For a good illuminating exception in the mushrooming dialogue industry see the proceedings of the Jakarta dialogue of 2003, Karlina Helmanita *et al.* (eds) *Dialogue in the World Disorder. A Response to Threat of Unilateralism and World Terrorism* (Jakarta: UIN, the Hadayatullah University, 2004). This volume includes B. Tibi, "Islamic Civilization and the Quest for Democratic Pluralism," pp. 159–201.

14 Peter Mandaville, *Transnational Muslim Politics. Re-Imagining the Umma* (London: Routledge, 2004).

15 Fleming Rose, "Die Stunde der Wahrheit," *Der Spiegel*, issue 22 (29 May 2006), pp. 136–7. Rose was the editor of the Danish daily *Jyllands Posten* that published the distasteful Mohammed cartoons.

16 This is the phrasing of Prof. Chabei Nemoto, to whom I am indebted for an invitation by the EU–Japan Committee to address in Tokyo the tenth Anniversary of the EU–Japan Dialogue 2003 on culture and globalization. Some ideas of this chapter were presented then in Tokyo in my paper, published in the volume of the proceedings (Tokyo, 2003, in Japanese).

17 B. Tibi, "A Migration Story. From Muslim Immigrants to European Citizens of the Heart," in: *The Fletcher Forum for World Affairs*, vol. 31, 1 (Winter 2007) pp. 147–168.

18 For more details B. Tibi, *Kreuzzug und Djihad. Der Islam und die christliche Welt* (Munich: Bertelsmann, 1999, new edition 2002), especially chapter II on Charlemagne, Christendom and Islam, and chapters V and VI on the West and Islam. On Charlemagne as founder of Europe see Horst Fuhrmann, *Einladung ins Mittelalter* (Munich: C.H. Beck, 1987). See also Peter Brown, *The Rise of Western Christendom* (Oxford: Blackwell, 1996).

19 Paul Fregosi, *Jihad in the West: Muslim Conquests from the 7ᵗʰ to the 21ˢᵗ Centuries* (New York: Prometheus Books, 1998) and in a similar mindset also Efraim Karsh, *Islamic Imperialism. A History* (New Haven, CT: Yale University Press, 2006).

20 Will Durant, *The Renaissance: A History of Civilization in Italy from 1304–1576 AD* (New York: Simon and Schuster, 1953, reprint 1981). This volume is a part of Durant's story of civilizations, referenced in note 29 below. On the impact of Islam on the Renaissance see Chapter V in B. Tibi, *Kreuzzug und Djihad* (note 18).

21 These symbols of "Jerusalem" and "Athens" stand for Christendom and the secular West respectively: they were established in this meaning by Leslie Lipson, *The Ethical Crises of Civilization* (London: Sage, 1993), p. 63. The next quote in the text is taken from page 62.

22 For references on the cross-cultural fertilization that took place in the Renaissance context, see note 20 and in general Toby E. Huff, *The Rise of Early Modern Science. Islam, China and the West* (Cambridge: Cambridge University Press, 1995), chapters 2 and 3.

23 Theodore H. von Laue, *The World Revolution of Westernization: The Twentieth Century in Global Perspective* (New York: Oxford University Press, 1987), chapters I (concept) and VII (the present).

24 See Marshall G.S. Hodgson, *Rethinking World History: Essays on Europe, Islam and World History* (Cambridge, IL: Cambridge University Press, 1993), Part II on Islam; see also his masterpiece *The Venture of Islam: Conscience and History in a World Civilization* (Chicago, IL: Chicago University Press, 1974), three volumes.

25 Geoffrey Parker, *The Military Revolution and The Rise of the West, 1500–1800* (Cambridge: Cambridge University Press, 1988), p. 115.

26 John Kelsay, *Islam and War: A Study in Comparative Ethics* (Louisville, KY: West-minster/John Knox Press, 1993), pp. 25–6.

27 See the study by Mahdi referenced in note 10 on the historical masterpiece of Ibn Khaldun, *al-Maqaddima* [Prolegomena], which exists in many editions and languages. These editions and the secondary literature on this subject are fully referenced in B. Tibi, *Der wahre Imam. Der Islam von Mohammed bis zur Gegenwart*, (Munich: Piper, 1996, new 2001), Chapter 6.

28 Ernest Gellner, *Postmodernism, Reason and Religion* (London and New York: Routledge, 1992), p. 85. See also David Gress, *From NATO to Plato. The Idea of the West and its Opponents* (New York: The Free Press, 1998).

29 B. Tibi, *Einladung in die islamische Geschichte* (Darmstadt: Primus, 2001). See also the eleven-volume work *Story of Civilization* (published from 1953) by Will Durant, also co-authored from volume 7 together with his wife Ariel Durant, reprinted by Simon and Schuster (New York, from 1963) and the volume by Fernand Braudel, *A History of Civilizations* (London: Penguin, 1994); see also note 1 above.

30 On the Islam diaspora in Europe see B. Tibi, *Islamische Zuwanderung. Die gescheiterte Integration* (Munich: DVA, 2002) and on the prospects of Europeanizing Islam see the reference in note 47 to the Cornell project. See also notes 45 and 46.

31 See B. Tibi, "Islamism, National and International Security after September 11," in Andreas Wenger and Guenther Baechler (eds) *Conflict and Cooperation. The Individual between Ideal and Reality, Festschrift in Honor of Prof. Kurt Spillmann* (Zurich: Neue Zuercher Zeitung, 2002), pp. 127–52.

32 Roman Herzog *et al.* (ed.) *Preventing the Clash of Civilizations: A Strategy for Peace for the Twenty-First Century* (New York: St Martin's Press, 1999); my chapter to this volume is referenced in the ensuing note.

33 See B. Tibi, "International Morality and Cross-Cultural Bridging," in Herzog (note 32), pp. 107–26.

34 Hedley Bull, *The Anarchical Society. A Study of Order in World Politics* (London: Macmillan, 1977), p. 273.

35 Benjamin Barber, *Jihad vs McWorld* (New York: Random House, 1995).

36 Max Horkheimer, *Kritik der instrumentellen Vernunft* (Frankfurt: Athenaeum Press, 1974).

37 Myron Weiner, *The Global Migration Crisis: Challenge to States and to Human Rights* (New York: HarperCollins, 1995). Weiner's approach is applied to Islamic migration to Europe in my book referenced in note 30 above.

38 This quote from my *Bosch Memorial Lecture* (1994) is referenced in note 1 above.

39 John Kelsay, *Islam and War* (note 26), p. 5.

40 Ibid., p. 118.

41 Jamey Keaton from Associated Press, "Rioting Spread to 20 Towns in Paris Region," *US Today*, 4 November 2005, p. 8a. It was continued on the 2006 anniversary. See Keaton's report "Violence in France," *The Ithaca Journal*, 23 October 2006, p. 8a.

42 For evidence and more details see B. Tibi, *Islamische Zuwanderung* (referenced in note 30).

43 Some authors believe they have seen the true face of Tariq Ramadan, such as Robert Spencer, *Onward Muslim Soldiers. How Jihad still Threatens America and the West* (Washington, DC: Regenery Publishers, 2003), pp. 64–9, Caroline Fourest, *Frère Tariq* (Paris: Grasset, 2004) and Ralph Ghadban, *Tariq Ramadan und die Islamisierung Europas* (Berlin: Schiler, 2006). I had an encounter with this person in Brussels. See also my report about a debate with Ramadan that took place there along with the enlightened Paris Imam Dalil Boubakeur, published in: *Neue Zuercher Sonntagszeitung* of 20 October 2002, p. 23.

44 Michael S. Teitelbaum and Jay Winter, *A Question of Numbers: High Migration, Low Fertility, and the Politics of National Identity* (New York: Hill and Wang: 1998). See chapter 12 on Islamic fundamentalism and the West, pp. 221–40.

45 The first source of the concept of Euro-Islam is B. Tibi, "Les conditions d'un Euro-Islam," in Robert Bistolfi and François Zabbal (eds) *Islams d'Europe: intégration ou insertion communautaire?* (Paris: Éditions de l'Aube, 1995), pp. 230–4 in Paris 1992. On Euro-Islam one reads in *Time* magazine: "Bassam Tibi ... who coined the term Euro-Islam, insist[s] that the integration of Europe's Muslims depends on the adoption of a form of Islam that embraces Western political values ... 'The options for

Muslims are unequivocal,' says Tibi. 'There is no middle way between Euro-Islam and a ghettoization of Muslim minorities'"; *Time* magazine, 25 December 2001, p. 49. This seems not to be the understanding of Tariq Ramadan on a European Islam (see note 43).

46 This project resulted in the volume: Nezar AlSayyad and Manuel Castells (eds) *Muslim Europe or Euro-Islam: Politics Culture and Citizenship in the Age of Globalization* (Lanham and Berkeley, CA: Lexington Books, 2002), wherein the chapter by B. Tibi, "Muslim Migrants in Europe: Between Euro-Islam and Ghettoization," pp. 31–52. For a continuation of this reasoning see next note.

47 In a Cornell research project on "transnational religion" the competition between Islamization and Europeanization has been addressed in a research paper published under the title "Europeanizing Islam or the Islamization of Europe: Political Democracy versus Cultural Difference," in Peter Katzenstein and Timothy A. Byrnes, *Religion in an Expanding Europe* (Cambridge: Cambridge University Press, 2006), chapter 8, pp. 204–24

48 On multi-culturalism see the contributions in Christian Joppke and Steven Lukes (eds) *Multi-cultural Questions* (Oxford: Oxford University Press, 1999).

49 Jürgen Habermas, *The Philosophical Discourse of Modernity* (Cambridge, MA: Massachusetts Institute of Technology Press, 1987).

50 See Jack Donelly, *Universal Human Rights in Theory and Practice* (Ithaca, NY: Cornell University Press, 1989) and Micheline R. Ishay (ed.) *The Human Rights Reader: Major Political Writings, Essays, Speeches and Documents from the Bible to the Present* (New York: Routledge, 1997).

51 Gellner, *Postmodernism* (note 28), p. 85.

52 Alain Finkielkraut, *La Défaite de la pensée* (Paris: Gallimard, 1989).

53 On the study of culture see Adam Kuper, *Culture. The Anthropologists' Account* (Cambridge, MA: Harvard University Press, 1999); and on the study of civilization see the reader edited by John Rundell and Stephen Mennell, *Classical Readings in Culture and Civilization* (London: Routledge, 1998).

54 See Clifford Geertz, *The Interpretation of Cultures: Selected Essays* (London: Fontana Press, 1973), in particular pp. 3–30. I employ this Geertzian approach in my book referenced in note 7, in particular in chapter 1.

55 Sayyid Qutb, *Ma'alim fi al-tariq* [Signposts along the Road] (Cairo: Dar al-Shuruq, thirteenth legal printing, 1989); on the political thought of Qutb see Roxanne L. Euben, *Enemy in the Mirror: Islamic Fundamentalism and the Limits of Modern Rationalism* (Princeton, NJ: Princeton University Press, 1999), pp. 49–92. On the difference between Islam and Islamism already addressed in the preface of the present book see B. Tibi, "Gibt es eine islamische bzw. islamistische Herausforderung an Europa? Ein Plaedoyer fuer eine euro-islamische Asabiyya im Konflikt der Zivilisationen," *Religion-Staat-Gesellschaft*, vol. 6, 1 (2005), pp. 19–62, and by the same author: "Euro-Islam, juridisch burgerschap en burgers van het hart," *Nexus*, No. 41 (2005), pp. 173–203. This contribution was completed for the summit at the end of the Dutch presidency of the European Union (2004) that took place in Rotterdam, December 2004.

56 On this Islamist notion of *Hakimiyyat*-rule see B. Tibi, *The Challenge of Fundamentalism* (note 12 above), chapters 7 and 8.

57 It is embarrassing, but nevertheless necessary, to refer to the authoritative history of Damascus by Mohammed A. Al-Taqiuladdin al-Husni, *Kitab Muntakhabat al-Tawarikh li Dimashq* (Damascus 1928), to prove, against the damaging gossip of the Islamists in Europe's diaspora, that I descend from the Islamic notability (Ashraf) of Damascus; see p. 877 on Banu al-Tibi.

58 B. Tibi, "The Attitudes of Sunni Arab Islamic Fundamentalism toward Modern Science and Technology," in Martin E. Marty and R. Scott Appleby, *The Fundamentalism Project*, five volumes, here vol. 2, *Fundamentalisms and Society*, in the section "Reclaiming the Sciences, the Family, and Education" (Chicago: Chicago University Press, 1993), pp. 73–102.

59 B. Tibi, "Islamic Dream of Semi-Modernity," *India International Centre Quarterly* (New Delhi), vol. 22, 1 (Spring 1995), pp. 79–87. For references on e-jihad see Gary R. Bunt, *Islam in the Digital Age. E-Jihad, Online Fetwas and Cyber Islamic Environments* (London: Pluto Press, 2003).

60 Qutb, *Ma'alim* (note 55), p. 5.
61 Ibid., pp. 6–7.
62 Daryush Shayegan, *Cultural Schizophrenia* (Syracuse, NY: Syracuse University Press, 1993).
63 Mohammed Abed al-Jabri, *Arab-Islamic Philosophy: A Contemporary Critique* (Austin, TX: University of Texas Press, 1999), pp. 120–30.
64 Immanuel Kant, "Entwurf zum Ewigen Frieden," in Richard Saage and Zwi Batscha (eds) *Friedensutopien* (Frankfurt: Suhrkamp, 1975) and on the inclusion of this concept in the contemporary debate Bruce Russett, *Grasping the Democratic Peace: Principles for a Post-Cold War World* (Princeton, NJ: Princeton University Press, 1993).
65 Samuel P. Huntington, *The Third Wave: Democratization in the Late Twentieth Century* (Norman: University of Oklahoma Press, 1991).
66 See Chapter 7 of the present book and B. Tibi, "Democracy and Democratization in Islam," in Michèle Schmiegelow (ed.) *Democracy in Asia* (New York: St Martin's Press, 1997), pp. 127–46 and more recently B. Tibi, "Democracy in an Age of Islamism," in Alan Olson *et al.* (eds) *Educating for Democracy* (Lanham, MD: Rowman and Littlefield, 2004), pp. 203–19. See also Chapter 2 of the present book.
67 B. Tibi, *Mit dem Kopftuch nach Europa. Die Tuerkei auf dem Weg in die EU* (Darmstadt: Primus, 2005, expanded and updated edition 2007).
68 See Roger Collins, *The Arab Conquest of Spain* (Oxford: Blackwell, 1994) and Sir Steven Runciman, *The Fall of Constantinople* (New York: Cambridge University Press, 1990).
69 See the references in note 19 and furthermore Alan Jamieson, *Faith and Sword. A Short History of Christian–Muslim Conflict* (London: Reaktion Books, 2006).
70 See the chapter on *hijra* in Islam by B. Tibi, *Islamische Zuwanderung* (note 30), pp. 258–90.
71 Jean François Revel, *Democracy Against Itself: The Future of the Democratic Impulse* (New York: Free Press, 1993), chapter 12.
72 Stephan Theil, "Tolerating the Intolerable," *Newsweek*, 5 November 2001, p. 46–8.
73 This is the title of Ramadan's presentation in Stockholm, 16 June 2006.
74 Tariq Ramadan, *Aux sources du renouveau musulman. D'al-Afghani à al-Banna* (Paris: Éditions Bayard, 1998), see also note 43 and 45. The alleged continuity between Afghani and al-Banna is not in line with historical facts and is therefore wrong; it is based on a false interpretation.
75 For full evidence see chapter 3 on jihadism rooted in the Muslim Brotherhood in B. Tibi, *Der neue Totalitarismus* (Darmstadt: Primus, 2004), pp. 106–37.
76 Hasan al-Banna, "Risalat al-jihad," included in his collection of essays, published as *Majmu'at Rasa'il al-Imam al-Shahid Hasan al-Banna* (Cairo: Dar al-Da'wa, 1990, legal edition), pp. 271–92.
77 The Muslim scholar Sachedina conceals this issue instead of revealing it and dealing with it analytically: Abdulaziz Sachedina, *The Islamic Roots of Democratic Pluralism* (Oxford: Oxford University Press, 2001). For a contrast see B. Tibi, "The Pertinence of Islam's Predicament with Democratic Pluralism," *Religion-Staat-Gesellschaft*, vol. 7, 1 (2006), pp. 83–117.

6 The European diaspora of Muslim migrants and the idea of Europe: could they become Europeans by choice? Euro-Islam, legal citizenship and "citizens of the heart"

1 See B. Tibi, "Europeanizing Islam or the Islamization of Europe: Political Democracy versus Cultural Difference," in Peter Katzenstein and Timothy Byrnes (eds) *Religion in an Expanding Europe* (New York: Cambridge University Press, 2006), pp. 204–24; and earlier by the same author, in Nezar AlSayyad and Manuel Castells (eds) *Muslim Europe or Euro-Islam: Politics, Culture, and Citizenship in the Age of Globalization* (Berkeley and New York: Lexington Books, 2002) on Euro-Islam, chapter 2, pp. 31–52.
2 See B. Tibi, *Europa ohne Identitaet?* (Munich 1998, and many new editions between 2000 and 2002); Dutch translation, *Europa Zonder Identiteit? De Crisis van de Multi-culuturele Samenleving* (Aarselaar, Belgium: Deltas, 2000).

3 Francis Fukuyama, "Identity, Immigration and Democracy," *Journal of Democracy*, vol. 17, 2 (2006), pp. 5–20.

4 On this notion see Muhsen Mahdi, *Ibn Khaldun's Philosophy of History. A Study in the Philosophic Foundations of the Science of Culture* (London: Allen and Unwin, 1957); the work of Ibn Khaldun is referenced in note 31.

5 This assumption is based on the findings of the "Culture Matters Research Project" (CMRP) in which my thinking on Islam has been incorporated. See the acknowledgement and the reference in note 9 to Chapter 5 of this volume.

6 Peter Neumann, "Europe's Jihadist Dilemma," *Survival*, vol. 48, 2 (2006), pp. 71–84.

7 See chapter 10 "The Islamization of Europe" in J. Millard Burr and Robert Collins, *Alms for Jihad, Charity and Terrorism in the Islamic World* (New York: Cambridge University Press, 2006).

8 See note 1 and B. Tibi, "Gibt es eine islamische bzw. Islamistische Herausforderung an die Identitaet Europas?" *Religion-Staat-Gesellschaft*, vol. 6, 1 (2005), pp. 19–62.

9 Gilles Kepel, *Les Banlieues de l'Islam. Naissance d'une réligion en France* (Paris: Editions du Seuil, 1987).

10 "Les conditions d'un Euro-Islam" (see note 45 to Chapter 5).

11 The term and concept of cultural modernity are employed here in line with Jürgen Habermas, *The Philosophical Discourse of Modernity* (Cambridge, MA: MIT Press, 1987).

12 John Kelsay, *Islam and War. A Study in Comparative Ethics* (Louisville, KY: John Knox Press, 1993), p. 118.

13 B. Tibi, "Islam: Between Religious-Cultural Practice and Identity Politics," in Y. Raj Isar and Helmut Anheier (eds) *Cultures and Globalization* (London: Sage, 2007).

14 On the Frankfurt School of Horkheimer and Adorno see Martin Jay, *The Dialectical Imagination. A History of the Frankfurt School* (Boston, MA: Little, Brown, 1973).

15 Max Horkheimer, *Kritische Theorie*, two volumes (Frankfurt aim Main: Fischer, 1968); here, preface, vol. I, p. xiii.

16 B. Tibi, *Der neue Totalitarismus. Heiliger Krieg und westliche Sicherheit* (Darmstadt: Primus, 2004). See also B. Tibi, "The Totalitaranism of Jihadist Islamism and its Challenge to Europe and to Islam," in: *Totalitarianism Movements and Political Religion* (2007) vol. 8, 1 pp. 35–54.

17 I am among the authors who contributed to the anti-Huntington volume by the former president of Germany, Roman Herzog *et al.*, *Preventing the Clash of Civilizations. A Peace Strategy for the Twenty-First Century* (New York: St Martin's Press, 1999), see note 35 below.

18 Michael Teitelbaum and Jay Winter, *A Question of Numbers. High Migration, Low Fertility and the Politics of National Identity* (New York: Hill and Wang, 1998), in particular pp. 221–39 on Islamic fundamentalism.

19 See Lawrence E. Harrison, *Underdevelopment is a State of Mind: The Latin American Case* (Cambridge, MA: Center for International Affairs, Harvard University, 1985) and the reference to the Culture Matters Research Project (CMRP); see note 5 above.

20 Gerard Delanty, *Inventing Europe: Idea, Identity, Reality* (New York: St Martin's Press, 1995).

21 B. Tibi, *Islam between Culture and Politics* (New York: Palgrave, second expanded edition, 2005).

22 On this see the volume edited by Joseph Mitchell and Helen Buss Mitchell, *Taking Sides. Clashing Views on Controversial Issues in Western Civilization* (Guilford, CT: McGraw Hill, 2000). As a Muslim I also see bridges based on the heritage of rationalism in Islam, specifically the Hellenization process; see Franz Rosenthal, *The Classical Heritage of Islam* (London: Routledge, 1975, reprinted 1994) and William Montgomery Watt, *Islamic Philosophy and Theology* (Edinburgh: Edinburgh University Press, 1962; reprinted 1979).

23 The controversy took place in Amsterdam and is published in Praemium Erasmianum Foundation (ed.) *The Limits of Pluralism. Neo-Absolutisms and Relativism* (Amsterdam: Erasmus, 1994). Among the contributors are C. Geertz, E. Gellner, Shlomo Avineri and B. Tibi.

24 Raymond Aron, *Paix et guerre entre les nations* (Paris: Calman-Lévy, 1962).

25 See the references in note 1 to Chapter 5.

26 See the chapter on migration in Malcolm Anderson, *Frontiers. Territory and State Formation in the Modern World* (Cambridge: Polity Press, 1996), pp. 127–50.

27 See John Kelsay, *Islam and War* (referenced in note 12).

28 Ibid.

29 See B. Tibi, *Islamische Zuwanderung. Die gescheiterte Integration* (Munich: DVA, 2002), chapter 3 and 4 on "parallel societies" as Islamic enclaves in Europe.

30 Leon de Winter, "Wir muessen fuer eine Weile die Tore schließen," *Die Welt*, 15 December 2004, front page.

31 See the reference in note 4 above and the reprint Ibn Khaldun, *al-Muqaddima* (Cairo: al-Maktabah al-Tijariyya, new printing, no date).

32 On the concept and potential of a Euro-Islamic *asabiyya* see my 2005 article referenced in note 55 to Chapter 5.

33 Elaine Sciolino, "School Scarf Ban in France. Official Report Calls for a Law," *New York Times*, also published in *International Herald Tribune* (*IHT*), 12 December 2003, front page and p. 6. See also the report on the following day "Threat on Head Scarves Angers French Muslims," *IHT*, 13 December 2003, p. 3.

34 Niluefer Goele, *The Forbidden Modern. Civilization and Veiling* (Ann Arbor, MI: Michigan University Press, 1996), p. 1. See also chapter 10 on the head-scarf in my book *Aufbruch am Bosporus. Die Tuerkei zwischen Europa und dem Islamismus* (Munich: Diana Press, 1998). This volume was also translated into Turkish and published in Istanbul in 2000.

35 See my chapter "International Morality and Cross-Cultural Bridging" in Roman Herzog *et al.*, *Preventing the Clash of Civilizations* (note 17), pp. 107–26.

36 See B. Tibi, "The Pertinence of Islam's Predicament with Democratic Pluralism," *Religion-Staat-Gesellschaft*, vol. 7, 1 (2006), pp. 83–117.

37 See my Cornell work referenced in note 1, and in contrast Seyla Ben-Habib (ed.) *Democracy and Difference* (Princeton, NJ: Princeton University Press, 1996).

38 On the origin of Euro-Islam see the references in note 10 and also the ensuing papers referenced in note 1 above.

39 See also Patricia Crone, *Pre-Industrial Societies. Anatomy of the Pre-Modern World* (Oxford: Oneworld, new printing, 2003) and Bassam Tibi, *The Crisis of Modern Islam. A Preindustrial Culture in the Scientific-Technological Age* (Salt Lake City, UT: University of Utah Press, 1988).

40 See Philip D. Curtin, *The World and the West. The European Challenge and the Overseas Response in the Age of Empire* (Cambridge: Cambridge University Press, 2000).

41 See for instance Tariq Modood (ed.) *The Politics of Multi-culturalism in the New Europe* (New York: St Martin's Press, 1997). According to Modood Europe has become "now a supranational community of cultures, sub-cultures and transcultures." The implication of this allegation and way of determining Europe is to deny Europe a civilizational identity of its own. The result is an anti-European sentiment. See my contrasting position in my book referenced in note 2 above, for which I use a question mark in the title *Europa ohne Identitaet?* "Europe without Identity?" See also Moodod's contribution (Chapter 6) to the volume of AlSayyad and Castells referenced in note 1 above.

42 Manuel Castells, *The Information Age: Economy, Society and Culture, Vol. Two: The Power of Identity* (Cambridge: MA: Blackwell, 1997), p. 8.

43 See William Montgomery Watt, *Muslim–Christian Encounters. Perceptions and Misperceptions* (London: Routledge, 1991) and Norman Daniel, *Islam and the West: The Making of an Image* (Oxford: Oneworld, new edition 1993).

44 Nezar AlSayyad, "Culture, Identity, and Urbanism in a Changing World," in Michael Cohen (ed.) *Preparing for the Urban Future* (Baltimore, MD: Johns Hopkins University Press, 1996), pp. 108–22, here p. 109.

45 Ibid., pp. 120f.

46 B. Tibi, "Euro-Islam. The Quest of Islamic Migrants and of Turkey to become European," *Turkish Policy Quarterly*, vol. 3, 1 (2004), pp. 13–28, see also note 38.

47 This is the term used by Tomas Gerholm and Yngve G. Lithman (eds) *The New Islamic Presence in Western Europe* (London: Mansell, 1988, paperback, 1990). This presence was the subject-matter of a research project run at the University of Leiden, Netherlands, from which the following two volumes grew: W.A.R. Shadid *et al.* (eds)

Muslims in the Margin. Political Responses to the Presence of Islam in Western Europe (Kampen, Netherlands: Kok Pharos, 1996) and W.A.R. Shadid *et al.* (eds) *Political Participation and Identities of Muslims in Non-Muslim States* (Kampen, Netherlands: Kok Pharos, 1997). I was a member of the project and contributed the chapter "Islam, Hinduism and the Limited Secularity in India: A Model for Muslim-European Relations?" vol. 1, pp. 130–45.

48 Bernard Lewis, "Europa wird am Ende des Jahrhunderts islamisch sein," *Die Welt*, 28 July 2004, p. 6, and in contrast B. Tibi, "Grenzen der Toleranz. Missbrauch des Rechtsstaates durch Djihadisten," *Welt am Sonntag*, 5 September 2004, p. 14. The controversy was covered by Christopher Caldwell, "Islamic Europe?" *Weekly Standard* (Washington), vol. 10, 4 (4 October 2004), pp. 15–16.

49 William G. Lockwood, *European Moslems* (New York: Academic Press, 1975) and Tone Bringa, *Being Muslim the Bosnian Way: Identity and Community in a Central Bosnian Village* (Princeton, NJ: Princeton University Press, 1995).

50 For more details see B. Tibi, *Islamische Zuwanderung* (referenced in note 29), chapter 8.

51 Alec G. Hargreaves, *Immigration, "Race" and Ethnicity in Contemporary France* (London: Routledge, 1995). See also Gilles Kepel, *Les Banlieues de l'Islam. Naissance d'une religion en France* (Paris: Editions du Seuil, 1987) and more recently Paul Silverstein, *Algeria in France* (Bloomington, IN: Indiana University Press 2004).

52 Philip Martin, "Germany: Reluctant Land of Immigration," in Wayne A. Cornelius *et al.* (eds) *Controlling Immigration. A Global Perspective* (Stanford, CA: Stanford University Press, 1994), pp. 189–225.

53 B. Tibi, "Die Schwierigkeit, an der deutschen Universitaet heimisch zu sein," in Namo Aziz (ed.) *Fremd in einem kalten Land. Ausländer in Deutschland* (Freiburg: Herder, 1992), pp. 121–36.

54 Ursula Spuler-Stegemann, *Muslime in Deutschland* (Freiburg: Herder, new edition 2002), in particular pp. 46–91.

55 The papers of this conference were published in a volume edited by John Docker and Gerhard Fischer, *Adventures of Identity. European Multi-cultural Experiences and Perspectives* (Tübingen: Stauffenberg Press, 2001). The volume includes B. Tibi, "Communitarianism and Euro-Islam," chapter 4, pp. 45–60.

56 On Muslim migrants in France and the United Kingdom see Gilles Kepel, *A l'ouest d'Allah* (Paris: Edition du Seuil, 1994); in France, Hargreaves and Silverstein (referenced in note 51); and in Germany Spuler-Stegemann (referenced in note 54). See also, on Britain, Philip Lewis, *Islamic Britain* (London: I.B. Tauris, new edition 2002).

57 There are two early comparisons of Turkish and North African Muslim migrants in Germany and France: Roger Brubaker, *Citizenship and Nationhood in France and Germany* (Cambridge, MA: Harvard University Press, 1992) and Klaus Manfrass, *Tuerken in der Bundesrepublik – Nordafrikaner in Frankreich* (Bonn: Bovier, 1991).

58 See the report, "Harte Hand gegen Hassprediger," *Der Spiegel*, no. 48 (2004), pp. 36–40.

59 Udo Ulfkotte, *Der Krieg in unseren Staedten. Wie radikale Islamisten Deutschland unterwandern* (Frankfurt am Main: Eichborn, 2003).

60 See the references in notes 11 and 14. Habermas is among the progressive Germans who support the integration of migrants; see his book: *Die Einbeziehung des Anderen* (Frankfurt/M.: Suhrkamp, 1996). It is, however, sad that Habermas fails to see the politicization of Islam in the diaspora community and thus overlooks the implications related to it. On this issue see Bassam Tibi, "Habermas and the Return of the Sacred. Is it a Religious Renaissance, a Pronouncement of a 'Post-Secular Society,' or the Emergence of Political Religion as a New Totalitarianism?" *Religion-Staat-Gesellschaft*, vol. 3, 2 (2002), pp. 265–97.

61 See Josef Schacht, *An Introduction to Islamic Law* (Oxford: Clarendon Press, 1964).

62 Ernest Gellner, *Postmodernism, Reason and Religion* (London: Routledge, 1992), p. 85.

63 Kelsay, *Islam and War* (referenced in note 12), p. 118.

64 Ibid., p. 5.

65 See the result of an inter-cultural effort for establishing a consensus shared by different cultures in the volume of An-Na'im and the contributors at the Wilson Center: Abdullahi An-Na'im and Francis Deng (eds) *Human Rights in Africa. Cross-Cultural Perspectives* (Washington, DC: Brookings Institution, 1990). The volume includes. B. Tibi, "The European Tradition of Human Rights and the Culture of Islam," pp. 104–32.

66 In his book on early Islam, Hichem Djait, *al-Fitna* (Beirut: Dar al-Talia, 1992), p. 49 points at the importance of *hijra*/migration for the spread of Islam in combination with jihad.

67 See chapter 10 on "The Islamization of Europe" in J. Millard Burr and Robert Collins, *Alms for Jihad. Charity and Terrorism in the Islamic World* (New York: Cambridge University Press, 2006), pp. 237–62. It is the mindset of the religious doctrine of *hijra* that is revived at present; see Muhammad Khalid Masud, "The Obligation to Migrate: The Doctrine of Hijra in Islamic Law," in James Piscatori and Dale Eickelman (eds) *Muslim Travellers* (Berkeley, CA: University of California Press, 1990), pp. 29–49; and chapter 6 in my book on *Islamische Zuwanderung*, referenced in note 29.

68 Efraim Karsh, *Islamic Imperialism. A History* (New Haven, CT: Yale University Press, 2006), in particular chapters 12 and 13 on the present day.

69 Speech delivered by the Hashemite Prince Hassan Ibn Talal at the Euro-Islamic Forum of the European Academy of Arts and Sciences in November 1996 in Salzburg, manuscript. By then I was director of that forum.

70 Leslie Lipson, *The Ethical Crises of Civilization* (London and Newbury Park, CA: Sage, 1993), p. 62.

71 On Islamic rationalism see Herbert A. Davidson, *Alfarabi, Avicenna and Averroës on Intellect* (New York: Oxford University Press, 1992).

72 See Mushrul Hasan, *Legacy of a Divided Nation. India's Muslims since Independence* (Boulder, CO: Westview Press, 1997) and the chapter on the pertinence of this Indian experience to Europe in my book *Europa ohne Identitaet?* (see note 2), pp. 223–40. See also the reference in the next note.

73 See Bassam Tibi, "Islam, Hinduism and Limited Secularity in India. A Model of Muslim-European Relations in the Age of Migration?" referenced in note 47 above.

74 See Bassam Tibi, "Foreigners – Today's Jews?" in Ulrich Wank (ed.) *The Resurgence of Right Wing Radicalism in Germany* (Atlantic Highlands, NJ: Humanities Press, 1996), pp. 85–102. I refuse to make this parallel, because the Jews were native Europeans, not migrants, but I do refer to it.

75 On Islamist anti-Semitism, see B. Tibi, "Die Maer des Islamismus von der juedischen und kreuzzueglerischen Weltverschwoerung gegen den Islam," in Julius Schoeps *et al.* (eds) *Alter-neuer Judenhass. Antisemitismus, arabisch-israelischer Konflikt und europaeische Politik* (Berlin: Verlag fuer Berlin-Brandenburg, 2006), pp. 179–202.

76 David Gress, *From Plato to NATO. The Idea of the West and its Opponents* (New York: The Free Press, 1998), pp. 503f.

77 Ernest Gellner, *Postmodernism* (referenced in note 62), pp. 84f.

78 B. Tibi, *The Challenge of Fundamentalism. Political Islam and the New World Disorder* (Berkeley, CA: University of California Press, 1998, updated edition 2002).

79 On the grounds of my study of political Islam I strongly disagree with the highly flawed book by John Esposito and John Voll, *Islam and Democracy* (New York: Oxford University Press, 1996). These authors do not distinguish between Islam and Islamism (see my review in *Journal of Religion* (1998), October issue, pp. 667–9).

80 The Algerian Islamist Ali Ben Haj and most others truly believe "*al-demoqratiyya kufr*/democracy is heresy." For a reference on this see Ahmidah Aiyashi, *al-Islamiyun al-jazairiyaun bain al-sulta wa al-rasas* [Algerian Islamists between Rule and Bullets] (Algiers: Dar al-Hikmah, 1992), pp. 57–60.

81 On the Islamist instrumental use of democracy as restricted to a procedure of voting and overlooking the nature of democracy as a political culture, see B. Tibi, "Démocracie et Démocratisation en Islam. La Quête d'un Islam éclairé et les contre-forces de l'autoritarisme et du fondamentalisme religieux," *Revue Internationale de Politique Comparée*, vol. 2, 2 (1995), pp. 285–99, and the debate in Chapter 7 of this volume.

82 In the book by the Oxford scholar Larry Siedentop, *Democracy in Europe* (London: Penguin Books, 2000), see the chapter "Europe, Christianity and Islam," pp. 189–214, where one finds highly pertinent and equally intelligent reasoning on this issue, but an over-emphasis on the "Christian component." If Siedentop were right, then the Islamic diaspora in Europe, including myself, would never be able become European.

83 See Alan Jamieson, *Faith and Sword. A Short History of Christian–Muslim Conflict* (London: Reaktion Books, 2006); he argues that the new conflict "between the post-Christian West and Islam is more a clash between secular materialism and a revived religion," p. 208. I prefer to speak of a civilizational values-based conflict.

7 Political Islam and democracy's decline to a voting procedure: the political culture of democracy is the solution for Islamic civilization

1 Jürgen Habermas, *The Philosophical Discourse of Modernity* (Cambridge, MA: MIT Press, 1987), pp. 1–22.

2 To be sure, the notion "pre-modern" is not used here in an evolutionist understanding. For more details see Patricia Crone, *Pre-Industrial Societies. Anatomy of the Pre-Modern World* (Oxford: Oneworld, new edition 2003) and B. Tibi, *The Crisis of Modern Islam. A Preindustrial Culture in the Scientific-Technological Age* (Salt Lake City, UT: Utah University Press, 1988).

3 On the Frankfurt School, established by Theodor W. Adorno and Max Horkheimer, see note 14 to Chapter 6. As a Muslim from Damascus I received my academic education in this school of thought with these great philosophers, who were my academic teachers in Frankfurt and had tremendous impact on the unfolding of my thinking.

4 B. Tibi, "The Interplay between Social and Cultural Change," in George Atiyeh and Ibrahim Oweis (eds) *Arab Civilization. Studies in Honor of Constantine Zurayk* (Albany: SUNY, 1988), pp. 166–82.

5 See the "Culture Matters Research Project" (CMRP), chaired by L. Harrison, in note 5 to Chapter 6 and note 9 to Chapter 5.

6 On this issue see the project-based publication by the Emirates Center for Political and Strategic Studies and Research (ECSSR) (ed.) *The Gulf. Challenges of the Future* (Abu Dhabi: ECSSR, 2005) which includes B. Tibi, "Political Reform in the Gulf: Society and State in a Changing World," chapter 17, pp. 313–30.

7 This reformatory mindset is reflected in the thoughts of the Muslim human rights activist Abdullahi An-Na'im, *Islamic Reformation* (Syracuse, NY: Syracuse University Press, 1990) and also in the contributions to Tore Lindholm and Kari Vogt (eds) *Islamic Law Reform and Human Rights* (Copenhagen: Nordic Human Rights Publications, 1993) by Abdullahi An-Na'im and also by Mohammed Arkoun and B. Tibi.

8 This is the assumption already verified in the research completed within the Fundamentalism Project at the American Academy of Arts and Sciences. The findings were published under the same title in five volumes, edited by Martin Marty and Scott Appleby (1991–5). The findings include B. Tibi, "The Worldview of Sunni–Arab Fundamentalists," in vol. 2 of this project, *Fundamentalisms and Society* (Chicago, IL: Chicago University Press, 1993), pp. 73–102.

9 The chapter *"al-istishraq ma'kusan"* [Orientalism in reverse] in Sadik Jalal al-Azm, *Dhihniyyat al-Tahrim* (London: Riad El-Rayyes, 1992), pp. 17–86. On this debate see also the additional Part V in the new edition of my book, *Islam between Culture and Politics* (New York: Palgrave, 2005, updated and expanded), chapter 11.

10 B. Tibi, "Genesis of the Arab Left. A Critical Viewpoint," in Edward Said (ed.) *The Arabs of Today. Alternatives for Tomorrow* (Columbus, OH: Forum Associates, 1973), pp. 31–42.

11 Robert Hefner, *Civil Islam. Muslims and Democratization in Indonesia* (Princeton, NJ: Princeton University Press, 2000). In his book *Two Worlds of Islam. Interaction Between Southeast Asia and the Middle East* (Miami: University Press of Florida, 1993), Fred von der Mehden rightly states: "religious education in the Middle East ... remains a major source of Muslim thought in Southeast Asia, especially in Indonesia" (p. 97). This has not changed over recent years. Political Islam is imported into Southeast Asia from the Middle East, but Indonesian civil Islam is not perceived in the Arab world.

12 On this "other-ing" of non-Muslims, in particular on the other-ing of the West in a Muslim worldview dominated by a mindset of self-victimization, see the illuminating study on Iranian Muslim intellectuals by the enlightened Iranian scholar Mehrzad Boroujerdi, *Iranian Intellectuals and the West: The Tormented Triumph of Nativism* (Syracuse, NY: Syracuse University Press, 1996), chapters 1, 2 and 3. This analysis applies to Arab intellectuals as well. See also the next note.

13 Graham E. Fuller, *A Sense of Siege. The Geopolitics of Islam and the West* (Boulder, CO: Westview Press, 1995).

14 This is the core topic of a comparative research project conducted by UCLA and the American University of Paris on "World Cultures." The findings were published in Raj Isar and Helmut Anheier (eds) *Culture, Conflict, Globalization* (London: Sage,

2007). The volume includes B. Tibi, "Islam: Between Religious-Cultural Practice and Identity Politics."

15 On this issue see B. Tibi, "The Totalitarianism of Jihadist Islamism and its Challenge to Europe and to Islam," *Totalitarian Movements and Political Religion*, vol. 8, 1 (2007), pp. 35–54; and on the spread of Islamism in the European diaspora, B. Tibi, "A Migration Story. From Muslim Immigrants to European 'Citizens of the Heart'?" *Fletcher Forum of World Affairs*, vol. 31, 1 (2007), pp. 147–68.

16 Samir al-Khalil, *The Republic of Fear. The Politics of Modern Iraq* (Berkeley, CA: University of California Press, 1989). This is a pseudonym for Kanan Makiya.

17 On this issue see my article, "Missionarisches Bewusstsein. Als Napoleon Bonaparte 1798 Kairo eroberte, hoffte er vergebens als Befreier gefeiert zu werden. Dem US-Praesidenten George W. Bush wird es in Bagdad aehnlich ergehen," *Financial Times Deutschland*, 10 April 2003, p. 8. On Napoleon in Egypt see B. Tibi, *Arab Nationalism. Between Islam and the Nation-State* (New York: St Martin's Press, third edition 1997), pp. 79–84.

18 United Nations Development Program, *Arab Human Development Report, Creating Opportunities for Future Generations* (New York: United Nations, 2002).

19 George Makdisi, *The Rise of Colleges. Institutions of Learning in Islam and the West* (Edinburgh: Edinburgh University Press, 1981), pp. 77–80.

20 B. Tibi, *Aufbruch am Bosporus. Die Tuerkei zwischen Europa und dem Islamismus* (Munich: Diana Press, 1998), chapter 9 (Turkish translation, Istanbul 2000).

21 Stephan Schwartz, *The Two Faces of Islam. The House of Sa'ud from Tradition to Terror* (New York: Doubleday, 2002), chapter 7. Schwartz also discusses indirect Saudi funding of terrorism.

22 See the publication by the Fundamentalism Project, 5 vols (referenced in note 8), in particular part 3 on education in vols 2 and 3, *Fundamentalisms and the State* (Chicago, IL: University of Chicago Press, 1993) on "remaking politics."

23 On education see chapter 8 in B. Tibi, *Islam between Culture and Politics* (referenced in note 9).

24 On the rejection of democracy as an imported solution see Yusuf al-Qaradawi, *al-Hall al-Islami wa al-hulul al-Mustawradah* [The Islamic and the Imported Solution] (Beirut: al-Risalah, reprint 1980) and on democracy as *kufr*/heresy see Ahmida Ayashi, *al-Islamiyun al jaza'riyun bain al-sulta wa al-rasas* [Algerian Islamists between State Authority and Bullets], Algiers 1991, pp. 33 and 58.

25 See Peter Brown, *The Rise of Western Christendom* (Oxford: Blackwell, 1996).

26 See William MacNeill, *The Rise of the West. A History of the Human Community* (Chicago: University of Chicago Press, 1963), in particular part III; and David Gress, *From Plato to NATO. The Idea of the West and its Opponents* (New York: Free Press, 1998).

27 Leslie Lipson, *The Ethical Crisis of Civilization. Moral Meltdown or Advance?* (London: Sage, 1993), p. 63.

28 Ibid., p. 62.

29 On this Hellenization see William Montgomery Watt, *Islamic Philosophy and Theology* (Edinburgh: Edinburgh University Press, 1962), parts 2 and 3.

30 On democracy see Anthony Birch, *The Concepts and Theories of Modern Democracy* (London: Routledge, 1993); on the global context, see David Held, *Democracy and the Global Order. From the Modern State to Cosmopolitan Governance* (Stanford, CA: Stanford University Press, 1995).

31 Hedley Bull, "The Revolt against the West," in Hedley Bull and Adam Watson (eds) *The Expansion of International Society* (New York: Oxford University Press, 1984), pp. 217–28.

32 See B. Tibi, "Post-Bipolar Order in Crisis. The Challenge of Politicized Islam," published in the special issue of the LSE journal *Millennium* on "Religion and International Relations," vol. 29, 3 (2000), pp. 843–59.

33 Therefore, I strongly reject the work of John Esposito and John Voll, *Islam and Democracy* (New York: Oxford University Press, 1996). See my critical review in *Journal of Religion*, vol. 78, 4 (1998), pp. 667–9.

34 The Moroccan philosopher Mohammed Abed al-Jabri rightly argues in his book *Arab Islamic Philosophy* (Austin, TX: University of Texas Press, 1999): "The future can only be Averroëist" (p. 120). The work of Averroës heralds the height of Islamic rationalism in Hellenized medieval Islam.

35 On Islamic rationalism see Herbert A. Davidson, *Alfarabi, Avicenna and Averroës on Intellect* (New York: Oxford University Press, 1992); and in general Franz Rosenthal, *The Classical Heritage of Islam* (Berkeley, CA: University of California Press, 1975), parts III, IV and V. On the transmission of this tradition to Europe see David Lindberg, *The Beginning of Western Science* (Chicago, IL: University of Chicago Press, 1992); and Toby E. Huff, *The Rise of Early Modern Science. Islam, China and the West* (Cambridge: Cambridge University Press, 1995).

36 See Daniel Bell, "The Return of the Sacred," in his collected essays, *The Winding Passage 1960–1980* (New York: Basic Books, 1980). On this resumed debate see B. Tibi, *Islam between Culture and Politics* (New York: Palgrave, 2001), chapter 11 to the updated edition of 2005.

37 Clifford Geertz, *The Interpretation of Cultures* (New York: Basic Books, 1973), chapter 4.

38 See my contribution to Helmut Anheier and Raj Isar (eds) *Culture, Conflict, Globalization* (referenced in note 14).

39 Ernest Gellner, *Postmodernism, Reason and Religion* (London: Routledge, 1992), p. 85.

40 See B. Tibi, "Culture and Knowledge: The Politics of Islamization of Knowledge. The Fundamentalist Claim to De-Westernization," *Theory, Culture and Society*, vol. 12, 1 (1995), pp. 1–24. On the splitting of modernity into, first, instruments and, second, values pursued in political Islam, see B. Tibi, "The Worldview of Sunni-Arab Fundamentalists: Attitudes Towards Modern Science and Technology," in Martin Marty and Scott Appleby, *Fundamentalism and Society* (vol. 2 of *The Fundamentalism Project*, see reference in note 8 above), pp. 73–102.

41 On this Islamist thought see the leading Islamist Yusuf al-Qaradawi, *al-Hulul al-Mustawradah* (referenced in note 24), pp. 49–110.

42 B. Tibi, "International Morality and Cross-Cultural Bridging," in Roman Herzog *et al.*, *Preventing the Clash of Civilizations. A Peace Strategy for the Twenty-First Century* (New York: St Martin's Press, 1999), pp. 107–26.

43 See Bruce Russett, *Grasping the Democratic Peace. Principles for a Post-Cold War World* (Princeton, NJ: Princeton University Press, 1993); and B. Tibi, "From Islamist Jihadism to Democratic Peace? Islam at the Crossroads in Post-Bipolar International Politics," *Ankara Paper 16* (London and Ankara: Frank Cass, 2005).

44 Hedley Bull, "The Revolt against the West" (referenced in note 31), p. 223.

45 Daniel Patrick Moyniham, *Pandaemonium. Ethnicity in International Politics* (New York: Oxford University Press, 1993); see also the reference in note 14.

46 B. Tibi, "The Attitudes of Middle Eastern Elites and Counter-Elites Towards Political Order: The Islamic-Fundamentalist Challenge to the Secular Domestic and International Order," in Samuel Huntington (ed.) *Project on Conflict or Convergence: Global Perspectives on War, Peace and International Order*, Harvard Academy for International and Area Studies, mimeographed Cambridge, MA, 1997; published version: "The Fundamentalist Challenge to the Secular Order in the Middle East," *Fletcher Forum of World Affairs*, vol. 23, 1 (1999), pp. 191–210.

47 Niluefer Goele, *The Forbidden Modern. Civilization and Veiling* (Ann Arbor: Michigan Press, 1996).

48 Efraim Karsh, *Islamic Imperialism. A History* (New Haven, CT: Yale University Press, 2006).

49 In their *Asalib al-ghazu al-fikri li al-'alam al-Islami* [Methods of the Intellectual Invasion of the Islamic World] (Cairo: Dar al-I'tisam, second edition 1978) the Saudi-Wahhabi professors 'Ali M. Jarisha and Muhammad Sh. Zaibaq reject learning from Europe, as does the Islamist Anwar al-Jundi, *Ahdaf al-taghrib fi al-'alam al-Islami* [The Goals of Westernization in the Islamic World] (Cairo: al-Azhar Press, 1987). For a justification of this attitude see also the reference in note 54.

50 See the book by Mehrzad Boroujerdi (referenced in note 12).

51 See my article on the story of Islamic migration to Europe (referenced in note 15).

52 In his editorial "Manifests from the Left too Sensible to Ignore," *International Herald Tribune*, 30–31 December 2007, p. 2, Roger Cohen distinguishes between two varieties of the contemporary left. Among the supporters of the first trend are "hyperventilating left-liberals ... rational argument goes out of the window." These people also engage in "disgraceful alliances with illiberal theocrats. These 'European pacifists' back the beheading brigade, the child-bombers and other fundamentalists." In contrast, the left of "the Easton Manifesto is united by strong support for freedom of

speech and ideas, democracy and pluralism, as well as by unqualified opposition to all forms of terrorism and totalitarianism." I place the critique of political Islam in this book in this tradition of the left, which I encountered and adopted at the Frankfurt School of the Holocaust survivors Max Horkheimer and Theodor W. Adorno, Jews who were – to me, as a Muslim in Frankfurt – my academic teachers.

53 Roger Scruton, *The West and the Rest. Globalization and Terrorist Threat* (Wilmington, DE: ISI Books, 2002), chapter 4.

54 On *asalah*/authenticity see Anwar al-Jundi, *al-Mu'asarah fi itar al-aslah* [Modernity in the Context of Authenticity] (Cairo: Dar al-Sahwa, 197). The author states "we need a return to the sources, not an enlightenment" and "we are the teachers of the West, not its disciples."

55 See Abdulhadi Abdulrahman, *Sultat al-nas* [The Authority of the Text] (Beirut: al-Markas al-Thaqafi, 1993), pp. 45ff.

56 Roxanne Euben, *Journeys to the Other Shores. Muslim and Western Travelers in the Search of Knowledge* (Princeton, NJ: Princeton University Press, 2006).

57 More on this in the important contribution of Makdisi, *The Rise of the College* (note 19 above); see also the chapter on education in B. Tibi, *Islam between Culture and Politics* (referenced in note 9), pp. 167–85.

58 On the institutionalization of knowledge in the course of cultural change see Robert Wuthnow, *Meaning and Moral Order* (Berkeley, CA: University of California Press, 1987), chapter 8.

59 See Philip D. Curtin, *The World and the West. The European Challenge and the Overseas Response in the Age of Empire* (Cambridge: Cambridge University Press, 2000).

60 Syed Sajjad Hussain and Syed Ali Ashraf, *Crisis in Muslim Education* (London: Hodder and Stoughton, 1979), pp. 2–3.

61 See Stephan Schwartz, *The Two Faces* (referenced note 21), chapter 7; and Daniel Pipes, *In the Path of God. Islam and Political Power* (New York: Basic Books, 1984), chapter 10: "The Great Oil Boom."

62 On the debate on Eurocentrism see Roy Preiswerk and Dominique Perrot, *Ethnocentrism in History* (New York: NOK Publishers International, 1978); and, more recently, James M. Blaut, *The Colonizer's Model of the World. Geographical Diffusionism and Eurocentric History* (New York: Guilford Press, 1993). On Westernization see Theodore H. von Laue, *The World Revolution of Westernization* (New York: Oxford University Press, 1987).

63 More on this in Rob Wilson and Wimal Dissanayake (eds) *Global–Local: Cultural Production and the Transnational Imaginary* (Durham, NC: Duke University Press, 1996).

64 See the reference to the work jointly done with the reform Muslim An-Na'im in note 7. See also Abdullahi A. An-Na'im and Francis Deng (eds) *Human Rights in Africa: Cross-Cultural Perspectives* (Washington, DC: Brookings Institution, 1990), especially my chapter "The European Tradition of Human Rights and the Culture of Islam," pp. 104–32.

65 On this simultaneity see chapters 1, 4, 5 in B. Tibi: *The Challenge of Fundamentalism. Political Islam and the New World Disorder* (Berkeley, CA: University of California Press, 1998).

66 Raymond Aron, *Paix et guerre entre les nations* (Paris: Calmann Lévy, 1962).

67 Hedley Bull, *The Anarchical Society: A Study of Order in World Politics* (New York: Columbia University Press, 1977), p. 273. See my chapter "Democracy and Democratization in Islam," in Michèle Schmiegelow (ed.) *Democracy in Asia* (New York: St Martin's Press, 1997), pp. 127–46.

68 See "Democracy and Democratization in Islam" (referenced in note 67).

69 B. Tibi, "The Totalitarianism of Jihadist Islamism" (referenced in note 15). See also Zeyno Baran, "Fighting the war of Ideas," in: *Foreign Affairs* (November/December 2005), pp. 68–78. See also Walid Phares, *The War of Ideas. Jihadism against Democracy* (New York: Palgrave, 2007).

70 These flaws are reflected in the work of the French scholars Olivier Roy and Gilles Kepel.

71 On religion and world politics see the references to the introduction to this book, as well as Eric O. Hanson, *Religion and Politics in the International Society Today* (Cambridge: Cambridge University Press, 2006).

72 On Hamas see Matthew Levitt, *Hamas. Politics, Charity and Terrorism in the Service of Jihad* (New Haven, CT: Yale University Press, 2006).
73 See chapters 9 and 10 in B. Tibi, *The Challenge of Fundamentalism* (referenced in note 65).
74 Benjamin R. Barber, *Jihad vs McWorld* (New York: Random House, 1995).
75 See Mohammed Arkoun, *Rethinking Islam* (Boulder, CO: Westview Press, 1994); and B. Tibi, *Islam and the Cultural Accommodation of Social Change* (Boulder, CO: Westview Press, 1990).
76 See the negative contention of the Turkish scholar Şerif Mardin on "Civil Society and Islam" and in contrast my positive views, both referenced in note 50 to the introduction.
77 See the reference on identity politics and conflict in note 14.

Bibliography

Abdillah, Masykuri, *Responses of Indonesian Muslim Intellectuals to the Concept of Democracy*, Hamburg: Abera Verlag, 1997.

Abrahamian, Ervand, *Khomeinism. Essays on the Islamic Republic*, Berkeley, CA: University of California Press, 1993.

Adler, Emmanuel and Crawford, Beverly, (eds) *The Convergence of Civilizations. Constructing a Mediterranean Region*, Toronto: University of Toronto Press, 2006.

Ajami, Fouad, *The Arab Predicament. Arab Political Thought and Practice since 1967*, Cambridge: Cambridge University Press, 1981.

—— *The Vanished Imam Musa Sadr and the Shia of Lebanon*, Ithaca, NY: Cornell University Press, 1986.

Akhavi, Shahrough, *Religion and Politics in Contemporary Iran*, Albany, NY: State University of New York Press, 1980.

AlSayyad, Nezar, "Culture, Identity, and Urbanism in a Changing World," in: Michael Cohen (ed.) *Preparing for the Urban Future*, Baltimore, MD: Johns Hopkins University Press, 1996, pp. 108–22.

Anderson, Liam and Stansfield, Gareth, *The Future of Iraq*, New York: Palgrave, 2004.

Anderson, Malcolm, *Frontiers. Territory and State Formation in the Modern World*, Cambridge: Polity Press, 1996.

Anheier, Helmut and Isar, Y. Raj (eds) *Culture, Conflict, Globalization*, London: Sage, 2007.

An-Na'im, Abdullahi A., *Toward an Islamic Reformation. Civil Liberties, Human Rights and International Law*, Syracuse, NY: Syracuse University Press, 1990.

An-Na'im, Abdullahi A. and Deng, Francis M. (eds) *Human Rights in Africa. Cross-Cultural Perspectives*, Washington, DC: Brookings, 1990.

Appleby, R. Scott (ed.) *Spokesmen for the Despised*, Chicago, IL: University of Chicago Press, 1997.

Apter, David E., *The Politics of Modernization*, Chicago, IL: University of Chicago Press, 1965.

Arjomand, Said Amir, *The Turban for the Crown. The Islamic Revolution in Iran*, New York: Oxford University Press, 1989.

Arkoun, Mohammed, *Rethinking Islam*, Boulder, CO: Westview, 1994.

Arnold, Anthony, *The Fateful Pebble. Afghanistan's Role in the Fall of the Soviet Empire*, Novato, CA: Presido, 1993.

Aron, Raymond, *Paix et guerre entre les nations*, Paris: Calman-Lévy, 1962.

Aust, Stefan and Schnibben, Cord, *11 September. Geschichte eines Terrorangriffs*, Munich: Deutsche Verlagsanstalt, 2002.

Ayubi, Nazih, *Political Islam, Religion and Politics in the Arab World* London: Routledge, 1991.

Baker, Raymond, *Islam Without Fear, Egypt and the New Islamists*, Cambridge, MA: Harvard University Press, 2003.

Bamualin, Chaider (ed.) *Islam and the West*, Jakarta: UIN Hidayatullah University, 2003.

Baram, Amatzia, *Culture, History and Ideology in the Formation of Ba'thist Iraq 1968–89*, New York: St Martin's Press, 1991.

Barber, Benjamin R., *Jihad vs. McWorld*, New York: Random House, 1995.

Be'eri, Eliezer, *Army Officers in Arab Politics and Society*, New York: Praeger, 1970.

Bell, Daniel, *The Winding Passage 1960–1980*, New York: Basic Books, 1980.

Ben-Dor, Gabriel, "Ethnopolitics and the Middle Eastern State," in Milton Esman and Itamar Rabinovich (eds) *Ethnicity, Pluralism and the State in the Middle East*, Ithaca, NY and London: Cornell University Press, 1988, pp. 71–92.

Ben-Habib, Seyla (ed.) *Democracy and Difference. Contesting the Boundaries of the Political*, Princeton, NJ: Princeton University Press, 1996.

Berkes, Niyazi, *The Development of Secularism in Turkey*, New York: Routledge, new edition 1998.

Bernard, Cheryl and Khalilzad, Zalmay, *The Government of God. Iran's Islamic Republic*, New York: Columbia University Press, 1984.

Binder, Leonard, *Islamic Liberalism. A Critique of Development Ideologies*, Chicago, IL: University of Chicago Press, 1988.

Birch, Anthony, *The Concepts and Theories of Modern Democracy*, London: Routledge, 1993.

Blankinship, Khalid Yahya, *The End of the Jihad State. The Reign of Hisham Ibn Abd al-Malik and the Collapse of the Umayyads*, Albany, NY: State University of New York Press, 1994.

Blaut, James M., *The Colonizer's Model of the World. Geographical Diffusionism and Eurocentric History*, New York: Guilford Press, 1993.

Bloch, Ernst, *Avicenna und die aristotelische Linke*, Frankfurt am Main: Suhrkamp, 1963.

Bodansky, Yossef, *Bin Laden. The Man Who Declared War on America*, Rocklin, CA: California Forum, 1999.

Boer, T.J. De, *Geschichte der Philosophie im Islam*, Stuttgart: Fromann, 1901.

Boroujerdi, Mehrzad, *Iranian Intellectuals and the West. The Tormented Triumph of Nativism*, Syracuse, NY: Syracuse University Press, 1996.

Braudel, Fernand, *A History of Civilizations*, New York: Penguin, 1994.

—— *The Mediterranean and the Mediterranean World in the Age of Philip II*, 2 vols, Berkeley, CA: University of California Press, 1995.

Bringa, Tone, *Being Muslim the Bosnian Way: Identity and Community in a Central Bosnian Village*, Princeton, NJ: Princeton University Press, 1995.

Brisard, Charles, *Zarqawi. The New Face of al-Qaida*, New York: Other Press, 2005.

Brown, Kenneth, "Profile of a Nineteenth-Century Moroccan Scholar," in Nikki Keddie (ed.) *Scholars, Saints and Sufis. Muslim Religious Institutions in the Middle East since 1500*, Berkeley and Los Angeles, CA: University of California Press, 1972, pp. 127–48.

Brown, Peter, *The Rise of Western Christendom*, Oxford: Blackwell, 1996.

Brubaker, Roger, *Citizenship and Nationhood in France and Germany*, Cambridge, MA: Harvard University Press, 1992.

Brzezinski, Zbigniew, *Out of Control. Global Turmoil on the Eve of the 21st Century*, New York: Charles Scribner's Sons, 1993.

Bull, Hedley, *The Anarchical Society. A Study of Order in World Politics*, New York: Columbia University Press, 1977.

Bull, Hedley and Watson, Adam (eds) *The Expansion of International Society*, Oxford: Clarendon Press, 1984.

Bunt, Gary R., *Islam in the Digital Age. E-Jihad, Online Fetwas and Cyber Islamic Environments*, London: Pluto Press, 2003.

Burgat, François and Dowell, William, *The Islamic Movement in North Africa*, Austin, TX: Center for Middle Eastern Studies, University of Texas at Austin, 1993.

Burr, J. Millard and Collins, Robert O., *Alms for Jihad. Charity and Terrorism in the Islamic World*, New York: Cambridge University Press, 2006.

Butterworth, Charles (ed.) *The Political Aspects of Islamic Philosophy. Essays in Honor of Muhsin S. Mahdi*, Harvard Middle Eastern Monographs, Cambridge, MA: Harvard University Press, 1992.

Buzan, Barry, *People, States and Fear. An Agenda for International Security Studies in the Post-Cold War Era*, Boulder, CO: Lynne Rienner, 1991.

Byrnes, Timothy A. and Katzenstein, Peter (eds) *Religion in an Expanding Europe*, New York: Cambridge University Press, 2006.

Castells, Manuel, *The Information Age: Economy, Society and Culture, Vol. Two: The Power of Identity*, Cambridge, MA: Blackwell, 1997.

Charney, Jean-Paul, *L'Islam et la guerre. De la guerre juste à la révolution sainte*, Paris: Fayard, 1986.

Chesler, Phyllis, *The New Antisemitism*, San Francisco, CA: Jossey Bass, 2003.

Choueiri, Youssef M., *Islamic Fundamentalism*, Boston, MA: Twayne, 1990.

Chubin, Shahram, *Iran's Nuclear Ambition*, Washington, DC: Carnegie Endowment for Peace, 2006.

Collins, Roger, *The Arab Conquest of Spain 710–797*, Oxford: Blackwell, 1989, reprinted 1994.

Creveld, Martin van, *The Transformation of War*, New York: The Free Press, 1991.

Creveld, Martin van and von Knop, Katherina (eds) *Countering Modern Terrorism. History, Current Issues and Future Threats*, Bielefeld: Bertelsmann, 2005.

Crone, Patricia, *Pre-Industrial Societies. Anatomy of the Pre-Modern World*, Oxford: Oneworld, 2003.

Curtin, Philip D., *The World and the West. The European Challenge and the Overseas Response in the Age of Empire*, Cambridge: Cambridge University Press, 2000.

Dallmayr, Fred, *Dialogue among Civilizations. Some Exemplary Voices*, New York: Palgrave, 2002.

Daly, M.W. and Sikainga, Ahmad A. (eds) *Civil War in the Sudan*, London: British Academic Press, 1993.

Daniel, Norman, *Islam and the West: The Making of an Image*, Oxford: Oneworld, new edition 1993.

Davidson, Herbert A., *Alfarabi, Avicenna and Averroës on Intellect. Their Cosmologies, Theories of the Active Mind, and Theories of Human Intellect*, New York: Oxford University Press, 1992.

Dawisha, Adeed I., (ed.) *Islam in Foreign Policy*, Cambridge: Cambridge University Press, 1983.

—— *Arab Nationalism. From Triumph to Despair*, Princeton, NJ: Princeton University Press, 2003.

Delanty, Gerard, *Inventing Europe: Idea, Identity, Reality*, New York: St Martin's Press, 1995.

Demant, Peter, *Islam vs Islamism. The Dilemma of the Muslim World*, Westport, CT: Praeger, 2006.

Diamond, Larry, Plattner, M. and Brumberg, D. (eds) *Islam and Democracy in the Middle East*, Baltimore, MD: Johns Hopkins University Press, 2003.

Docker, John and Fischer, Gerhard (eds) *Adventures of Identity. European Multicultural Experiences and Perspectives*, Tübingen: Stauffenburg-Verlag, 2001.

Donelly, Jack, *Universal Human Rights in Theory and Practice*, Ithaca, NY: Cornell University Press, 1989.

Donner, Fred, *The Early Islamic Conquests*, Princeton, NJ: Princeton University Press, 1981.

Duran, Michael, "Somebody Else's Civil War," *Foreign Affairs* (2002), vol. 82, 1, pp. 22–42.

Durant, Will, *The Story of Civilization*, 11 volumes, New York: Simon and Schuster, 1953–67; Vol 5: *The Renaissance: A History of Civilization in Italy from 1304–1576 AD* (New York: Simon and Schuster, 1953, reprint 1981.

Ehrenburg, John, *The Idea of Civil Society. The Critical History of an Idea*, New York: New York University Press, 1999.

Ehteshami, Anoushiravan, *After Khomeini. The Iranian Second Republic*, London: Routledge, 1995.

Elshtain, Jean B., *Just War against Terror*, New York: Basic Books, 2003.

Emerson, Michael (ed.) *Democratization in the European Neighborhood*, Brussels: CEPS, 2005.

Enayat, Hamid, *Modern Islamic Political Thought*, Austin, TX: University of Texas Press, 1982.

—— "Iran. Khumayni's Concept of the 'Guardianship of the Jurisconsult'," in James P. Piscatori (ed.) *Islam in the Political Process*, Cambridge: Cambridge University Press, 1983, pp. 160–80.

Erasmus Foundation (ed.) *The Limits of Pluralism. Neo-Absolutism and Relativism*, Erasmus Ascension Symposium 11–15 May, 1994, Amsterdam: Praemium Erasmianum Foundation, 1995.

Esposito, John (ed.) *The Iranian Revolution. Its Global Impact*, Miami, FL: Florida International University Press, 1990.

—— *The Islamic Threat. Myth or Reality?*, New York: Oxford University Press, 1992.

Esposito, John and Voll, John, *Islam and Democracy*, New York: Oxford University Press, 1996.

Euben, Roxanne L., *Enemy in the Mirror. Islamic Fundamentalism and the Limits of Modern Rationalism. A Work of Comparative Political Theory*, Princeton, NJ: Princeton University Press, 1999.

—— *Journeys to the Other Shores. Muslim and Western Travelers in the Search of Knowledge*, Princeton, NJ: Princeton University Press, 2006.

al-Farabi, *al-madina al-fadila*, English edition *Al-Farabi on the Perfect State*, ed. and trans. Michael Walzer, Oxford: Oxford University Press, 1985.

Feldman, Noah, *After Jihad. America and the Struggle for Islamic Democracy*, New York: Farrar and Straus, 2004.

Fetscher, Iring and Muenkler, Herfried (eds) *Piper Handbuch der politischen Ideen: Das Mittelalter*, vol. II, Munich: Piper Verlag, 1993.

Finkielkraut, Alain, *La Défaite de la pensée*, Paris: Gallimard, 1989.

Firestone, Reuven, *Jihad. The Origins of Holy War in Islam*, New York: Oxford University Press, 1999.

Foroutan, Naika, *Kulturdialoge zwischen dem Westen und der islamischen Welt*, Wiesbaden: DUV, 2004.

Fourest, Caroline, *Frère Tariq. Discours, Stratégie et Méthode de Tariq Ramadan*, Paris: Grasset, 2004.

Fregosi, Paul, *Jihad in the West. Muslim Conquests from the 7th to the 21st centuries*, Amherst, NY: Prometheus Books, 1998.

Fuhrmann, Horst, *Einladung ins Mittelalter*, Munich: C.H. Beck, 1987.

Fukuyama, Francis, *The End of History and the Last Man*, New York: Avon Books, 1992.

—— "Identity, Immigration and Democracy," *Journal of Democracy* (2006), vol. 17, 2, pp. 5–20.

Fuller, Graham E., *The Center of the Universe. The Geopolitics of Iran*, Boulder, CO: Westview Press, 1991.

Fuller, Graham E. and Francke, Rend Rahim (eds) *The Arab Shi'a. The Forgotten Muslims*, New York: St Martin's Press, 1999.

Fuller, Graham E. and Lesser, Ian, *A Sense of Siege. The Geopolitics of Islam and the West*, Boulder, CO: Westview Press, 1995.

Geertz, Clifford, *The Interpretation of Cultures: Selected Essays*, London: Fontana Press, 1973.

—— *Islam Observed. Religious Development in Morocco and Indonesia*, Chicago, IL: University of Chicago Press, 1989.

Gellner, Ernest, *Postmodernism, Reason and Religion*, London and New York: Routledge, 1992.

—— "Expiation through Subjectivism," in Erasmus Foundation (ed.) *The Limits of Pluralism. Relativism and Neo-Absolutisms*, Amsterdam: Praemium Erasmianum Foundation, 1994, pp. 163–5.

Gerges, Fawaz, *America and Political Islam. Clash of Cultures or Clash of Interests?*, Cambridge: Cambridge University Press, 1999.

Gerholm, Tomas and Lithman, Yngve G. (eds) *The New Islamic Presence in Western Europe,* London: Mansell, 1988.

Ghadban, Ralph, *Tariq Ramadan und die Islamisierung Europas*, Berlin: Schiler Verlag, 2006.

Gibb, Sir Hamilton A.R., *Studies on the Civilization of Islam*, Princeton, NJ: Princeton University Press, 1962, reprint 1982.

Giddens, Anthony, *Nation State and Violence*, Berkeley, CA: University of California Press, 1987.

Goele, Niluefer, *The Forbidden Modern. Civilization and Veiling*, Ann Arbor, MI: University of Michigan Press, 1996.

Goldberg, Ellis, Kasaba, R. and Migdal, J.S. (eds) *Rules and Rights in the Middle East: Democracy, Law, and Society*, Seattle, WA: University of Washington Press, 1993.

Goody, Jack, *Islam in Europe*, Cambridge: Polity Press, 2004.

Gress, David, *From Plato to NATO. The Idea of the West and its Opponents*, New York: The Free Press, 1998.

Habeck, Mary, *Knowing the Enemy. Jihadist Ideology and the War on Terror*, New Haven, CT: Yale University Press, 2006.

Habermas, Jürgen, *The Philosophical Discourse of Modernity. Twelve Lectures*, Cambridge, MA: MIT Press, 1987.

—— *Die Einbeziehung des Anderen*, Frankfurt aim Main: Suhrkamp, 1996.

—— *Glauben und Wissen*, Frankfurt aim Main: Suhrkamp, 2001.

Hall, John (ed.) *Civil Society*, Cambridge: Polity Press, 1995.

Halliday, Fred, *Islam and the Myth of Confrontation. Religion and Politics in the Middle East*, London: Tauris, 1995.

—— *Nation and Religion in the Middle East*, London: Saqi Books, 2000.

Hamidullah, Muhammad, *The Muslim Conduct of State*, Lahore: Sh. Muhammad Ashraf, 1977.

Hanson, Eric O., *Religion and Politics in the International System Today*, New York: Cambridge University Press, 2006.

Haqqani, Husain, *Pakistan between Mosque and Military*, Washington, DC: Carnegie Endowment, 2005.

Hargreaves, Alec G., *Immigration, "Race" and Ethnicity in Contemporary France*, London: Routledge, 1995.

Harrison, Lawrence E., *Underdevelopment is a State of Mind: The Latin American Case*, Cambridge, MA: Center for International Affairs, Harvard University, 1985.

Harrison, Lawrence E., Berger, P. and Kagan, J. (eds) *Developing Cultures*, Vol. One: *Essays on Cultural Change*, Vol. Two: *Case Studies*, New York: Routledge, 2006.

Hasan, Mushrul, *Legacy of a Divided Nation. India's Muslims since Independence*, Boulder, CO: Westview Press, 1997.

Hashmi, Sahail (ed.), *Islamic Political Ethics*, Princeton, NJ: Princeton University Press, 2002.

Haynes, Jeff, *Religion in Global Politics*, London: Longman, 1998.

Hefner, Robert, *Civil Islam. Muslims and Democratization in Indonesia*, Princeton, NJ: Princeton University Press, 2000.

—— *Remaking Muslim Politics. Pluralism, Contestation, Democratization*, Princeton, NJ: Princeton University Press, 2005.

Held, David, *Democracy and the Global Order. From the Modern State to Cosmopolitan Governance*, Stanford, CA: Stanford University Press, 1995.

Helmanita, Karlina, Abubakar, I. and Afrianty, D. (eds), *Dialogue in the World Disorder. A Response to Threat of Unilateralism and World Terrorism*, Jakarta: UIN Hidayatullah University, 2004.

Herzog, Roman, *Preventing the Clash of Civilizations. A Peace Strategy for the Twenty-First Century*, ed. H. Schmiegelow with comments by Amitai Etzioni, Hans Küng, Bassam Tibi and Masakazu Yamazaki, New York: St Martin's Press, 1999.

Hinsley, F.H., *Sovereignty*, Cambridge: Cambridge University Press, second edition 1986.

Hodgson, Marshall, *The Venture of Islam. Conscience and History in a World Civilization*, 3 vols, Chicago, IL: Chicago University Press, 1974.

—— *Rethinking World History: Essays on Europe, Islam and World History*, Cambridge: Cambridge University Press, 1993.

Hoffer, Eric, *The True Believer. Thoughts on the Nature of Mass Movements*, New York: Perennial Library, 2002, reprint of the original of 1951.

Hoffman, Bruce, *Inside Terrorism*, New York: Columbia University Press, 1998.

Hoffmann, Stanley, *Janus and Minerva. Essays in the Theory and Practice of International Politics*, Boulder, CO: Westview Press, 1987.

—— *World Disorders. Troubled Peace in the Post-Cold War Era*, New York: Rowman & Littlefield, 1998.

Holsti, Kalevi J., *The State, War and the State of War*, Cambridge: Cambridge University Press, 1996.

Hooglund, Eric, *The Iranian Revolution and the Islamic Republic*, Syracuse, NY: Syracuse University Press, 1986.

Horkheimer, Max, *Kritische Theorie*, 2 vols, Frankfurt aim Main: Fischer, 1968

—— *Kritik der instrumentellen Vernunft*, Frankfurt aim Main: Athenaeum, 1974.

Hourani, Albert, *Arabic Thought in the Liberal Age, 1798–1939*, Oxford: Oxford University Press, 1962.

—— *Europe and the Middle East*, Berkeley, CA: University of California Press, 1980.

Howe, Marvine, *Turkey Today. A Nation Divided over Islam's Revival*, Boulder, CO: Westview Press, 2000.

Hudson, Michael C., *Arab Politics. The Search for Legitimacy*, New Haven, CT: Yale University Press, 1977.

Huff, Toby E., *The Rise of Early Modern Science. Islam, China and the West*, Cambridge: Cambridge University Press, 1995.

Hunter, Shireen Tahmasseb, *Iran and the World. Continuity in a Revolutionary Decade*, Bloomington, IN: Indiana University Press, 1990.

—— *The Future of Islam and the West. Clash of Civilizations or Peaceful Coexistence?* London: Praeger, 1998.

Huntington, Samuel P., *Political Order in Changing Societies*, New Haven, CT: Yale University Press, 1968.

—— *The Third Wave. Democratization in the Late Twentieth Century*, Norman, OK: University of Oklahoma Press, 1991.

—— *Clash of Civilizations*, New York: Simon and Schuster, 1996.

Hussain, Syed Sajjad and Ashraf, Syed Ali, *Crisis in Muslim Education*, London: Hodder and Stoughton, 1979.

Ibn Khaldun, *al-Muqaddima* [Prolegomena], Arabic reprints, Cairo: al-Maktaba al-Tijariyya, with no date, English translation, *The Muqaddimah: An Introduction to History*, trans. Franz Rosenthal, 3 vols, Princeton, NJ and New York: Princeton University Press, 1958.

Ibrahim, Saad Eddin, "Anatomy of Egypt's Militant Islamic Groups," *International Journal of Middle East Studies* (1980), vol. 12, p. 449. Reprinted in Saad Eddin Ibrahim, *Egypt, Islam and Democracy,* Cairo: AUC Press, 1996, pp. 1–33.

Imara, Mohammed, *al-sahwa al-Islamiyya* [The Islamic Awakening], Cairo: Dar al-Shuruq, 1991.

Ishay, Micheline R. (ed.) *The Human Rights Reader: Major Political Writings, Essays, Speeches and Documents from the Bible to the Present*, New York: Routledge, 1997.

Jabar, Faleh, *The Shi'ite Movement in Iraq*, London: Saqi, 2003.

Jaber, Hala, *Hezbollah. Born with a Vengeance*, New York: Columbia University Press, 1997.

al-Jabri, Mohammed Abed, *Arab Islamic Philosophy, A Contemporary Critique*, Austin, TX: Center for Middle Eastern Studies, University of Texas at Austin, 1999.

Jackson, Robert H., *Quasi-States: Sovereignty, International Relations, and the Third World*, Cambridge: Cambridge University Press, 1990.

Jamal, Amal, *The Palestinean National Movement. Politics and Contention 1967–2005*, Bloomington, IN: Indiana University Press, 2005.

Jamieson, Alan G., *Faith and Sword. A Short History of Christian-Muslim Conflict*, London: Reaktion Books, 2006.

Jansen, Johannes, *The Dual Nature of Islamic Fundamentalism*, Ithaca and New York: Cornell University Press, 1997.

Jay, Martin, *The Dialectical Imagination. A History of the Frankfurt School*, Boston, MA: Little, Brown, 1973.

Johnson, James Turner, *The Holy War Idea in Western and Islamic Traditions*, University Park, PA: Pennsylvania State University Press, 2001.

Joppke, Christian and Lukes, Steven (eds) *Multi-cultural Questions*, Oxford: Oxford University Press, 1999.

Juergensmeyer, Mark, *The New Cold War? Religious Nationalism Confronts the Secular State*, Berkeley, CA: University of California Press, 1993.

—— *Terror in the Mind of God. The Global Rise of Religious Violence*, Berkeley, CA: University of California Press, 2000.

Kaldor, Mary, *Global Civil Society*, Cambridge: Polity Press, 2003.

Kant, Immanuel, "Entwurf zum Ewigen Frieden," in Richard Saage and Zwi Batscha (eds) *Friedensutopien*, Frankfurt aim Main: Suhrkamp, 1975.

Kaplan, Robert, *The Coming Anarchy. Shuttering the Dreams of Post Cold War*, New York: Random House, 2000.

Karsh, Efraim, *Islamic Imperialism. A History*, New Haven, CT: Yale University Press, 2006.

Kassab, Mohammed Y., *L'Islam face au nouvel ordre mondial*, Algier: Editions Salama, 1991.

Katzenstein, Peter and Byrnes, Timothy A. (eds) *Religion in an Expanding Europe*, New York: Cambridge University Press, 2006.

Keddie, Nikki (ed.) *An Islamic Response to Imperialism. Political and Religious Writings of al-Afghani*, Berkeley, CA: University of California Press, 1968.

—— *Roots of Revolution. An Interpretative History of Modern Iran*, New Haven, CT: Yale University Press, 1981.

Kelsay, John, *Islam and War. A Study in Comparative Ethics*, Louisville, KY: John Knox Press, 1993.

Kepel, Gilles, *Les Banlieus de l'Islam. Naissance d'une réligion en France*, Paris: Seuil, 1987.

—— *A l'ouest d'Allah*, Paris: Edition du Seuil, 1994.

—— *Jihad, expansion et déclin de l'Islamisme*, Paris: Gallimard, 2000.

Khadduri, Majid, *War and Peace in the Law of Islam*, Baltimore, MD: Johns Hopkins University Press, 1955.

al-Khalil, Samir, *The Republic of Fear. The Politics of Modern Iraq*, Berkeley, CA: University of California Press, 1989.

Khoury, Philip and Kostiner, Josef (eds) *The Formation of States in the Middle East*, Berkeley, CA: University of California Press, 1990.

Klausen, Jytte, *The Islamic Challenge in Politics and Religion in Western Europe*, Oxford: Oxford University Press, 2005.

Kramer, Martin, "Hizbullah: The Calculus of Jihad," in Martin Marty and R. Scott Appleby (eds) *The Fundamentalism Project, Vol. Three: Fundamentalisms and the State. Remaking Polities, Economies, and Militance*, Chicago, IL: University of Chicago Press, 1993.
—— *Arab Awakening and Islamic Revival*, New Brunswick, NY: Transaction Publishers, 1996.
Kuegelgen, Anke von, *Averroës und die arabische Moderne. Ansaetze zu einer Neugruendung des Rationalismus im Islam*, Leiden: Brill Press, 1994.
Kuper, Adam, *Culture. The Anthropologists' Account*, Cambridge, MA: Harvard University Press, 1999.
Kurdi, Abdulrahman A., *The Islamic State*, London: Mansell, 1984.
Kurzman, Charles (ed.) *Liberal Islam*, New York: Oxford University Press, 1998.
Laue, Theodore Hermann von, *The World Revolution of Westernization. The Twentieth Century in Global Perspective*, New York: Oxford University Press, 1987.
Lehring, Gary, "Identity Politics," in M. Hawkesworth and M. Kagan (eds) *Routledge Encyclopedia of Government and Politics*, 2 vols, London: Routledge, 2004, vol. 1, pp. 576–86.
Levitt, Matthew, *Hamas. Politics, Charity and Terrorism in the Service of Jihad*, New Haven, CT: Yale University Press, 2006.
Lewis, Bernard, "Politics and War," in Joseph Schacht and Clifford E. Bosworth (eds) *The Legacy of Islam*, second edition, Oxford: Clarendon Press, 1974, pp. 156–209.
—— *Islam, Volume One: Politics and War*, New York: Oxford University Press, 1987.
—— *Multiple Identities in the Middle East*, New York: Shaken Books, 1998.
—— *What Went Wrong? Western Impact and Middle Eastern Response* Oxford: Oxford University Press, 2002.
—— *The Crisis of Islam. Holy War and Unholy Terror*, London: Weidenfeld and Nicolson, 2003.
Lewis, Philip, *Islamic Britain: Religion, Politics and Identity among British Muslims*, new edition, London: I.B. Tauris, 2002.
Lincoln, Bruce, *Holy Terrors. Thinking about Religion after September 11*, Chicago, IL: University of Chicago Press, 2003.
Lindberg, David, *The Beginning of Western Science*, Chicago, IL: University of Chicago Press, 1992.
Lindholm, Tore and Vogt, Kari (eds) *Islamic Law Reform and Human Rights*, Copenhagen: Nordic Human Rights Publications 1993.
Lipset, Seymour Martin (ed.) *The Encyclopedia of Democracy*, 4 vols, Washington, DC: The Congressional Quarterly, 1995.
Lipson, Leslie, *The Ethical Crises of Civilizations. Moral Meltdown or Advance?*, London: Sage, 1993.
Lockwood, William G., *European Moslems*, New York: Academic Press, 1975.
Lyons, Gene M. and Mastanduno, Michael (eds) *Beyond Westphalia*, Baltimore, MD: Johns Hopkins University Press, 1995.
MacNeill, William H., *The Rise of the West. A History of the Human Community*, Chicago, IL: University of Chicago Press, 1963.
Mahdi, Muhsen, *Ibn Khaldun's Philosophy of History. A Study in the Philosophic Foundations of the Science of Culture*, London: George Allen Unwin, 1957.
Mahfuz, Mohammed, *al-lathin zulimu. al-tanzimat al-Islamiyya fi misr* [The Opressed. Islamist Organizations in Egypt], London: el-Rayyes Books, 1988.
Makdisi, George, *The Rise of Colleges. Institutions of Learning in Islam and the West*, Edinburgh: Edinburgh University Press, 1981.
Mallat, Chibli, *The Middle East into the 21st Century. The Japan lectures and other studies on the Arab-Israeli conflict, the Gulf crisis and political Islam*, Reading: Ithaca Press, 1996.
Mandaville, Peter, *Transnational Muslim Politics, Reimagining the Umma*, New York: Routledge, 2004.
Manfrass, Klaus, *Tuerken in der Bundesrepublik – Nordafrikaner in Frankreich*, Bonn: Bovier, 1991.
Mardin, Şerif, "Civil Society in Islam," in John Hall (ed.) *Civil Society. Theory, History, Comparison*, Cambridge: Polity Press, 1995, pp. 278–9.
Marr, Phebe, *The Modern History of Iraq*, Boulder, CO: Westview Press, 1985.
Martin, Leonore (ed.) *New Frontiers in Middle Eastern Security*, New York: St Martin's Press, 1999.
Martin, Philip, "Germany: Reluctant Land of Immigration," in Wayne A. Cornelius, T. Takeyuki, P. Martin and J. Hollifield (eds) *Controlling Immigration. A Global Perspective*, Stanford, CA: Stanford University Press, 1994, pp. 189–225.

Marty, Martin and Appleby, R. Scott (eds) *The Fundamentalism Project*, 5 vols, Chicago, IL: University of Chicago Press, 1991–5.

Masud, Muhammad Khalid, "The Obligation to Migrate: The Doctrine of Hijra in Islamic Law," in James Piscatori and Dale Eickelman (eds) *Muslim Travellers: Pilgrimage, Migration, and the Religious Imagination*, Berkeley, CA: University of California Press, 1990, pp. 29–49.

Mayer, Ann E., "The Shari'a: A Methodology or a Body of Substantive Rules?," in Nicholas Heer (ed.) *Islamic Law and Jurisprudence*, Seattle, WA: University of Washington Press, 1990, pp. 177–98.

—— *Islam and Human Rights. Tradition and Politics*, Boulder, CO: Westview Press, 1991.

—— *War and Peace in the Islamic Tradition: International Law*, mimeograph, ref. no. 141, Philadelphia, PA: University of Pennsylvania, Wharton School, Department of Legal Studies, no date.

Mehden, Fred R. von der, *Two Worlds of Islam. Interaction between Southeast Asia and the Middle East*, Miami-Jacksonville, FL: University of Florida Press, 1993.

Miller, Lynn H., *Global Order. Values and Power in International Politics*, Boulder, CO: Westview, 1990.

Milton-Edwards, Beverley, *Islamic Politics in Palestine*, London: Tauris, 1996.

Mitchell, Joseph and Buss Mitchell, Helen (eds) *Taking Sides. Clashing Views on Controversial Issues in Western Civilization*, Guilford, CT: McGraw Hill, 2000.

Mitchell, Richard P., *The Society of the Muslim Brothers*, Oxford: Oxford University Press, 1969.

Modood, Tariq (ed.) *The Politics of Multi-culturalism in the New Europe*, New York: St Martin's Press, 1997.

Momen, Moojan, *An Introduction to Shi'i Islam: The History and Doctrines of Twelver Shi'ism*, New Haven, CT: Yale University Press, 1983.

Mortimer, Edward, *Faith and Power. The Politics of Islam*, New York: Vintage, 1982.

Moyniham, Daniel Patrick, *Pandaemonium. Ethnicity in International Politics*, New York: Oxford University Press, 1993.

Nakash, Yitzhak, *The Shi'is of Iraq*, Princeton, NJ: Princeton University Press, 1994.

—— *Reaching for Power. The Shi'a in the Modern Arab World*, Princeton, NJ: Princeton University Press, 2006.

Nardin, Terry (ed.) *The Ethics of War and Peace*, Princeton, NJ: Princeton University Press, 1998.

Neumann, Peter, "Europe's Jihadist Dilemma," *Survival* (2006), vol. 48, 2, pp. 71–84.

Norris, Pippa and Inglehart, Ronald, *Sacred and Secular. Religion and Politics Worldwide*, New York: Cambridge University Press, 2004.

O'Ballance, Edgar, *Islamic Fundamentalist Terrorism. 1979–95. The Iranian Connection*, Washington Square, NY: New York University Press, 1997.

—— *Sudan, Civil War and Terrorism (1956–1999)*, New York: St Martin's Press, 2000.

Papastergiadis, Nikos, *The Turbulance of Migration*, Cambridge: Polity Press, 2000.

Pape, Robert, *Dying to Win. The Strategic Logic of Suicide Terrorism*, New York: Random House, 2005.

Parker, Geoffrey, *The Military Revolution. Military Innovation and the Rise of the West, 1500–1800*, Cambridge: Cambridge University Press, 1988.

Partner, Peter, *God of Battles. Holy Wars in Christianity and Islam*, Princeton, NJ: Princeton University Press, 1997.

Peters, Rudolph, *Islam and Colonialism. The Doctrine of Jihad and Modern History*, The Hague: Mouton, 1979.

—— *Jihad in Classical and Modern Islam*, Princeton, NJ: Markus Wiener, 1996.

Petterson, Dan, *Inside Sudan. Political Islam. Conflict and Catastrophe*, Boulder, CO: Westview, 2003.

Philpott, Daniel, "The Challenge of September 11 to Secularism in International Relations," *World Politics* (2002), vol. 55, 1, pp. 66–95.

Pipes, Daniel, *In the Path of God. Islam and Political Power*, New York: Basic Books, 1984.

Pirenne, Henri, *Mahomet et Charlemagne*, Paris: Presses Universitaires de France, 1937, reprint 1992; English translation *Mohammed and Charlemagne*, London: Dover, 1939, reprint 2001.

Piscatori, James, *Islam in the World of Nation-States*, Cambridge: Cambridge University Press, 1986.

Popper, Karl, *The Open Society and its Enemies*, 2 vols, London: Routledge and Kegan Paul, 1945.

Powers, Roger and Vogle, William (eds) *Protest, Power and Change. An Encyclopedia of Non-Violent Action*, New York: Garland, 1997.

Preiswerk, Roy and Perrot, Dominique, *Ethnocentrism in History*, New York: NOK Publishers International, 1978.

Qur'an, English translation by N.J. Dawood, fourth edition, London and New York: Penguin, 1974.

Rahman, Fazlur, *Islam and Modernity. Transformation of an Intellectual Tradition*, Chicago, IL: University of Chicago Press, 1982.

Ralston, David B., *Importing the European Army. The Introduction of European Army Techniques into the Extra-European World 1600–1914*, Chicago, IL: University of Chicago Press, 1990.

Ramadan, Tariq, *Aux Sources du Renouveau Musulman. D'al Afghani à Hassan al-Banna. Un Siècle de Réformisme Islamique*, Paris: Bayard, 1998.

Ramazani, Rouhollah Karegar, "Khumayni's Islam in Iran's Foreign Policy," in Adeed I. Dawisha (ed.) *Islam in Foreign Policy*, Cambridge: Cambridge University Press, 1983.

—— *Revolutionary Iran. Challenge and Response in the Middle East*, Baltimore, MD: Johns Hopkins University Press, 1987.

Ranger, Terence and Hobsbawm, Eric (eds) *The Invention of Tradition*, Cambridge: Cambridge University Press, reprint 1999.

Ranstorp, Magnus, *Hizb'Allah in Lebanon. The Politics of the Western Hostage Crisis*, New York: St Martin's Press, 1997.

Rashid, Ahmed, *Taliban. Militant Islam*, New Haven, CT: Yale University Press, 2000.

Revel, Jean François, *Democracy Against Itself: The Future of the Democratic Impulse*, New York: Free Press, 1993.

Ricklefs, M.C., *A History of Modern Indonesia*, second edition, Stanford, CA: Stanford University Press, 1993.

Rodinson, Maxime, *Mohammed*, second edition, London: Allen Lane, 1971.

—— *Mahomet*, Paris: Éditions du Seuil, 1975.

—— *La Fascination de l'Islam*, Paris: Maspero, 1980.

Rosefsky Wickham, Carrie, *Mobilizing Islam. Religion, Activism and Political Change in Egypt*, New York: Columbia University Press, 2002.

Rosenthal, Franz, *The Classical Heritage of Islam*, London: Routledge, 1975, reprinted 1994.

Roy, Olivier, *The Failure of Political Islam*, Cambridge, MA: Harvard University Press, 1994.

Rubin, Barnett R., *The Fragmentation of Afghanistan*, New Haven, CT: Yale University Press, 1995.

Rubin, Barry, *Islamic Fundamentalism in Egyptian Politics*, London: Macmillan, 1990.

Runciman, Sir Steven, *The Fall of Constantinople*, New York: Cambridge University Press, 1990.

Rundell, John and Mennell, Stephen (eds) *Classical Readings in Culture and Civilization*, London: Routledge, 1998.

Russett, Bruce, *Grasping the Democratic Peace. Principles for a Post-Cold War World*, Princeton, NJ: Princeton University Press, 1993.

Sachedina, Abdulaziz, *The Islamic Roots of Democratic Pluralism*, Oxford: Oxford University Press, 2001.

Safran, Nadav, *Egypt in the Search for Political Community*, Cambridge, MA: Harvard University Press, 1961.

Sageman, Mark, *Understanding Terror Networks*, Philadelphia, PA: University of Pennsylvania Press, 2004.

Said, Edward, *Covering Islam*, New York: Pantheon, 1981.

Schacht, Joseph, *An Introduction to Islamic Law*, Oxford: Clarendon Press, 1964.

Schaebler, Birgit and Stenberg, Leif (eds) "al-Qaradawi, Yusuf, 'The Global Mufti'," in *Globalization and the Muslim World*, Syracuse, NY: Syracuse University Press, 2004, pp. 153–65.

Schwartz, Stephen, *The Two Faces of Islam. The House of Sa'ud From Tradition to Terror*, New York: Doubleday, 2002.

Scruton, Roger, *The West and the Rest. Globalization and the Terrorist Threat*, Wilmington, DE: ISI-books, 2002.

Shadid, Wasif Abdelrahman R. and van Koningsveld, P. (eds) *Muslims in the Margin. Political Responses to the Presence of Islam in Western Europe*, Kampen, Netherlands: Kok Pharos, 1996.
—— *Political Participation and Identities of Muslims in Non-Muslim States*, Kampen, Netherlands: Kok Pharos, 1997.
Sharabi, Hisham, *Neopatriarchy. A Theory of Distorted Change in Arab Society*, New York: Oxford University Press, 1992.
Shayegan, Daryush, *Cultural Schizophrenia. Islamic Societies Confronting the West*, Syracuse, NY: Syracuse University Press, 1992.
Siedentop, Larry, *Democracy in Europe*, London: Penguin, 2000.
Silverstein, Paul, *Algeria in France*, Bloomington, IN: Indiana University Press 2004.
Skocpol, Theda, *States and Social Revolutions*, Cambridge: Cambridge University Press, reprint 1987.
Sorel, Georges, *Réflexions sur la violence*, Paris: Editions du Trident, 1987; English translation *Reflections on Violence*, ed. and trans. Jeremy Jennings, Cambridge: Cambridge University Press, 1999.
Soroush, Abdolkarim, *Reason, Freedom and Democracy in Islam*, New York: Oxford University Press, 2000.
Spencer, Robert, *Onward Muslim Soldiers. How Jihad Still Threatens America and the West*, Washington, DC: Regenery, 2003.
Spuler-Stegemann, Ursula, *Muslime in Deutschland*, Freiburg im Breisgau: Herder, new edition 2002.
Stowasser, Karl, *Ein Muslim entdeckt Europa* Munich: C.H. Beck Verlag, 1989, p. 223.
Teitelbaum, Michael and Winter, Jay, *A Question of Numbers. High Migration, Low Fertility and the Politics of National Identity*, New York: Hill and Wang, 1998.
Tibi, Bassam, *Militaer und Sozialismus in der Dritten Welt*, Frankfurt aim Main: Suhrkamp, 1973.
—— "Genesis of the Arab Left. A Critical Viewpoint," in Edward Said (ed.) *The Arabs of Today. Alternatives for Tomorrow*, Columbus, OH: Forum Associates, 1973, pp. 31–42.
—— "Secularization and the Functional Differentiation of the Social System," *Archives for the Philosophy of Law and Social Philosophy* (1980), vol. LXVI, pp. 207–22.
—— "The Iranian Revolution and the Arabs. The Search for Islamic Identity and the Search for an Islamic Government," *Arab Studies Quarterly* (1986), vol. 8, 1, pp. 29–44 (first presented at MESA, Chicago 1983).
—— "Politische Ideen in der 'Dritten Welt' waehrend der Dekolonisation," in Iring Fetscher and Herfried Muenkler (eds) *Pipers Handbuch der politischen Ideen*, Munich: Piper Verlag, 1987, pp. 363–402.
—— *The Crisis of Modern Islam. A Preindustrial Culture in the Scientific-Technological Age*, Salt Lake City, UT: University of Utah Press, 1988.
—— "The Interplay between Social and Cultural Change," in George Atiyeh and Ibrahim Oweis (eds) *Arab Civilization. Studies in Honor of Constantine Zurayk*, Albany: SUNY, 1988, pp. 166–82.
—— "The European Tradition of Human Rights and the Culture of Islam," in Abdullahi A. An-Na'im and Francis M. Deng (eds) *Human Rights in Africa. Cross-Cultural Perspectives*, Washington, DC: Brookings, 1990, pp. 104–32.
—— "The Simultaneity of the Unsimultaneous. Old Tribes and Imposed Nation-States in the Middle East," in Philip Khoury and Joseph Kostiner (eds) *Tribes and State Formation in the Middle East*, Berkeley, CA: University of California Press, 1990, pp. 127–52.
—— *Islam and the Cultural Accommodation of Social Change*, Boulder, CO: Westview Press, 1990.
—— "Die Schwierigkeit, an der deutschen Universitaet heimisch zu sein," in Namo Aziz (ed.) *Fremd in einem kalten Land. Ausländer in Deutschland*, Freiburg im Breisgau: Herder, 1992, pp. 121–36.
—— "Universality of Human Rights and Authenticity of non-Western Cultures. Islam and the Western Concept of Human Rights" (review article on Ann E. Mayer), *Harvard Human Rights Journal* (1992), vol. 5, pp. 221–6.
—— "Zwischen islamischem Erbe und kultureller Erneuerung: Die Chancen der Demokratisierung im Nahen Osten nach dem Golfkrieg," in Herfried Muenkler (ed.) *Die Chancen der Freiheit. Grundprobleme der Demokratie, Festschrift fuer Professor Iring Fetscher*, Munich: Piper Verlag, 1992, pp. 199–23.

—— "The Worldview of Sunni Arab Fundamentalists: Attitudes Towards Modern Science and Technology," in Martin E. Marty and R. Scott Appleby (eds) *The Fundamentalism Project*, 5 vols, Vol. 2: *Fundamentalisms and Society*, Chicago, IL: Chicago University Press, 1993, pp. 73–102.

—— "Political Islam as an Expression of Fundamentalism," in Erasmus Foundation (ed.) *The Limits of Pluralism. Relativism and Neo-Absolutisms*, Amsterdam: Praemium Erasmianum Foundation, 1994, pp. 29–35.

—— "Islamic Law/Shari'a, Human Rights, Universal Morality and International Relations," *Human Rights Quarterly* (May 1994), vol. 16, 2, pp. 277–99.

—— *Das Mittelmeer als Grenze oder als Bruecke Europas zur Welt des Islam*, Bosch Memorial Lecture, Stuttgart: Bosch Foundation, 1994, p. 30.

—— "Culture and Knowledge: The Politics of the Islamization of Knowledge. The Fundamentalist Claim to De-Westernization," *Theory, Culture & Society* (1995), vol. 12, 1, pp. 1–24.

—— "Les Conditions d'un Euro-Islam," in Robert Bistolfi and François Zabbal (eds) *Islams d'Europe: intégration ou insertion communautaire?* Paris: Éditions de l'Aube, 1995, pp. 230–4.

—— "Démocracie et démocratisation en Islam. La Quête d'un Islam éclairé et les contreforces de l'autoritarisme et du fondamentalisme religieux," *Revue Internationale de Politique Comparée* (1995), vol. 2, 2, pp. 285–99.

—— "Islamic Dream of Semi-Modernity," *India International Centre Quarterly* (New Dehli) (Spring 1995), vol. 22, 1, pp. 79–87.

—— *Der wahre Imam. Der Islam von Mohammed bis zur Gegenwart*, Munich: Piper, 1996.

—— "Foreigners – Today's Jews?" in Ulrich Wank (ed.) *The Resurgence of Right Wing Radicalism in Germany*, Atlantic Highlands, NJ: Humanities Press, 1996, pp. 85–102.

—— "Islam, Hinduism and the Limited Secularity in India: A Model for Muslim–European Relations?," in W.A.R. Shadid and P. van Koningsveld (eds) *Muslims in the Margin. Political Responses to the Presence of Islam in Western Europe*, Kampen, Netherlands: Kok Pharos, 1996, pp. 130–45.

—— *Das arabische Staatensystem*, Mannheim: Bibliographisches Institut, 1996.

—— "War and Peace in Islam," in Terry Nardin (ed.) *The Ethics of War and Peace*, Princeton, NJ: Princeton University Press, 1996 and 1998.

—— *Arab Nationalism. Between Islam and the Nation-State*, New York: Macmillan Press, third edition 1997.

—— "The Cultural Underpinning of Civil Society in Islamic Civilization," in Elisabeth Ozdalga and Sune Person (eds) *Civil Society, Democracy and the Muslim World*, Istanbul: Swedish Research Institute, 1997, pp. 23–32.

—— "Democracy and Democratization in Islam," in Michèle Schmiegelow (ed.) *Democracy in Asia*, New York: St Martin's Press, 1997, pp. 127–46.

—— "Entry on Jihad," in Roger Powers and William B. Vogele (eds) *Protest, Power and Change. An Encyclopedia of Nonviolent Action*, New York: Garland, 1997, pp. 277–81.

—— *Conflict and War in the Middle East. From Interstate War to New Security*, New York: St Martin's Press, second enlarged edition 1998.

—— *Europa ohne Identitaet?*, Munich: Bertelsmann, 1998.

—— *The Challenge of Fundamentalism. Political Islam and the New World Disorder*, Berkeley: University of California Press, 1998, updated edition 2002.

—— "The Failed Export of the Islamic Revolution," in Frédéric Grare (ed.) *Islamism and Security*, Geneva: Programme for Strategic and International Security Studies, 1999, pp. 63–102.

—— *Kreuzzug und Djihad. Der Islam und die christliche Welt*, Munich: Bertelsmann, 1999.

—— "International Morality and Cross-Cultural Bridging," in Roman Herzog, *Preventing the Clash of Civilizations*, ed. Henrik Schmiegelow, with comments by Amitai Etzioni, Hans Küng, Bassam Tibi and Masakazu Yamazaki, New York: St Martin's Press, 1999, pp. 107–26.

—— "The Fundamentalist Challenge to Secular Order in the Middle East," *Fletcher Forum of World Affairs* (1999), vol. 23, 1, pp. 191–210.

—— "Secularization and De-Secularization in Islam," *Religion-Staat-Gesellschaft* (2000), vol. 1, 1, pp. 95–117.

—— "Post-Bipolar Order in Crisis: The Challenge of Politicized Islam," *Millennium, Journal of International Affairs* (2000), vol. 29, 3, pp. 843–59.

—— *Einladung in die islamische Geschichte*, Darmstadt: Primus, 2001.
—— "Communitarianism and Euro-Islam," in John Docker and Gerhard Fischer (eds) *Adventures of Identity. European Multicultural Experiences and Perspectives*, Tübingen: Stauffenburg-Verlag, 2001, pp. 45–60.
—— *Islamische Zuwanderung. Die gescheiterte Integration*, Munich: Deutsche Verlagsanstalt, 2002.
—— "Habermas and the Return of the Sacred. Is it a Religious Renaissance, a Pronouncement of a 'Post-Secular Society,' or the Emergence of Political Religion as a New Totalitarianism?" *Religion-Staat-Gesellschaft* (2002), vol. 3, 2, pp. 265–96.
—— "Between Islam and Islamism: A Dialogue with Islam and a Security Approach vis-à-vis Islamism," in Tami A. Jacoby and Brent E. Sasley (eds) *Redefining Security in the Middle East*, Manchester: Manchester University Press, 2002, pp. 62–82.
—— "Islamism, National and International Security after September 11," in Guenther Baechler and Andreas Wenger (eds) *Conflict and Cooperation. The Individual between Ideal and Reality, Festschrift in honor of Kurt R. Spillmann*, Zurich: Neue Zuercher Zeitung, 2002, pp. 127–52.
—— "Muslim Migrants in Europe: Between Euro-Islam and Ghettoization," in Nezar AlSayyad and Manuel Castells (eds) *Muslim Europe or Euro-Islam: Politics, Culture, and Citizenship in the Age of Globalization*, Lanham, ND and Berkeley, CA: Lexington Books, 2002, pp. 31–52.
—— "Islamism, Democracy and the Clash of Civilizations," in Jakarta Center for Languages and Cultures/UIN (ed.) *Islam and the West. Obstacles and Solutions in Search for a New World Civilization*, Jakarta: UIN and Adenauer Foundation, 2003, pp. 3–13.
—— "Obstacles and Solutions," in Jakarta Center for Languages and Cultures/UIN (ed.) *Islam and the West. Obstacles and Solutions in Search for a New World Civilization*, Jakarta: UIN and Adenauer Foundation, 2003, pp. 196–200.
—— *Die fundamentalistische Herausforderung. Der Islam und die Weltpolitik*, Munich: C.H. Beck, fourth fully rewritten new edition 2003.
—— *Der Neue Totalitarismus. Heiliger Krieg und westliche Sicherheit*, Darmstadt: Primus, 2004.
—— "Islamic Fundamentalism," in Mary Hawkesworth and Maurice Kogan (eds) *Encyclopedia of Government*, 2 vols, second edition, London: Routledge, 2004, vol. 1, pp. 184–204.
—— "The Open Society and its Enemies within," *Wall Street Journal*, 17 March 2004, p. A10.
—— "Euro-Islam. The Quest of Islamic Migrants and of Turkey to become European," *Turkish Policy Quarterly* (2004), vol. 3, 1, pp. 13–28.
—— "Islamic Civilization and the Quest for Democratic Pluralism," in Karlina Helmanita, I. Abubakar and D. Afrianty (eds) *Dialogue in the World Disorder, A Response to Threat of Unilateralism and World Terrorism*, Jakarta: UIN Hidayatullah University, 2004, pp. 159–201.
—— *Mit dem Kopftuch nach Europa? Die Türkei auf dem Weg zur Europäischen Union*, Darmstadt: Primus; 2005 new enlarged edition 2007.
—— *Islam between Culture and Politics*, New York: Palgrave, second expanded edition 2005 [2001].
—— "Islam, Freedom and Democracy in the Arab World," in Michael Emerson (ed.) *Democratization in the European Neighborhood*, Brussels: CEPS, 2005, pp. 93–116.
—— "Euro-Islam, juridisch burgerschap en burgers van het hart," *Nexus* (2005), no. 41, pp. 173–203.
—— "From Islamist Jihadism to Democratic Peace? Islam at the Crossroads in Post-Bipolar International Politics," *Ankara Paper* 16, London: Taylor and Francis 2005, pp. 1–41.
—— "Countering Terrorism as War of Ideas and Worldviews," in Martin van Creveld and Katherina von Knop (eds) *Countering Modern Terrorism. History, Current Issues and Future Threats*, Bielefeld: Bertelsmann, 2005, pp. 131–72.
—— "Gibt es eine islamische bzw. islamistische Herausforderung an die Identität Europas? Ein Plädoyer für eine euro-islamische Asabiyya im Konflikt der Zivilisationen," *Religion-Staat-Gesellschaft* (2005), vol. 6, 1, pp. 19–62.
—— "Political Reform in the Gulf: Society and State in a Changing World" in Emirates Center for Political and Strategic Studies and Research (ECSSR) (ed.) *The Gulf. Challenges of the Future*, Abu Dhabi: ECSSR, 2005, pp. 313–30.

—— "Education and Democratization in an Age of Islamism," in Alan Olson, David Steiner and Irina Tuuli (eds) *Educating for Democracy*, Lanham: Rowman & Littlefield, 2005, pp. 203–19.

—— "Europeanizing Islam or the Islamization of Europe: Political Democracy versus Cultural Difference," in Peter Katzenstein and Timothy A. Byrnes (eds) *Religion in an Expanding Europe*, Cambridge: Cambridge University Press, 2006, pp. 204–24.

—— "Die Maer des Islamismus von der juedischen und kreuzzueglerischen Weltverschwoerung gegen den Islam," in Klaus Faber, Julius Schoeps and Sacha Stawski (eds) *Neu-alter Judenhass. Antisemitismus, arabisch-israelischer Konflikt und europaeische Politik*, Berlin: Verlag Berlin-Brandenburg, 2006, pp. 179–202.

—— "The Pertinence of Islam's Predicament with Democratic Pluralism," *Religion-Staat-Gesellschaft: Journal for the Study of Beliefs and Worldviews* (2006), vol. 7, 1, pp. 83–117.

—— "The Totalitarianism of Jihadist Islamism and its Challenge to Europe and to Islam," *Totalitarian Movements and Political Religion* (2007), vol. 8, 1, pp. 35–54.

—— "A Migration Story. From Muslim Immigrants to European 'Citizens of the Heart'?" *Fletcher Forum of World Affairs* (2007), vol. 31, 1, pp. 147–68.

—— "Islam: Between Religious-Cultural Practice and Identity Politics," in Helmut Anheier and Yudhushthir Raj Isar, *Cultures and Globalization*, vol. 1: *Conflicts and Tensions*, London: Sage, 2007.

Tilly, Charles, *The Formation of National States in Western Europe*, Princeton, NJ: Princeton University Press, 1985.

Toynbee, Arnold J., *A Study of History*, 12 vols, London: Oxford University Press, 1951–61.

Ulfkotte, Udo, *Der Krieg in unseren Städten. Wie Islamisten Deutschland unterwandern*, Frankfurt aim Main: Eichborn, 2003.

United Nations, *Arab Human Development Report 2002. Creating Opportunities for Future Generations*, New York: United Nations, 2002.

Walzer, Michael, *Just and Unjust Wars. A Moral Argument with Historical Illustrations*, third edition, New York: Basic Books, 2003.

—— (ed. and transl.) *Al-Farabi on the Perfect State*, Oxford: Oxford University Press, 1985.

Watson, Adam, *The Evolution of International Society: A Comparative Historical Analysis*, London: Routledge, 1992.

Watt, William Montgomery, *Islamic Philosophy and Theology*, Edinburgh: Edinburgh University Press, 1962, reprint 1979.

—— "Muslims and the Third World," *Third World Affairs 1986 Yearbook*, London: Third World Foundation, 1986, pp. 207–14.

—— *Islamic Fundamentalism and Modernity*, London: Routledge, 1988.

—— *Muslim–Christian Encounters. Perceptions and Misperceptions*, London: Routledge, 1991.

—— (ed.) *Bell's Introduction to the Qur'an*, completely rev. and enlarged, Edinburgh: Edinburgh University Press, 1994.

Weiner, Myron, *The Global Migration Crisis. Challenge to States and to Human Rights*, New York: HarperCollins, 1995.

Whittacker, David J. (ed.) *The Terrorism Reader*, London: Routledge, 2001.

Willis, Michael, *The Islamist Challenge in Algeria. A Political History*, New York: New York University Press, 1997.

Wilson, Rob and Dissanayake, Wimal (eds) *Global/Local: Cultural Production and the Transnational Imaginary*, Durham, NC: Duke University Press, 1996.

Wordlaw, Grant, *Political Terrorism*, Cambridge: Cambridge University Press, 1982, second edition 1989.

Worsley, Peter, *The Third World*, Chicago, IL: Chicago University Press, second edition 1967.

Wuthnow, Robert, *Meaning and Moral Order. Explorations in Cultural Analysis*, Berkeley, CA: University of California Press, 1987.

Ye'or, Bat, *Islam and Dhimmitude. Where Civilizations Colide*, Cranbury, NJ: Associated University Presses, 2002.

—— *Eurabia. The Euro-Arab Axis*, Cranbury, NJ: Associated University Presses, 2005.

Quotations from Arabic sources

Abdulfattah, Nabil, *al-mashaf wa al saif* [The Holy Book of the Sword], Cairo: Madbuli, 1984.

Abdulrahman, Abdulhadi, *Sultat al-nas* [The Authority of the Text], Beirut: al-Markas al-Thaqafi, 1993.

al-Aqqad, Abbas Mahmud, *al-demoqratiyya fi al-Islam* [Democracy in Islam], Cairo: 1952.

al-Armanazi, Najib, *al-Shar' al-duwali fi al-Islam* [International Law in Islam], reprint of the 1930 Damascus edition, London: Riad El-Rayyes Books, 1990, originally in French as a PhD dissertation.

al-Ashmawi, Mohammed Said, *Usul al-shari'a* [The Origins of Shari'a], Cairo: Madbuli, 1983.

—— *al-Islam al-siyasi* [Political Islam], Cairo: Sinah, 1987.

—— *Jauhar al-Islam* [The Core of Islam], Cairo: Sinah, 1992.

al-Awwa, Mohammed Salim, *Fi al-nizam al-siyasi li al-dawla al-Islamiyya* [On the Political System of the Islamic State], Cairo: al-Maktab al-Masri, 1975, sixth reprinting 1983.

Ayashi, Ahmida, *al-Islamiyun al jaza'riyun bain al-sulta wa al-rasas* [Algerian Islamists between State Authority and Bullets], Algiers: Dat al-Hikmah 1991.

al-Azm, Sadik Jalal, *Dhihniyyat al-Tahrim* [The Mentality of Taboos], London: Riad El-Rayyes, 1992.

al-Banna, Hasan, *Majmu'at Rasa'il al-Imam al-Shahid Hasan al-Banna* [Collected Writings], Cairo: Dar al-Da'wa, legal edition, 1990. Essay on Jihad on: pp. 271–92.

Dharif, Muhammad, *al-Islam al-siyasi fi al-watan al-arabi* [Political Islam in the Arab World], Casablanca: Maktabat al-Ummas and al-Ma'arif, 1992.

Djait, Hichem, *al-Fitna* [The Inter-Islamic War], Beirut: Dar al-Talia, 1992.

Hanafi, Hasan, *al-din wa al-thaura* [Religion and Revolution], 8 vols, Cairo: Madbuli, 1977–88.

Husni, Abdullatif, *al-Islam wa al-alaqat al-duwaliyya. Namudhaj Ahmed bin Khalid al-Nasiri* [Islam and International Relations. The Model of al-Nasiri], Casablanca: Afriqya al-Sharq, 1991.

Ibn Khaldun, *al-Muqaddima* [Book of Examples], Cairo: al-Maktabah al-Tijariyya, new printing, no date.

Ibrahim, Saad Eddin (ed.) *Humum al-aqaliyyat fi al-watan al-Arabi* [The Concerns of Minorities in the Arab World], Cairo: Ibn Khaldun Center, second printing, 1994.

Imara, Mohammed, *al-Islam wa al-uruba* [Islam and Arabism], Cairo: Dar al-Wihda, 1981.

Institute for Arab Unity Studies (ed.) *Azmat al-demoqratiyya fi al-watan al-Arabi* [Crisis of Democracy in the Arab World], Beirut: Institute for Arab Unity Studies, 1984.

al-Jabri, Mohammed Abed, *Takwin al-aql al-Arabi* [The Creation of the Arab Mind], Beirut: al-Talia, 1984.

—— *al-turath wa al-hadatha* [Heritage and Modernity], Beirut: al-Markaz al-Thaqafi, 1991.

Jadulhaq, Jadul-haq Ali, ed. for *al-Azhar, Bayan ila al-nas* [Declaration to Humanity], two vols, Cairo: al-Azhar, 1984, 1988.

Janinah, Nu'mat-Allah, *Tanzim al-jihad* [The Organization of Jihad], Cairo: Dar al-Hurriyya, 1988.

Jarisha, 'Ali M. and Zaibaq, Muhammad Sh., *Asalib al-ghazu al-fikri li al-'alam al-Islami* [Methods of the Intellectual Invasion of the Islamic World], Cairo: Dar al-I'tisam, second edition 1978.

al-Jundi, Anwar, *Ahdaf al-taghrib fi al-'alam al-Islami* [The Goals of Westernization in the Islamic World], Cairo: al-Azhar Press, 1987.

—— *al-Mu'asarah fi itar al-aslah* [Modernity in the Context of Authenticity], Cairo: Dar al-Sahwa, 1987.

Mahmud, Abdulhalim, *al-jihad wa al-nasr* [Jihad to Victory], Cairo: Dar al-Kitab al-Arabi, 1968.

al-Mawdudi, Abu al-A'la, *al-Islam wa al-madaniyya al-haditha* [Islam and Modern Civilization], Cairo: reprint, no date.

al-Mu'mini, Colonel (al-Muqaddam) Ahmad, *al-ta'bi'a al – jihadiyya fi al-Islam* [The Jihadist Mobilization for Islam], Constantine, Algeria: Mu'asasat al-Isra, 1991.

al-Nasiri, Ahmed bin Khalid, *al-istiqsa fi akhbar al-Maghreb al-aqsa* [Inquiry into the History of Maghreb], nine vols, Casablanca: Dar al-Kitab, 1955.

al-Qaradawi, Yusuf, *Hatmiyyat al-hall al-Islami wa al-hulul al-mustawradah* [The Islamic Solution and the Imported Solutions], new printing, Cairo: Mu'assat al-Risalah, reprint 1980.

Qutb, Sayyid, *al-mustaqbal li hadha al-din* [The Future Belongs to This Religion], Cairo: Dar al-Shuruq, 1981.

—— *al-Islam wa mushiklat al-hadarah* [Islam and the Problems of Civilizations] ninth legal edition, Cairo: Dar al-Shuruq, 1988.

—— *Ma'alim fi al-tariq* [Signposts along the Road], Cairo: Dar al-Shuruq, thirteenth legal edition 1989.

—— *al-salam al-alami wa al-Islam* [World Peace and Islam], Cairo: Dar al-Shuruq, tenth reprint 1992, legal edition.

—— *al-jihad fi sabil Allah* [Jihad on the Path of God], Cairo: Dar al-Isma, reprint 1992.

Shadid, Mohammed, *al-jihad fi al-Islam* [Jihad in Islam], seventh edition, Cairo: Dar al-tawzi al-Islamiyya, 1989.

Shahrur, Mohammed, *al-dawla wa al-mujtama* [State and Society], Damascus: al-Ahali, 1994.

—— *al-kitab wa al-Qur'an, qira'a mu'asira* [The Book of the Qur'an. A Modern Reasoning], Beirut: Sharikat al-Matbu'at, sixth edition 2000.

Shaltut, Mahmud, *al-Islam aqidah wa shari'a* [Islam as Religious Belief and Law], tenth printing, Cairo: Dar al-Shuruq, 1980.

al-Sharqawi, Hasan, *al-Muslimun, ulama wa hukama* [Muslims as Ulema and Wise Men], Cairo: Mu'ssasat Mukhtar, 1987.

al-Tahtawi, Rifa'a Rafi, *Takhlis al-ibriz ila talkis Paris* [Paris Diary], Beirut: Ibn Zaidun, reprint, no date.

Tu'aymah, Sabir, *al-shari'a fi asr al-ilm* [Islamic Shari'a in the Age of Science], Beirut: Dar al-Jil, 1979.

Yasin, Muhammad Na'im, *al-jihad. Mayadinahu wa asalibahu* [The Fields and Methods of Jihad], Algiers: Dar al-Irschad, 1990.

Index